100
BEST
Resorts of the
Caribbean

a photo essay

Biras Creek Resort
p. 77

Almond Morgan Bay
p. 226

Hotel Kura Hulanda
Spa and Casino
p. 98

Cobblers Cove
p. 56

The Buccaneer
p. 286

Biras Creek Resort
p. 77

One&Only
Ocean Club
p. 50

Petit St. Vincent
Resort
p. 261

The Bitter End
Yacht Club
p. 80

Carlisle Bay
p. 18

Strawberry Hill
p. 132

Hotel Saint-Barth
Isle de France
p. 213

La Samanna
p. 240

The Buccaneer
p. 286

One&Only
Ocean Club
p. 50

Hotel Saint-Barth
Isle de France
p. 213

Almond Morgan Bay
p. 226

Petit St. Vincent
Resort
p. 261

100 BEST RESORTS SERIES

Eighth Edition

B E S T

Resorts of the
Caribbean

Kay Showker

travel

Guilford, Connecticut

The prices, rates, and hours listed in this guidebook were confirmed at press time. We recommend, however, that you call establishments to obtain current information before traveling.

To buy books in quantity for corporate use
or incentives, call **(800) 962-0973**
or e-mail **premiums@GlobePequot.com**.

Text design by Nancy Freeborn
Map by Stefanie Ward © Morris Book Publishing, LLC
Photo layout by Joanna Beyer

ISSN 1546-5799
ISBN 978-0-7627-4883-9

Printed in the United States of America
10 9 8 7 6 5 4 3 2 1

CONTENTS

THE RESORTS BY ISLAND

A WORD OF THANKS

When a book covers 100 resorts on thirty-nine islands, it goes almost without saying that the author needs the help of many people to complete the task. I am certainly no exception. This book has required an incredible amount of research, discussions with knowledgeable people, and follow-up. Dozens of people were tireless in their efforts to help me. I only wish I could name them all, but I would be remiss not to mention some.

First, I would like to express my everlasting gratitude to the late Marcella Martinez of Marcella Martinez Associates, New York, and her staff, who helped me every step of the way.

The questionnaire for the Green Leaf Awards was based on months of discussions with environmentalists, experienced hotel managers, architects, and others working in the conservation field. But none of it would have been possible without the help of Stan Selengut, the proprietor of Maho Bay Camp and a recognized authority and adviser to governments and tourism officials around the world on ecotourism, and Peggy Bendel of Development Counsellors International, whose work for the U.S. Virgin Islands formed the basis of my questionnaire.

Others who made generous efforts on my behalf are Katharine Dyson; Kim Duvall-Hutchinson, Premier World Marketing, Miami; Mary Brennan and Roberta Garzaroli, The Atrebor Group, New York; Virginia Haynes, Montgomery Communications, New York; Marilyn Marx, Marilyn Marx Associates, New York; Candice Adams and her staff, Adams Unlimited, New York; Laura Davidson and her staff, Laura Davidson Public Relations, New York; Cheryl Andrews and her staff, Cheryl Andrews Marketing, Coral Gables, Florida, and most of the general managers and their staff of the resorts included in the book.

Text Contributions

Because the time constraints of writing and updating this book made it impossible for me to revisit every resort prior to my deadline, as I had wanted to do, I called on my writing colleagues for help. Some contributed specific material written for this book; others allowed me to use material from articles that had been published recently elsewhere. In every case they are writers who specialize in the Caribbean and are as qualified as I to write this book. Indeed, several have written books on the Caribbean.

Several entries are based on articles that first appeared in *Caribbean Travel and Life,* and I am particularly grateful to the authors for their generous cooperation. Specifically these are Eden Rock (St. Barts) by Susan Pierres; and the late Stan Murray for his input on Casa de Campo (Dominican Republic), Altamer (Anguilla), and Parrot Cay (Turks and Caicos). There were also contributions from John Buchanan for Hotel Kura Hulanda (Curaçao) and Gay Myers for Raffles Resort (Canouan, The Grenadines); and James Olearchik for Four Seasons Resort Great Exuma (Bahamas). Suzanne McManus, Jamaica, advised and helped me with the research on all the resorts in Jamaica.

Katharine Gordon Dyson not only helped me edit much of the material in the book but also contributed Sandcastle (Jost Van Dyke, B.V.I.) and Mount Cinnamon (Grenada).

UNITED
STATES

Grand
Bahama — Little Abaco

—Great Abaco

Paradise Island
Nassau — Harbour Island

Andros
Island

THE BAHAMAS

• Exumas

CUBA

TURKS AND
CAICOS ISLANDS

ATLANTIC OCEAN

CAYMAN
ISLANDS — Little
Cayman

Grand
Cayman

Montego
Bay

Runaway
Bay

Ocho Rios

Port-au-Prince

HAITI

Negril

Port
Antonio

JAMAICA

Kingston

Puerto Plata

DOMINICAN
REPUBLIC

Santo
Domingo

Rincón

La
Romana

Punta
Cana

PUERTO
RICO

San Juan

Fajardo

Jost Van Dyke

Tortola

Virgin Gorda

St. John

St. Thomas

St. Barts

St. Croix

St. Kitts

Nevis

BRITISH
VIRGIN
ISLANDS

Anguilla

St. Maarten/St. Martin

Antigua

Montserrat

Guadeloupe

Dominica

U.S. VIRGIN
ISLANDS

Martinique

St. Lucia

St. Vincent

The
Grenadines

Barbados

Bequia

CARIBBEAN

SEA

Aruba

Curaçao

• Bonaire

Grenada

Tobago

Trinidad

SOUTH AMERICA

INTRODUCTION

Ask any ten Caribbean cognoscente to name the best or even their favorite resort in the Caribbean and you will probably get ten different answers. You will certainly start an argument.

In the thirty years or so that I've been writing about the Caribbean, the questions I'm asked most often are "What's your favorite place?" and "What's the best place to stay?" It is not surprising, since the choice of a hotel is usually a traveler's first concern. But the best resort, like beauty, is in the eye of the beholder. And resorts, like people, differ. Not every resort suits everyone's needs and style.

Any of us can recognize high quality and good service. We all appreciate good architectural design and interior decor. But to be the best, a hotel or resort must have that "something special" that is almost impossible to define and strikes each of us differently.

Then, too, there was a time not long ago when the choices in the Caribbean were clearer, because good resorts were few. But now, after two decades of steady building throughout the region, the number has more than doubled. (The Caribbean Hotel Association's reference guide lists over 2,000 entries.) The choice is more difficult, but, happily, the selection is more interesting.

Consider, too, that these hotels, inns, and resorts are spread over nearly forty separate islands, or island groups, and you will see that the task is daunting. *100 Best Resorts of the Caribbean* is meant to make the choice easier. Most people do not want or need the standard long list of hotels with brief descriptions that appear in most Caribbean guidebooks; they prefer some

selectivity, and selectivity is precisely the aim of this book.

Since standards vary so much from island to island, it is difficult to set up arbitrary rules or criteria to apply across the board. What passes as the best in Guadeloupe may be only acceptable in Anguilla. What has some travelers turned on in St. Barts would be turned down in Jamaica. A great deal also has to do with an island's tradition—British, French, Dutch, Spanish—and the kind of tourists it attracts.

The Caribbean best are recognized by the same attention to detail and quality of service, food, care, comfort, and facilities that distinguish the best hotels and resorts around the world. But in judging the Caribbean, you have to be generous. There are many problems in trying to operate a top-quality resort in the Tropics. This, coupled with the region's high operating costs, means that the best tend to be equated with the most expensive.

Yet it would have been a mistake to include only the most expensive resorts. The selection would have been easy, but you don't need me to tell you which are the 100 most expensive hotels in the Caribbean. Any good travel agent can tell you that. What's more, being expensive is no guarantee of being the best—or even good—and there are some real dogs out there. Rather, consideration was given to ambience, historic setting, management style, uniqueness, and other elements that make some resorts the best for other than traditional reasons.

What impresses me, even after all these years, is the enormous variety that the Caribbean offers. I wanted the 100 resorts in this book to reflect that variety and to represent a broad range of establishments: large and small, beachside and hillside, modest and deluxe, homey and elegant.

I made a conscious effort to provide diversity, choosing the resorts I considered the best in each category across the broadest possible spectrum on as many islands as possible. The selections run the gamut from rustic retreats to private island hideaways to large, full-service layouts. They range in their degree of luxury from minimal to extravagant. That's why you will find such widely differing entries as back-to-nature Maho Bay Camp on St. John, U.S. Virgin Islands, at one end of the spectrum and posh Malliouhana on Anguilla at the other.

What Is a Resort?

But first, what is a resort? Because my selection covers such a broad range, you may wonder how I define *resort,* and you will certainly want to know the criteria I used.

Webster's defines *resort* as a place providing recreation and entertainment, especially to vacationers. *Roget's Thesaurus* and Rodale's *The Synonym Finder* list as synonyms *hotel, inn, club, lodge, spa, watering place, camp.* This book includes places fitting all these appellations, along with *haven, hideaway,* and *retreat.*

But let me make it simple. I define *resort* as "a place to go for a vacation." It is a broad definition, but it reflects a reality— namely, that vacationers are an extremely diverse group whose ideas of a vacation differ as much as their interests, needs, and expectations. What is paradise for one person might be hell for another.

For some people the ideal resort is a pleasure palace by the sea—the more luxurious, the more pampering, the more exclusive, the better. For others it is the exact opposite. They willingly trade creature comforts to be close to nature with as few man-made intrusions as possible.

Then there are the honeymooners, golfers, divers, birders, hikers; those who want action; those who want serenity; others who care about cuisine; those who take family vacations; those who want to be directly on the beach; others who want a vacation in the mountains; those who select a resort by the variety of sports and recreation available; those who care little about activities. All of these people will find resorts in this guide to suit them. Yet travelers' needs did not guide my initial selection—only the fine-tuning. My first concern was the quality of the resort itself.

Criteria

So what were my criteria? To be the best a resort needs a combination of factors: location, setting, layout, service, appearance, ambience, dining experience, sports facilities, management, and staff. But then it must have something beyond these—the intangibles, that *je ne sais quoi.*

Maybe it's warmth, maybe it's style. It is a certain quality, a feeling that is hard to define but that you know instinctively when you find it. When I described my dilemma to a fellow writer, he replied instantly, "Yes, I know what you mean. Would you want to spend a week there?"

"That's it," I replied. "That's it." Would you want to spend a week there? And perhaps more important, at the end of the week, do you long to return? Every entry in this book was put to that test. There were other tests, too. Does the resort live up to the goals it designed for itself? Does it fulfill its role—whatever the style, price, category—better than any other?

Another important criterion: The resort had to have been in business for at least one year. Most of those included here have been around much longer than a year; they have stood the test of time. A few, which barely got in under the time requirement, were included because the owners have established track records for running outstanding hotels and because the inn or resort is of such quality and distinction that it merits early recognition. Others that have opened in the last year and hold promise of being among the best are listed in the "On the Horizon" section at the end of the book.

Certainly some testing was influenced by my personal likes and dislikes. When I go to the Caribbean, I want to know I'm in the Caribbean. I want to feast on its beauty as well as its bounty, to feel the balmy air and hear the sea. My ideal resort takes advantage of its location; it lets the trade winds cool the air and blow away the sand flies. Its rooms and restaurants are open to the sea, with breezy balconies and splendid views. Architecture is to me as important as ambience—the two work together to make a place special. Good architectural design fits its environment and helps create the ambience. I also care a great deal about the Caribbean's heritage—natural, historical, cultural—and have more to say about this later in the Green Leaf Awards section.

I like places that make me feel good as soon as my taxi pulls up to the front door. I like places that look as though they are expecting you, from an alert doorman to a friendly check-in desk to a bellhop who tells me everything I need to know about my room and points out the features of the hotel that I am likely to need soon after my arrival. I appreciate one who takes the time to find the luggage rack and place my suitcase on it, and checks the ice bucket or water in the fridge to ensure that I can have a cool drink of water after my long trip.

Little things mean a lot: good reading lights, firm mattresses, efficient bathrooms with a place for toiletries, fresh flowers, lit footpaths or flashlights to light the way. I

like omnipresent but unobtrusive managers, and I want to shake hands with the person minding the store.

Although I let my experience guide me, I sought the opinions and advice of many others—travel agents and other writers who specialize in the Caribbean, hoteliers with long Caribbean experience, friends who live in the Caribbean part or all of the year, and, most important, dozens of vacationers I met along the way. They gave me their overall impressions and were particularly helpful in highlighting the features that had made their visit to a particular resort memorable. But in the end the choices are mine. So, too, are the comments and criticism.

The Goal

My principal objective in the resort profiles was to define a resort's personality and stress the elements that make it different and distinctive from other resorts to enable you to identify with those best suited for you. But defining a resort's personality is not an exact science. Sometimes it is the history of the structure that helped shape the resort's character, sometimes the owner or manager whose imprint is indelible, sometimes the setting, the staff, the ambience, or a specific feature—or all of the above.

In the beginning I thought finding 100 different ways to describe 100 different resorts would be the hardest part about writing this book. Instead, I found that the resorts have such distinctive personalities, the descriptions almost wrote themselves. In a way the ease of writing about them further confirmed my choices.

Small Versus Large

Those who know the Caribbean well will not be surprised to learn that out of the total 100 resorts in this book, more than half have fewer than fifty rooms, and forty-one have fewer than thirty rooms. Less than a fourth are large resorts with a hundred or more rooms. This was not a deliberate decision. In fact, I had not even analyzed the numbers until after I had written all the entries.

There's no mystery about the results. Big resorts are better known because they have the muscle to market and promote themselves, but small ones of fewer than fifty rooms are more typical of the Caribbean and are its strength, providing a more authentic Caribbean experience.

Small hotels have a personality—that's what makes them worthy of attention—while large ones tend to be homogenized. Let me quickly add, however, that the large resorts included here run counter to the norm; they, too, have strong character.

The size of a hotel makes a difference in the type of Caribbean holiday you have. Large hotels have a greater array of activities and facilities, a busier atmosphere, and more round-the-clock staff and services than a small hotel, where the atmosphere is usually quiet and very relaxed.

At the smallest ones you get more personal care and attention from the manager, who is often the owner, and from the staff, who will call you by name and learn your preferences from the first day of your visit. Usually you feel as though you are a guest in a friend's home or at a weekend house party. The service may not be as polished as at large resorts, but it is warm and genuine.

Commitment

The Caribbean is full of wonderful stories about people with a dream. Owning a small hotel in the Caribbean is a fantasy that's right up there in popularity with buying a boat and sailing around the world. So irrepressible is the idea that many, many people have done it and continue to do it. Most give up after a few years when they learn

how difficult it is to run a really good hotel in the Caribbean. The innkeepers in this book are people who made it; invariably, they reflect the high degree of personal commitment it takes to succeed.

Amenities

Many small hotels, including some of the most expensive, do not have air-conditioning, television, or phones in the rooms. Not having a phone is a blessing to some people, an inconvenience to others. The Calabash in Grenada has the ideal solution: All guest rooms have telephones—along with a printed note that says, "The phone will be removed if you find it a nuisance." On the other hand, many hotels have recognized the inevitable and have installed wireless Internet access and accept the use of cell phones with specific restrictions as to where and when they can be use. Not all cell phones work on all islands, however.

As for air-conditioning, you may be surprised (I was amazed) to discover how many resorts don't have it—and don't need it. Ceiling fans and natural breezes do a better job. Generally, the absence of air-conditioning in a good hotel says the structure was built to be architecturally sensitive to its setting.

In the past Caribbean hoteliers believed they could not attract guests, particularly Americans, if they did not have air-conditioning. But during the oil crises of the 1970s, when skyrocketing fuel bills almost put them out of business, many returned to Mother Nature out of necessity. The response from guests was so positive that more followed suit and frequently went to solar power—a trend that has picked up momentum with the recent escalating cost of oil and concern over protecting the fragile Caribbean environment.

Architects with Caribbean experience have long since abandoned square concrete-block hotels in favor of styles that suit the natural environment, stressing open-air dining, louvered windows and doors, shaded terraces, and tile and terracotta floors. What a joy!

Paradise Isn't Perfect

Even the best resorts aren't perfect. Where I feel it's warranted, I point out weaknesses. And you may notice that I save my toughest judgment for the posh corners of paradise, where prices unhappily have risen to heights as heavenly as the pleasures. To me, expensive resorts have a greater responsibility to deliver what they promise than those that keep rates low and don't try to be fancy. Higher rates, however, are usually justified as the degree of luxury increases, since almost everything is imported, and catering to Americans—a demanding lot—is costly. Nonetheless, people who seek luxury still want their money's worth.

Maintenance in the Tropics, government taxes, and service charges also drive up costs. High labor costs and restrictive policies—often more politically than economically motivated, since hotels are usually the island's largest employers—are contributing factors, too. Which brings me to the matter of service.

Service

The Caribbean offers service at a stroll. Swift, at-the-snap-of-a-finger, professional service is unusual. If that's your yardstick for judging service, you'll be disappointed even in the best of the best places. If you require this kind of service to be happy, the Caribbean is the wrong place for you.

Caring, cheerful, and thoughtful service from a friendly staff, not speed or polish, are the criteria on which to make a judgment here. Turn off your motor, leave your watch at home, relax. This is not a cop-out or apology for service in the Caribbean.

Rather, it is said to help you enjoy your vacation by knowing the parameters within which Caribbean resorts operate.

Careers in service industries are only now getting the respect they deserve from people who, having passed from colonialism to independence, traditionally equated such work with servitude. Fortunately, this attitude is fading as islanders have come to recognize their need for tourism and as local ownership of hotels has broadened. Professionalism, too, is increasing as training and opportunities grow and the hospitality profession, as it matures, offers meaningful advancement to young people.

Cuisine

The time has come for travelers and travel writers to stop saying, "You can't get a good meal in the Caribbean." It simply isn't true. I've enjoyed wonderful meals from the Bahamas to Trinidad. It's neither difficult, nor impossible; too many restaurants and hotels have demonstrated otherwise.

In judging a resort I gave cuisine a great deal of attention. Some places have brought a quality and creativity to their cuisine not associated with the Caribbean in the past. Many have young, imaginative chefs who are turning out great dishes. Now, too, culinary competitions islandwide and regionwide are regular events and have stimulated participants to be creative and innovative.

Trouble in Paradise

Idyllic places today must be more than pretty to get our attention and gain our loyalty. They must be reasonably efficient, if not always convenient, and secure. Trouble in paradise is troubling whenever it rears its ugly head, but with the exception of a few islands—ironically, those that have the most tourists—crime is less of a problem at hotels in the Caribbean than in any major city in the United States.

We who live by security systems and double-bolted doors have forgotten what it's like not to worry about security. But imagine! There are still Caribbean islands where people don't lock their doors. And there are still resorts where you aren't given a room key because they don't have them—or need them. When I visit some of my favorite places where there are no locks on the doors, I find it unsettling at first, until I realize I can shed those city fears. The freedom is exhilarating.

Crawling Critters

Welcome to the Tropics. If this is your first visit, I have some explaining to do. If you have been to Florida or the Mississippi Delta, you already know about bugs and other creatures that thrive in warm, humid climates. Ninety-nine percent are harmless. They may not be cheering to see, but they won't hurt you. "I saw a roach 2 inches long," I've heard visitors new to the Tropics say. And I reply, "Yes, I see them often."

This is true even at the best Caribbean resorts. Recently, at one of the very finest, most expensive resorts in this book, I opened a drawer, and there it was—a huge water bug flat on its back, dead.

You'll also see geckos or chameleons and, after the first shock, you'll grow fond of them, like pets. They are wonderfully interesting to watch; some have great color, too.

At certain times of the year, mosquitoes can be fierce, particularly after a rain. I know; they love me. I never go anywhere without insect repellent. Most good hotels provide a can of repellent in their guest rooms and usually have a can on hand at the bar. People with allergies may have a problem using repellents and should consult their doctors. Needless to say, in air-conditioned places you are less likely to be bothered. It's the best reason I know for air-conditioning.

How the Book Is Organized

100 Best Resorts of the Caribbean is organized alphabetically by island or island group. Each island or island group starts with a profile intended as no more than a quick introduction. I have made the assumption that you have been to the Caribbean before or have other guidebooks by me or other writers with the nitty-gritty details for planning a vacation. Within each island or island group, the resorts are also listed alphabetically.

At the end of each resort's entry, you will find an information block providing standard information on the resort that is not included in the text, such as where to make reservations or how much local tax or service charges are levied. Other information, such as room amenities like television and air-conditioning or sports facilities such as tennis courts and water-sports equipment, is also listed for quick reference. If, however, a resort is known for a particular sport like golf or diving, more information on its special features is provided in the text.

Seasons and Symbols

There is absolutely no uniformity in designating the beginning and ending of high season and low season in the Caribbean. The dates differ from island to island and hotel to hotel. Unless specified to the contrary, the definitions throughout this book are those used generally in the region: High season is the winter months from mid-December to mid-April; low season is comprised of the balance of the year when hotel rates are reduced by 30 percent or more. More and more resorts are adding a third season, known as the shoulder season (mid-April to late May and/or September to October), when rates are also reduced substantially.

Rates peak during holiday periods, particularly during Christmas and New Year's and in February, when most resorts require a one-week or longer stay. When your priority is a winter vacation, paradise can be pricey, but you can often save a bundle by shifting slightly from March to mid-April or by going in November instead of December. And do not overlook packages. Even the fanciest resorts have them, particularly in the shoulder and low seasons. They usually represent meaningful savings and have additional bonus features.

Rates found at the end of each resort indicate the resort's price range rather than the rates for each different type of accommodation. All rates are subject to change, and if the past is prologue, they will change. Consult the resort or its U.S. reservations or a travel agent who can get the most current information. Prices are quoted in U.S. dollars unless indicated otherwise.

The symbols used are as follows:

EP (European Plan): Room only, no meals.

CP (Continental Plan): Room with continental breakfast.

FAB (Full American Breakfast): Room with full American breakfast.

MAP (Modified American Plan): Room with breakfast and dinner.

A (American Plan): Room with three meals daily.

FAP (Full American Plan): Room with three meals; full American breakfast daily.

ALL-INCLUSIVE

The rate includes accommodations, all meals, on-premises sports and entertainment, drinks, tax, and service.

You should know that many resorts call themselves all-inclusive or say they have all-inclusive packages when in fact they do not. The hotel's brochure spells out what is and is not included. It is important to read the fine print.

Facilities

Almost any of the resorts in this book can arrange those sports not available at their property and island tours or boat trips to nearby islands. Most have tennis and beachside sports, but it is important when you compare prices to factor in these additional costs when the use of facilities is not included in room rates.

Dress Code

Specific guidelines are given under each resort, as the code does vary, but generally throughout the Caribbean, dress during the day and evening is casual and informal. This, however, does not mean sloppy, tacky, or tasteless. West Indians are often quite offended by the way some tourists dress. Hotel owners are also. They ask that beachwear be kept for the beach. Many resorts require a jacket for dinner in the winter season, but only a very few still require ties for men. Some of the smallest, least pretentious hotels have the strictest dress codes for evening.

Children

More and more couples are vacationing with their children. Most Caribbean resorts welcome children, but a few do not, or they limit the age or the time period. The policy is spelled out for every resort in this book. Those that welcome families often have special rates for children; some have special meals and supervised activities. All that take children can arrange babysitters, although some resorts request that you notify them in advance.

Meetings

Almost all resorts now take meetings, but some small ones are likely to take them only at certain times of the year. Alternatively, you can book the entire hotel—not a bad idea for small groups.

Stargazing

Since I have already selected 100 resorts out of the 2,000 plus hotels in the Caribbean, you may wonder why I added stars. I'm wondering, too, since it will probably cause me nothing but grief—from readers who will tell me I overrated this or that resort, and from hoteliers who will think I've underrated them. I agonized over each one, but I don't claim that I always got it right.

The distinctions are as follows:

***** A league of their own. Not only do they stand out as the best on their island, but they stand up to each other as well.

**** Close to the top but not quite in a league all their own.

*** All-around good but not quite in the top league.

** All-around good but on a modest scale.

* Small, very modest.

N/S/T A few resorts were not given stars because they are (N) too new to be judged, (S) too specialized to be classified in the usual manner, or (T) in transition under new owners or management.

Green Leaf Awards 🌿

Protecting the environment is not a fad but a concern that we must maintain day in and day out. In no place in the world is this more essential than the Caribbean. The natural environment is this area's number one asset and protecting it must be its number one priority. The need is as great, if not greater, for the people who live there as for visitors. Without it, they have nothing.

More and more people are becoming aware of their role as travelers, and many (myself included) want to support those who demonstrate an environmental awareness and are making an effort to protect this heritage through their daily actions.

In researching this book I created an environmental profile that I asked every resort to complete; their participation was entirely voluntary. To my knowledge it was the first time a guidebook has made such an attempt in any part of the world. My purpose was not to serve as critic, since there are some recently created internationally recognized standards by which to judge, nor do I consider myself an expert, only a concerned citizen. Rather, I wanted to survey this group in particular to learn if the 100 that are the best at operating their resorts treat their environment with the same care they give their guests. I awarded Green Leaves to those who demonstrate an ongoing concern through their conservation policies and practices.

I was surprised and pleased by the results. Of the one hundred resorts, seventy-five responded. Environmental awareness and conservation among these hotels is at a much higher level than I had realized. I welcome your suggestions for future editions.

Author's Postscript

I want to assure you that there was no charge for a hotel to be in this guide—a practice not uncommon for books of this kind, particularly in Europe. Nor did I incur any obligation whatsoever in the course of researching the resorts and making my selections.

The choices are entirely my own. I sought opinions often and listened to advice. I tried to cast myself into the mold of the people for whom a resort was designed. But in the end the process was subjective. I don't claim to be all-knowing; nor do I expect everyone to agree with all my selections. However, I can say without hesitation that there is no resort in this book I wouldn't be happy to return to many times. Indeed, I believe that sentiment is the most valuable criterion a writer can use.

From time to time the Caribbean region experiences hurricanes and tropical storms that can cause damage. If there has been a hurricane or storm recently in the area you plan to travel to, you should phone ahead or consult the resort's Web site to make sure that the resort you'd like to visit is open and that any storm damage has been repaired.

The prices and rates listed in this guidebook were confirmed at press time but under no circumstances are they guaranteed. We recommend that you contact establishments before traveling to obtain current information.

ANGUILLA

Sea, sand, and serenity—these are the assets of this tranquil hideaway in the north-eastern corner of the Caribbean. Anguilla (pronounced Ann-GWEE-la), 5 miles north of St. Martin, is a dry, low-lying coral island that receives only 35 inches of rainfall per year.

What Anguilla lacks in mountains and tropical foliage, it makes up for in powdery white beaches, which you can have almost to yourself, and fantastically clear aqua and cobalt-blue waters that have attracted yachtsmen for decades and fishermen for centuries. More recently the spectacular waters have been luring snorkelers and scuba divers to the large reefs that lie off Anguilla's coast.

Yet until it burst on the scene in the 1980s with some superdeluxe resorts, Anguilla was the best-kept secret in the Caribbean. Since then trendsetters have been flocking to this little-known spot to learn what all the fuss is about. A beach-comber's island at heart, Anguilla even now is so laid-back that you might need to practice doing nothing to enjoy its tranquillity. Over the years the island has gained an array of good restaurants, shops, and tourist facilities—all low-key—and it even has a budding artist colony. Yet, the island only got its first golf course in 2006 and still has no casinos or shopping arcades, and all but a few small cruise ships pass it by. If you want a change of pace, though, Anguilla is only a twenty-minute ferry ride from the casinos and duty-free shopping of St. Martin.

Traditionally among the region's most skilled boatmen and fishermen, the Anguil-lans supply the markets and restaurants of St. Martin with much of their fish. You can watch the fishing boats come in at Island Harbor on the eastern end. The Anguil-lans also make boats, including an unusual racing vessel that gets tested during Anguilla's annual Race Week in August. Sleek yachts and humble fishing boats are available to take you to nearby atolls for a picnic and a day of snorkeling.

For a destination whose total number of guest rooms is less than that of a large hotel, Anguilla has a surprising range of accommodations, from guest houses to posh hotels.

Information

Anguilla Tourist Information, (877) 4-ANGUILLA or (914) 287-2400; Fax: (914) 287-2404; www.anguilla-vacation.com; e-mail: mwturnstyle@aol.com

ALTAMER

Shoal Bay West, Anguilla, B.W.I.

The story of Altamer reads like a dream. More than a decade ago, an American couple, Michael and Rebecca Eggleton (he, an international banker; she, a CPA) were vacationing on Anguilla when they decided to buy some property and build a beach house. Their six acres abut crescent-shaped Shoal Bay West, a secluded beach on the western end of Anguilla with views of St. Martin in the distance across the Caribbean Sea.

They envisioned a reasonably modest home, but by the time they decided to build, the government had enacted laws requiring all beachfront property to be operated as a hotel or villa available for rent to visitors.

Near their property were the futuristic, snow-white villas of Covecastles, designed by well-known architect Myron Goldfinger with interiors by his wife, June. The Eggletons wanted their villa to be consistent with the nearby architecture, but unique in its design. With Goldfinger as the architect, they planned Altamer—a beach house like no other.

Rebecca Eggleton and June Goldfinger set off on several worldwide odysseys to find artists, furniture makers, and artisans to duplicate historical items for use in the decor and to arrange for such extravagances as handmade $10,000 Murano glass light fixtures for the living room. For the African Sapphire villa, Altamer commissioned artisans in South Africa to create a chandelier designed by June Goldfinger that has over half-million beads, all made by hand.

The resulting collections are stunning. Throughout, the furnishings combine stylish modern pieces with fine antiques and rare art from around the world, with an emphasis on Turkey, Russia, Africa, Brazil, and Italy. To say that these beach houses are over the top might be an understatement. Now comprised of three large, ultramodern villas, all rooms have floor-to-ceiling windows facing the blue Caribbean waters.

In Russian Amethyst, the first villa, the eye is greeted with a fantasy-like opulence, with oversize rattan furniture awash in a sea of multihued plush cushions—pink, periwinkle, and purple—arranged in conversation groupings. Vases of floral bouquets are everywhere.

On the first floor of the main villa are the Great Room with a soaring 21-foot ceiling, sitting areas, a formal dining room with a custom-designed table for twelve, views of the beach from the large sliding glass doors and windows, and a state-of-the-art professional gourmet kitchen where the villa's chef turns out his fabulous creations. Forget calories.

Behind the elongated oval glass dining table is a large three-part painting, *Cloud Triptych,* by Jan Aronson. It is the perfect complement to the ceiling, which seems to touch the sky. There is a second Aronson painting in the room and a priceless antique Russian chest to keep board games of all kinds. Here, too, is a magnificent gilded candelabra—a little something that Rebecca and June picked up in Russia. It's 18-karat gold on bronze and was formerly owned by one of the czars. Whew!

There are no rugs or carpets, simply a spotlessly clean tile floor. When asked why, the senior butler is quick to reply, "After all, it's a beach house."

Outside this first floor is the swimming pool, which runs almost the length of the building and is ringed with chaise lounges with canary-yellow cushions. On the far side of the pool is a grove of palm trees with the vibrant blue sea peeking through. It's the Yellow Brick Road, Bali Hai, and Shangri-La in one!

The second floor, with full views of St. Martin and the Caribbean, has a triangle-shaped game room with a wet bar, pool table, and home theater with flat-screen television and a DVD player. Guest rooms One and Two, also with full sea views, are on this level, each with a marble bathroom with a Jacuzzi tub and separate shower. Extending out toward the sea and accessible only from this level is a 50-foot-long skywalk, allowing guests to lounge, dine, bird-watch, or catch the sunrise at the water's edge.

On the third level is the grand master bedroom, which more than lives up to its name. Measuring 26 feet by 26 feet, it has a 19-foot ceiling, a curved balcony, and bar above, and three large skylights for natural lighting. A king-size bed swathed in fine Italian linens has a television at its foot. In the marble bathroom are long twin vanities, a Jacuzzi for two, separate walk-in shower, and wall-mounted television. Directly off the bedroom is a huge private balcony with extensive views. Guest rooms Four and Five with high ceilings and skylights are also on this level.

The fourth-floor balcony over the master bedroom has a sitting area and can be converted into an office with a computer with high-speed Internet access, printer, scanner, and fax. The balcony also has a stainless steel and marble wet bar.

A caveat: The other bedrooms, while comfortable, cannot compare to the master bedroom. Those planning to take the villa with friends might want to draw straws to decide who gets the master bedroom first, and then rotate (the butlers will switch the clothing) so all have their turn at the ultimate Altamer luxury.

Near the entrance to the villa in a separate building is a guest room that can accommodate two additional persons. It also houses a fitness center for this villa.

But all this was merely the beginning. The Eggletons added a small reception and executive meeting facility in 2002; and two more villas in 2003 and 2004, each slightly larger than the first villa. Brazilian Emerald has five bedrooms and seven baths; while the third villa, African Sapphire, has eight bedrooms and nine baths. Each villa has a fitness room, a private pool, and hot tub. The last villa takes Africa as its inspiration with museum-quality art and artifacts throughout, each more interesting and unusual than the last.

Altamer's Conference Centre, designed and state-of-the-art equipped, provides video conferencing, high-speed Internet access, videotaping facilities, starfish speakers, computer projector and screen, VCR, DVD, desktop computers, facsimile, copier, and resort sound system. The main room, measuring 800 square feet, has boardroom seating for up to thirty around the custom-built teak board table or seating for eighty people theater style. There are two small breakout rooms used for a four-person meeting or as private office space. The centre can provide a conference coordinator, IT coordinator, and secretarial services.

The staff of ten for each villa includes four butlers, a resident manager, concierge, two housekeepers, and two gardeners. A chef and assistant are available for an additional charge. Head of villa operations and chief service officer, Carl Irish, is a Montserrat native and natural people-person, who will probably meet you at the airport on arrival. Preston Brookes, a butler, is an Anguillan, as are the other staff members.

Executive chef Maurice Leduc, whose forty years of experience ranges from an apprenticeship at Maxim's in Paris to an award-winning French restaurant in Boston and several gold medal awards, is in charge of all catering for weddings, anniversaries, and other special events at the resort.

From the island's main road, the turnoff to Altamer is onto a paved road marked by an Altamer sign and leads to the resort's small gatehouse. Since guests fill out in advance a guest preference form, which includes credit card information as well as menu choices, arrival is like being welcomed into the home of a rich uncle. There are no formalities, save for the entire staff being on hand to greet you.

You are offered iced towels and drinks. Depending on the time of arrival, you will probably sit down for a "snack" on the terrace.

By the time you get to your bedroom, your suitcases will have been unpacked and your clothes neatly folded in drawers or placed on hangers in the closet.

Evenings are spent watching movies from the extensive DVD library, or lazing in the Great Room listening to CDs from a collection that numbers in the hundreds. The remote that controls music throughout each villa can be operated from anywhere in it. The refrigerator in the kitchen is yours to raid at any hour, and Maurice thoughtfully leaves a sweet and some late-night snacks in plain view.

When the time comes to leave, Carl and Preston make it easier by packing your gear while you have breakfast or take a last swim.

In July 2007, Altamer held a ground breaking ceremony to announce a joint venture partnership with Island Global Yachting (IGY) for a five-star mega-yacht marina, the first such facility on Anguilla, and real estate development that will include six new villas and a 164-unit luxury resort hotel, retail and residential components. The target date for the marina is late 2009. The 101-slip marina will accommodate yachts up to 300 feet and will be an official port of entry to the island. Headquartered in Fort Lauderdale, IGY (www.igymarinas.com) operates under the signature Yacht Haven Grande collection and was the developer of the new marina in St. Thomas.

Most people cannot imagine the experience Altamer offers. Call it contemporary sybaritism with no detail overlooked, no amenity too small, and no need too great. Service is impeccable. You soon discover that you rarely have to ask for anything. The butlers not only anticipate every need, they seem to read your mind.

The sheer elegance and grandeur of Altamer can be overwhelming, but it will appeal to those who crave barefoot elegance in superb surroundings with extreme comfort and excellent service—provided, of course, they can afford it.

Altamer *****

Box 3001, Shoal Bay West, Anguilla, B.W.I.; or 6800 SW 40th Street, Box 333, Miami, FL 33155
Phone: (264) 498-4000, (888) 652-6888; Fax: (264) 498-4010; e-mail: info@altamer.com; www.altamer.com

Owners: Michael and Rebecca Eggleton

General Manager: Rebecca Eggleton

Open: Year-round

Credit Cards: American Express, Visa, MasterCard, Discover

U.S. Reservations: (888) 652-6888, rings to Anguilla office for reservations

Deposit: 50 percent to secure reservation; sixty days balance Minimum Stay: Seven nights during high season

Arrival/Departure: Altamer meets guests at airport and arranges taxi. (Note: Anguilla hotels cannot provide their own transportation for guests due to taxi regulations.)

Distance from Airport: 8 miles; twenty minutes by taxi

Accommodations: Three villas accommodating forty people (two villas with five bedrooms and seven baths with Jacuzzi tubs and separate showers; two bedrooms available in separate quarters; and one villa with eight bedrooms and nine baths)

Amenities: Air-conditioning, ceiling fans; professional kitchen; high-speed Internet connection; flat-screen television with DVD player, state of the art digital sound system with 30,000 song titles; safe; butler and maid service 7:00 a.m.–10:00 p.m.; hot tub; game room with custom-built pool table; marble bathrooms with Jacuzzi bathtubs; wet bars on multiple levels; handicap accessibility; elevators in each villa

Electricity: 110 volts

Fitness Facilities/Spa Services: Fitness center in each villa; massage and spa services on request

Sports: Beach, swimming pool; two tennis courts; snorkeling, deep-sea fishing, sailing, diving arranged. Each villa has a fitness center, tennis court with pavilion, 45-foot swimming pool, and hot tub.

Dress Code: Casual

Children: All ages

Meetings: Conference table seating for twenty, thirty in total. Theatre-style configuration increases capacity to seventy to eighty depending on setup.

Day Visitors: None

Handicapped Facilities: Yes

Packages: Weddings; corporate

Rates: Per day, All-inclusive. *High Season* (December–April): weekly $42,350–$48,400. *Low Season:* $30,250–$36,300. For holidays, Christmas/New Year's, inquire

Service Charge: 10 percent

Government Tax: 10 percent

CAP JULUCA
Maunday's Bay, Anguilla, B.W.I.

Cap Juluca could win any contest for being the most beautiful resort in the Caribbean, if not the world. It is sensual, romantic, and glamorous. Situated on 179 acres at Maunday's Bay, on Anguilla's leeward shores, with St. Martin in the distance, Cap Juluca is a villa resort stretching for a mile along the curve of a magnificent beach.

The posh resort is comprised of superdeluxe villas in Moorish style, complete with arches, domes, turrets, and keyhole doorways in a fairyland of colors. The blue skies, azure sea, magenta bougainvillea, and green gardens seem all the more intense against the snow-white villas. Cap Juluca is fittingly named for the Arawak god of the rainbow.

Guest rooms, in two-story "hotel" villas and pool villas with up to five bedrooms, come in a bewildering variety: from a bedroom with shower to a large villa with a private pool.

The sumptuous interiors vary, but they all have Italian tile floors and louvered doors of Brazilian walnut. Generally, those east of the main pool have built-in banquettes of white masonry with colorful cushions and pillows that give the interior a clean, sophisticated look. Moroccan artifacts and design elements inspired by colorful Moorish motifs are set against pure white walls, conveying the impression of a palace in Tangier. The newer villas are furnished rather grandly in European colonial style, which seems to my eye a bit heavy and pretentious for the airy, dreamy ambience that Cap Juluca is meant to convey.

The huge, luxurious bathrooms found in some suites are second to none. They are fabulous, if not downright decadent. They feature a king's ransom of Italian marble and mirrors along with an oversize bathtub, double sinks, a separate shower, and a bidet. Some even have a double bathtub with headrests and a private solarium.

You can sink into the mile of soft, deep white sand at your doorstep, or loll about the large freshwater pool. A continental breakfast served in your room or on your terrace or patio is part of the luxury at Cap Juluca. You can also have breakfast and lunch at Georges, a restaurant under an onion-shaped dome by the central pool pavilion. Roving beach waiters offer chilled towels, complimentary mineral water and sorbet, and drinks on request.

The eastern end of the beach is anchored by Pimm's, the main restaurant. Named for a refreshing drink popular with the British in the days of the raj, Pimm's has an enchanting setting directly by the sea, looking across the sweep of Cap Juluca by the bay. In the evening the candlelit tables and the sound of the water lapping at the rocks make it even more romantic.

Lunch and dinner menus feature seafood selections based on the island's supply of fresh fish, along with chicken, lamb, veal, and beef specialties, and too many yummy desserts—but all prepared with a light touch. Georges, at the center of the beach, serves Mediterranean cuisine tinged with Caribbean flavors and lighter fare at lunch. Two special nights are held here weekly—a seafood beach buffet on Fridays and a grand marché on Mondays after the manager's cocktail party. Chefs from areas of different cuisine (local, Indian, etc) have their own stations and serve appetizers, entrees, and desserts, and guests vote on the dish they like best for each course. The resort's other restaurant, Kemia (meaning tapa or mezza), is located next to Pimm's.

Should you care to leave your villa or haven by the pool, Cap Juluca has three Omni-turf tennis courts (two lighted) and a pro shop. The use of Sunfish, snorkeling gear, windsurfers, and Hobie Cats is included in the rate. Excursions farther afield are available on Cap Juluca's two boats. You could also work on your golf stroke at Cap Juluca's aqua driving range.

The resort has an herb garden and self-guided walking trails that lead to a lagoon behind the resort—a popular bird-watching location. The garden supplies fresh herbs for the chef and is a novelty for guests.

There is not much entertainment at Cap Juluca. Several evenings feature dancing at Georges and television is available in the media room, as are VCRs and cassettes on request. The main building also has a library and boutique and reception area, where you check in while you sip a welcome drink. To the east side of the media room is an expanded fitness center with cardio equipment and four spa treatment rooms. Cardi, an Anguillan and a cricket player who played professionally in England, is available as a personal trainer. A well-trained staff of professionals offer many Asian and other trendy specialty treatments. Treatments can also be given in one's room. Pilates or yoga and beach fitness session with Cardi are available almost daily.

In April 2008, Cap Juluca Properties Ltd., an investor syndicate and newly formed Anguillian company, acquired the Cap Juluca. The new owner's group, headed by travel industry executive Adam M. Aron, plans an $80 million renovation and upgrade of the resort along with the addition of new guest amenities, a new spa, retail shops, resort pool, and the development of Cove Bay Beach, Cap Juluca's second undeveloped beach. A limited number of residential villas will be available for sale. The renovation will be undertaken in phases, enabling the resort to remain open throughout. The hotel's present employees have been retained. Aron , formerly Chairman and CEO of Vail Resorts, including its RockResorts, serves on the Board of Directors of Starwood Hotels and Resorts, Norwegian Cruise Line, and Prestige Cruise Holdings, owner of Regent Seven Seas Cruises and Oceania Cruises. Among the major investors are Manfredi Lefebvre, Chairman of Silversea Cruises and Silversea Investments and the Government of Anguilla, which is expected to have 20 percent ownership in Cap Juluca Properties Ltd. Cap Juluca has been designed as a secluded, stylish retreat for sophisticated travelers and is meant to have a mystique of exotic, erotic luxury about it. There's every reason to believe that the new owners expect to keep it that way.

Cap Juluca *****
P.O. Box 240, Maunday's Bay, Anguilla, B.W.I.
Phone: (264) 497-6666; Fax: (264) 497-6617; e-mail: capjuluca@anguillanet.com; www.capjuluca.com

Owner: Cap Juluca Holdings, Ltd.

General Manager: Hans Maissen

Open: Year-round except September and October

Credit Cards: American Express, MasterCard, Visa

U.S. Reservations: Cap Juluca, (888) 8-JULUCA (888) 858-5822, (866) 458-5822, (305) 466-0916

Deposit: Three nights; thirty days cancellation

Minimum Stay: Seven nights during Christmas/New Year's

Arrival/Departure: Guests met at airport in Anguilla by hotel representative; complimentary transfer service in packages. On request, transfers can be arranged from St. Maarten airport on the Cap Juluca Sea Shuttle for $75 per person one-way (or private boat transfer for $355).

Distance from Airport: (Wallblake Airport) 5 miles: taxi one-way, $24; via ferry from Marigot, St. Martin: 4 miles (twenty minutes), $12; taxi from the ferry terminal in Anguilla to hotel, $20

Distance from the Valley: 5 miles; taxi one-way, $24

Accommodations: 58 rooms and junior suites and 7 suites in hotel villas and six pool villas; with terraces or patios; all have king-size beds; some suites have extra queen-size daybed

Amenities: Air-conditioning, ceiling fans; refrigerator with initially stocked minibar; telephone; some baths with tub, some with solarium and double tub, some with shower only; hair dryer, deluxe toiletries, bathrobe and slippers; nightly turndown service, room service as requested; bottle of rum and fruit in room; kitchen in villas

Electricity: 110/220 volts

Fitness Facilities/Spa Services: Fitness center; in-room treatments upon request

Sports: Freshwater swimming pool, six villa pools; tennis, Sunfish, Hobie Cats, snorkeling gear, waterskiing free; scuba, fishing, golf arranged for charge

Dress Code: Casual by day; casually elegant in evening; no jacket or tie required

Children: All ages, but advance inquiry requested for those under three; cribs; babysitters; supervised children's program several times a year

Meetings: Up to forty people

Day Visitors: No

Handicapped Facilities: No

Packages: Romantic Retreat; weekend getaway; weddings; and others

Rates: Per room, daily, CP. *High Season* (January 4–March 31): $825–$2,590. *Shoulder Season* (April 1–30 and November 15–mid-December): $535–$1,765. *Low Season:* $400–$1,245. One-bedroom/private pool suites and three- and five-bedroom villas priced separately; inquire

Service Charge: 10 percent

Government Tax: 10 percent

CUISINART RESORT & SPA
Rendezvous Bay, Anguilla, B.W.I.

A resort for the twenty-first century, CuisinArt is a hideaway for baby boomers who want it all—large comfortable rooms with the latest electronic gadgets, huge marble bathrooms, a beautiful beach, a vanishing-edge swimming pool, gourmet cuisine by a celebrated chef, a hydroponic farm (no pollution, no pesticides), a full-service spa for pampering, with a fitness center and par course for just enough exercise not to feel guilty. What else could you ask for?

Set on the beautiful white sands of Rendezvous Bay on Anguilla's southern coast with views of St. Martin across the Caribbean Sea, the stylish resort's lavishness makes it clear that no costs were spared, no shortcuts taken.

The resort is approached by a drive along a flower-bordered boulevard that leads to the grand entrance of the blue-domed main building with the reception and concierge desks, three boutiques, a video library, a game room with a billiards table, a bar, a lounge, and restaurants. Everywhere the whitewashed walls are ablaze with vivid, decorative paintings by Italian artists, establishing one of CuisinArt's dual goals—art patronage. And you thought it was named for a kitchen appliance!

(I will let you in on a little secret. Many people seem puzzled by the name, CuisinArt. The quick explanation: The resort's owner, Leandro Rizzuto, owns Conair, the parent company of Le Cuisinart.)

The resort is set around tropical gardens centered by a large swimming pool from which a series of small pools and waterfalls drop to the beach. To each side are large whitewashed villas of Mediterranean-inspired architecture. Flower-filled courtyards at each entrance are framed by an archway with a wooden door that adds an accent and stairs whose art deco brick glass is integrated into the white stucco walls.

All ten villas are directly on the beach; each has eight spacious units. The first and second floors have junior suites while the top floor has one-bedroom and luxury junior suites with patios or terraces that convert to two-bedroom suites. The verandas are large enough for a table with two chairs and two chaise lounges. All have cable television with forty-seven channels, telephone, and high-speed Internet connection. Large bathrooms are set in soft-toned Italian marble and have double sinks, deep oval tubs, and a separate shower. Luxury junior suites and one-bedroom suites also have a private solarium for sunning.

The three-story main building has eleven accommodations: nine luxury rooms and two spectacular penthouses. Of the latter, one is a 4,300-square-foot, three-bedroom suite, the other a 7,600-square-foot, two-bedroom suite. Each has a living room, a fully equipped kitchen (with Cuisinart appliances), and wraparound terraces with expansive views. Two additional guest rooms are available for penthouse guests.

The spacious accommodations—double the size of most hotel rooms—are furnished in a comfortably elegant style with fine rattan and wood furniture imported from Mexico and brightly colored Italian fabrics, predominantly in blue and yellow. There are three venues for dining. Santorini, the resort's gourmet restaurant, offers a creative menu of contemporary cuisine infused with the flamboyant flavors and spices of the Caribbean. Santorini also has a "Chef's Table" where twice weekly, executive chef Denise Carr presents a six-course dinner with wine pairings from the resort's new 3,600-bottle cellar, and hands-on cooking classes are also offered twice a week for lunch. Cafe Mediterraneo, overlooking the pool, serves seafood, grilled items, pizza, and salads of fresh home-grown vegetables. Bring money: Prices here are on a par with those of top eateries in New York.

The third venue is the new Tapas Lounge and Rum Bar where, as the name implies, small plates of finger food are served,

accompanied by live music several nights during the week. The Hydroponic "farm" (which looked like a greenhouse to me), grows much of the vegetables, edible flowers, and herbs used by the resort in its restaurants and by the spa to create some of its organic lotions and oils.

CuisinArt has three lighted tennis courts, a boccie court next to the swimming pool, a championship croquet field, and a 1-mile par course with exercise stations. Nonmotorized water sports are complimentary for guests.

The resort's full-service Venus spa and fitness center is situated in a three-story building with five treatment rooms, of which three have outdoor showers. The top floor is used as an outdoor treatment space. The trained staff offers massages, seaweed wraps, reflexology, aromatherapy, hot stone therapy, sea salt scrubs, and an array of other treatments. An expansion tripling the spa's size was completed in autumn of 2008. The spa now has a total of sixteen treatment rooms including couples and VIP suites, a thalassotherapy pool, a yoga/Pilates studio, a fitness center with Technogym equipment, and more.

CuisinArt's gardens, created by landscape designer and horticulturalist Caryl Clement as an oasis within Anquilla's dry environment, showcase more than 150 species of trees, fragrant flowers, and exotic plants.

CuisinArt's prices might give you sticker shock, but money seems not to be a problem for the new millionaires, celebrities, and other people who come here—the highest-priced suites are the first to go.

CuisinArt Resort & Spa ***
P.O. Box 2000, Rendezvous Bay,
Anguilla, B.W.I
Phone: (264) 498-2000; Fax: (264) 498-2010; e-mail: reservations@cuisinart.ai;
www.cuisinartresort.com

Owner: Leandro Rizzuto

General Manager: Stephane Zaharia

Open: Year-round except early September–October

Credit Cards: American Express, Master-Card, Visa

U.S. Reservations: (800) 943-3210, (212) 972-0880

Deposit: Three nights; thirty days cancellation

Minimum Stay: Ten nights during Christmas/New Year's

Arrival/Departure: Guests met at Anguilla airport by hotel representative

Distance from Airport: (Wallblake Airport) 6 miles (20-minute drive): taxi one-way, $22; via ferry from Marigot, St. Martin, to Blowing Point Ferry terminal, (twenty-five minutes), $15. Boat shuttle from St. Maarten Airport to Blowing Point Ferry Terminal (20 minutes) $68 per person. Taxi from Blowing Point to resort, $20.

Distance from the Valley: 4 miles; taxi one-way, $20

Accommodations: 93 rooms and suites, all with terraces

Amenities: Air-conditioning, ceiling fans; refrigerator; telephone, high-speed Internet; bath with tub and separate shower, hair dryer, deluxe toiletries, bathrobe; nightly turndown service, room service; concierge

Electricity: 110/220 volts

Fitness Facilities/Spa Services: Full-service spa, fitness center, scheduled classes, 1-mile par course, hair salon, Jacuzzi

Sports: Freshwater swimming pool; three lighted tennis courts, pro and clinics; boccie court; championship croquet field; snorkeling, windsurfing, sailing; golf arranged

Dress Code: Casual by day; casually elegant in evening; no jacket or tie required

Meetings: Up to twenty-five people

Children: All ages; supervised children's program during holiday periods only

Day Visitors: No

Handicapped Facilities: No

Packages: Year-round

Rates: Per room, daily, CP. *Winter* (January 4–March 31): $705–$3,500. *Spring* (April 1–30): $485–$2,500. *Summer* (May–Nov 16) $400–$2,300;. *Holiday* (mid-December–January 3): $1,095–$5,280. Holiday rates require a ten-night minimum stay.

Service Charge: 10 percent

Government Tax: 10 percent

MALLIOUHANA
Mead's Bay, Anguilla, B.W.I.

Located on Anguilla's northwestern coast on a twenty-five-acre bluff overlooking two spectacular beaches, Malliouhana (the Arawak Indian name for Anguilla) is a sybaritic fantasy in Mediterranean design set in a garden of Eden.

Almost from the day it opened in 1984, the resort won rave reviews for its extraordinary interiors, style, refinement, gourmet cuisine, and attention to detail. It raised deluxe to a lofty new level that few can equal.

Before creating Malliouhana, British industrialist and well-traveled bon vivant Leon Roydon and his late wife, Lyane, had dreamed of building a Caribbean resort with the standards to which they were accustomed in Europe. Like most people, the Roydons fell in love with Anguilla when they visited it for the first time, in 1980.

There are no signs pointing the way to Malliouhana. A driveway passes through landscaped gardens exploding with color and shaded by stately palms to a cluster of white stucco buildings with arched galleries and red tile roofs that look more like palatial Mediterranean hilltop mansions than a hotel.

From the elegant lobby you step through a series of tall, cool white arches that rise to cathedral ceilings of warm Brazilian walnut. They lead to terraced gardens and high-ceilinged, breeze-filled lounges with light terra-cotta tile floors and upholstered rattan furniture.

Malliouhana's accommodations all feature huge bedrooms with king-size beds; they are located in wings of the main building and other buildings on the cliff and in villas with one-bedroom suites and two double rooms directly on the beach. Junior suites have large bedrooms and dressing rooms; one-bedroom and two-bedroom suites have separate bedrooms, living-dining rooms, and covered patios. Guest rooms have marbled and mirrored bathrooms almost as large as the bedrooms, and terraces overlooking Anguilla's peacock-blue waters.

Exquisitely designed tropical furniture of the highest-quality rush and bamboo and rich Brazilian mahogany louvered doors and windows with solid-brass fittings contrast with the stark white bedcovers, tile floors, and walls adorned with subdued Asian prints and vibrant Haitian paintings.

The resort has a mile of powder-fine beach on one side and a small, intimate cove, accessible only from the hotel (or by boat), on the other. There are four Laykold tennis courts (lighted), which are managed by a Peter Burwash International pro. You'll also find a water-sports center and fitness center. The hotel's launch is available for trips to nearby islets and reefs for snorkeling and picnics and for excursions to St. Martin.

At cocktails guests enjoy light musical entertainment, but the evening's highlight is dining on haute cuisine in the casually elegant terrace restaurant overlooking the sea. Chef Alain Laurent has continued the tradition of his teacher, the late Jo Rostang of La Bonne Auberge—a two-star Michelin restaurant on the French Riviera—who developed Malliouhana's cuisine. In the winter season, staff from La Bonne Auberge come to work with the Anguillan staff, some of whom have been given training in France. Malliouhana also has an outstanding wine cellar, stocked with 25,000 bottles of fine wine selected and shipped by connoisseur Leon Roydon, mostly from France.

For those who prefer a casual day, the resort has another pool and poolside cafe, Le Bistro, by the beach. The second floor of the cafe has a large room for meetings; it can be converted into a disco.

If you had any doubt that times are changing, Malliouhana's children's addition is proof positive. For the increasing number of guests traveling with their children and grandchildren, the posh hideaway added the Children's Place, a well-equipped beachfront playground with its own pirate ship beached on the sand, a paddling pool, and two Playworld Systems areas: one for ages two through five, the other for ages five through twelve. The playground is supervised daily from 9:00 a.m. to 5:30 p.m. and is free for guests.

In another bow to trends, the resort built an elaborate 15,000-square-foot spa. The facility offers massage, skin and hair care, and body treatments that use island herbs, spices, flowers, and fruits creatively. Roydon clearly understands the needs of his discerning guests. A staff-to-guest ratio of more than two to one and the high level of service by the resort's staff of 200 Anguillans, more than half of whom have been with the resort since it opened, ensure that those needs are met in a gracious atmosphere.

From the time it opened, Malliouhana has attracted celebrities, movie stars, and a loyal following of well-heeled, sophisticated travelers. Leon Roydon and his son Nigel manage the hotel with meticulous care. One of them is on hand to greet guests on arrival and to say farewell at the end of their stay. At other times, however, the managers keep their distance, believing that people come to Malliouhana for privacy. As a result, some people find Malliouhana cold. Malliouhana's ambience is not for everyone, especially if you prefer your beachside elegance to be barefoot.

Malliouhana *****
P.O. Box 173, Mead's Bay, Anguilla, B.W.I.
Phone: (800) 835-0796, (264) 497-6111; Fax: (264) 497-6011; e-mail: malliouhana@anguillanet.com; www.malliouhana.com

Owner: Leon Roydon

General Manager: Nigel Roydon

Open: Year-round except September–October

Credit Cards: Most major

U.S. Reservations: Direct to hotel, (800) 835-0796

Deposit: Three nights; thirty days cancellation

Minimum Stay: Seven nights, December–March

Arrival/Departure: Transfers not available

Distance from Airport: 8 miles from Wallblake Airport and Blowing Point Ferry terminal; taxi one-way, $20

Distance from Main Town: 9 miles; taxi one-way, $20

Accommodations: 55 rooms (including 34 double rooms, six junior suites, seven one-bedroom suites, three Jacuzzi suites, one pool suite, and two two-bedroom suites)

Amenities: Air-conditioning, ceiling fans (also in bathrooms); telephone; stocked minibars; ample closet space; bathroom vanities with makeup lights, deep tub, shower stall, bidet, plush towels, bathrobes, hair dryer, toiletries; room service until 10:30 p.m.; beauty salon; designer boutique, sundries shop; cable television in television room and library; some televisions and VCRs for rent

Electricity: 110 volts

Fitness Facilities/Spa Services: Fitness center and full-service spa; personal trainer

Sports: Three freshwater pools and large heated Jacuzzi; snorkeling; four tennis courts (lighted); fishing gear, waterskiing, windsurfing, Sunfish, Lasers, Prindle catamarans; deep-sea fishing, diving arranged for fee

Dress Code: Casual but chic sportswear by day; casually elegant in evening

Children: All ages; babysitters available; children's pool and playground

Meetings: Small groups on request

Day Visitors: No

Handicapped Facilities: No

Packages: Romance (honeymoon, anniversary); June 1–August 31, packages of four or more nights and Spa, five nights (April–mid-December); Family & Friends, 5 nights (May–mid-November)

Rates: Single or double, daily, EP. *High Season* (mid-December–March 31): $720–$3,340. *Shoulder Season* (April 1–April 30 and November 19–mid-December): $465–$2,015. *Low Season* (May 1–August 31 and November 1–19): $345–$1,465. Surcharge for Christmas holiday period.

Service Charge: 10 percent

Government Tax: 10 percent

SIRENA RESORT AND VILLAS
Mead's Bay, Anguilla, B.W.I.

Soothing to your mind and gentle on your pocketbook, this small ridgetop resort refutes the ill-founded image that Anguilla is a hideaway only for the filthy rich.

Only a short slope—200 yards, maybe—from powdery sands, Sirena Resort and Villas gives you fabulous Mead's Bay Beach but at a third of the cost of Malliouhana, the pricey preserve of celebrities and moguls that anchors the beach's eastern end.

To be absolutely accurate and not to mislead, Sirena has accommodations of two types in two locations. There are villas near the shore; the walk to the beach for villa guests takes about one minute. At the top of the rise is the main hotel, an attractive complex of two- and three-story buildings housing the restaurants, bar, lounge, a boutique, small spa, Internet cafe, and most accommodations. Guests here take a three-minute walk along a path to the same fine beach—hardly an inconvenience.

Designed by a Swiss architect, Sirena combines Mediterranean tradition with Caribbean touches: white stucco walls and arches, peaked ceilings, weathered red tile roofs, and generous balconies trimmed with white latticework.

The main building has guest rooms on three floors, each with a balcony overlooking the gardens and the large swimming pool. Rooms are modest and uncluttered.

They have terra-cotta tile floors and tiled bathrooms, and are furnished with Indonesian furniture, Egyptian cotton linens, green plants, and fresh flowers. All rooms have safes, and most standard and superior rooms, plus the villas, have air-conditioning and cable television at no extra charge. Room service is available for breakfast only.

I would have been happy had the rooms been just a wee bit larger with a tad more closet space (pack lightly). They are functional and immaculate. Sirena even includes single rooms—an almost unheard-of commodity in Caribbean resorts. The singles are small with a queen-size bed and a tiny terrace. The most desirable double rooms are the top-floor ones, which have high ceilings and the best views. Rooms 301 and 302 have access to a roof terrace with expansive views. Even more desirable are the junior suites, two on the top floor of the main building and two in a new building in the gardens. These now have a new roof that has given them much higher ceilings.

Stone pathways through the gardens lead to the four comfortable, but rather modest, villas and the mile-long beach. Two villas have two bedrooms with two baths, and two have three bedrooms, each with a bath and a separate entrance. The villas have lounges, fully equipped kitchens, a private patio or rooftop sundeck, a telephone, barbecue equipment, daily maid service, and their own freshwater pool. Dishwashers and cable television are available at an extra charge. The villas are particularly well suited for families.

The hotel's restaurant, Mahi Mahi, offers French cuisine with a Caribbean flavor. The manager's cocktail party and a Caribbean evening on Monday includes music by a steel band, and Thursday night features performances by local music groups.

The resort has spa services such as massage and reflexology at its Massage Center.

Sirena is well suited for families. In the summer months the resort offers a children's program that includes snorkeling trips, glass-bottom boat excursions, and other activities. Up to two children under twelve stay free in a room with two adults.

Opened in 1989 by a young, personable Swiss couple and operated by them, Sirena acquired new owners in 2007.

Sirena may not have the panache of its ritzy neighbors, but many people would probably find its casual and comfortable digs far more suitable for a relaxed beachside vacation.

Generally, Sirena Resort and Villas receives more Europeans, particularly in the summer, than Americans. Its low-key, friendly atmosphere is well suited to singles who want a quiet vacation, young couples, and families with children who are happy building sand castles on the beach and can go without a daily fix of television or Nintendo.

Sirena Resort and Villas **
P.O. Box 200, Mead's Bay, Anguilla, B.W.I. Phone: (264) 497-6827; Fax: (264) 497-6829; e-mail: info@sirenaresort.com; www .sirenaresort.com

Owner/General Manager: Ian Malpass

Open: Year-round

Credit Cards: All major

Reservations: Direct to hotel, (800) 331-9358; or International Travel and Resorts (ITR), (800) 223-9815, (212) 251-1800; Fax: (212) 545-8467

Deposit: Three nights; ten days confirmation; thirty days cancellation

Minimum Stay: Ten nights during Christmas/New Year's

Arrival/Departure: Transfer arranged upon request for fee

Distance from Airport: (Wallblake Airport) 9 miles; taxi one-way, $20

Distance from Main Town: 9 miles; taxi one-way, $20

Accommodations: 20 units with balcony or patio in three-story main building (16 doubles with queen, king, or two full-size beds; four singles with queen); four junior suites (with king and queen sleeper sofa); and six villas with 15 bedrooms, each with two queens or one king

Amenities: Ceiling fans; telephone; clock-radio; bath with shower only, hair dryer, basket of toiletries; minibar; room service for breakfast only; safe; air-conditioning in most standard and superior rooms, plus all suites and villas; cable television in villas and available in hotel rooms for charge; Jacuzzi tubs in junior suites; massage center

Electricity: 110 volts

Sports: Two freshwater swimming pools; free snorkeling gear; bicycles for fee; tennis, boating, fishing, horseback riding arranged; full-service PADI Dive Center on premises

Dress Code: Informal

Children: All ages; cribs; babysitters; children's activity program in summer; up to two children under twelve stay free in room with two adults

Meetings: No

Day Visitors: Welcome

Handicapped Facilities: No

Packages: Summer, pre-Christmas, winter

Rates: Per person, daily, EP. *High Season* (mid-December–March 31): $260–$350 (rooms); $400-$470 (suites); $400–$500 (villas). *Low Season:* $159–$240 (rooms); $279–$319 (suites); $399–$624 (villas). Single rates available; inquire. Check out specials on its Web site.

Service Charge: 10 percent

Government Tax: 10 percent; Tourism Tax: $1 per room per night

ANTIGUA

Shaped somewhat like a maple leaf, Antigua has protruding fingers that provide its coastline with sheltered bays, natural harbors, and extra miles of beautiful beaches—one for every day of the year, the Antiguans say—fringed by coral reefs. These assets have made Antigua one of the most popular beach and water-sports centers in the Caribbean. As a bonus, low humidity and year-round trade winds create the ideal climate for tennis, golf, horseback riding, and a variety of other sports and sightseeing.

Antigua (pronounced Ann-TEE-ga) is the largest of the Leeward Islands. Located east of Puerto Rico, between the U.S. Virgin Islands and the French and Dutch West Indies, Antigua is a transportation hub of the region and the home of LIAT (Leeward Islands Air Transport), the regional carrier of several Eastern Caribbean states.

After English settlers from St. Kitts established a colony near Old Town on the southern coast in 1632, Antigua remained a British possession until 1981, when full independence was achieved. Today the island's British heritage and historic character are most evident at English Harbour, once the headquarters of the British navy, where the buildings of the old wharf (now known as Nelson's Dockyard) have been restored to house shops, inns, restaurants, and museums.

St. John's, the capital and once a sleepy West Indian village, has become a popular tourist mecca. Charming historic buildings of West Indian architecture house attractive boutiques and restaurants.

This relaxed and quietly sophisticated island has a few large resorts and casinos, but most of Antigua's hotels are small and operated by their owners—a feature that helps give the island a less commercial atmosphere than some other Caribbean destinations.

Information

Antigua and Barbuda Department of Tourism, 305 East 47th Street, Suite 6A, New York, NY 10017; (212) 541-4117, (888) 268-4227; Fax: (646) 215-6008; www.antigua-barbuda.org
(Also see Hermitage Bay on p. 300 and
Hodges Bay Club on p. 301 in On the Horizon.)

CARLISLE BAY

St. Mary's, Antigua

Set on a secluded beach on the south coast of Antigua, with a backdrop of rolling hills, Carlisle Bay byof British hotelier Gordon Campbell Gray, best known for One Aldwych, one of London's leading contemporary luxury hotels, brings urban chic to the Tropics—and his first Caribbean venture.

Upon arrival at Carlisle Bay, you will cross a short bridge over a small pond into the Pavilion, a large, high-ceilinged, open reception area with contemporary sofas in white and dark wood tables and chairs set against pickled gray walls. To the right of the Pavilion entrance is the reception desk, of an Asian design. At the opposite end is the Pavilion Bar, where light snacks are served, and beyond, the swimming pool. At the center is a large round table with vases of orchids and coffee table books. Dominating the room at the entrance and in the Pavilion are huge, 7-foot-high, dark wood Indonesian planters—all very dramatic.

Off the lobby and overlooking the large swimming pool is East, the resort's gourmet dinner restaurant, serving Asian fusion cuisine. Guests enter through a pair of massive, carved Indonesian wooden doors flanked by a glass wall. On the floor of maple, stained dark to boat finish, are dark wood tables and tomato pink, slipcovered chairs to enhance East's exotic look.

Indigo on the Beach is an open-to-the-breezes beachfront bar and restaurant serving three meals with an accent on grills, fresh seafood, and salads. The restaurant's decor repeats the gray pickled wood on the floor, dark wood Caribbean chairs with gray-striped cushions, and dark wood tables with polished Indigo blue tops—hence the name.

The pretty, free-form swimming pool, tiled in dark green and gray mosaic, is surrounded by natural hardwood lounge chairs shaded by white umbrellas. Next to the pool, a pergola with seating is set in a mass of white bougainvillea.

There are two sets of guest rooms, some directly on the beach in the buildings of the former hotel situated here, and now renovated from top to bottom; others set back a few steps from the beach in large, three-story villas in landscaped gardens, all with private terrace or balcony facing the sea. The resort takes advantage of the two sets of accommodations by designating the first group directly on the beach as "family suites" intended for guests with children; while the three-story villas are designed for couples and individuals who probably fit the "urban sophisticate" profile for whom the resort was designed.

All accommodations are spacious suites—from junior to three-bedroom—in a cool contemporary style designed by London interior designer Mary Fox Linton, using four subdued color schemes—lavender, sunset, aqua, and gray-blue—and accented by straight-line dark wood furniture with white Frette bed linens and textured silk curtains of Thai silk from Jim Thompson. The suites are equipped with CD and DVD players, satellite television, and minibar. Fiber optic reading lights on each side of the king-size bed, high-speed wireless Internet access, an espresso machine, and exotic toiletries are among the suites' unusual amenities. The large bathroom has a separate shower, bathtub, and toilet—all in glass and stainless steel fixtures giving the room a rather severe, masculine look.

The suites' wardrobe doors are covered in specially commissioned black-and-white photographs of Antiguan plant life by Jason

Taylor. His images of Antigua also hang in the suites, intended, perhaps, to give the room an existential aura. The outdoor terraces are furnished with wide, dark wood day beds, a gray rattan table and chairs covered in silver-gray cotton, and more of the 7-foot-high Indonesian planters that greet visitors at the entrance and in the Pavilion.

The three-bedroom Carlisle Suites are designed to accommodate six guests and have two king-bedded rooms and one twin-bedded room. They are not available to parties of more than six, and no discounts are offered for reduced occupancy.

In addition to family-friendly accommodation, the resort welcomes children with Cool Kids Club, a purpose-built, professional staff facility catering to children from six months to twelve years old. The air-conditioned center with a shaded terrace is equipped with jungle gym, sandpit, paddling pool and four mini tennis courts and is open daily. There is no charge for children three years and older. For babies and toddlers and for evening babysitter, the rate is $15 per hour plus service & tax. Children are split into age groups: Six months through three years, activities include finger painting, water play, treasure hunts, and beach games; four through seven years, activities include art projects, song and dance, junior tennis, and swimming; eight through twelve years, activities include outdoor sports, indoor activities, and two excursions per week such as Hobie cat sailing, mini-hikes, or swimming with stingrays (there is a charge for off-site visits). Teenagers may join younger children on excursions and participate in tennis and water-sports clinics. Blue, the spa, gym, and wellness center in a glass-walled pavilion near the tennis courts, has six treatment rooms including a couples' room. It offers a wide range of health and beauty treatments using pure and natural products. It also has a beauty salon.

The state-of-the-art gymnasium, with 360-degree views over the beach and hills, has a chill-out room, separate men's and women's plunge pools and saunas, Pilates area, and a juice bar. Yoga is offered in a new, open-sided pavilion in the gardens. The spa reception desk and juice bar are made of marble and resin composite in duck egg blue; gray tones dominate the spa.

Carlisle Bay has nine tennis courts with Har-Tru surfaces; two are lighted for night play. Water sports include snorkeling, dinghy and catamaran sailing, windsurfing, and diving with a qualified dive instructor. Kite-surfing, deep-sea fishing, and scuba diving are available, but no motorized water sports. The casual Jetty Bar is on the beach by the water-sports center.

The glass-fronted library, with a collection ranging from great works to great beach reads, has two computer desks with flat-screen iMac computers and Internet access, and an unusual feature: Lucite and glass bookshelves that are backlit and slowly change color. The room is furnished with white sofas and armchairs and a glass table with a driftwood base.

Another glass-sided facility, the Carlisle Room, overlooks the tennis courts and is used for meetings or private dining. It comfortably seats thirty dining guests in chairs with hyacinth blue slipcovers. The air-conditioned Screening Room, like the original at One Aldwych, has forty-five Italian-designed blue leather chairs. Current films and old favorites are screened every evening and children's movies are offered during the day, particularly at the warmest time of day.

Carlisle Bay ****
Old Road, St. Mary's, Antigua, W.I.
Phone: (268) 484-0000; Fax: (268) 484-0001; e-mail: info@carlisle-bay.com; www .carlisle-bay.com

Owner: Gordon Campbell Gray

General Manager: Andrew Hedley

Open: Year-round except September to mid-October

Credit Cards: Most major

U.S. Reservations: Direct to hotel; Leading Small Hotels of the World; Crown International, (800) 628-8929

Deposit: Full payment in advance

Minimum Stay: Ten nights, Christmas/New Year's

Arrival/Departure: No private hotel transfer service due to local regulations; however, airport meet/assist service available

Distance from Airport: Thirty minutes from International Airport; taxi $48 for up to four passengers

Distance from St. John's: Thirty minutes; twenty minutes from English Harbour

Accommodations: 88 suites (27 beach; 48 ocean; four three-bedroom Carlisle suites; nine Bay suites being added)

Amenities: King-size or twin beds, Frette bed linens; air-conditioning, ceiling fan; Living Nature toiletries; direct-dialing phone, Internet access, satellite television; minibar; espresso machine; safe; twenty-four-hour room service; terrace or balcony with double daybed

Electricity: 110 volts

Fitness Facilities/Spa Services: Spa with six treatment rooms; separate men's and women's plunge pools and saunas; gym, yoga and Pilates area; juice bar

Sports: Freshwater swimming pool; nine tennis courts, two floodlit; snorkeling, sailing, windsurfing, diving, kite-surfing, deep-sea fishing, and scuba diving available; no motorized water sports

Dress Code: Smart casual

Children: All ages; professionally staffed kids club

Meetings: Up to forty-five people in Carlisle Room; forty-five-seat screening room

Day Visitors: Restaurants with reservations

Handicapped Facilities: No

Packages: Spa, tennis, yoga, couples, celebration/honeymoon; four and seven nights

Rates: Per room, double, FAP and afternoon tea. *High Season* (mid-December–late March): $1,050–$1,125; Carlisle suite $2,300–$2,800. *Spring/Autumn:* $840–$895; Carlisle suites $1,975–$2,1785. *Low Season:* $775–$830; Carlisle suite $1,750–$1,950. Third person and meal plans available.

Service Charge: 10 percent

Government Tax: 10.5 percent

CURTAIN BLUFF
St. John's, Antigua, W.I.

Ideally located on a secluded promontory on Antigua's southern coast, with Atlantic surf washing the beach on one side and the tranquil Caribbean lapping the shore on the other, Curtain Bluff is an exclusive enclave of tropical splendor spread across twenty beachfront acres against a backdrop of verdant hills.

The time-tested resort has been called Antigua's blue-chip address for conservative travelers by some and a tropical paradise with a country club ambience by others, but perhaps the best description was offered by the guest who said, "This is a place where you fall in love with your wife all over again." Not a bad vote of confidence for a resort that set a new standard for the Caribbean when it was opened in 1961, watched a host of competitors blossom—and wither like dandelions—and is still going strong.

Whatever Curtain Bluff is, for sure it is a reflection of its creator, Howard Hulford. A legend in his own time, he has been called by many the best hotelier in the Caribbean. Gruff, opinionated, love-me-if-you-dare, Hulford is as famous for his silver mustache as he is for his manner. He and his fine staff have made sure his standard of excellence has been maintained at Curtain Bluff for almost five decades. As a result the resort is usually booked a year in advance, primarily by repeat visitors.

Curtain Bluff operates as an all-inclusive resort. Included in the price are all meals, afternoon tea, and table wine; most sports; deep-sea fishing; and even postage stamps. Room service is available for all meals, and bar service is provided at no extra charge—an unusual amenity for an all-inclusive resort.

Accommodations include seafront double rooms with sitting areas as well as one- and two-bedroom suites in two-story, low-rise buildings, all with terraces and dreamy views. The tastefully appointed rooms have tile floors and wicker furniture dressed in pastels. The two-bedroom, two-level suites offer a breeze-cooled patio with a hammock just waiting to be used; the second bedroom can be rented as a separate accommodation.

The most luxurious: deluxe suites perched in stair-step fashion near the top of the bluff. Each unit has a bedroom larger than most New York apartments, with great reading lights mounted by the headboard, a spacious living room that opens directly onto a large terrace with spectacular views, five ceiling fans, and a well-equipped marbled bathroom with separate tubs and showers. The counters, with double sinks, are topped with gorgeous, unusual green or blue variegated marble. One of the newest buildings has eighteen marvelous junior suites, of whichseven are connecting pairs and accommodate families. Another group of twenty-two junior suites, each with 750 square feet have nine pairs connecting. Above the two floors of junior suites are two extravagant suites, Grace Bay and Morris Bay, comprising the entire third floor; each is the equivalent in size of three junior suites.

Your introduction to Curtain Bluff begins at the central building, surrounded by a riot of flowers and gardens. At the reception and concierge desk, you will be greeted by the amiable Wendy Eardley, the resort's very efficient assistant manager who seems to have the answer to your every need. Beyond is a small patio, shaded by a large tamarind tree, and the dining terrace. To one side is a boutique and the Sugar Mill Bar, the gathering spot for predinner drinks and hors d'oeuvres. Both the dining terrace and bar are open to the view and have stairs that lead down to the gardens and the beachside rooms—an added convenience for guests here.

Daytime activities are centered on the calm, palm-fringed Caribbean beach, which offers the Beach Club, where informal lunches are served; the Wednesday barbecue buffet is a beach party with steel band music. You'll find umbrellas, changing rooms, showers, and water-sports equipment. Here, too, is the large swimming pool in a pretty grove overlooking the beach.

Tennis is one of Curtain Bluff's main attractions. It has four all-weather championship courts (lighted), a squash court, viewing stands, a resident pro, and a pro shop. Beyond the tennis courts is an air-conditioned fitness center with a full line of exercise equipment and an outdoor area where aerobic, Pilates, and yoga sessions are held with a professional trainer six times weekly.

Meals are served in the main restaurant, tea on the Bar Terrace. The kitchen at Curtain Bluff is directed by Christophe Blatz, the former sous-chef, following the retirement of chef Reudi Portmann, who had been with Curtain Bluff for thirty-seven years. Blatz, like Portmann, keeps his menus limited, changing them daily to maximize the use of fresh products.

Lunches are light, but dinners are a real treat with your choice of hot and cold soups, appetizers, salads, six different entrees, and too many yummy desserts each night. The wine cellar, with approximately 30,000 bottles of the finest vintages, is Hulford's pride, second only to his fabulous gardens.

Times are changing, even at Curtain Bluff. Recently, the resort has added air-conditioning to all bedrooms and has added wireless Internet access in each room. But the new spa with its fabulous location tops the list of new amenities. Perched on the bluff at the south end of the property with wide-angle views of the Caribbean and the island of Montserrat in the distance, the Spa at Curtain Bluff has five treatment rooms: four single and one for couples—each has its own private balcony. Open-air walkways and waterfalls enhance the setting, while a relaxation room, a ten-person hot tub, and an outdoor veranda overlooking the water provide ideal spots to relax and enjoy the spa's freshly brewed lemongrass tea made from herbs grown in the resort's garden. "Spa Bites," a changing menu of fruit and vegetable snacks developed by spa director Novie Jones and Curtain Bluff's chef are served after treatments. Among the spa's signature treatments are a caviar-and-champagne massage when one's body is saturated with special oils and champagne poured over it; a soothing wrap of water lily, green tea, and chamomile; a Caribbean green coffee wrap for a cellulite treatment; and an antiaging with Myoxy caviar mask, among other treatments. The spa also offers treatments for children that parents can observe. The spa uses Pevonia products and is open daily from 10:00 a.m. to 7:00 p.m.

Curtain Bluff is not for everyone, but it does not try to be. The ambience may seem a little old-fashioned to some, but it appeals to Curtain Bluff's loyal patrons, who are now in their third generation and who enjoy dressing for dinner and dancing under the stars to the sounds of the oldies, updated for the young and young-at-heart with jazz, rock, reggae, and calypso.

Curtain Bluff *****
P.O. Box 288, Old Road, St. John's, Antigua, W.I.
Phone: (268) 462-8400, -8403, (888) 289-9898, (212) 289-8888; Fax: (268) 462-8409; www.curtainbluff.com; curtain bluff@curtainbluff.com

Owner: Howard Hulford

Managing Director: Rob Sherman

General Manager: Calvert A. Roberts

Open: November 1–late August

Credit Cards: All major

U.S. Reservations: Direct to hotel or (212) 289-8888

Deposit: Three nights; thirty days cancellation except mid-December–January 1, for which payment must be received before November 1

Minimum Stay: Ten nights during Christmas

Arrival/Departure: Hotel transfers not available due to local taxi regulations

Distance from Airport: 16 miles (thirty-five minutes); taxi one-way, $50

Distance from St. John's: 13 miles; taxi one-way, $30

Accommodations: 72 rooms and suites, all with terraces. All accommodations have either a king or two twin beds.

Amenities: Ceiling fans; telephones (suites have them in bath); wall safes; bath with tub and shower, bathrobes, umbrella, miniature flashlight, hair dryers available; fresh flowers daily; full room service; suites have minibars; no television (television room); room service for food during meal times, for bar 10:00 a.m.–11:00 p.m.; Internet in-room connection (charge for high-speed)

Electricity: 110 volts

Fitness Facilities/Spa Services: See text

Sports: Tennis (see text); squash; croquet; putting green; Hobie cats, snorkeling, waterskiing, windsurfing; diving for certified divers only; deep-sea fishing; 47-foot ketch for optional whole- and half-day sails; swimming pool; hiking trips in nearby hills; area offers some of the best birding locations in Antigua

Dress Code: Casual by day; cover-up required in dining room; long pants and collared shirts for gentlemen (jacket and tie optional) required after 7:00 p.m. in public areas

Children: All ages, except February, when only those twelve years and older welcome; cribs; babysitters

Meetings: Up to twenty people

Day Visitors: No

Handicapped Facilities: Limited

Rates: Per room double, daily, All-inclusive. *High Season* (mid-December–mid-April): $995–$1,725. *Low Season* (mid-April–May and mid-October–mid-December): $745–$1,220. Single-room rate $100 less than double-room rate.

Service Charge: 10 percent

Government Tax: 10.5 percent

GALLEY BAY RESORT & SPA
St. John's, Antigua, W.I.

By the time you have made the long drive from the airport, through St. John's and down the narrow country road to Galley Bay, you may be having second thoughts. But press on. It's worth it.

Galley Bay (not to be confused with Galleon Beach on the eastern side of Antigua) has one of the prettiest away-from-it-all settings in the Caribbean. Tucked away on the western coast on forty tropical acres—some landscaped, some natural—the resort is bordered on one side by ½ mile of uninterrupted white-sand beach and, on the other, by a lagoon and bird sanctuary, banded by green hills.

After a hurricane all but leveled the resort in 1995, it was completely rebuilt by its new owners whose group has other hotels in Antigua, Palm Island in the Grenadines, and hotels on three other islands. The rebuilding modernized Galley Bay without changing its essential character, although it is no longer rustic, as it was in the past. The beautiful new entryway with a land bridge spanning the lagoon is downright elegant. All the facilities were upgraded, the gardens tamed and greatly embellished, and a much-needed swimming pool added, as well as six cottages with twenty-four deluxe guest rooms directly on the southern beach. A further expansion is underway on the north side where a second swimming pool and thirty-two premium suites have been added.

Galley Bay offers three types of accommodations: beachfront rooms, suites directly on the beach, and thatched-roof huts called Gauguin Cottages, resting under shade trees by the lagoon, a stone's throw from the sea. The original beachfront rooms, in two-unit cottages with patios, have terra-cotta floors, rush rugs, and a fresh look with rattan furniture covered with attractive prints and louvered windows that catch the breezes.

Rooms in the newest cottages are about a third larger and have huge marble bathrooms with a long, wide counter over two sinks and a big shower. There is a walk-in closet and enough hangers for a year's stay. All have air-conditioning, ceiling fans, telephone, television, coffeemakers, and minifridges stocked with soft drinks and beer. Another beachfront group of sixteen more luxurious one-bedroom suites are located on the south side of the beach. The thirty-two most recently added suites on the north side near the new, second swmming pool, are the most luxurious of all, with mahogany furniture and 400-thread-count sheets, as well as flat-screen, wall-mounted television, iPod docking stations, DVD players, and wireless Internet access. The oversized baths have his and hers showers and soaking tubs for two.

The Gauguin Cottages are much more comfortable than you might expect upon first sight. They are two rooms whose masonry walls are covered with white stucco and wooden strips and topped with thatched roofs made to look like huts; they are connected by a thatch-covered breezeway-patio. One "hut" is a spacious bedroom with a sitting area; the other has a bath/dressing room where you will find extra-plush towels and toiletries. The upgraded Gauguin Cottages have private splash pools. Except for their style and location, they vary little from the other accommodations. But they do have a sort of South Sea islands feeling—if you use your imagination.

The resort has a hard-surface tennis court, racquets, and balls; bicycles; a rough track around the lagoon for walking and jogging; a shaded Ping-Pong table in its own thatched hut; and a small, air-conditioned exercise pavilion beside the lagoon. The most recent addition is Indulge, a small spa with two elevated massage decks overlooking the lagoon and bird sanctuary and two pods for massages—one for couples. The spa uses Pevonia Botanica products; a spa menu is available.

Galley Bay has a splendid beach, but be aware that in the winter months the sea is often rough with swells, which is why the swimming pools are such welcome additions. Equipment for snorkeling, windsurfing, and sailing is provided.

Another of Galley Bay's distinctive features is its open-air beachside bar, which sits under a high pyramid of weathered wood and plaited palms and adds to the rustic ambience. Next door, the open-air lounge, furnished with easy chairs, traditional planter's chairs, and comfortable sofas, is the gathering place for most activities—drinks, daytime chats, afternoon tea, and lots of doing nothing. By cocktail time in the evening, when folks have gotten dressed a bit fancier, there's something of a house-party atmosphere for after-dinner socializing and dancing.

The open-sided dining room, bordered by an attractive boardwalk of weathered wood, is the venue for all meals and offers full menus and table service—in other words, no buffets, a feature that distinguishes Galley Bay from most all-inclusive resorts. Menus change daily and offer an imaginative selection. Dine by candlelight with the sea lapping at the shore and the stars twinkling overhead—it's as romantic a setting as you will find in the Caribbean. The service is outstanding. There is piano music most nights; live entertainment, featured three or four evenings a week, might be a calypso singer, a combo, or a steel band.

The Gauguin, a second, rustic restaurant serving grilled food, is situated at the far end of the beach. Here some tables by the sea are under their own separate thatched roof, giving them an intimate, romantic feeling. And now, a third small restaurant, Ismay's, featuring trendy Caribbean fusion cuisine, has been added.

Galley Bay is a comfortable, laid-back, informal retreat. Most guests in winter are British and European; in summer more are American.

Galley Bay has the advantage of seeming to be on a remote island when, in fact, it is only about fifteen or twenty minutes by car (which you will need) from town and nightlife at nearby hotels. That should be ideal for active urbanites who are attracted to a totally relaxed lifestyle but unaccustomed to vegging out and might get restless.

In my opinion Galley Bay is better, prettier, and more comfortable than ever. What's more, the staff is one of the best, most friendly, and most caring I have encountered anywhere in visiting the Caribbean.

The Elite Island Resorts group recently added The Verandah Resort & Spa on the northeast coast of Antigua. The eco-friendly resort has 200 villa-style accommodations, each with a large verandah as the name suggests. (www.verandahresortandspa.com)

Galley Bay Resort & Spa ★★★★
Box 305, Five Islands, St. John's, Antigua, W.I.
Phone: (268) 462-0302; Fax: (268) 462-4551; e-mail: galleybay@candw.ag; www.eliteisland.com

Owners: Rob Barrett and James Lane

General Manager: Britton Foreman

Open: Year-round

Credit Cards: All major

U.S. Reservations: (800) 345-0356, (954) 481-8787

Deposit: Three nights; thirty days cancellation; for arrivals during February, reservations and complete payment must be received no later than forty-five days prior to arrival. Cancellations within thirty days will result in a three-night penalty fee.

Minimum Stay: Five nights winter; three nights summer; eight nights mid-December–January 1; and February seven nights

Arrival/Departure: Transfer service not provided

Distance from Airport: (Bird Airport) 8 miles; taxi one-way, $21

Distance from St. John's: 4 miles; taxi one-way, $15

Accommodations: 98 rooms and suites with patios (including 10 superior and 29 deluxe beachfront rooms; 48 beachfront suites; 13 thatched cottages) with king-size beds and 13 with splash pools

Amenities: Ceiling fans, air-conditioning; bath with shower (some with tub); bathrobe, safe, hair dryer, deluxe basket of toiletries;

minifridge, coffeemaker. Premium suites have large tubs and his and hers showers. Open-air library

Electricity: 110 volts

Fitness Facilities/Spa Services: Air-conditioned room with exercise equipment; spa with various moderately priced treatments, facial; hair salon

Sports: Tennis, sailing, snorkeling, wind-surfing, kayaking, bicycling equipment included; diving, golf arranged; pool; Ping-Pong; jogging track; bird sanctuary

Dress Code: Casual by day; after 7:00 p.m. long pants or stylish jeans, collared shirt, shoes; no shorts or T-shirts in bar and restaurant areas

Children: None under sixteen years of age except at Christmas holidays

Meetings: No

Day Visitors: No

Handicapped Facilities: No

Packages: All-inclusive

Rates: Two people, per room, daily, All-inclusive. *High Season* (mid-December–mid-April): $965–$1,175. *Low Season:* $840–$1,045. For single, deduct $100 per day.

Service Charge: Included

Government Tax: Included

JUMBY BAY
Antigua, W.I.

Less than a mile off the northern coast of Antigua is the ultimate private-island resort, Jumby Bay. Situated on a 300-acre dot of land scalloped with pearly beaches, the exclusive eighty-eight-acre resort was created in 1983. The name, Long Island, was changed to Jumby Bay. After several other owners, the resort was sold in 2002 back to the island's fourteen homeowners from whom it had been purchased. The homeowners engaged Rosewood Hotels & Resorts of Dallas to manage the property. (Rosewood's other Caribbean properties are Caneel Bay and Little Dix Bay.) Jumby was given a multimillion-dollar refurbishment, which followed the extensive renovations made earlier that restored Jumby Bay to its former luster. Jumby Bay has never been more luxurious or looked better.

Jumby Bay offers quietly luxurious accommodations, facilities, and amenities, as fine as can be found in the Caribbean, for one all-inclusive price. That means all meals, cocktails and wine with meals, afternoon tea, cocktail beverages in your room, all sports and recreational facilities on the property, transfers, and even post-age stamps. At the airport in Antigua, you are met by a Jumby Bay representative and whisked off to the nearby Beachcomber dock, where the Jumby Bay high-speed cat-amaran is waiting.

Jumby Bay has three groups of accom-modations, all near, but not directly on, the beach. Semi-rondavel villas, each with two suites, are set along paved paths lead-ing from the main beach to a 200-year-old plantation house, the centerpiece. More rooms and suites are located in Pond Bay House, a graceful Spanish-mission-style structure on a finger of land overlooking a long beach. All accommodations, except the second-floor rooms in Pond Bay House, have outdoor/indoor showers; some have an outdoor tub as well.

The beautifully appointed rooms, all with sitting areas, are furnished in custom-designed rattan with pillows and bedcovers in understated quality fabrics and most with four-poster, king-size beds. Another four superdeluxe villas inspired by traditional West Indian architecture are the most luxurious of the lot. Set alongside Pond Bay House, each villa has two spacious suites and a veranda facing the sea. The four attached villas share a swimming pool. On the south side of the island are the Harbor Bay and Harbor Beach villas—one three-bedroom villa and ten huge two-bedroom suites with large living rooms and kitchens and infinite-edge swimming pools at three of the suites. Also, six of the large, private estates, ranging from three to six bedrooms, are available for rent.

Each cluster of villas is different, but all of the resort's accommodations have walls of louvered doors and windows of Brazilian walnut, adding a rich accent to the decor and providing cross ventilation. High, beamed ceilings create a sense of space and airiness. Bathrooms are unusually large. Bicycles are standing outside the doors, and you'll find a hammock, too.

The beautifully restored Estate House, with its red tile roof, whitewashed arches, and delightful garden courtyard, is reminiscent of a Mediterranean palazzo. The courtyard opens onto a pretty indoor-outdoor dining terrace used for dinner. Courtyard steps lead to a second-floor lounge with a cozy bar, library, and television.

Daytime activity is centered in the large, flower-bedecked Verandah Bar, a beach pavilion near the entry dock and main beach.

Breakfast, lunch, afternoon tea, and, from mid-December to April 31, dinner are served on its open-air terraces—and shared with a host of bananaquits and hummingbirds. Early dining for children is available. The Veranda restaurant has been enlarged to almost double its size. Next to the beach pavilion are three Laykold tennis courts (lighted); a full-time pro is available. Beyond is a large freshwater swimming pool, bordered by white canvas "chalets" providing shade and privacy to attractive chaise lounges. The Beach Hut serves as the sports center. If you feel less ambitious, you can take up residence on a lounge chair beneath a thatched umbrella by the 1,800-foot white-sand beach.

Jumby Bay maintains an impressive nursery to grow an enormous variety of tropical plants. Except for the flower-festooned resort grounds and lush gardens of the private mansions, the island is covered with dry woods; nature trails and biking paths meander past sumptuous villas and lead to beaches. One path goes to Pasture Bay, where the endangered hawksbill turtle comes to lay her eggs from May to November. (A record fifty-eight turtles came in 2005.) Under a watch by WIDECAST (Wide Caribbean Sea Turtle Conservation Network), Jumby Bay hosts marine biology students studying the endangered species during the nesting season.

Jumby Bay, with its gracious informality and aura of well-being, is made for honeymooners and romantics, but it appeals equally to those who simply want to get away from it all in spacious, sophisticated surroundings.

Jumby Bay ✳✳✳✳
Box 243, Jumby Bay Island, Antigua, W.I.
Phone: (268) 462-6000, -6002, -6003;
Fax: (268) 462-6020; e-mail: jumbygs@
candw.ag; www.jumbybayresort.com

Management: Rosewood Hotel & Resorts

Managing Director: Carlos Salazar

Open: Year-round

Credit Cards: Most major

U.S. Reservations: Direct to hotel, (800) 237-3237; (888) ROSEWOOD (767-3966)

Deposit: Three nights; thirty days cancellation

Minimum Stay: Ten nights during Christmas/New Year's

Arrival/Departure: Transfer service $50 adults, per person, round-trip; $25 per child two to twelve. Those arriving by private plane, inquire

Distance from Airport: Less than 1 mile (five-minute ride) to ferry dock; ten-minute boat ride to Jumby Bay dock; Jumby Bay operates its own scheduled water shuttle between resort and Beachcomber dock in Antigua

Distance from St. John's: 7 miles (fifteen minutes) from Beachcomber dock in Antigua; taxi one-way, $20

Accommodations: 40 rooms and suites (with king-size beds; two queens in second bedroom when booked as two-bedroom unit); 11 two-bedroom suites in Harbor Bay and Harbor Beach villas; six private villas with three to six bedrooms

Amenities: Air-conditioning, ceiling fans; hair dryers, deluxe toiletries, bathrobes, plush towels changed twice daily; wall safe; umbrellas, walking sticks; cable television in suites and villas, coffeemakers, telephones, CD player; ice service daily; golf carts for guests in villas; twenty-four-hour concierge; room service 7:00 a.m. –10:00 p.m. for $10 minimum surcharge plus costs of food

Electricity: 110 volts

Fitness Facilities/Spa Services: Fitness center; spa services available

Sports: Freshwater swimming pool, putting green, croquet court, three tennis courts, windsurfing, snorkeling, Sunfish, hiking trails, bicycles included; scuba diving, deep-sea fishing, golf in Antigua arranged for fee

Dress Code: Casual by day; slightly more formal for evening; no jacket or tie required

Children: All ages; playground. Children under two years old free; two to twelve years old, $150 per night holiday/winter, $75 in spring/summer.

Meetings: Pond Bay House or entire island can be rented

Day Visitors: No

Handicapped Facilities: Most facilities accessible

Packages: Honeymoon, wedding

Rates: Per room, double, daily, inclusive. *High Season* (mid-December–March 31): $1,250–$1,975. *Shoulder Season* (early April–May 31; mid-November–mid-December): $925–$1,600. *Low Season:* $755–$1,350. Two-bedroom, inquire

Service Charge: 10 percent

Government Tax: 10.5 percent

ARUBA

Aruba was little more than a sleepy sandbar in the 1950s before the gracious Arubans began to develop their tourism industry. Now they have created one of the most popular, fun-loving playgrounds in the Tropics. And they never stop: This Dutch island is booming with new resorts, marinas, smart boutiques, and more.

Fifteen miles off the Venezuelan coast, this dry, low-lying island in the Netherlands Antilles has surprisingly diverse landscapes and natural attractions for an island only 20 miles long. Similar to the American Southwest, with rocky desert terrain and less than 20 inches of annual rainfall, the island has two totally different faces.

On the southern coast tranquil beaches, sophisticated resorts, and glittering casinos line Palm Beach, a beautiful 5-mile band of sand where most of the hotels are located. In sharp contrast, the rugged northern shore reveals moonscape terrain with pounding surf, shifting sand dunes, caves with prehistoric drawings, and strange gigantic rock formations sculpted by the strong winds. The countryside is dotted with tiny farm villages of Dutch colonial architecture. They're surrounded by cactus fields, which turn overnight from a lifeless gray to flowering green following a good rain, and the distinctive ever-present divi-divi tree. The outback can be fun to visit on horseback or by jeep safari with a naturalist guide.

Aruba is ringed by coral reefs, making snorkeling and diving popular; deep-sea fishing is good, too. But the most popular sport is windsurfing and the relatively new sport of kiteboarding; the strong winds that shape the divi-divi trees and keep the island cool have made Aruba one of the leading windsurfing and kiteboarding locations in the Caribbean. In June an annual international windsurfing competition is held at Eagle Beach, where winds can exceed 25 knots.

In the capital of Oranjestad, a redesigned town center and shopping plaza showcase Aruba's Dutch colonial past. The Aruba Historical Museum, housed in Fort Zoutman, and William III Towers, one of the island's oldest landmarks, reveal its ancient past. The museum and other examples of historical preservation reflect Aruba's increased emphasis on its cultural and historical heritage. Folkloric shows presented regularly at hotels, as well as restaurants serving authentic Arubian dishes, are other indications.

Information

Aruba Tourist Authority, 100 Plaza Drive, First floor, Secaucus, NJ 07094;
(800) TO-ARUBA, (201) 330-0800, (201) 558-1110;
Fax: (201) 558-4767; www.aruba.com
Offices in Atlanta, Chicago, Ft. Lauderdale, Miami, Houston,
West Hollywood, California.

HYATT REGENCY ARUBA
Palm Beach, Aruba

Located on Palm Beach, along twelve beautiful beachfront acres on Aruba's southwestern coast, the Aruba Hyatt proves that you can have your cake and eat it, too. In other words, with good design it is possible to have a large, full-service resort and still retain the warmth and grace of a small hotel.

Opened in 1990, the hotel recently completed a $20 million, two-year "extreme makeover," as the hotel terms it, that retained the hotel's handsome Spanish-mission-inspired architecture while creating a sophisticated, contemporary look for almost all the interiors.

The Hyatt Regency Aruba consists of a nine-story tower flanked by two wings of four and five stories, that overlook the hotel's centerpiece: a landscaped, multi-level pool and lagoon. It starts as a waterfall by the open-air lobby, flows into a series of interconnected pools in flower-filled gardens, and leads to a wide, white-sand beach. You can slip quietly into the pool at one end and splash down a two-story winding water slide at the other, or swim up to the bar on yet another side.

In the public areas the new decor of the lobby and lounges have been enhanced by a light and airy look with white marble floors, white muslin curtains, and contemporary white sofas against brown wicker furniture and dark wooden floors.

By the Ruinas del Mar restaurant, a rock wall, which seems to float in the lagoon near the center of the gardens, is built of a native limestone called Aruba rock, quarried on the island's northern coast. Here, the design plays on Aruba's gold-mining days at the turn of the century. Mock ruins, special carvings, textured and tinted concrete, and weather-beaten rocks in the gardens and around the pool create the look of the old mines still found in several locations on the island. All guest rooms have water or garden views, and most have balconies. Their contemporary decor combines avocado and olive green with soft orange and brown, plus a signature orchid in each room. The newest additions are plasma television, Hyatt's signature Grand Bed™ (one king or two queens), and high-speed Internet. The renovated bathrooms have granite countertops, marble floors, rainshower heads, and Moen fixtures throughout.

The Regency Club, Hyatt's executive rooms enhanced with more luxurious amenities, is located on the ninth floor. It has a private concierge and a lounge where complimentary continental breakfast and evening cocktails and tasty hors d'oeuvres are served daily.

There are four specialty suites ranging in size from 1,150 to 2,500 square feet and with one to four bedrooms, large living rooms with cathedral ceilings, stocked wet bars, and guest baths, as well as rooftop terraces with wraparound views of Palm Beach and the Caribbean. One of the master bedrooms, furnished with a king-size bed, has a spacious bathroom with a whirlpool tub.

Low-key compared to other large Aruban resorts, the Hyatt has as many services and facilities as its flashier neighbors, if not more. The Ruinas del Mar, an indoor-outdoor restaurant, offers a breakfast buffet and nightly dinner and especially popular Sunday champagne brunch. Nearby is Cafe Piccolo, a small Italian cafe specializing in regional cuisine, particularly northern Italian dishes and pizza hot from a large brick oven, and Cafe Japengo, a seafood and sushi restaurant. The casual Palms, a beachfront grill with an exhibition kitchen has been redesigned as a Latin bistro offering creative South American and Caribbean cuisine and specializing in seafood. Live merengue and salsa entertainment, along with demonstrations and lessons by professional dancers, is staged on Thursday, Friday, and Saturday nights. The restaurant is open from early morning until midnight, except for dinner on Wednesday. The poolside Balashi Bar, a swim-up or walk-up bar adjacent to the swimming pool, serves grilled meat and seafood, sandwiches, and salads during the day. Footprints Grill offers "barefoot dining" right on the beach, under a thatched roof beside tiki torches.

In the evening you can take in a sunset cruise, a comedy show, or the disco. Especially popular at sunset with a daily specialty drink is Piets Pier Bar by the ocean. The recently expanded Casino Copacabana has a nightly live musical show and offers introductory clinics on casino games. The alfresco Lobby Bar overlooking the pools, an open-air lounge and bar adjacent to the lobby, redesigned in a South-Beach-meets-the-Caribbean fashion with canopied day beds and colorful lighting, offers live musical entertainment nightly.

The resort offers a full service dive and water-sports facility operated by Red Sail Sports, including dive programs for the disabled with instructors certified by the Handicapped Scuba Association, and special-interest dives such as a PADI underwater naturalist course. It can arrange golf, deep-sea fishing, sailing, and other sporting excursions. The Stillwater Spa offers a wide range of body and beauty treatments and state-of-the-art exercise equipment, a sauna and steam room, massage rooms, men's and women's locker rooms, and showers.

Pool and beach aerobics, volleyball, pool basketball, and other activities are offered daily. In conjunction with the health club, the Hyatt maintains an arrival/departure lounge with lockers and showers, allowing early-arriving or late-departing guests full access to hotel facilities.

While you are checking out the gym, you can check the kids into Camp Hyatt, a program of supervised day and evening activities for children ages three to twelve, available daily year-round. Camp Hyatt facilities include a children's outdoor playground, arts and crafts, a Nintendo play station, and more than a hundred different types of games and toys. Activities, led by professional counselors, include nature walks, Papiamento lessons, pool and beach games, swimming and windsurfing lessons, and movies. Prices range from $45 for a half day to $75 for a full day with meals, and $30 in the evening. Children get special menus, special room rates, and special check-in packets.

Casual and friendly, the Aruba Hyatt has a certain glamour and attracts a wide range of guests, mostly from the United States and Latin America. It appeals to couples, families with children, and water-sports enthusiasts.

Hyatt Regency Aruba ★★★★

J. E. Irausquin Boulevard #85, Palm Beach, Aruba

Phone: (297) 586-1234; Fax: (297) 586-1682; www.aruba.hyatt.com

Owner: Aruba Beachfront Resorts

General Manager: Susan Santiago

Open: Year-round

Credit Cards: All major

U.S. Reservations: Hyatt Worldwide, (800) 233-1234

Deposit: Varies, depending on season; fourteen days cancellation, except sixty days for Christmas

Minimum Stay: Ten nights during Christmas

Arrival/Departure: No transfer service

Distance from Airport: 7 miles; taxi one-way, $20

Distance from Oranjestad: 4½ miles; taxi one-way, $8.00

Accommodations: 360 guest rooms and suites with queen- or king-size beds, most with terrace; Regency Club floor (29 rooms)

Amenities: Air-conditioning, ceiling fans; bath with tub and shower, basket of toiletries, hair dryer; makeup mirror; telephones; stocked minibar; coffeemaker; iron and ironing board; personal safe; television with CNN and other cable services, clock, radio, plasma television, high-speed Internet; nightly turndown service, twenty-four-hour room service; floor of nonsmoking rooms; concierge; business services; quality boutiques; hair salon. Regency Club: Club lounge; continental breakfast, evening cocktails and hors d'oeuvres; concierge; upgraded amenities and linens

Electricity: 110 volts

Fitness Facilities/Spa Services: Full-service health club and spa (see text)

Sports: Three-level pool with waterfalls and slide; wide white-sand beach; two free tennis courts (lighted); biking; water sports; dive resort and specialty courses; PADI certification for fee; dive boat departs from beach on trips daily; luxury glass-bottom catamaran with private-yacht amenities; deep-sea fishing arranged; eighteen-hole golf course 2 miles from resort

Children: All ages; cribs, high chairs; babysitters; Camp Hyatt for ages three to twelve. Children under eighteen may stay free in parent's room or purchase second room at 50 percent discount, depending on availability.

Meetings: Up to 600 people

Day Visitors: Yes

Handicapped Facilities: Fully accessible; dive program for disabled

Packages: Honeymoon, dive, wedding

Rates: Per person, daily, EP. *High Season* (mid-December–mid-April): $525–$545. *Low Season* (mid-April–mid-December): $350–$395.

Service Charge: 12 percent on room

Government Tax: 7 percent

THE BAHAMAS

An archipelago of more than 700 tropical islands stretches south from the eastern coast of Florida over 100,000 square miles of peacock-green and cobalt-blue seas. The Bahamas are so close to the U.S. mainland that many people hop to them in their own boats or private planes for the weekend.

Proximity, together with the foreign but familiar cultural influence of Great Britain (which ruled the Bahamas for more than two centuries), helps make this island nation the tropical destination most visited by Americans—almost five million a year. The variety and range of activities are further attractions.

Most people's introduction to the Bahamas includes Nassau, the capital and commercial center, and Paradise Island, across the harbor. Both bustle with activity day and night, but when you want to exchange the razzle-dazzle for tranquillity, you need only escape to the "other Bahamas," where life is so laid-back and serene that ten people make a crowd. The Out Islands, as they are called, offer lazy, sunny days of sailing, snorkeling, scuba diving, fishing, windsurfing, or doing nothing at all, and evenings of dining on fresh fish and homemade island specialties.

The Abacos: At the northern end of the archipelago, a group of islands is strung in boomerang fashion for 130 miles around the Sea of Abaco, whose sheltered waters offer some of the Bahamas' best sailing. Marsh Harbour is the hub, and New Plymouth is a Cape Cod–like village with palm trees.

Andros: Directly west of Nassau, Andros is the largest of the Bahamas but one of the least developed islands. The interior is covered with forests and mangroves. The Barrier Reef, third largest in the world, and, just beyond, the Tongue of the Ocean, 1,000 fathoms deep, lie off the eastern coast and attract divers and sport fishermen from afar. The towns, hotels, and airstrips are also on the eastern coast.

Eleuthera: First-timers in search of the other Bahamas will delight in the quiet and beauty of this island paradise with its 300 years of history, comfortable hotels, and good dining and sports facilities. Eleuthera, 60 miles east of Nassau, is a 110-mile-long slice of land never more than 2 miles wide (except for splays at both ends).

Governor's Harbour, near the center of the island, is the main town and commercial hub. Harbour Island, almost touching the northeastern tip, is one of the Bahamas' most beautiful spots and the site of Dunmore Town, its original capital.

Exumas: About 35 miles south of Nassau, the Exumas spread southeast across 130 square miles of the beautiful turquoise waters popular with yachtsmen, snorklers, and divers. Georgetown, the center, is a quiet village of fewer than one thousand people.

Information

Bahamas Tourist Office, 1200 South Pine Island Road, Suite 750, Plantation, FL 33324;
(800) 4-BAHAMAS, (954) 236-9292; Fax: (954) 236-9282; www.bahamas.com.
Offices also in Chicago, Dallas, Los Angeles, New York, and Toronto

GREEN TURTLE CLUB AND MARINA

Abaco, Bahamas

Set on a point overlooking White Sound on the south and Coco Bay on the north, and surrounded by white sand beaches and green forested hills, the Green Turtle Club has been a favorite of yachtsmen since it started as a boathouse bar in the 1960s.

The Charlesworth family, who formerly owned the resort, came to the Bahamas from Britain in search of a family vacation house. When you see Green Turtle Cay, you will understand immediately why they decided to stay. It has one of the most idyllic settings in the Abacos, if not the entire Bahamas. It was apparently enough to attract the new owners, Adam Showell and his sister, Ann Showell Mariner, who bought the hotel in September 2004. They also own "Castle in the Sand Hotel" in Ocean City, Maryland.

There is a variety of accommodations spread over the fourteen-acre property. The wooden cottages with deluxe rooms and suites are painted a fresh yellow with white trim; inside, the spacious rooms are furnished with attractive colonial-style mahogany furniture, Meissen prints, and Oriental rugs.

Some rooms and suites, as well as cottages with kitchens for up to four people, are located on a small rise by the swimming pool. Other villas directly on the water have private docks and kitchens and can accommodate up to eight to ten people.

A deluxe beach villa has three separate accommodations—all with kitchen—and can be rented together or as one unit. It has its own swimming pool for the use of the guests staying in the villa and their guests. The pine-paneled dining rooms with high-pitched ceilings and colonial-style furnishings accommodate the many day visitors, mainly boaters, along with guests of the hotel. Dinner menus are changed daily, and you are asked to make your selection by 5:00 p.m. each day. There are two seatings: 7:00 and 7:30 p.m., when dinner is served promptly.

The resort is constantly being refurbished and upgraded without changing its atmosphere. Among the recent additions are a 20,000-gallon-per-day watermaker and wireless Internet service, free for hotel and marina guests. Green Turtle has the ambience of a club, and indeed, it has a private membership club, Green Turtle Yacht Club, to which all hotel guests pay $1 per day temporary membership. It is also associated with the Birdham Yacht Club in England, the Palm Beach Yacht Club, and some other boating clubs in Florida.

The bar, with its dark wood and beamed ceiling, is in the original boathouse and decorated with flags from yacht clubs around the world. Its walls are papered with one-pound British sterling notes, U.S. dollars, and other currency, maintaining a tradition begun in World War II when RAF pilots, about to depart on a mission, left money for a round of drinks in their memory in case they did not return. Just outside the bar is a patio restaurant.

The bar is the social center in winter, but in summer the crowd moves out to the pretty terrace by the marina. At sunset and after dinner, this is probably the liveliest place in the Abacos, particularly on the nights when there is live music for listening and dancing. A lounge by the bar has cable television.

Tucked in the corner to one side of the terrace is a quiet cove with a small beach where lounge chairs and thatched umbrellas draw sun worshipers during the day. Up a small hill where the rooms are located, there is a pretty, tiled lap swimming pool. For those who are more energetic, a path behind the cottages leads to secluded Coco Bay, a beautiful white-sand beach where there is good snorkeling. A narrow dirt road leads to New Plymouth, the main settlement on Green Turtle Cay, about an hour's walk from the resort. Water sports, boats for fishing, and dive excursions are available daily. Brendal's Golf can be arranged at Treasure Cay, a twenty-minute boat ride away.

The nearest airport is on Treasure Cay; from there you take a taxi to the ferry dock, a ferry to New Plymouth, and a water taxi to the club. But after a couple of the resort's famous Tipsy Turtle Rum Punches, you'll forget about the long trip and be happy that you discovered the club.

Green Turtle Club and Marina **

Green Turtle Cay, Abaco, Bahamas Out Islands

Phone: (242) 365-4271; Fax: (242) 365-4272, (866) 528-0539, (800) 254-2617; e-mail: info@greenturtleclub.com; www.greenturtleclub.com

Owners: The Showell family

General Manager: Lynn Johnson

Open: Year-round

Credit Cards: All major

U.S. Reservations: Direct to hotel 866-528-0539 or its Web site

Deposit: Five nights for Christmas/New Year; two nights, balance of year; thirty days

cancellation for holidays, fourteen days balance of year

Minimum Stay: Five nights during holidays, two nights balance of year

Arrival/Departure: Green Turtle Ferry Service can be arranged by hotel reception; $11 per person one way, payable locally. Taxi from Ferry Dock to airport, $4 per person with $8 minimum charge

Distance from Airport: (Treasure Cay Airport) 3½ miles; taxi and ferry, see information above. Distance from New Plymouth: 2 miles; water taxi daily

Accommodations: 34 rooms with deck or terrace in cottages and villas (all with queen or king); some with kitchens

Amenities: Air-conditioning, ceiling fans; six rooms have bath with tub, twenty-two have shower only; small refrigerator; no telephones, television, room service

Electricity: 110 volts

Sports: Freshwater swimming pool; boat rentals, snorkeling, diving, bonefishing, kayaking, deep-sea fishing available for fee

Dress Code: Casual

Children: All ages; cribs and babysitters can be arranged

Meetings: Up to fifty people

Day Visitors: Welcome; reservations required for meals

Handicapped Facilities: No

Packages: See description on resort's Web site

Rates: One or two people, daily, EP. *High Season* (January–early August): $240–$495. *Low Season* (mid-August–late December): $180–$325. For two- and three-bedroom accommodations, inquire. Guests who pay for six nights may get the seventh night free.

Service and Government Tax: 25 percent

SMALL HOPE BAY LODGE

Andros, Nassau, Bahamas

The very antithesis of the glitz and glitter of Nassau and Paradise Island is Small Hope Bay Lodge, a rustic retreat in an idyllic setting on the eastern coast of Andros. Here, friendly conversation replaces casinos and floor shows, and natural means not only an almost undisturbed landscape but also genuine people and an ambience where guests blend into the "family" and love it—or quickly find they are in the wrong place.

When the late Dick Birch decided to give up cold Canadian winters and the fast track to create a resort on an undeveloped island, he found the ideal spot: a white-sand beach on Andros, facing the third longest barrier reef in the world, only an hour's flight from Florida.

Hidden under pine and palm trees on the shallow bay from which it takes its name, Small Hope Bay Lodge has twenty bungalows for forty guests at the edge of a crescent beach. Birch, an engineer by profession, built the bungalows and lodge himself out of local pine and coral stone. The bungalows have large rooms with tiled floors and are decorated with colorful handmade batiks created at Androsia, the factory begun by Birch's former wife, Rosie, and now a mainstay of the island's economy. Hammocks wide enough for two are placed about the property. Romantic? You bet.

The lodge, the focal point of the resort, has a large living room rather than a hotel lobby. (Check-in means having your name hung up at the bar.) The homey lounge has a large stone fireplace and walls lined with well-read books: everything from scientific treatises to science fiction. An old fishing boat, the *Panacea,* serves as the bar (drinks are included in the all-inclusive price).

Meals are informal, in keeping with the resort's laid-back ambience. Breakfast always has a "Bahamian Special" consisting of down-home island tastes with a full continental buffet and full range of choices from the grill. Lunch and dinner are served buffet style. By early evening guests have gathered in the lodge to sample a Bahama Mama or another cocktail at the bar, along with conch fritters and a veggie platter served every evening before dinner.

Dinner is a communal affair at which guests dine family style with family members, dive masters, and staff. It is just slightly more formal than other meals, with Androsia table linens and the chef coming to the bar and announcing the details of the upcoming meal. The chef favors fresh seafood supplied by local fishermen, with fresh vegetables from the island's farms, along with Bahamian influenced continental cuisine. At least once per week is Bahamian night with complete Bahamian fare, including fresh conch salad.

Entertainment after dinner might be an impromptu party or slide show in the lounge. On cool winter evenings guests settle on huge cushions by a warm fire to continue their conversations. Others play chess, backgammon, or Ping-Pong. Someone strumming a guitar might bring on a song; a CD might inspire dancing.

Children are easily included in the informal atmosphere. There is plenty for them to do, but they must be ten years old to dive. Children nine and under have a separate dinner hour. Some Birch grandchildren are likely to be around.

The star attraction is the 142-mile-long barrier reef, less than fifteen minutes from the lodge. A conservationist and record-setting diver, Birch (and his family) worked hard to have the Bahamian government declare the Andros reef a national reserve. The reef has a tremendous variety of coral and fish, and virgin dive sites are frequently found.

The dive center offers excursions several times daily, ranging from 10 feet on one side of the reef to "over the wall," a dive to 185 feet that looks down a sheer vertical 6,000-foot drop into the Tongue of the Ocean. You can have a personalized video of your dive made by the lodge's resident diver-photographer. Nondivers snorkel in shallow water either from shore or from the dive/snorkel boat out on the reef, or they can take a Discover Scuba course at no cost. Equipment is provided. A special program provides one-on-one or -two diving with a dive master to some of the Blue Holes, part of the intricate cave system beneath Andros. The center also offers shark diving under controlled, environmentally conscious conditions. It offers Nitrox and numerous advanced certifications.

Bonefishing is as popular as diving, and you can't find better waters for the sport than those of Andros. Small Hope can arrange everything you need, along with some of the best bonefishing guides in the Bahamas.

The resort has a variety of special week packages and guided tours: yoga groups, a birding and ecology week with experts, bonefishing clinics, safari into the interior of Fresh Creek, or overnight camping in the wilderness on western Andros.

Small Hope continues its environmental stewardship with zeal and a great deal of pride that is reflected in its complete recycling program. For example, all beer bottles are sent back to the manufacturer, aluminum cans go to Nassau for "cans for Kids" and steel cans are sent to a recycling company; vegetables are composted. The resort also has an Environmental Management System, which causes it to be sensitive

and creative in making the fifty-year-old property ever more sensitive to the environment. For example, it monitors all usage of electricity per person, water per person, and production of waste.

Small Hope operates as an all-inclusive resort; rates include accommodations, meals and hors d'oeuvres, open bar, hotel taxes, and use of windsurfers, bikes, sailboats, kayaks, nature trails, beachfront hot tub, self-guided bike and walking nature trails, and free introductory dive or snorkel lessons.

Following Dick's sudden death in 1996, his son, Jeff, and other members of the family have carried on the spirit of this unspoiled paradise, which is not just a business but a way of life. It's like spending the weekend at a beach cottage with friends from all over the world. While diving continues to be the main attraction, nondivers in search of tropical bliss and beauty, good food, and good company will be happy here, too. "Rest, relaxation, and rediscovery" is the resort's motto, and it delivers.

Small Hope Bay Lodge ** 🌿
Fresh Creek, Andros Island; P.O. Box FC23301, Fresh Creek, Andros Island, Bahamas
Phone: (800) 223-6961, (242) 368-2014; Fax: (242) 368-2015; e-mail: SHBinfo@ SmallHope.com; www.smallhope.com

Owners: The Birch family

General Manager: Jeff Birch

Open: October to U.S. Labor Day in September

Credit Cards: All major

U.S. Reservations: Direct to lodge, (800) 223-6961

Deposit: One night per person within fourteen days of reservation

Minimum Stay: Five nights during Christmas/New Year's and Easter

Arrival/Departure: Free taxi transfer

Distance from Airport: 5 miles; Western Air, twice daily, about $140, from Nassau or Continental Airlines from Fort Lauderdale, $300 per person, round-trip. Be sure to bring passport. There is also ferry service from Nassau on Bahamas Ferries three times per week.

Accommodations: 20 cottages with twin beds or king (good mattresses), all with patios; four two-bedroom cottages for families with children

Amenities: Ceiling fans; bath with shower; oceanfront hot tub; tile floors; air-conditioning in half of the rooms (small energy surcharge); room service on request; no telephones, television, locks on doors

Electricity: 110 volts/60 cycles

Fitness Facilities/Spa Services: Masseuse available; hot tub on beach

Sports: Diving and snorkeling (see text); windsurfing (equipment free), Laser sailboat, kayaks, Hobie catamaran; nature walks; birding; biking; no swimming pool; great bonefishing, $275 half day for two

people, boat, guide, equipment; reef fishing, deep-sea fishing available; guided eco-trips available for extra fee

Dress Code: Informal resort wear, day and evening. Small Hope has only one rule: no ties.

Children: All ages; cribs; playroom and supervised activities; babysitters available; children's rates; special rates for single parents; equipment and lessons for scuba/snorkeling for children under age ten

Packages: Scuba, wedding, fishing, family, honeymoon, snorkeling

Meetings: Up to forty people when renting entire resort

Day Visitors: Welcome

Handicapped Facilities: Limited

Rates: All-inclusive, per adult, per night, nondivers. *High Season* (mid-December–late April): $229. *Low Season:* $209. Divers: $289–$309 (including three dives per day). Rates for snorkelers and children are available.

Service Charge: Included; 4 percent discretionary gratuity added to bill

Government Tax: Included

FOUR SEASONS RESORT
GREAT EXUMA AT EMERALD BAY

Great Exuma, Bahamas

You don't even realize you've arrived at Four Seasons Resort Great Exuma at Emerald Bay in the Bahamas until you have turned off Queen's Highway and started down the long lane to the main building.

Quietly settled on 470 acres, the classic resort blends in well with its quaint Out

Island surroundings of Great Exuma. This is, in fact, surprising, since the opening of the Four Seasons completely transformed life on this small island. While suddenly the A-list crowd was abuzz about an island they had never heard of until November 2003 when the resort opened, Great Exuma has embraced its new-found fame with genuine Bahamian pleasure and grace.

Upon approaching the resort's main building in muted Bahamian British colonial style, the eighteen-hole Greg Norman–designed golf course spreads out on either side and behind. Created by Smallwood Reynolds Stewart & Stewart, the Four Seasons Resort manages to be elegantly discreet and seaside comfortable at the same time. The main building and centerpiece of the resort opens onto a lovely small lobby with the reception desk and concierge service. Here, too, is Il Cielo, the upscale restaurant that serves Italian cuisine for dinner.

To one side of the main building is the indoor meeting space area with eight rooms for business meetings and an additional large outdoor area for events. To the other side of the main building are a small shop and the divine spa. Specializing in Balinese techniques and Bahamian ingredients, this 32,406-square-foot oasis offers a full range of treatments in seventeen indoor treatment rooms and three outdoor treatment cabanas. It even has a secluded Tranquil Garden for Zen time between treatments or rounds of golf. It includes a fitness club and beauty salon, as well.

Beyond the lobby, the true charm of the Four Seasons becomes evident. Spread in both directions in a crescent shape, everything becomes focused on the heavenly blues of the waters of Emerald Bay. At the center the large, free-form "Active Pool" meanders in different directions and is outlined by the yellow-and-white striped cloth cabanas that provide needed respite from the strong Bahamian sun. A second freshwater pool, off to one side of the resort, is the "Quiet Pool" for adults away from the din of the families at the Active Pool.

To the left and right are lovely pale-yellow, three-story buildings with white Bahamian sloped, tile roofs and shuttered soft pastel stucco that house the majority of the 183 guest rooms. These buildings are not directly on the water or beach but rather tucked a bit back, with large lawns separating them. All of the guest rooms are tastefully done in understated elegance of classic, comfortable decor. The oversize rooms use light sky-blue or seagrass color schemes, accented by stone floors, custom area rugs, and dark-stained, handcrafted wood furnishings. The comfortable beds are available in king-size or two doubles. The rooms are equipped with televisions, DVD/CD players, air-conditioning, ceiling fans, seating areas, and louvered sliding doors out onto a balcony or terrace. Some higher-category rooms also have separate parlor areas.

The large marble bathrooms are designed in typical Four Seasons style with large dual-sink vanities, large deep-soaking tubs, separate glass-enclosed showers, and a separate toilet. Guests can indulge in the abundant L'Occitane amenities and then wrap up in the 100 percent cotton oversize bath towels and cotton bathrobes.

The pristine beach is an undeveloped stretch of sand that leaves one feeling as if there isn't any other place in the world. Waiters walk up and down the beach, serving drinks, treats, and food, while activities staff help guests with kayaks, windsurfing, and other nonmotorized water sports.

Next to the pool is the colorful and casual Sea Breeze Grill, where you can dine indoors or out on Caribbean fare, with choices ranging from a variety of grilled meat and seafood to pizza and sandwiches. The bar here is popular for before- and after-dinner drinks and a great place to mingle with other guests.

Just beyond this area, directly on the beach, are six one-bedroom suites and one three-bedroom villa with private pool.

Designed in pastel blue that mimics the waters of the bay, these spacious suites are the top of the line for the resort.

On the far side of the Active Pool, the complimentary Kids for All Seasons club welcomes youngsters, ages five to twelve, daily from 9:00 a.m. to 5:00 p.m. Here they can take part in a range of games, activities, and cultural lessons, and splash in the adorable Turtle Pond wading pool. Babysitting services are available for an extra charge.

The first phase of the twenty-three-acre Marina at Emerald Bay has been completed. Located a short distance from the resort, the marina provides 160 wet slips and 190 dry slips and can accommodate mega-yachts of 260 feet in length. Serving as a point of entry for customs and immigration, the marina offers daily docking and full marina services, including water and electricity, telephone and cable television, fuel dock, Dockmaster's office, the Harbormaster's Lounge restaurant, a ship's chandlery, a produce market, floating docks, and dry dock storage.

The true beauty of this resort is the beauty of the Bahamas and its people. Four Seasons has taken every opportunity to incorporate the local flavor and culture into its resort while still maintaining its well-established service and style.

Four Seasons Resort Great Exuma at Emerald Bay
P.O. Box EX29005, Great Exuma, Bahamas
Phone: (242) 336-6800; Fax: (242) 336-6801; e-mail: reservations.exu@fourseasons.com; www.fourseasons.com/greatexuma

Owner/Management: Emerald Bay Resort/Four Seasons

General Manager: James Kostecky

Open: Year-round

Credit Cards: All major

U.S. Reservations: reservations.exu@fourseasons.com; (800) 332-3442

Deposit: Two nights; thirty days cancellation

Minimum Stay: None, except during major holidays; inquire

Arrival/Departure: Transfers available. Great Exuma is served by American Eagle from Miami, Continental Connection from Fort Lauderdale, and Bahamas Air and Sky Unlimited from Nassau.

Distance from Airport: (Exuma International) fifteen minutes; taxi one-way, $43

Accommodations: 183 rooms and suites (140 rooms; 36 executive suites with separate living rooms and two bathrooms; six one-bedroom beachfront suites; one three-bedroom villa with private pool), all with either king or two doubles; eighteen two- and three-bedroom condominiums in rental pool intermittently

Amenities: Air-conditioning, ceiling fan; feather duvets and pillows; multiline phones with speakerphone and conference call capabilities; CD and DVD players, clock-radio; safe; umbrellas; iron and ironing board; tea and coffeemaker, stocked minibar; cable television with pay-per-view movies, high-speed Internet access, voice mail; tiled bathrooms with separate tub and shower, two sinks, toilet, hair dryer, L'Occitane bath products, oversize cotton bath towels and bathrobes; twice-daily housekeeping, twenty-four-hour room service

Electricity: 110 volts

Fitness Facilities/Spa Services: See text

Sports: Greg Norman eighteen-hole golf course; diving, bone- and sports fishing, snorkeling, kayaking, windsurfing; tennis

Dress Code: Smart casual

Children: All ages; Kids for All Seasons program

Meetings: Up to 400

Day Visitors: Welcome, but guests have priority at all facilities

Handicapped Facilities: Two guest rooms; property is handicap accessible

Packages: Romance, golf, others

Rates: Per person, double, daily, EP: *High Season* (early January–mid-April): $520–$6,950. *Shoulder Season* (May and November–): $375–$6,450. *Low Season:* $275–$5,300, Holiday Season (mid-December–January 1): $520–$6,950.

Service Charge: 10 percent on room rate; 15 percent on food and beverages

Government Tax: 10 percent

ROYAL PLANTATION ISLAND
Fowl Cay, Exumas, Bahamas

When I first set off for Fowl Cay, I had no idea what to expect. I could not find it on a map. I had been told it was a small, remote, rustic island in the Exumas that had not been developed. Yet, I was assured there were overnight accommodations, if somewhat rustic. I knew that Gordon "Butch" Stewart, the owner of Sandals Resorts, had bought the island to develop it as a member of his Royal Plantation Collection, a new group of upscale resorts he had launched. But "rustic" and "royal" seem to be a non-sequitur. That peaked my curiosity all the more.

Imagine my surprise upon arrival when I saw a handsome clubhouse and swimming pool and six attractive villas set amidst the island's well-behaved shrubbery and low-laying trees along well maintained gravel roads that pass a tennis court and lead to the beach. A small, remote island—yes. Rustic, hardly.

Tiny compared to New York City's Central Park, Fowl Cay is an unspoiled fifty-two-acre private island paradise, surrounded by the spectacularly beautiful waters of the Exumas, 70 miles south east of Nassau and about midway down the Exuma chain.

Stewart purchased the island after vacationing there and falling in love with it. Fowl Cay, which has since been renamed Royal Plantation Island, can be reached by plane from Nassau or Fort Lauderdale to Staniel Cay, a stone's throw away where general manager Steve Huggins or his wife, Julie, meet guests for the five minute boat ride to the boat dock on Fowl Cay.

The name "Fowl Cay" was derived, we are told, a century or two ago when fowl and other animals were raised on the island to provide food for marauding sailors and settlers on nearby islands. Today, there's no fowl to be seen, except for occasional gulls and other sea birds, but a neighboring speck of land, Big Major Spot, has a family of pigs that hurry out to greet Huggins' boat when he takes guests touring.

The six very comfortable villas are available for rent: Blue Moon (with a backside patio directly on to a private beach) and Sweetwater, both with three bedrooms, three bathrooms, and Lindon with one bedroom, one bathroom are located in the vicinity of North Beach. Starlight and Sea Breeze, both with two bedrooms, two bathrooms are located at Ridge Top, about in the center of the island facing south/south-west. Near the boat dock, the bi-level Bird-cage with two bedrooms, two bathrooms sits at the edge of a bluff on the island's high-est point providing great sea views on three sides. The entire island and all six houses, accommodating a total of thirty-four people, may be rented and would be ideal for a fam-ily gathering or group.

The grey-shingled roof houses, similar in layout to upscale Jamaican villas, are nicely furnished like a well-tended home. The decor is different in each, but the layout is similar—a central living room/dining room and fully equipped kitchen, with bedrooms in the wings on both sides. Each villa has central air-conditioning, a fully equipped kitchen, breakfast and snack provisions, satellite television, DVD and CD players, luxury linens in the bedrooms, and plush towels and Molton Brown amenities in the bath. Each villa has its own dedicated golf cart, beach-cruiser bicycles, and a motor-boat for excursions and fishing. By next year, all villas will have free Wi-Fi access.

The Clubhouse, dubbed the Harbour Club Eating and Drinking House, has a large lounge, a bar with chess board and billiards table, and a dining room where guests can indulge on generous quantities of the Bahamian-style cooking. Its reputation has already spread, so salts sailing in the neigh-borhood frequently tie up for dinner.

Most nights, Steve Huggins, a genial, witty Brit who is the perfect general man-ager for the resort, can be found tending bar, often assisted by one of the guests, and creating an atmosphere for instant camara-derie among all the guests.

At the front of the Harbour Club is a freshwater swimming pool and across the front a long veranda with white wicker rocking chairs, just waiting for occupants to while away a lazy afternoon gazing out at the gorgeous turquoise waters of the

Exumas. For the more ambitious, there's an exercise room, a clay tennis court (rac-quets and balls available), walking trails, and at South Beach, horseshoes to play and kayaks, snorkel equipment, and sailboats to use. Deep-sea fishing and diving can be arranged, and for the really restless, a few miles out to sea is the 112,000-acre Exuma Cays Land and Sea Park, a protected world of coral reefs teeming with sea life.

In addition to its air strip, Staniel Cay is a charming community of about fifty native Bahamian residents and thirty vacation homeowners. It has a church, several shops, a general store, Natajia's Sweet Tooth, and the Staniel Cay Yacht Club, which has served as action central for the area since the 1960s—and making Jimmy Buffett's list of top ten favorite island bars. Close by is Thunderball Grotto, where the 1965 James Bond film *Thunderball* was filmed (so was *Splash*), located between Big Major Spot and Staniel Cay.

Royal Plantation Island operates as an all-inclusive. Rates include all food and drinks, which guests can tailor to their per-sonal preferences prior to arrival, access to all the resort's facilities, use of sports equipment, a golf cart, and motorboat for each house. By the end of 2009, the resort expects to add a beachfront bar and grill, several new villas, a Red Lane® Spa, ame-nities such as private butlers, and satel-lite phones. (Most U.S. cell phones do not work on the island.) Fowl Cay has a second white-sand beach on the north side; smaller beaches are being created by clearing brush on the western end of the island.

Less than a quarter of the island has been developed, but there are plans to add more villas, including some over-water pavilions, while keeping the owner's com-mitment to preserving the environment. Progress will be slow due to the island's remote location, which makes getting building supplies and builders to the island difficult and takes time. Given the sheer joy that visitors derive from the privacy, serenity, and tranquillity of this small paradise, progress can't be slow enough.

Royal Plantation Island

Fowl Cay, N I Cay, The Exumas, Bahamas
Phone: (242) 357-0095; Fax: (954) 208-8216; www.royalplantation.com; www.fowl cay.com; info@fowlcay.com

Owner: Gordon "Butch" Stewart

General Managers: Steve and Julie Huggins

Open: Year-round

Credit Cards: All major

U.S. Reservations: (888) 48-ROYAL; Direct to hotel (242) 357-0095; or reservations@ fowlcay.com; VHF CH16

Deposit: 25 percent of total booking

Cancellation: 60 days prior to arrival; holiday booking deposit nonrefundable

Minimum Stay: Christmas and New Year's, seven-night minimum

Arrival/Departure: From Nassau, Flamingo Air flies twice daily to Staniel Cay in 40 minutes, $90 one-way. www.flamingoairbah .com. From Fort Lauderdale, Watermakers Air, a charter airline, has two flights daily to Staniel Cay, $500 round-trip (954) 467-8920. Boat transfer from Staniel Cay provided by Royal Plantation Island for guests.

Distance from Staniel Airport: 1½ miles

Accommodations: Six villas (1–3 bedrooms with fully equipped kitchens)

Amenities: All villas have air-conditioning, ceiling fans, satellite television, DVD and CD players, Molton Brown toiletries, golf cart, bicycles, motorboat, and by 2009, free Wi-Fi.

Electricity: 110 volts

Fitness/Spa Facilities: Exercise room; Red Lane® Spa in 2009

Sports: Freshwater swimming pool, several beaches, boating, snorkel equipment, tennis court, walking trails, horseshoes, kayaks, and sailboats. Deep-sea fishing and diving for fee

Dress Code: Casual

Children: All ages

Meetings: Entire island rental for up to thirty-four persons

Day Visitors: Reservations required for meals

Handicapped Facilities: No

Packages: None

Rates: *High/Low Season,* from $1,000/$650 per person, per day or $10,150/$9,220 per week for one-bedroom house for two people, to $500/$451 and $15,500/$12,633 for a two-bedroom, four people, to $500/$382 and $19,250/$16,045 for three-bedroom for six people.

Service Charge: Included

Government Tax: Included

DUNMORE BEACH CLUB

Harbour Island, Eleuthera, Bahamas

This small cottage colony has won the hearts of its many loyal fans and the coveted Hideaway Small Inn of the Year Award for good reason. Still, to understand what it is and is not, let's step back briefly in time.

Three decades ago Long Islander Basil Albury converted a house on the crest of the ridge overlooking Harbour Island's famous pink-sand beach into a small inn and added some cottages. For twenty-five years he ran it like a private club, preferring guests who were in the social registry and not accepting anyone who was not recommended. Albury did not like tourists, did not allow Bahamians, and was outspoken to a fault.

Still, the resort garnered praise, loyal fans, and legions of repeaters—more than 90 percent. Most say it was the outstanding food. So concerned was Albury that Dunmore remain as it was that when he decided to sell, he looked for and found buyers from among his previous guests.

Today some of the "our club" atmosphere remains, but the new owners introduced a more open attitude and fresh spirit—not to mention lots of fresh paint and professionalism. The Club now takes anyone, with or without recommendations, who fits. Fitting in has more to do with understanding what the club is than with who you are.

Dunmore Beach is a small, quiet—very quiet—resort set high above the beach on eighteen well-kept acres shaded by tropical trees and colorful flowers. The eight guest cottages, each with two units, are spaced far enough apart from one another to provide a great deal of privacy.

The structures are squares, more or less, painted in pretty pastels, each a different color. What they lack in architectural merit on the outside, they make up for in their comfortable interiors—all with pitched roofs, air-conditioning, and modern bathrooms.

The guest rooms are large suites with pickled-wood-beamed ceilings. Each is individually furnished in attractive and cheerful English country style, with tropical touches and island paintings. All units have a separate sitting room and an enlarged bathroom with a 6-foot-long Jacuzzi tub, oversize shower stall, vanity with double sinks, and lighted mirror, as well as a refrigerator. Each one has a breezy porch with fabulous views, where it is easy to spend hours reading, sipping a cool drink, snoozing, watching the changing colors of the beautiful sea, and feeling completely removed from the cares of the world.

The main house serves as clubhouse and social center. It has a large, comfortable living room with a library. A lounge with a bar is invitingly furnished with white rattan and pretty prints. The lounge extends to an indoor dining room with an oceanfront terrace. The clubhouse was recently enlarged and a business center added to provide computers with Internet and e-mail access. A lacy gazebo by the dining terrace is another good perch for viewing the gorgeous beach and deep blue sea. The bar is open on a self-service honor basis all day, but is attended during prelunch and predinner cocktail hours, which quickly take on a house-party ambience.

The resort's reputation for having the best cuisine on the island is well deserved. Guests enjoy creative and imaginative interpretations of Bahamian dishes and international classics. The staff members who serve the meals are also wonderful: attentive, caring, and delightful.

Weather permitting, breakfast, lunch, and dinner are served on the outdoor terrace, in full view of the pretty pink-sand beach and the sea, or in the rather spartan dining room with walls reaching to a high-pitched hip roof with a pickled-wood-beamed ceiling. Snow-white wooden tables, with white captain's chairs, are brightened with bouquets of fresh pink hibiscus.

At dinner the room gets much dressier and more formal, as do the guests. Dunmore Beach is one of the few places in the Tropics that still requires a jacket for dinner during the winter. Most of the guests would not have it any other way. The dining room tables are dressed in white linen and candlelight, and meals are served on fine china with crystal stemware and silver flatware. Dinner is served at one sitting, between 7:00 and 8:30 p.m. When space is available, nonresident guests are accepted if they have reservations. There is a special early dinner for children under twelve years of age.

From the dining room terrace, steps lead down to the beach—as nice a spot for walking or jogging as it is for sunning and swimming. There are beach chairs and umbrellas for lounging. The resort offers tennis and snorkeling and other water sports; bonefishing and deep-sea fishing can be arranged.

Dunmore owns another nine acres, where there are two new cottages: The two-story Ocean House has a large ground floor bedroom and sitting room, both with ocean views. The upper level also has a large master bedroom, kitchenette, small study, and a private sundeck with a spectacular view. The cottage can be rented as a two-bedroom house or as two private suites. Next door is a four-bedroom villa, Sitting Pretty, which is also available for rent.

Dunmore Beach has an informal, clubby atmosphere, and if you feel you belong, you'll love it. Although the owners are from Locust Valley, New York, southern accents predominate. Guests are affluent, mostly professionals and CEOs. Families with children come frequently.

Dunmore Beach Club **

P.O. Box EL-27122, Harbour Island, Eleuthera, Bahamas
Phone: (242) 333-2200, toll free (877) 891-3100; Fax: (242) 333-2429; e-mail: info@dunmorebeach.com; www.dunmore beach.com

Owner: Dunmore Beach Club, Ltd.

General Manager: Mrs. Quincie Stubbs

Open: Year-round except September–October

Credit Cards: Visa, MasterCard only

U.S. Reservations: Direct to hotel, toll free (877) 891-3100

Deposit: Three nights; thirty days cancellation

Minimum Stay: None

Arrival/Departure: No transfer service

Distance from Airport: (North Eleuthera International Airport) 3 miles; from airport to ferry, 1 mile, $5; from dock to Harbour Island, 2 miles, $5; from Harbour Island to hotel: taxi one-way, $4

Distance from Dunmore Town: ½ mile; taxi one-way, $4

Accommodations: 14 units in seven cottages, all with terraces; with twins or kings; one two-bedroom villa and one four-bedroom villa

Amenities: Air-conditioning, ceiling fans; bath with Jacuzzi tub and separate shower, hair dryer, robes, basket of toiletries; refrigerator, ice service; radio and clock; no telephone, television

Electricity: 110 volts

Sports: Tennis courts, free; no swimming pool

Dress Code: In winter jackets and collared shirts required for dinner; May–August, collared shirts requested

Children: All ages; children under twelve years old dine separately; cribs, high chairs; babysitters

Meetings: Up to twenty-eight people

Day Visitors: No

Handicapped Facilities: Yes, but beach access difficult

Packages: Special rates for weddings; inquire

Rates: Per room, two people, daily, FAP. *High Season* (November 1–April 30): $519–$819. *Low Season:* $295–$450. Villas, daily, two bedrooms (four people) FAP. *High Season:* $1,700; *Low Season:* $1,000. Four bedrooms, no meals included, *High Season:* $1,700, *Low Season:* $1,200. Additional occupants and children's rates; inquire

Service Charge: 20 percent for gratuities and government tax

Government Tax: Included in service charge

BRITISH COLONIAL HILTON NASSAU
Nassau, Bahamas

In October 1999 Hilton International opened its first Bahamian property, the British Colonial Hilton Nassau, after completing an eighteen-month, $68 million restoration that converted the historic property into a deluxe business and leisure hotel with downtown Nassau's only private beach. A decade later, the hotel is about to undergo another major renovation.

Located in the heart of downtown Nassau's business center, the British Colonial Hilton is the city's oldest continuously operating hotel, first opened in 1922. It is part of a development project that housed the first stock exchange in the Bahamas, along with offices. Formerly known as the British Colonial Hotel and built on the historic site of old Fort Nassau, the seven-story Hilton preserves the Caribbean colonial charm of the old landmark while adding the amenities that today's travelers want and expect.

The latest renovations, which are suppose to be completed by December 2008, will include a makeover of the guest rooms, meeting rooms, restaurants, and a redesign of the lobby that's sure to be magnificent. The sixth and seventh floors have sixty-eight executive rooms, along with an Executive Club Lounge, where guests enjoy private check-in and check-out as well as complimentary breakfast, evening hors d'oeuvres, and drinks on the lounge's outdoor terrace.

In addition to the private beach, the landmark property has a large freshwater swimming pool set in pretty tropical gardens, a fitness center, and a snorkeling facility. Portofino restaurant serving a buffet and a la carte international selections, is open for breakfast, lunch, and dinner. The outdoor Patio Bar and Grille offers Bahamian and American-style snacks. For cocktails there's Blackbeard's Cove Bar and the Palm Court

Lounge. You can enjoy evening entertainment by local jazz sensation Pam Woods on Tuesday, Wednesday, and Thursday evening.

The British Colonial Hilton has a fully equipped business center. Its meeting facilities include the spacious Governor's Ballroom, the Victoria Room with garden and ocean views, the Sir Harry Oakes Boardroom, Sir Milo Butler Boardroom, the New Windsor Room, and five other meeting rooms. Situated at the head of Bay Street, the hotel is within easy walking distance of Nassau's famous Straw Market, duty-free shops, historic sites, and the port. Golf and nightlife are only a few minutes away by car.

The British Colonial was the setting for two James Bond films with Sean Connery: *Thunderball* (1965) and *Never Say Never Again* (1983). (Connery has a home on the island.) A 007 suite has been created at the hotel decorated with posters and other memorabilia that pay homage to the acting legend and the movies made there.

The hotel can arrange for Stuart Cove (who trained the Bond movie doubles) to take divers down to see the 120-foot freighter that was sunk for the movie *Never Say Never Again* as well as the Valkin Bomber airplane from *Thunderball*. Both wrecks are the actual sets from the movies and lie 40 feet beneath the surface.

British Colonial Hilton Nassau ***
One Bay Street, Nassau, Bahamas
Phone: (242) 322-3301; Fax: (242) 322-2286; www.hilton.com

Owners: Adurion Capital Limited

Management: Hilton Hotels Corporation

General Manager: Peter Webster

Credit Cards: All major

U.S. Reservations: Hilton Reservations Worldwide, (800) HILTONS

Deposit: One night

Minimum Stay: None, except Christmas/New Year's

Arrival/Departure: Guests referred to local company for transfer service

Distance from Airport: (Nassau International Airport) 10 miles; taxi one-way, $22

Accommodations: 288 rooms (including 47 executive level rooms, 20 suites, the Prime Ministers Suite, and the Executive Lounge)

Amenities: Air-conditioning; telephones; television; hair dryer, toiletries; room service, nightly turndown service; high-speed Internet; oversize desks; modems, fax machines on request

Electricity: 120 volts

Fitness Facilities/Spa Services: See text

Sports: Beach, swimming pool; free nonmotorized water sports and snorkeling facility on premise

Children: All ages stay free when staying with parents

Dress Code: Business casual

Meetings: Facilities for up to 400 people; five meeting rooms; boardroom; business center

Day Visitors: Yes

Handicapped Facilities: Yes

Packages: Yes

Rates: Per room, double, daily: *High Season* (January–May 31): $219–$1,200. *Low Season* (June 1–September 30): $149–$1,200. *Shoulder Season* (October 1–December 21): $189–$1,200; *Christmas holidays* (December 22–31): $229–$1,200. Single rates available.

Service Charge: Maid gratuity, $4 per person per day

Government Tax: 12 percent

Energy Surcharge: $4 per person per day

GRAYCLIFF HOTEL

Nassau, Bahamas

If you are a romantic and care more about ambience, history, and in-town location than glitter, casinos, or the beach, Graycliff will be your kind of hotel.

Situated in one of the oldest structures in Nassau (and listed in the National Register of Historic Places), Graycliff is one of the most unusual hotels in the Bahamas, if not the Caribbean. Just up the hill from Bay Street, Nassau's main thoroughfare, and 1 block from Government House, the landmark mansion is thought to have been built around 1666 by Captain John Howard Graysmith, an infamous pirate who commanded the schooner, *Graywolf,* which plundered treasure ships along the Spanish Main. Partially destroyed by the Spaniards in 1703, segments of the original mansion can still be seen in the Graycliff structure. In 1776, when Nassau was captured by the American Navy, Graycliff became their headquarters and garrison—hence the bars on the windows of the hotel's wine cellar.

Graycliff was Nassau's first inn when it opened in 1844. Later it was commandeered as an officers' mess for the West Indian Regiment during the American Civil War. During the roaring 1920s, Graycliff opened to the public again by then-owner Polly Leach, a close companion to Al Capone, and became a popular gathering spot for the rich and famous.

Later the mansion became the private residence of a wealthy Canadian couple who renovated the mansion and added the swimming pool, and in 1966, Graycliff was purchased by Lord and Lady Dudley, Third Earl of Staffordshire, who hosted such luminaries as the Duke and Duchess of Windsor, Lord Mountbatten, and Sir Winston Churchill there. Lady Grace Dudley added an English accent to the decor and priceless antiques, some of which still decorate guest rooms and public areas.

In 1973 Graycliff was purchased by its current owners, Enrico and Anna Maria Garzaroli, who turned the private home into the elegant hotel and restaurant that it is today. The hotel has twenty varied, newly renovated rooms and pool cottage suites, two restaurants, a gym, and two swimming pools. The Graycliff Cigar Company was added in 1998.

The hotel has two sections: Graycliff Hotel with rooms in the old section named to evoke the romance of the tropics, and Graycliff Cigar Company Hotel, the newer part where the names reflect the cigars made there. Rooms have views of the gardens, pool, or Nassau Harbor. Each is different in arrangement and individually decorated, blending the old and the new; all are air-conditioned and have private baths. The old can be enjoyed in the Pool Cottage, where Winston Churchill stayed, and usually considered the bridal suite or the Baillou, the original master bedroom in the main house, with an enormous, elegant bedroom, parlor, and marble bathroom larger than most New York apartments. The new, huge Mandarino Cottage has an extra large bathroom with whirlpool and separate shower, and a dining terrace, especially popular with honeymooners. Luxury rooms and suites have sitting areas; the Graycliff Suite also includes a dining area, private balcony, and very large bathroom.

Dining at Graycliff is a treat. The Graycliff Restaurant serves fine (and expensive) continental and Bahamian cuisine in very elegant surroundings (some might say a bit pretentious). The evening begins with cocktails in the Old World parlor while you peruse the menu and place your dinner order and enjoy piano music in the background. Be sure to try the house specialty. The restaurant has four air-conditioned dining rooms and an outdoor dining area. The decor reflects the era when Graycliff was a private home. Following dinner you are invited to relax and enjoy the evening with an after-dinner cognac or cigar. Dinner for two costs $150 and up.

Graycliff's award-winning Wine Cellar has an inventory of more than 200,000 bottles from more than 400 vintners in fifteen countries. These include rare wines such as an 1865 Château Lafite to today's most popular vintages. Private tours of the wine cellar and Cigar Company are available and you can have a private cigar-rolling lesson for a fee. Recently, the wine cellar became a venue for private wine tasting dinners for up to eighteen people. The cost for the room is $1,000 plus the dinner and wine. You can also explore Graycliff's Wine Cellar online.

The second restaurant, Humidor Churrascaria, offers a complete change of pace and is a fun and festive dining experience. When the restaurant opened in 2005, it brought a brand-new concept to Nassau and was an immediate hit. The cuisine is Brazilian Churrascaria with a Bahamian flair. Churrascaria (choo-rah-scah-ree-ah) refers to a restaurant that specializes in Rodizio—a Brazilian barbecue method of grilling, cutting, and serving several varieties of meats.

The restaurant does not have a traditional menu; rather, a steady stream of energetic waiters bring you a large quantity and variety of meats such as chicken, pork, beef, and lamb hot from the grill. There's also a large salad bar, vegetables, and fresh fish. The all-you-can-eat prix fixe meal costs $39.95 per person. Dessert, drinks,

and gratuities are not included. Dinner is served nightly Monday through Saturday. Both restaurants are open to the public, but breakfast is served to hotel guests only.

Needless to say, the romantic setting makes Graycliff very popular for weddings, and the wedding coordinator can customize the couple's wedding. Graycliff's newest addition is a Chef's Table in the kitchen, and coming soon, a chocolate factory across the street in an old building that is being renovated. Other amenities include a gym with treadmills, bikes, free weights, weight machines with television or music, sauna, and Jacuzzi; and the Graycliff's Gift Shop & Gallery, with items ranging from fine postcards to original artwork and, of course, cigars. In addition to brands created by Graycliff's Cigar Company, the shop has a selection of Cuban cigars.

Although the surroundings are elegant, the ambience at Graycliff is friendly. And you don't really have to give up Nassau's glittering nightlife or gorgeous white-sand beaches. Both are less than ten minutes away in almost any direction.

Graycliff Hotel ***
8–12 West Hill Street, Nassau, NP, Bahamas; P.O. Box N-10246, Nassau, Bahamas Phone: (800) 476-0446, (242) 302-9150; Fax: (242) 326-6110; e-mail: info@gray cliff.com; www.graycliff.com

Owners: Enrico and Anna Maria Garzaroli

General Manager: Paolo Garzaroli

Open: Year-round, restaurants closed to public Christmas day.

Credit Cards: Most major

U.S. Reservations: (800) 476-0446

Deposit: One night

Minimum Stay: One night, except three nights from December 20–January 3

Arrival/Departure: Arranged on request for fee

Distance from Airport: Twenty minutes from Nassau International; Taxi one-way $22–$25

Distance from Nassau: Located in Nassau

Accommodations: 20 rooms and suites (nine with sitting areas; six with balconies or terrace. Most have king bed; several with double beds; and two are singles)

Amenities: Air-conditioning, private bath (eleven with Jacuzzis), minibar; safe; direct-dial phone, alarm clock, dataport, cable television; hair dryer, toiletries, iron and ironing board; daily housekeeping, evening turndown, room service, coffee/tea service, laundry/dry cleaning available; shop; free on-site parking; Wi-Fi throughout the property

Electricity: 110 volts

Fitness Facilities/Spa Services: In-room massages available; weight room/gym. Personal trainer on request

Sports: Two swimming pools; nearby tennis, golf, and water sports

Dress Code: Dress code strictly enforced. For lunch, casually elegant. For dinner, resort elegant; jackets suggested but not required. No shorts (dinner); shoes must be worn at all times.

Children: Allowed but no facilities

Meetings: Up to 300

Day Visitors: In restaurants

Handicapped Facilities: Limited

Packages: Wedding, honeymoon

Rates: Per room, daily. *High Season* (mid-December–April 30): $375–$700; *Low Season* (May 1–mid-December): $325–$575

Service Charge: $4.25 per person, per day on rooms; 18 percent on food and beverages

Government Tax: 12 percent on room

ONE&ONLY OCEAN CLUB
Paradise Island, Nassau, Bahamas

Paradise on Paradise. In the ups and downs of the Bahamas' development, the posh One&Only Ocean Club has been the one resort that's kept its panache. Located on thirty-five acres along a white-sand beach across the bridge from Nassau, this tony resort is one of the most beautiful in the Tropics. It has style.

Now one of the One&Only group, the signature of Kerzner International luxury hotels, the Club has undergone extensive renovation and expansion over the years that has included beachfront rooms, a beachfront restaurant headed by a noted chef, an elaborate spa, a KidsOnly program, and a redesigned golf course. The project was part of a $100 million development, which included the construction of Ocean Club Estates—luxurious homes and a marina. More recently, the resort has added a boardroom for twenty-two people; a logo shop; a family pool; and a group of ultraluxury, beachfront, three- and four-bedroom villas with their own infinity-edge pool and dedicated butler.

Long a hideaway for the rich and famous, the club was originally the private winter home of a wealthy Swedish industrialist, who named it Shangri-La. In the 1960s A&P heir Huntington Hartford built the Ocean Club adjacent to Shangri-La, got government permission to rename the island Paradise Island (originally called Hog Island), and turned it into a premier resort for his wealthy friends. In 1968 Resorts International acquired the majority interest in Hartford's holdings and expanded Paradise Island into a major resort. In 1988, in a highly publicized deal with Donald Trump, the late showman/producer Merv Griffin bought Resorts International, which included the Ocean Club; and in 1994 Sun International bought out Merv Griffin and built the nearby mammoth resort complex, Atlantis. The Ocean Club was left in its secluded splendor.

Kerzner International (formerly Sun International) reinvented the resort, preserving its timeless elegance while updating it with new facilities and fresh amenities for a new generation of travelers in the twenty-first century.

Located on the eastern end of Paradise Island, a forty-minute drive from Nassau International Airport, hotel services begin upon your arrival at the airport with limo transfer (for a fee) to the resort.

As soon as you turn into the long drive through gardens and manicured lawns to the main entrance, you know you have arrived at a special place. The club's style begins with check-in. If you have been a guest before, the staff will remember your name and probably your preferences for breakfast, newspapers, sports, and any special services you require.

The main building is a graceful two-story mansion, with rooms set around a tropical garden courtyard with an ornamental pool and fountain at the center. The rooms overlook turquoise waters edged by 2 miles of beach along lawns where hammocks swing

in the breeze under palms and giant eucalyptus trees. Rooms have verandas and are furnished in colonial-style mahogany.

The Crescent, made up of five two-story buildings by the beach, has forty ocean-front rooms (each measuring a spacious 550 square feet) and ten suites (each with a huge 1,100 square feet)—all with private balcony or terrace with unobstructed views of the club's long white-sand beach. Dressed in subdued colors and British-colonial decor but still Caribbean in feeling, the accommodations have large marble bathrooms, separate showers, double-sink vanities, and the latest technology—Internet access, portable telephone, DVD and CD players, and DMX music. Crescent suites also have steam shower, Jacuzzi bathtub, a bathroom television, and a Bose entertainment system.

All accommodations enjoy butler service, which includes packing and unpacking, dinner and activity reservations, personal wake-up calls, daily fruit bowl delivery, shoeshine service, afternoon tea, champagne, and strawberries delivered to guest rooms. There is thrice-daily maid service, including nightly turndown, and guests can borrow from the CD and DVD library. Laptops are available for guest in-room use. Guests in suites and garden cottages have in-room check-in.

To the south is the freshwater swimming pool, which has a wonderful setting overlooking the terraced Versailles Gardens, which flow for ¼ mile in seven tiers to an authentic twelfth-century French cloister on the highest rise at the far southern end. The cloister, with its graceful arches and columns, was part of a monastery brought, piece by piece, from France to the United States by William Randolph Hearst. Hartford purchased the stone structure, shipped it from Florida, and had it reassembled here. The Pool Terrace, adjacent to the pool and tennis courts, is open throughout the day for light fare and drinks.

The resort has a family pool near the tennis courts and a complimentary KidsOnly program. Housed in its own facility, it offers imaginative half- and full-day interactive, educational, and recreational experiences for ages four to twelve, daily throughout the year. The beachfront restaurant, Dune, created by renowned chef and restaurateur Jean-Georges Vongerichten and designed by famed French interior designer Christian Liaigre, is stunning. Set in the dunes at the edge of the beach, the decor interprets the British-colonial heritage of the Bahamas in a modern context, rendering it casual and elegant at the same time. Liaigre, who is known as the most environmentally sensitive of designers, blends natural woods and fibers with a sophisticated patina of color that ranges from the ash of weathered wood around the bar to the slate of chairs and the charcoal of highly polished Ivory Coast hardwood table tops in the dining room. Running full length across the back of the restaurant is the display kitchen, encased in glass partitions that reflect the ocean into the room.

Daily at breakfast, lunch, and dinner, diners may sit inside under a high-pitched, beamed ceiling and look in one direction to the turquoise sea and in the other direction to the activity in the kitchen. Or they can dine under white umbrella tables on the outdoor patio overlooking the beach. At one end of the building is an outdoor white marble bar, which has become a popular rendezvous almost any time of day.

The menu offers Jean-Georges's signature dishes from his top-rated New York restaurants—Jean Georges, Mercer Kitchen, Vong, and JoJo—with Bahamian ingredients whenever possible. To underscore his commitment to using local products, Jean-Georges engaged Bahamian Teresa Kemp

to create a garden of local herbs in front of the restaurant. Jean-Georges was also responsible for training the Bahamian staff. The Ocean Club Golf Course was totally revamped into an eighteen-hole championship course by pro golfer and course designer Tom Weiskopf. The course (7,123 yard/par 72), designed for every caliber of player, takes advantage of the Bahamian landscape and crosswinds, challenging golfers' precision and accuracy. It offers seaside greens and tees, alternating fairways, lakes, and a clubhouse. The course is available for play only to Ocean Club and Atlantis guests and villa owners.

The One&Only Ocean Club's spa, operated by Mandara, has an open air pavilion; eight private spa suites, each with a garden Jacuzzi and outdoor waterfall shower. The spa suites use natural materials—Javanese teak massage tables, Thai-silk pillows, and coconut bowls filled with fresh flowers and floating candles. In the serene atmosphere for which it is known, Mandara offers a full range of body and beauty treatments.

On the beach—one of the most beautiful in the world—you are served afternoon sorbet and cooled off with Evian misting. Beach attendants and food and beverage service are available. Water sports include sailing, kayaking, and snorkeling; diving can be arranged. A fitness room with Nautilus equipment has men's and women's lockers and changing facilities. Bicycles are available without charge.

The Tennis Club has nine Har-Tru courts (four lighted for night play); a staff pro available for private lessons; and a pro shop with racquet rentals and full line of apparel.

One&Only Ocean Club guests have the best of both worlds: peace and tranquility in a romantic setting and a glittering nightlife at the nearby Atlantis. Guests have access to Atlantis's other facilities and restaurants as well. Free shuttles run every half hour to Atlantis, the golf course, and the casino.

In addition to its romance, this fashionable resort appeals to people who like a quietly elegant and slightly European ambience.

One&Only Ocean Club ★★★★
Box N-4777, Paradise Island, Nassau, Bahamas
Phone: (242) 363-2501, (800) 321-3000; Fax: (242) 363-2424; www.oneandonly oceanclub.com

Owner: Kerzner International Bahamas

General Manager: James Scott

Open: Year-round

Credit Cards: Most major

U.S. Reservations: Kerzner International, (800) 321-3000

Deposit: Two nights

Minimum Stay: None, except at Christmas/New Year's; inquire

Arrival/Departure: Transfer service via town car, $60 one-way

Distance from Airport: (Nassau International Airport) Forty minutes; taxi one-way, $22; five minutes from Paradise Island Airport

Distance from Nassau: 3 miles; taxi one-way, $6.00 plus $2.50 bridge toll; water taxi between Paradise Island and Nassau one-way, $2.50

Accommodations: 105 rooms and suites and two three-bedroom and one four-bedroom villa, all with terraces and king-size beds

Amenities: Air-conditioning, ceiling fans; television (including one in bathroom); marbled bath with tub and shower, hair dryer, toiletries; telephones (including one in bathroom); stocked minibar; room service, terry robes, thrice-daily maid service; butler service; daily fruit bowl, afternoon champagne and strawberries; laptop for use in suites and villas, shoeshine service. Crescent: VCR, Jacuzzi baths, steam shower, Bose entertainment system, in-room check-in; Internet access, DVD and CD player, iPods, and DMX music

Electricity: 110 volts

Fitness Facilities/Spa Services: Fitness room operated by New York-based La Palestra; men's and women's lockers and changing facilities; full-service Mandara spa

Sports: Beach, two freshwater pools (one for children); tennis, golf, walking paths, bikes, water sports

Children: KidsOnly program; babysitters; Discovery Channel Camp operated by Atlantis

Dress Code: Casual but always chic; jackets requested in evening

Meetings: Small executive groups

Day Visitors: Not encouraged

Handicapped Facilities: Limited

Packages: Golf, tennis, honeymoon, wedding

Rates: Per room or suite, daily, EP. $500–$2,500. For villa rates, inquire

Service Charge: $7 per couple daily housekeeping gratuity

Government Tax: 12 percent resort tax based on room rate

BARBADOS

Barbados is an elegant place in a quiet sort of way. Whether it is the 300 years of British rule, the Bajans' pride and natural grace, or the blue-stocking vacationers who return annually like homing birds to their roost, this Caribbean island feels something like *Masterpiece Theatre* in the Tropics.

Independent since 1966, Barbados still seems as British as the queen. Bridgetown, the capital, has a Trafalgar Square, now renamed National Heroes Square. Bewigged judges preside over the country's law courts, hotels stop for afternoon tea, and a police band gives outdoor concerts.

The 166-square-mile island of green rolling hills even resembles the English countryside and is a pleasure to explore. On an island only 21 miles long, you can visit stately homes and gardens, more than fifty important historic sites, and the outstanding Barbados Museum.

A coral island 100 miles east of the Lesser Antilles, Barbados is the easternmost land in the Caribbean. Its western coast, fringed with attractive beaches, is bathed by calm Caribbean waters; the eastern shores are washed by the whitecapped rollers of the Atlantic. It is one of the main locations for windsurfing in the Caribbean and often a venue for international competitions. The island is surrounded by coral reefs good for snorkeling and learning to scuba dive. Sailing, fishing, golf, tennis, horseback riding, and polo are also available.

Barbados has one of the widest selections of accommodations of any island in the Caribbean, ranging from modest guest houses to ultraposh resorts with great style. Each is different and distinctive. Their ambience is often more European than that found in hotels on Caribbean islands closer to the United States, because the majority of Barbados's visitors come from Britain and other European countries.

Information

Barbados Tourism Authority, 800 Second Avenue, New York, NY 10017;
(800) 221-9831, (212) 986-6516; Fax: (212) 573-9850;
and 3440 Wilshire Boulevard, #1215, Los Angeles, CA 90010;
(800) 221-9831, (213) 380-2198; Fax: (213) 384-2763; www.barbados.org
(Also see Almond Casuarina Beach Resort on p. 302 in On the Horizon.)

COBBLERS COVE

St. Peter, Barbados

This cozy complex of two-story cottages in gardens overlooking the beach can induce love at first sight in those who want a casual, romantic resort with just enough history to lend it charm—but with attractive, modern, spacious accommodations to boot.

The centerpiece of this quiet resort is a pale pink villa built in the early part of the twentieth century by a Bajan sugar baron as a summer home. The former living room, similar to an English country drawing room, now serves as a reading lounge with daily U.S. and European newspapers.

The villa's open-air, seaside terrace doubles as the dining pavilion and bar, a favorite meeting place for hotel guests and local friends. During the winter season you'll hear a strong British upstairs accent, but in summer the voices are likely to have a more familiar American ring.

In the evening the pavilion and another terrace next to the lounge become romantic settings for candlelight dining. Blending traditional European dishes with fresh local products, the chef has developed an innovative, sophisticated cuisine. Because all dishes are cooked to order, guests give their selections to the head waiter while they enjoy a drink at the bar adjacent to the dining terrace. Friday night is particularly special with a seafood (fresh catch from Barbados waters) and caviar (from around the world) dinner. Cobblers Cove has a dinner exchange with a number of other deluxe island hotels.

The cottages, each with four suites, sit snugly in a V in three acres of tropical gardens alongside the main house and around a small pool overlooking the Caribbean. The pool area can be crowded when the hotel is full, but a new, large wooden deck helps, providing much needed space for lounging near the beach, only 10 yards away.

All accommodations are suites with large bedrooms, ample closets, newly renovated and upgraded bathrooms, and special drying racks for wet bathing suits and towels. Each suite overlooks the garden or sea and has a wet bar and separate sitting room with louvered doors that, when folded back, open onto a furnished patio or balcony to create one large, airy space.

The most sensational accommodations are the bilevel Camelot and Colleton Suites on the top floor of the main villa by architect Ian Morrison, known for his handsome design of nearby Glitter Bay and Royal Pavilion hotels. These posh love nests offer the ultimate in privacy, along with marble floors; a king-size, canopied four-poster bed; and a lounge area with a settee, writing desk, and chaise lounge—all in fresh blue and white decor. The huge bathrooms have whirlpool tubs, twin sinks, bidets, and his and hers showers with twin showerheads. Each suite has a small plunge pool and wet bar that overlooks a wonderful view of the sea. These suites may well be the most heavenly honeymoon hideaways in the Tropics. The price is up there, too.

The resort's sports facilities include complimentary water sports and day and night tennis. You can go snorkeling directly off the beach. Cobblers has a gift shop, exercise room, and spa facilities housed in a pair of colorful chattel houses. Exercise equipment is top of the line. Recently, two new treatment rooms were added along with an expanded selection of treatments. Also in a chattel house is an Internet room on the top floor and on the first floor, a kids corner, which operates in the summer and during holidays when arts and crafts are offered a few hours per day.

Life at Cobblers Cove is very low-key. There's the manager's weekly cocktail party and occasional live musical entertainment, but essentially the resort is a friendly, easy-living sort of place where guests meet and mingle or go their own way.

The resort's informality is suited to families, while its cozy, romantic ambience attracts couples of all ages. Cobblers Cove is a member of the prestigious Relais et Châteaux.

Cobblers Cove ✳✳✳

Road View, St. Peter, Barbados
Phone: (246) 422-2291; Fax: (246) 422-1460; e-mail: cobblers@caribsurf.com; www.barbados.org/hotels/cobblers.htm

Owner: Hayton, Ltd.

General Manager: Randall Wilkie

Open: Year-round except September–mid-October

Credit Cards: All major

U.S. Reservations: Karen Bull Associates, (800) 890-6060; Fax: (404) 237-1841

Deposit: Three nights in winter, except seven nights during Christmas; one night in summer; twenty-eight days cancellation in winter, fourteen days in summer

Minimum Stay: Fourteen nights during Christmas/New Year's

Arrival/Departure: Transfer service arranged for fee

Distance from Airport: 18 miles (forty-five minutes); taxi one-way, $40

Distance from Bridgetown: 12 miles (twenty-five minutes); taxi one-way, $20

Accommodations: 38 suites in two-story cottages (22 garden view, 16 deluxe and oceanfront) with twin beds in ten, all with terraces and patios; two superdeluxe suites with plunge pool

Amenities: Air-conditioning, ceiling fans; direct-dial telephones; individual safes; television arranged on request; radio at front desk; bath with tub and shower, hair dryer, terry robes, basket of toiletries; stocked minibar, ice service, room service 8:00 a.m.–9:00 p.m.

Electricity: 110 volts/50 cycles

Fitness Facilities/Spa Services: Fitness facility with exercise equipment and spa services with new treatment rooms and expanded treatments

Sports: Freshwater swimming pool; free waterskiing, windsurfing, Sunfish, snorkeling, tennis; special fees for golf at Sandy Lane and Royal Westmoreland courses; diving/water sports can be arranged

Dress Code: Informal by day; elegantly casual in evening; men wear slacks and open-neck shirts. Jeans, shorts, and swimwear are not allowed in bar area after 7:00 p.m.

Children: All ages except mid-January–mid-March, when none under twelve years old; cribs; babysitters with advance notice

Meetings: No

Day Visitors: With reservations

Handicapped Facilities: Yes

Packages: Honeymooners, gourmet, golf, summer

Rates: Per room, two people, daily. **High Season** (early January–mid-April): $740–$1,050; Camelot and Colleton Suites, $2,100 and $2,450. **Low Season** (mid-April–September 30): $420–$620; suites, $980 and $1,400. EP **Shoulder Season**

(October 1–mid-December): $450–$600; suites, $1,200–$1,400. Single, two-bedroom, Christmas, MAP, low, and shoulder rates available; inquire

Service Charge: 10 percent included in all rates; additional at guests' discretion

Government Tax: Included

CORAL REEF CLUB
St. James, Barbados

This is a family affair. The O'Hara family—mother, two sons, a daughter, two daughters-in-law, and a son-in-law—own and operate this resort and give it a special cachet.

The Coral Reef Club, together with the Sandpiper, its sister hotel next door, enjoys a coveted location on Barbados's Caribbean coast, amid a string of fashionable resorts and trendy restaurants. Spread over twelve acres of flowering trees and gardens and fronting a mile of casuarina- and mahogany-shaded powdery sands, the resort blends an upscale British style with a comfortable, relaxing, friendly atmosphere.

Coral Reef Club was born almost by accident in the 1950s when an Englishman and owner of Coral Reef's original coral-stone house, began taking in guests to help defray expenses. Over the next three decades, the beachfront property grew from a four-bedroom beach house to a sixty-nine-room resort. The late Budge O'Hara, the patriarch of the family who arrived as manager with his bride, Cynthia, in 1956, eventually acquired both hotels.

After their father passed away in 1995, the younger O'Haras and their spouses assumed day-to-day management of Coral Reef and Sandpiper, putting their training to use, refurbishing, redecorating, updating, and expanding the properties, while their mother became chairman.

Patrick and Mark jointly manage Coral Reef, along with sister Karen, Patrick's wife, Sharon, and Mark's wife, Maria, an artist, who all help with refurbishing, housekeeping, and gardening. Sharon's sister, Sue Jardine, is sales and marketing manager, and Karen's husband, Wayne Capaldi, manages the Sandpiper. As we said, Coral Reef is a family affair.

A tree-lined drive leads to the original coral-stone villa overlooking the beach, passing the cottages and the newer, two-story buildings nesting in the gardens. The main building houses the island- and antique-dressed lobby, lounge, restaurant, and bar, which open onto a balustrade terrace overlooking the beach and gardens.

Accommodations are in garden rooms and cottages providing the most privacy; rooms in the main house; and the newer two-story colonial-style buildings with gingerbread trim. Some, built around a large swimming pool, house luxury junior suites and the newest category of luxury plantation suites. Another group of thirteen luxury cottages/suites have their own plunge pools and wraparound terraces. Located in the front half of the gardens toward the sea, they are well suited for families as they have a separate living room where two children can sleep. Also, there are two four-bedroom villas with kitchens. A few single rooms with double bed are also available.

All accommodations have tile floors, patios or balconies, king-size or twin beds, air-conditioning, ceiling fans; small refrigerators, direct-dial telephones, safes, hair dryers, CD players, clock radios, and homey touches, such as toasters, a shelf of paperback books, and fresh flowers.

The resort's most posh accommodations are five enormous, superdeluxe Plantation Suites with private pools. Situated on the second floor of two separate buildings with sea views, plus a fifth by the sea, the beautifully furnished, luxury suites have four-poster canopied beds, spacious living rooms, a dressing area, huge bathrooms with separate tub and large shower, and a complimentary starter bar. Two similar posh suites but with contemporary decor have been added to Sandpiper.

The breeze-cooled restaurant serves all three meals plus afternoon tea and a Sunday brunch buffet; during the winter season it also serves a buffet lunch daily. Dinner offers an a la carte menu nightly except Monday, when a buffet of Bajan dishes, plus English standards of roast beef and Yorkshire pudding, are featured. For a change of scenery, Coral Reef has a dining exchange with neighboring Sandpiper, as well as with Treasure Beach and Cobblers Cove up the road. Room service for meals is available during restaurant hours.

The main bar is open twenty-four hours, and musical entertainment and dancing are offered nightly in the winter, less frequently in other months. A folklore show and beach barbecue are staged weekly. The resort has a television room, billiards room, and Wi-Fi and a computer/Internet-access room for guests to use. A boutique in the style of a Barbados chattel house is found in the gardens. A complimentary shuttle to Bridgetown goes daily for shopping.

Those in search of an active vacation will find two freshwater swimming pools and two lighted tennis courts, as well as a ten-station, air-conditioned exercise room. They can enjoy free use of small sailboats, windsurfers, kayaks, and equipment for water skiing and for snorkeling on the resort's reef, only a few yards from the beach. They have access to a 32-foot catamaran, and scuba diving can be arranged for a fee, as can golf at the Royal Westmoreland and Sandy Lane courses.

Not ones to rest on their laurels, the owners closed Coral Reef Club from mid-May to mid-October in 2008 to create a spa with a fitness center and beauty salon, a new tennis court, and new administration buildings. The spa building, a departure from the colonial style of the accommodations, has an understated, slightly modern look and reflects a Zen-like atmosphere. Coral Arms, near the entrance which housed the fitness centre and hair salon, was demolished to make way for the new facilities.

Coral Reef has many loyal fans who, like the owners, are into the second and third generations. Most are Brits but many are affluent Americans who appreciate the resort's certain Old World character blended into a New World setting and its friendly family ambience. The O'Haras usually greet guests on arrival, invite them to their home for the manager's cocktail parties, and give gifts to those staying at Christmas. Many of the staff have been with the hotel for years.

Coral Reef Club ★★★★
St. James, Barbados
Phone: (246) 422-2372; Fax: (246) 422-1776; e-mail: coral@caribsurf.com; www.coralreefbarbados.com

Owners: O'Hara family

Managing Directors: Patrick and Mark O'Hara

Open: Year-round except late May–mid-July

Credit Cards: All major

U.S. Reservations: Ralph Locke, (800) 223-1108; Fax: (310) 440-4220

Deposit: Three nights, seven at Christmas; twenty-eight days cancellation winter, fourteen in summer

Minimum Stay: Fourteen days at Christmas, seven nights February 1–28, Easter, Thanksgiving

Arrival/Departure: No transfer service due to government regulations

Distance from Airport: 18 miles (forty-five minutes); taxi one-way $40

Distance from Bridgetown: 8 miles (twenty minutes)

Accommodations: 88 units, all with terraces, patios, or balconies (25 king or twin double; four singles; 6 superior junior suites; 33 luxury junior suites; 13 cottage suites with living room and plunge pool; five Plantation Suites with sundeck and plunge pool; two four-bedroom villas)

Amenities: Air-conditioning, ceiling fans; direct-dial phones; safe; refrigerator, toaster; hair dryer, bath with tub and shower, bathrobes, basket of toiletries; daily newspaper; nightly turndown service; television on request; hair salon; boutique; twenty-four-hour room service; e-mail and Internet access

Electricity: 110 volts/50 cycles

Fitness Facilities/Spa Services: New spa and fitness (see text)

Sports: Two freshwater swimming pools; two tennis courts with free pro program, lighted; snorkeling, Sunfish, kayaking, waterskiing, and windsurfing included; golf, diving, deep-sea fishing arranged for fee

Dress Code: Smart casual by day; elegantly casual in evening; jacket and tie or black tie Christmas and New Year's

Children: Children welcome year-round except January 15–March 15 when those under twelve years old cannot be accommodated; children under five not allowed in restaurant or lounge after 7:00 p.m.

Meetings: Up to twenty-four people

Handicapped Facilities: Certain accommodations suitable

Packages: Honeymoon, wedding

Rates: Per room, for two, BP rates, including breakfast, service charge and taxes. *High Season* (December 15–mid-April): $760–$2,600. *Low Season* (mid-April–October 6) $420–$1,265; (October 7-December 14): $440-$1,300. For two-bedroom, single, third person, and children rates, inquire

Service Charge: Included

Government Tax: Included

FAIRMONT ROYAL PAVILION
St. James, Barbados

Designed by architect Ian Morrison, known for his Italian-inspired style, the Royal Pavilion is aimed directly at today's affluent travelers. Although grand luxe in the European tradition, it has made a point of being more contemporary in style and attitude than the grandes dames of Barbados's hotels.

Set amid twelve acres of immaculate tropical gardens directly on a white-sand beach in a quiet cove, the pastel pink Royal Pavilion combines Spanish mission and Mediterranean elements in its design. An imposing avenue of royal palms leads to the flower-encircled portico of the main entrance. There you step into a marbled reception hall with a concierge desk and a colonnaded Andalusian courtyard cooled by a fountain. If you wish to have your arrival match the hotel's grand entrance, you can be met at the airport by a luxury car and have access to the airport's VIP lounge.

The resort's accommodations, all facing the sea, are in two wings of three-story buildings. All are large, deluxe rooms with terraces. Completing the roster is a villa with three additional accommodations.

A major renovation in 2003 involved extensive refurbishment of all guest rooms, restaurants, and public areas as well as landscaping.

The guest rooms are furnished in Asian wood and cane furniture, sisal rugs on light ceramic floor tiles, and a wall of built-in shelves with decorative rattan door panels. Rooms have Internet and fax access, DVD players, and 27-inch flat-screen televisions. Their balconies allow for unobstructed views of the sea. Bathrooms have a glass-enclosed shower, tub, and large vanity—all finished in Jerusalem bone marble with Italian marble accents.

The lobby is wireless-equipped, and two laptop computers are available for guests' use.

Royal Pavilion's triumph is the Palm Terrace, an elegant, pink marble dining room by the sea. Here the romantic palm-court effect is enhanced by a skylight pavilion roof shaded by living palm trees that are part of the decor. Adjacent to the restaurant is a spacious lounge with graceful arched doorways and windows opening onto views of the gardens and sea. Here guests enjoy afternoon tea, cocktails, and after-dinner drinks. The Palm Terrace restaurant and bar have a casual but sophisticated atmosphere. The restaurant serves contemporary cuisine with a Caribbean flair and some Thai and French influences.

On the northern side of the resort, Cafe Taboras is a casual, open-air restaurant where breakfast and lunch and some dinners are served, as well as offering a beach and poolside snack menu. It is named for Fernando Tabora, a well-known Latin American landscape architect who designed the exquisite gardens for Royal Pavilion. Cafe Taboras is terraced by the sea on one side, with the swimming pool, a new twelve-person plunge pool, and a large sunning deck on the other.

The hotel has two hard-surface tennis courts (lighted) and complimentary water sports. One of the courtyards has a cluster of fashionable boutiques and a hair salon. Through an arrangement with the nearby Royal Westmoreland Club, Royal Pavilion guests have access to that club's excellent golf course, designed by Robert Trent Jones II.

Royal Pavilion is tony but not snobbish and enjoys a high number of repeat guests, mostly from Britain, Italy, and the United States. It is well suited for those who want a relaxing vacation in a stylish yet casual ambience, where the emphasis is on pretty surroundings, comfort, and sophisticated cuisine.

Fairmont Royal Pavilion ★★★★
Porters, St. James, Barbados, BB24051
Phone: (246) 422-5555; Fax: (246) 422-0118; www.fairmont.com

Owner: Fairmont Hotels & Resorts

General Manager: Jennifer Harding

Open: Year-round

Credit Cards: All major

U.S. Reservations: Fairmont Hotels, (800) 441-1414

Deposit: Three nights, thirty days cancellation in winter; one night, fourteen days cancellation in summer

Minimum Stay: Twelve nights during Christmas

Arrival/Departure: Luxury car and limousine transfer services arranged for fee

Distance from Airport: 12 miles; taxi one-way, $40

Distance from Bridgetown: 8 miles; taxi one-way, $25

Accommodations: 72 oceanfront deluxe rooms with king-size beds and private balconies in two three-story buildings; one garden-view three-bedroom villa

Amenities: Air-conditioning; bath with tub and shower, hair dryer, basket of toiletries, bathrobe; direct-dial telephone, radio, cable television; Internet and fax access; DVD player; safe; stocked minibar; twice-daily maid service, twenty-four-hour room service; concierge

Electricity: 110 volts/50 cycles

Fitness Facilities/Spa Services: Air-conditioned fitness center; in-room massage

Sports: Freshwater swimming pool; complimentary tennis and equipment (lessons extra), Hobie Cats, Sunfish, snorkeling, waterskiing, windsurfing; diving additional; horseback riding, golf, fishing arranged

Dress Code: Informal by day, casually elegant in evening; for dining, jeans, T-shirts, rubber shoes, sneakers not accepted; no shorts in bar after 6:00 p.m., no swimwear at lunch or afternoon tea

Children: No children under thirteen years old except from May 1 to October 31; cribs; babysitters

Meetings: Up to fifty people; equipment available

Day Visitors: With reservations

Handicapped Facilities: Limited; one ground-floor room

Packages: Honeymoon, wedding

Rates: Per room, daily, EP. *High Season* (mid-December–mid-April): $864–$1,669. *Low Season* (May 1–early November): $519–$669. Shoulder Season (April 7–30): $1,209–$1,479. Inquire for two- and three-bedrooms rates.

Service Charge: 10 percent, included

Government Tax: 7.5 percent on room, included

BONAIRE

The second largest island in the Netherlands Antilles, Bonaire is located 50 miles north of Venezuela and 86 miles east of Aruba. For decades it has been a haven for divers, who come to enjoy the island's remarkable marine life. The entire coastline, from the high-tide mark to a depth of 200 feet, is a marine park with more than eighty dive sites.

Most island hotels cater to divers and have excellent operations on their premises. In some places the reefs are so near you can wade to them; others are only a swim or short boat ride away. Thus, divers can enjoy unlimited diving from the beach at any time of day or night—the kind of ease and convenience few places in the world can duplicate. Indeed, there's no better place in the Caribbean to learn scuba.

Even for travelers with no higher aspiration than snorkeling, this 24-mile crescent-shaped island offers plenty. Two of its attractions are certainly unusual, if not unique, and easily accessible. The hilly northern end is covered by the Washington/Slagbaai National Park, a 13,500-acre wildlife sanctuary that includes the island's highest point, 784-foot-high Brandaris Hill. The park is a showcase of island flora and fauna with a variety of unusual formations and 130 species of birds.

The flat, dry southern part of the island has an equally interesting attraction. Salt pans, more than 150 years old and covered with white sparkling mountains of salt, are worked commercially, but amid the pans is a 135-acre flamingo sanctuary and breeding ground for about 10,000 birds. You can tour the perimeter of the pans to watch and photograph the birds.

A quiet island of 10,400 inhabitants, Bonaire's peaceful ambience belies its turbulent past. Discovered in 1499 by Amerigo Vespucci—for whom the Americas were named—it was colonized by the Spaniards, who carted off the entire Arawak population to Hispaniola. Later the island was captured by the Dutch, fought over by the French and British, and leased to a New York merchant. Finally, in 1816, the Dutch took it over and kept it.

Kralendijk, the capital, is a colorful miniature city with distinctive Dutch colonial architecture. Among the oldest structures is historic Fort Oranje and the original administration building, which dates to 1837. It has been restored as the Government Office. The island has a surprising variety of good restaurants and a neat little shopping area in the heart of town.

Information

Tourism Corporation of Bonaire, 80 Broad Street, Suite 3202, New York, NY 10004; (212) 956-5911, (800) BONAIRE; www.tourismbonaire.com; usa@tourismbonaire.com

CAPTAIN DON'S HABITAT

Kralendijk, Bonaire, N.A.

A resort for divers, Captain Don's Habitat was founded by a diver who has become a legend in his own time.

I met Don Stewart, a salty California expatriate, on my first trip to Bonaire in the early 1970s, long before Habitat was born. He had wandered into Bonaire in 1962 from a 70-foot schooner called the *Valerie Queen* because, as he said in his wry way, "I was thirsty and heard they had water." The good ship *Valerie* sank; Stewart stayed. He started Bonaire's first hotel and later opened his own very rustic inn for divers, one of the first of its kind.

Stewart, known to all as Captain Don, bent my ear most of the day and evening on the wonders of scuba diving, the unique qualities of Bonaire, the need to protect the marine environment, and just about anything else that came to his mind. He was not a man at a loss for words.

Since then not much has changed, except that this interesting character has managed to get enough of the right people to listen. Today, after almost four decades of adhering to careful management of its reefs and sea life, Bonaire has one of the most magnificent marine parks in the world; diving is its number one industry. On the thirtieth anniversary of his arrival on the island and in appreciation for his contributions, the Bonaire government honored Stewart by proclaiming "Capt. Don Week" with all the associated fanfare; a memorial plaque sponsored by the Council of Underwater Resort Operators was placed on a reef bearing his name.

Along the way Stewart's once dinky little inn grew into quite a nice resort. Perched on a coral bluff north of town, overlooking a ½-mile shoreline of great diving,

Captain Don's Habitat is a very casual, relaxed resort. It is designed as clusters of white stucco town houses, some in attractive Dutch colonial architecture with high-pitched red roofs, others more modern with Spanish features such as courtyards and dark wood doors and windows.

In the past few years, the hotel has been substantially updated, upgraded, and expanded, now offering enough variety and flexibility to meet almost any need. There are two-bedroom garden-view cottages with kitchenettes set back from the water; deluxe ocean-view rooms with two queen-size beds, a refrigerator, and a furnished balcony or patio overlooking a large fresh-water swimming pool; and two-bedroom/two-bathroom garden-view apartments with kitchens each with a balcony or patio; and three- and four-bedroom villas. All rooms have air-conditioning and cable television; all rooms, except villa rooms and apartments, have telephones.

The interiors are spacious, particularly in the newest units, with wood-beamed ceilings and French doors leading to a patio overlooking the sea. Separated from their neighbors by greenery and walkways, the units convey a feeling of privacy and offer an unexpected level of luxury for their moderate rates. All the guest rooms are tastefully furnished, mostly with rattan. The traditional, island-style of cottages were renovated and upgraded in 2007; now they all have two bedrooms and two baths.

Wireless Internet service is available throughout the resort and guests can enjoy massage and spa services at the Intermezzo Day Spa, which is located on the property.

Happy hour at the Decompression Stop Bar, the oceanfront watering hole, attracts divers from far and wide. Rum Runners, the open-air seaside restaurant, offers an eclectic menu of Italian, Cajun, and local dishes, along with freshly made pizza. A barbecue on Monday after the manager's cocktail party is a merry evening that is well attended. Captain Don usually appears for these special nights with Stetson, fringe, and his custom-made peg leg. You can't miss him.

The dive operation is one of the main PADI five-star training facilities in the Caribbean. You can dive at Captain Don's twenty-four hours a day, any day of the year. The resort has three new, state-of-the-art boats and a photo shop and offers every level of instruction, including underwater photography courses. Most guests come on packages that include tank, weights, belt, unlimited free air, and at least one boat dive daily. Nitrox and rebreathers are available for rent with instruction. Trimix is also available for the technical divers.

One such weekly package, "7th Night Free" available from late April through June is priced from about $778 per person, based on double occupancy and includes ocean-view accommodations, buffet breakfast daily, welcome drink, manager's rum punch party, six single-tank boat dives, six days of twenty-four-hour unlimited shore diving, tanks, weights and belt, government taxes, service charges, and energy surcharge.

A sister resort, Habitat Curaçao on the western coast of Curaçao, offers similar programs.

Although Habitat caters mainly to divers and would-be divers, it offers other diversions such as ocean kayaking and windsurfing. You can swim in the main pool, set into a wooden deck by the sea, or soak up the sun on the resort's tiny strand of sand, appropriately named Seven Body Beach.

Captain Don, as loquacious as ever, is still a man with a mission, although retired from the daily operation of Habitat.

Couples between the ages of thirty and fifty and families with kids old enough to dive make up the majority of guests. Most come on packages, which represent good value. You should, too.

Captain Don's Habitat ** 🖋

P.O. Box 88, Kralendijk, Bonaire, N.A. Phone: (599) 717-8290; Fax: (599) 717-8240; e-mail: info@maduro.com; www .habitatdiveresorts.com

Owner: Maduro Holdings, Ltd.

General Manager: Jack Chalk

Open: Year-round

Credit Cards: Most major

U.S. Reservations: Captain Don's Habitat, Maduro Dive FantaSeas, (800) 327-6709, (305) 981-9113; Fax: (305) 981-9397

Deposit: $100 per person; full payment thirty-one days prior to arrival

Minimum Stay: None, except Christmas/ New Year's, seven nights

Arrival/Departure: Transfer normally included in packages

Distance from Airport: 6 miles; taxi one-way, $20

Distance from Kralendijk: 1 mile; taxi one-way, $10

Accommodations: 63 rooms and suites in cottages and villas (variety of sizes and layouts from studios to two bedrooms/two bathrooms)

Amenities: Air-conditioning, ceiling fans; some baths with tub, most with shower, toiletries; television; coffeemaker; hair dryer; safe big enough for laptop; telephones in deluxe ocean-view rooms and cottages; photo shop; no room service; wireless Internet

Electricity: 127 volts; 50Hz

Sports: Freshwater swimming pool; full scuba program (see text); boating, kayaking, snorkeling, windsurfing, deep-sea fishing, hiking arranged

Dress Code: Bathing suits and shorts appropriate at all times

Children: All ages, but must be ten or older to scuba dive

Meetings: Up to one hundred people; seminar and conference facilities

Day Visitors: Yes

Handicapped Facilities: Yes

Packages: Dive, nondivers, family

Rates: Per room, per night double (excluding meals, transfers, or diving). *High Season* (mid-December–March 31): $190–$265. *Low Season:* $149–$240. For a minimal cost, car rental can be added and Harley-Davidson motorcycles are available for rent. Inquire for weekly dive packages.

Service and Energy Surcharge: Included

Government Tax: Included

BRITISH VIRGIN ISLANDS

This archipelago of about fifty green, mountainous islands and cays scalloped with idyllic coves of white-sand beaches is spread over 59 square miles along Drake's Channel and the Anegada Passage between the Caribbean Sea and the Atlantic Ocean. Mostly volcanic in origin and uninhabited, the British Virgin Islands are almost as virgin as the day Christopher Columbus first saw them. Popular hiding places of pirates in olden days, these gems are today favorite hideaways of yachtsmen for their good anchorage and of vacationers fleeing the crowd.

The largest and most populated islands of this British Crown Colony are Tortola, the capital, and Virgin Gorda, to the east of Tortola. Several islands, such as Guana Island off Tortola's northeastern coast and Peter Island to the southeast, have been developed as private resorts.

Tortola is best known as a yacht-chartering center. Its main town and port, Road Town, is the British Virgin Islands' commercial and residential hub. Other entry points are West End, where ferries from St. Thomas stop, and the airport on Beef Island, connected to Tortola's eastern end by a small bridge.

Virgin Gorda's largest settlement, Spanish Town, is located about midisland. Little more than a hamlet a decade ago, the town has grown by leaps and bounds as the island has prospered from sheltering several of the Caribbean's most celebrated hideaways.

The B.V.I., as aficionados call them, do not appeal to everyone. They have no golf courses or casinos, and nighttime activity is very low-key. But they more than make up for the lack of razzle-dazzle with fabulous scenery and facilities, particularly for water sports.

Information

British Virgin Islands Tourist Board, 1270 Broadway, 705, New York, NY 10001;
(212) 696-0400, (800) 835-8530; Fax: (212) 563-2263;
e-mail: bvitouristboard@worldnet.att.net; www.bviwelcome.com

SANDCASTLE

Jost Van Dyke, B.V.I.

Feel like dropping out? Want to hide out for a few days? Try Sandcastle. It's on tiny Jost Van Dyke, a remote island northeast of Tortola that's home to only 200 people.

That number is just fine for those who find their way to this heavenly haven. There are no casinos, no native floor shows, no discos here. And until recently, there was no electricity either.

Sandcastle sits on White Bay, a gorgeous ½-mile stretch of powdery white sand with a lot of palm trees and tropical flowers, which seem to grow where they will. You stay in one of the four cottages, two of which have two rooms, or in one of two new spacious rooms. They are modestly but adequately furnished with almost everything you'd need on a castaway island: king-size beds and a twin-size day bed, comfy chairs, a coffee table, books, and an efficient toilet.

All rooms have electricity for lights and fans; the newest two rooms, in a storm-resistant building, even have air-conditioning. The water comes from heaven and the resort or island's desalinization plant. Outdoor shower stalls are attached to each cottage. The newest rooms have full baths with indoor hot-water showers. All accommodations now have hot-water showers.

The Soggy Dollar, the beachfront restaurant and bar, is the hotel's focal point and the food one of its highlights. Dinner finds many other guests from yachts anchored offshore sitting down to savor dishes such as fresh grilled fish and key lime pie.

Sandcastle's reputation for superb food is well known in yachting circles; sailors simply pull their boats into the bay and transfer to shore via their dinghies. There is no dock; you must usually take a step or two in the water before hitting dry land. It's all very romantic. Conversation can be lively or quiet, depending on the mix of guests.

You won't be at Sandcastle long before you'll be tempted to try the hotel's specialty drink, the Painkiller. This yummy concoction (rum, coconut cream, fruit juice, and nutmeg) may have originated here. Two at midday and it's hammock time.

There's wonderful snorkeling on a reef within swimming distance of the beach. The first reef is in only 12 feet of water; the sea bottom then slopes to about 40 feet for a second reef, and about 400 yards farther out is a wall with an 80-foot drop. It's great diving, too, if you come with dive gear.

For excitement it's a forty-five-minute walk or a quick taxi ride to Foxy's Tamarind Bar, the most famous watering hole in this part of the Caribbean. Foxy, the consummate Caribbean character, has a well-deserved reputation for his quick wit and talent on the guitar.

You could take an excursion or two to neighboring islands, but for most people the combination of sand, sea, and sun, along with the great cooking and friendly owners and staff, is enough.

Getting to Sandcastle requires a bit of scheduling and a lot of determination. You can fly to Tortola or St. Thomas. From Beef Island Airport on Tortola, it's a forty-five-minute taxi ride to the West End Ferry dock. From St. Thomas there's a ferry to West End several times daily, which takes one hour.

At West End the Jost Van Dyke ferry boat will meet you, and a half hour or so later, you'll kick off your shoes and wade ashore. Alternatively, from Red Hook on St. Thomas, the Mona Queen runs via St. John twice on Friday, Saturday, and Sunday directly to Jost Van Dyke in forty-five minutes.

Pack light. You won't need much—just bathing suits and shorts. This is barefoot living at its best. Obviously, Sandcastle is not for everyone, but for some it's as near paradise as they need to be.

In 2006 Sandcastle acquired new owners, the O'Connells, who say they plan to keep this little corner of paradise much the same as they found and fell in love with it.

Sandcastle *
6501 Red Hook Plaza, Suite 201, St. Thomas, U.S.V.I. 00802
Phone: (284) 495-9888; Fax: (284) 495-9999; e-mail: relax@soggydollar.com; www.soggydollar.com

For speediest mail: Cyril E. King Airport Cargo Bay 4, P.O. Box 11156-355, St. Thomas, U.S.V.I. 00801-4156

Owners/Managers: Jerry and Tish O'Connell

General Managers: Roger and Sandy Garside

Open: Year-round

Credit Cards: Visa, MasterCard

U.S. Reservations: Direct to hotel

Deposit: $500 to confirm reservations; sixty days cancellation

Minimum Stay: Three nights during winter

Arrival/Departure: See text

Distance from West End: (Tortola) Thirty minutes by boat; from Red Hook, St. Thomas: forty-five minutes

Accommodations: Four cottages (two directly on beach with sitting rooms, king-size beds, and daybed); two garden rooms with kings and air-conditioning

Amenities: Electricity for lights and fans; outside shower stalls connected to each cottage; gift and sportswear shop

Electricity: 110 volts/60 Hz (same as U.S.)

Sports: Kayaking and snorkeling equipment included; hammocks on beach

Dress Code: Very casual: bathing suits and bare feet

Children: None under sixteen years of age

Meetings: No

Day Visitors: Welcome at restaurant and bar

Handicapped Facilities: No

Packages: Seven-night MAP, including transportation from Tortola

Rates: Two people, daily, EP. *High Season* (mid-December–mid-May): $245–$295. *Low Season:* $160–$220. MAP and singles rate available; inquire

Service Charge: 10 percent on room, 15 percent on food and beverages

Government Tax: 7 percent on room

GUANA ISLAND
Guana Island, B.V.I.

A secluded resort tucked into a far-from-it-all setting, Guana Island is one of the Caribbean's true hideaways. Located off the northeastern coast of Tortola, 850-acre Guana Island began as a private club in the 1930s. After purchasing it in 1975, its new owner modernized the facilities while retaining its homey style and made it into a private nature sanctuary, leaving all but the seventy-acre resort area crowning the topmost ridge and some lowland orchard and sports areas undeveloped.

White-washed stone cottages, surrounded by gardens of hibiscus, oleander, and flowering trees, accommodate a total of thirty-two guests. The cottages vary in size and layout, but each has its own special appeal. My favorite is Eleuthera, where you wake up to a fabulous view across the island and sea and in the evening take in 200 degrees of magnificent scenery bathed in sunset orange and red.

The guest rooms are actually junior suites with large verandas. The rooms are earthy, airy, comfortable, and cozy, furnished in rattan and local art against whitewashed stucco walls, set off by wood-beamed ceilings. All accommodations are very comfortable and the bathrooms modernized. Two generators supply the island's power and a reverse osmosis system along with rainwater provides drinking water. A biological sewage treatment plant enables the resort to treat and recycle all waste, using the final clear water, which is high in nitrates, to water the "Orchard" and vegetable garden where papaya grows to the size of footballs. The garden produces most of the fruits and vegetables used by the resort and is a big attraction for guests who go there to meet and learn from Dr. Liao, the caretaker who shows them around and offers them tea, coconut milk, and freshly picked fruit.

Grenada House, which has a pool, rents as a two-bedroom unit with the pool or as two separate guest rooms without it. North Beach Cottage, a very private, one-bedroom house with a living room, kitchen, and bath is on its own ⅓ mile of beach with a private freshwater pool and a sea pool. North Beach

Cottage is surrounded by open and covered decks for lounging or sunbathing and dining. Meals can be arranged there, or you can eat at the resort's main dining terrace. The trail to the cottage from the main resort winds along an old Quaker stone wall. North Beach Cottage guests are provided with a golf cart to drive across the Flat to White Bay Beach activities and tennis courts. Recent additions are Harbour House and Jost House, two and three bedroom villas, each with their own pools and hot tubs plus use of a golf cart and villa services.

Guest cottages have no phones, but guests may use their cell phones or rent one from the resort to use, so long as they do not use it within "sight or earshot of other guests." Then too, Guana has added Wi-Fi Internet service for guests who bring their own computers, or they can use the guest computer in the Guest Office. There's no television, except in the villas, but the resort offers outdoor "Old Movie Nights" upon guests' request.

The main house, Dominica, is the social center. It includes a homey lounge with an honor bar, a library where a rare winter evening chill could be warmed by a fireplace, and dining terraces where all meals and afternoon tea are served.

The lively atmosphere at cocktails in the lounge before dinner is more like a weekend house party than a hotel. Dinner seating is arranged by the manager nightly. You may choose to dine with other guests or on your own. You dine by candlelight on a menu that includes fresh seafood, home-baked breads, locally grown fruits and vegetables, and good wine. There is a weekly beach barbecue with music and crab races.

Guana Island boasts six untrampled porcelain beaches. Reef-protected White Bay, the "arrival" beach below the main house, is a powdery ½-mile crescent bathed by gin-clear waters ideal for swimming and snorkeling. A golf cart or club jitney will shuttle you to and fro, or you can walk on one of the island's two paved roads. The more isolated beaches can be reached on hiking trails or by boat; two are accessible only by boat. A stone stairway of about 150 steps wanders down a cliff on the northern end of Guana and leads to Chicken Rock—so named because it looks like a sitting hen—where at the end of a long hike you can cool off in pristine sea pools before hiking back or being picked up by boat.

The owners' interest in conservation led them to make Guana a nature and wildlife preserve and garnered them awards from major magazines for their stewardship. They underwrite programs that, due to the island's unusual nature—an ecosystem almost undisturbed for a century—brings a small army of scientists from prominent universities, The Conservation Agency, and other institutions from afar to study and document its rich flora, fauna, and marine life. They are also helping to restore the natural environment and reintroduce native species, including a half-dozen or so flamingo, the red-legged tortoise, and the rock iguana.

About fifty bird species and thirty-one butterfly species can be seen regularly, and another fifty bird species come at different times of year. The pristine reefs near shore have about 125 species of fish and dozens of species of coral. Maps of the island's two dozen trails are available. Be sure to bring comfortable walking shoes or sneakers with tread and binoculars.

While the personable managers are attentive and the friendly staff—most of whom have been at Guana for years—are helpful, no one pampers you. You set your own pace, doing as little or as much as you want. There's lots of walking—hiking would be more accurate—to get to meals and the beach. (Transportation is available, too.)

But then, nature is what Guana is all about. If you need entertainment or waiters at your beck and call, this is not the place for you.

Guana is designed for travelers who seek tranquillity and can operate on their own juices. Your company will be mostly Americans, with a few British and other Europeans mostly in the thirty-to-sixty age group. Younger guests and honeymooners tend to come in spring and summer. If it's privacy you want, you can rent the entire island—as CEOs, wedding parties, and families on reunion often do.

Guana Island *** 🖋

Guana Island, B.V.I.

Phone: (284) 494-2354; Fax: (284) 495-2900; e-mail: guana@guana.com; www.guana.com

Owners: Henry and Gloria Jarecki

Resident Manager: Jason Goldberg

Open: Year-round except September–October

Credit Cards: American Express, Visa, and MasterCard; personal and travelers checks U.S. Reservations: Guana Island, (800) 54-GUANA, (914) 967-6050; Fax: (914) 967-8048

Deposit: Three nights per booking; thirty days cancellation unless resort is able to rebook accommodation. Policy differs for Christmas/New Year's; inquire

Minimum Stay: Four nights—less at some times of year; inquire

Arrival/Departure: Guests met at Beef Island Airport by Guana Island representative and taken to nearby dock to board resort's launch for ten-minute ride to island; $60 per person, round-trip transfer fee added to final bill.

Distance from Airport: Ten minutes by boat

Distance from Road Town: Forty-five minutes by boat and road; from launch dock to town one-way, $60

Accommodations: 15 rooms in seven hillside cottages, all with twin or king-size beds and verandas; one bedroom in North Beach Cottage; two bedrooms Harbour House; three bedrooms Jost House. (A total of 42 guests can be accommodated.)

Amenities: Bathrobes, hair dryers, shower amenities; welcome gifts; cell phone, Wi-Fi service, ceiling fan; shower-only baths, some with air-conditioning; no radio, television. Villas have phone and television.

Electricity: 110 volts

Sports: Two tennis courts (clay and all-weather Omni-turf); self-service beach bar with water-sports equipment, dressing and restrooms, lounging chairs, hammocks; use of courts, racquets, fishing rods, snorkeling gear, sailboats, kayaks, water skis, windsurfers; deep-sea fishing charters and diving arranged

Fitness/Spa Facilities: Beach spa for massage and other treatments; also available in room

Dress Code: Casual; cover-up and shoes at breakfast and lunch; dinner smart casual

Children: Inquire in advance

Meetings: Up to thirty-two people can rent whole island

Day Visitors: No

Handicapped Facilities: Very limited; inquire

Packages: Romance, honeymoon

Rates: Two people, daily, AP. *High Season* (December 20–January 3): $1,450; (January 4–March) $1,250. *Shoulder Season* (April 1–June 15): $1,025. *Low Season* (June 16–August 31): $695. North Beach Cottage and Villas, inquire. Entire island (daily up to thirty-two people): $21,050–$31,750, depending on the season

Service Charge: 10 percent; no additional tipping

Government Tax: 7 percent room tax

PETER ISLAND RESORT
Road Town, Tortola, B.V.I.

Set on some of the most beautiful beaches in the Caribbean and surrounded by forested hills with pretty vistas at every turn, posh Peter Island has evolved from a small, exclusive yacht haven created in 1971 into a full-scale resort and spa.

Covering 1,050 of the private island's 1,800 green, hilly acres, Peter Island is perennially named as one of the Caribbean's top resorts. It was all but blown away by Hurricane Hugo in 1989. But it was rebuilt by its then-owners, Amway Hotel Corporation, and has had several major renovations over the years, each upgrading and making it better. The last added a large, elaborate spa on its own separate beach. Ownership of Peter Island Resort passed to family members of the Amway owners in 2000 and is now privately owned.

The resort is laid out in two areas: the original A-frame cottages overlooking the yacht basin, and the more deluxe suites hidden beneath a forest of palm trees on Deadman's Bay, the main beach. The latter have the spacious beachfront junior suites that were improved with an open floor plan with large windows and doors that look out at the lush surroundings and ocean views. The rooms have lavish bathrooms with imported Spanish tile and original hand-laid stonework, walk-in double showers, Jacuzzi tubs, and walls of glass that open on to ocean or garden views. A certain formal look in period furnishings is blended with Caribbean decor to create a sophisticated yet comfortable ambience. Although the resort has not abandoned its long-standing policy of no-television-in-guest-rooms, Peter Island is looking to the future—fiber-optic cable lines and dataports in room and telephones were part of the upgrading. Some signature items such as Peter Island beach sandals and a compact disk of Caribbean music await you upon check-in.

The A-frames are less expensive than the beachfront rooms. Each cottage has four large bedrooms: two on the ground floor with patios and two above with high, beamed ceilings and decks overlooking the harbor on the south and Drake's Channel on the north.

Peter Island also has villas, each more spectacular than the other. The Crow's Nest is a fabulous villa with four bedrooms, each with a private balcony and bath, game room, entertainment system, library, wine cellar, and saltwater pool surrounded by flagstone terraces. The villa's former center garden was redesigned into an enormous living room and dining room. It is staffed with two maids, a gardener, and a cook; a jeep for your exclusive use is provided. Situated on the highest point of the resort, with spectacular views, its price is spectacular, too.

The two hillside villas at Hawk's Nest are suitable for families. One has two bedrooms, two baths, and the other, three bedrooms, living room, television, kitchenette, sundeck, and air-conditioning.

The newest villa, Falcon's Nest, the first of several multimillion dollar homes the resort intents to add as the demand warrants, is a six-bedroom residence with its own chef, housekeeper, valet and butler, and villa manager. Perched 350 feet above the Caribbean maximizing spectacular views, the villa combines a sophisticated, tropical island feel with a contemporary structure by interior designer Cooper Carry. Among its features are a custom-made twelve-person, hand-crafted Tiger maple dining room set, flat-screen television monitor that rises out of a built-in cabinet, two-story living room with elevated terrace, large outdoor living space with covered dining area, BBQ and swim-up bar; zero-entry pool with a waterfall, grotto, and large Jacuzzi. Each of the six bedroom suites has a terrace and luxurious bathroom with indoor/outdoor space, panoramic views, and rain shower with 150 colorful laser-lit jets. There's a couples spa treatment room; state-of-the-art exercise room; nanny quarters, chef's kitchen and quarters. Private charters, special menus and rare vintage wines are some of the special services Peter Island's villa program can offer guests.

At the resort, the open-air lobby, next to the infinity pool, is convenient to the dock and A-frame cottages. The adjacent library has a flat-screen television that carries CNN and other cable programs. The air-conditioned Tradewinds restaurant has large waterfront windows with views of Drake's Channel and Tortola. Tradewinds, which also has outdoor dining, offers twice-weekly vintner's wine-pairing dinners, focusing on a particular region to showcase wines from that area. Each course is prepared to complement the wines being served. The cost is $75 per person for hotel guests and $115 including wine for nonguests to participate. The Beach Bar and Grill on Deadman's Bay Beach, which has an open kitchen and wood-fired oven, is the casual setting for lunch. It offers an interesting menu as varied as pizza, roti, and fresh fish, along with a salad bar and dessert table. Tea is served daily in the bar area near the pool. Dinner by candlelight is set in both the main dining room and alfresco by the pool, weather permitting. Menus are changed daily, with light fare and a classic as well as a contemporary repertoire.

Peter Island's lovely spa is set in gardens on its own beach. Each of the twelve large treatment rooms has its own whirlpool. Two are in separate, small thatched-roof cottages directly by the sea. Two extraordinarily large treatment rooms are designed for two people. Based as it is away from the main resort, it has a superb, tranquil setting in a natural environment. There is a large infinite-edge swimming pool (with very cold water), outside showers encased in natural stone, and an outdoor terrace where lunch is served. The spa offers a wide selection of massages, scrubs, wraps, facials, and more.

Peter Island operates as an all-inclusive resort. In addition to meals and tea, water sports, tennis, mountain biking, and use of the fitness center are included. Hotel guests must reserve for dinner, because the dining terrace is a popular stop for yachts sailing in and around the Virgin Islands.

Each of Peter Island's five beaches is memorable. On Deadman's Bay Beach you will find thatched umbrellas and lounge chairs near the bar and the water-sports center; hammocks are hidden among the trees. The resort's fitness center, with an array of exercise equipment, is located at the eastern end of Deadman's Bay Beach. Farther east, Little Deadman's Bay is a mini-mirror image of the main beach, and farther on, secluded Honeymoon Beach has one thatched umbrella and two chairs. It's for all romantics, not just honeymooners, but only one couple at a time, please.

Peter Island Resort ★★★★
P.O. Box 211, Road Town, Tortola, B.V.I.; or P.O. Box 9409, St. Thomas, U.S.V.I. 00801
Phone: (284) 495-2000, (800) 346-4451; Fax: (284) 495-2500; e-mail: reservations@peterisland.com; www.peterisland.com

Owner: Van Andel family

Managing Director: Wayne Kafcsak

General Manager: Sandra Grisham-Clothier

Open: Year-round

Credit Cards: All major

U.S. Reservations: Peter Island Resort Worldwide; Phone: (800) 346-4451, (770) 476-4488; Fax: (770) 476-4979

Deposit: Three nights within five days of reservation

Minimum Stay: Ten nights during Christmas/New Year's

Arrival/Departure: Guests arriving at Beef Island Airport transfer directly to resort's motor launch for 6-mile trip across Drake's Channel to Peter Island. Resort also operates up to eight round-trips of free ferry service to its dock at Baughers Bay in Tortola. Transfer by helicopter directly to resort's lighted helipad arranged from St. Thomas, San Juan, or neighboring islands.

Distance from Airport: (Beef Island) Approximately 6 miles

Accommodations: 52 rooms (22 in A-frames with kings; 20 junior suites in beachfront buildings with kings); one three-bedroom villa with two-bedroom guest cottage; one four-bedroom and one six bedroom villa, all with verandas

Amenities: Air-conditioning, ceiling fans; minibar, coffeemaker; telephone; bath with double sinks, tub, shower, hair dryers, bathrobes, toiletries; room service for continental breakfast; no television; beachfront juniors have showers and Jacuzzis for two

Electricity: 110 volts

Fitness Facilities/Spa Services: New spa fitness center with exercise machines; massage and beauty treatments (see text)

Sports: Four tennis courts (two lighted), tennis pro, equipment; small boats, windsurfers, and free introductory lessons; fishing charters and motor launch sightseeing; snorkeling gear free; on-site dive operator

Dress Code: Men requested to wear sport coats (tie not necessary) in winter season for dinner

Children: Inquire

Meetings: Entire island can be rented for up to 100 people

Day Visitors: Welcome

Handicapped Facilities: Limited

Packages: Honeymoon, wedding, dive, sailing, four and seven nights off-season

Rates: All-inclusive, double occupancy, per day. *High Season* (January 4–March 31): $920–$1,335. *Low Season* (June 1– October 31): $575–$875. Call for rates November 1–March. Villa rates; inquire

Service Charge: 10 percent

Government Tax: 8 percent

SUGAR MILL HOTEL
Apple Bay, Tortola, B.V.I.

Set on a hillside overlooking Apple Bay on Tortola's quiet northern coast, Sugar Mill is a cozy country inn as well known for its restaurant as for its hotel. It is owned and operated by veteran travel and food writers Jinx and Jeff Morgan.

Sugar Mill is divided into two sections by the small road that skirts the northern coast of Tortola. Instead of a lobby, at the hotel entrance you will find an outdoor gazebo-lounge all but concealed in a riot of flowers and tropical greenery. It is adjacent to the bar, which doubles as the reception area, library, and boutique, and leads to an open-air terrace where breakfast is served. Behind it is the restored remnant of a 370-year-old sugar mill for which the inn is named and that houses the Sugar Mill Restaurant.

Hugging the steep hillside above the mill are clusters of two-story buildings containing the hotel's rooms and suites—all with balconies overlooking the lovely gardens and a small terraced, freshwater swimming pool. The rooms, furnished mainly in wicker, are comfortable but not fancy. They have air-conditioning, ceiling fan, private bathroom, hair dryer, iron, ironing board, clock radio, and a choice of king or twin beds. The rooms contain small kitchen units that families with children particularly appreciate.

Plantation House, near the hotel entrance gazebo, designed with fine stonework has two deluxe air-conditioned bedrooms, each with a patio, that can be rented individually or as a two-bedroom unit. Each has an open-plan layout, and is furnished with a king-size bed, a living room area with sofa and chairs, cable television, large bathroom with double sinks, and kitchenette and coffee maker.

The Cottage, a one-bedroom suite in classic Caribbean decor with mahogany furniture, has a queen-size, four-poster bed and sitting area as well as television, kitchenette, a bathroom with outside stone shower, and a garden veranda with table, chairs, and lounger.

The newest accommodations are four air-conditioned, pool suites decorated in warm tones, with bedroom (king or twin), living room with queen-size sofa-bed, television, breakfast-bar kitchenette, bathroom with twin sinks and a stone-faced outside showers with its own garden. The large balconies have ceiling fans with table and chairs overlooking the fresh water pool.

The resort also has a deluxe villa with two air-conditioned bedrooms with bathroom, living area with a queen-size sofa bed, a full kitchen, cable television, and large balcony with a wide-angle views of the ocean and neighboring islands. Pictures and helpful descriptions of the accommodations are available on Sugar Mill's Web site.

The lower section of the hotel sits at the edge of the sea alongside a small reef-protected beach with lounging chairs; here, too, is Islands, an informal, open-to-the-breezes restaurant where, as the name suggests, the specialties are Caribbean fare. It is open for lunch daily from noon to 2:00 p.m.

The old stone sugar mill, under a high roof with ceiling fans, the warm glow of candlelight, fresh flowers, colorful Haitian paintings, and classical music playing in the background—all this makes up the inviting setting in which you will enjoy the inn's celebrated cuisine. The Sugar Mill is usually filled with patrons from other hotels and residents of Tortola.

Menus are a la carte and change daily. There are four appetizers and five entrees from which to chose, featuring such specialties as grilled shrimp on coconut risotto with sesame sauce; cashew crusted halibut with mango and jalapeno sauce, and pumpkin risotto, to name a few. Many of the recipes are included in the *Sugar Mill Caribbean Cookbook.*

Given Jeff's expertise in California wines (he has written three books on the subject), it's no surprise that the extensive wine list highlights California vintages. Jeff has provided brief descriptions of each wine to help guests make their selections.

Sugar Mill gets a great variety of guests—celebrity friends, movie stars, artists, writers, and just plain folks. Many are repeaters—Americans, Canadians, and British—who appreciate the food and enjoy the inn's homey, informal atmosphere. Some come for the workshops conducted by established artists and sponsored by the Morgans from time to time.

Sugar Mill is a bit remote—for many that's part of its charm. Car rental can be arranged through the concierge; you'll need it if you want to explore the island.

Sugar Mill Hotel **
Box 425, Road Town, Apple Bay, Tortola, B.V.I.
Phone: (284) 495-4355, (800) 462-8834; Fax: (284) 495-4696; e-mail: sugmill@ surfbvi.com; www.sugarmillhotel.com

Owners: Jinx and Jeff Morgan

Managing Director: Patrick Conway

Open: Year-round except August– September

Credit Cards: Most major

U.S. Reservations: (800) 462-8834, (284) 495-4355

Deposit: Three nights; thirty days cancellation in order to issue full refund

Minimum Stay: Seven nights during Christmas/New Year's; three nights rest of high season

Arrival/Departure: Transfer arranged on request for fee

Distance from Airport: (Beef Island Airport) 18 miles (forty-five minutes); taxi one-way, $40

Distance from Road Town: 10 miles, taxi one-way, $20; from West End ferry dock, 3 miles, taxi one-way, $9

Accommodations: 23 rooms (including studios, deluxe villa, The Cottage; 19 double rooms with terrace and kitchen; four family suites); one two-bedroom villa; two Plantation House suites); twin and king-size beds

Amenities: Ceiling fans, air-conditioning; bath with shower only, hair dryers; telephone with dataport; clock-radio; iron and ironing boards; refrigerator and coffeemaker; microwave in all rooms; wireless Internet

Electricity: 110 volts/60 cycles

Sports: Freshwater swimming pool, small beach, beautiful long strands nearby; free snorkeling gear; scuba, deep-sea fishing, hiking, other sports arranged

Dress Code: Casual

Children: Over eleven years old in winter; babysitters

Meetings: No

Day Visitors: Welcome in small numbers

Handicapped Facilities: Inquire

Packages: Honeymoon, adventure

Rates: Two people per unit, daily, EP. *High Season* (mid-December–mid-April): $340–$385. *Shoulder Season* (mid-April–May 31 and November 1–mid-December): $275–$335. *Low Season* (June 1–July 31 and October 1–31): $255. Two bedroom, $690 and $695 winter; $535 summer. Single, triple, and quad rates are also available.

Service Charge: 10 percent

Government Tax: 7 percent

BIRAS CREEK RESORT
Virgin Gorda, B.V.I.

A masterpiece of British understatement far off the beaten path, Biras Creek is a hideaway in every sense. Small and secluded, the quietly posh resort is designed for relaxing and luxuriating in privacy in a casual, unpretentious, yet sophisticated ambience.

Much of the resort's privacy is all but guaranteed by its location: It's accessible only by boat or helicopter and reached by the resort's private launch—or by your own yacht. Set in 140 acres of nature preserve on an isthmus of green hills that brackets the northern end of Virgin Gorda, the resort overlooks North Sound, a huge deep-water bay that has long been a yachtsman's mecca. On the north and east is the Atlantic, and to the west—the side on which you arrive—the Caribbean.

When you approach from the water, all you see is a fortresslike stone structure with a steep carousel roof atop a small rise at the center of the property. Built in terraces and approached by several sets of interconnected stone steps, the "castle" serves as reception, dining, and social center with an indoor-outdoor terraced restaurant and bar commanding a lovely panoramic view.

The resort's size and layout also help ensure privacy. Hidden under enormous almond and sea grape trees that provide shade and maximize privacy are sixteen cottages, each with two suites. They skirt the crest of Bercher's Bay, where the Atlantic roars in—too rough for swimming but great for cooling breezes to lull you to sleep. Cottage 11A is so close to the sea, it's like being on a ship—in a storm.

Each suite has a large bedroom and sitting room with comfortable chairs, ottoman, and mountains of pillows. Sliding glass doors open onto an ocean-view terrace with lounging chairs—the perfect nook for afternoon reading or dozing. The bathroom features a delightful open-air shower with a tropical garden, enclosed by an 8-foot patio wall but open overhead to trees and blue skies.

Terra-cotta tile floors and the ocean breezes sailing through the screen doors and louvered windows keep the tree-shaded rooms cool. Near your cottage door you'll find two Caloi bicycles for your exclusive use.

In 2006, after being bought by Pam and David V. Johnson, owners of Michigan-based Victor International Corp, a real estate, resort development, and management company, Biras Creek was given a million-dollar renovation that updated the resort without changing its character. All the guest rooms were converted into non-smoking rooms and now have 300-thread-count cotton linens, Sealy Plush pillow-top mattresses, feathered down pillows, over-sized cotton towels, tropical waffle-weave robes, and iPod sound systems. Among other nice touches, the oceanfront room

patios have low wooden railings and terra-cotta tiles line the patios and entrances.

The two grand suites—17A and 17B—are superdeluxe with a private plunge pool, luxuriously spacious sitting room, bedroom, and bath and handsome, decor. A premier suite, ideal for a family, has two bedrooms two baths, and a spacious living area bordered by three terraces.

The Arawak Room, a lounge, has new Donghia furniture and Janus et Cie outdoor furniture on the Arawak deck—an ideal spot to relax and enjoy afternoon tea. The Arawak has wireless Internet connection for guests. Across from the Arawak room is a new air-conditioned fitness center with Nautilus elliptical and treadmill machines. Near to it is the spa, which has two treatment rooms and offers a full roster of services using using Decléor therapeutic treatments.

Running from the castle to the hillsides are twenty-five landscaped acres watched over by Biras Creek's gardener, Alvin Harrigan, who has tended the gardens since the resort opened in 1974. Harrigan guides guests on a weekly garden tour. The remaining 115 acres of the estate have been left to nature and include hiking trails and walking paths.

Biras Creek's freshwater pool, at the foot of the castle, has lounge chairs and thatched-roof sun shelters. A secluded beach at tranquil Deep Bay is a ten-minute walk or a five-minute bike ride from your cottage. En route you pass the tennis courts and a small estuary, a favorite spot for bird-watchers. Next to the beach a large thatched-roof pavilion has a bar (open daily) and picnic tables where lunch barbecues are served several days per week.

Biras Creek's open-air dining room in the hilltop castle is cheerful by day, with sunlight flooding the open terraces, and romantic by night, with candlelit tables and soft background music. The restaurant, which has been refurbished, serves three meals daily, as well as afternoon tea. A new private dining room for intimate and exclusive dining has been added. The new room can also accommodate private meetings and small conferences.

From its inception Biras Creek established a reputation for fine cuisine and an impressive wine list. The bar adjoining the main dining room is a delightful open-air lounge and a popular gathering spot before dinner. There's a weekly manager's party and several nights music accompanies dancing under the stars.

Biras offers several packages in the off-season that are good values. Among the most popular is the Sailaway package, which gives you the best of both worlds— a stay at the resort plus overnight sailing through the British Virgin Islands on the resort's own crewed yacht. The resort has its own helicopter landing pad.

Biras Creek appeals to experienced travelers who relish comfort and fine cuisine while at the same time appreciate being surrounded by nature's beauty.

Biras Creek Resort **** 🍃
Box 54, Virgin Gorda, B.V.I. 1150
Phone: (284) 494-3555; Fax: (284) 494-3557; e-mail: biras@biras.com; www.biras.com

Owners: Pam and David V. Johnson

General Manager: Rik Blyth

Open: Year-round

Credit Cards: All major

U.S. Reservations: (877) 883-0756; Fax: (248) 364-2471; or Relais et Châteaux, (800) 735-2478

Deposit: Three nights

Minimum Stay: Ten nights during Christmas

Arrival/Departure: Transfer included with four-night stay. From Virgin Gorda Airport take twenty-five-minute jitney bus ride to dock at Gun Creek on northern end (almost length of island). There, resort's water taxi picks you up for ten-minute ride to Biras Creek. From Tortola the resort's water taxi zips you from dock near Beef Island Airport directly to Biras Creek.

Distance from Airport: (Spanish Town) 8 miles; taxi one-way, $24; ferry from Beef Island one-way, $35

Accommodations: 31 suites in 16 cottages with twin or king-size beds; one two-bedroom ocean-view suite; three suites interconnect

Amenities: Ceiling fans, air-conditioning in bedrooms; coffeemakers, small refrigerator; phones; iron and ironing board; e-mail and Internet access; in-room dataport; safes; hair dryers, showers; robes; no locks on doors or room service

Electricity: 110 volts/60 cycles

Fitness Facilities/Spa Services: Small spa

Sports: Freshwater pool; two lighted tennis courts, free use of courts, equipment; sailing, snorkeling, windsurfing equipment and instruction; hiking trails; new motorized Boston Whalers; snorkeling trips three times a week and frequent trips to nearby secluded sands; fishing charters, day and sunset cruises; dive courses with certification arranged for fee; Dive BVI dive masters conduct free introductory scuba lessons

Dress Code: Casual by day; cover-up and footwear required in dining room and bar; informally elegant for evening; tie and jacket not required

Children: Over eight years old

Meetings: Up to sixteen people

Day Visitors: None

Handicapped Facilities: No

Packages: Off-season, honeymoon, Saila-way, family, wedding, weekend

Rates: Per person, double, daily, FAP. **High Season** (mid-December–early April): $980–$1,950. **Low Season:** $615–$1,185. Rates include use of tennis courts and water-sports equipment and round-trip airport transfers. Weekly and single rates available.

Service Charge: 10 percent

Government Tax: 7 percent

THE BITTER END YACHT CLUB
Virgin Gorda, B.V.I.

Although the Bitter End Yacht Club shares the waters of North Sound with Biras Creek, the two resorts are as different as you could imagine. Bitter End, stretching almost a mile along the northern shore of the sound, is as big and busy as Biras Creek is small and serene.

The eighty-nine-acre Bitter End began in the 1960s as a watering hole for yachts-men. In 1972, Chicago businessman, Myron Hokin, sailed by on a fishing trip. He recognized the value of Bitter End's superb anchorage—the last outpost before the Atlantic—and bought the property.

In 1988, Bitter End merged with neigh-boring Tradewinds, a more upscale resort, and overnight doubled in size. In addition to more facilities and rooms, Bitter End gained a wider range of style, broadening its appeal and transforming it from a boating haven to a full-scale resort.

Only steps from the beach, the original thatched cottages and Beachfront Villas, which continue to be the most popular accommodations, have recently been reno-vated, modernized, and greatly upgraded as part of the resort-wide multimillion-dollar renovation, introducing a bit of island sophistication to the resort's once tradi-tional decor, without compromising the hideaway's historical charm and unpreten-tious, barefoot elegance.

The refreshed decor, created by well-known Miami-based interior designer Bar-bara Hulanicki, integrates Italian-tiled bathrooms, teak vanities, custom-designed bedroom and common area furniture with all materials designed by Hulanicki exclu-sively for the Bitter End. Using bright blue, orange, and gold colors, the Asian and Caribbean–inspired fabrics in the bed-spreads and pillow are coordinated with the new art on the walls and the sea views from every accommodation's wraparound porch and hammock. Those familiar with Villas 8 through 12 may recall that they had a back entrance. To expand the dressing room and bathroom, new access was created through side doors and air-conditioning was added. Climbing the wooded hillsides above the Clubhouse restaurant to the southeast are the deluxe North Sound Suites in jungle gardens; they're connected to one another by wooden walkways and catwalks, much like tree houses. Similar to the Beachfront Villas, each of the North Sound Suites vil-las has two accommodations with balconies and fabulous views of the sound. The two units—one with two queen-size beds and one with a king—can be combined into a two-bedroom cottage. The rooms have peaked, wooden ceilings and are tastefully decorated in wicker with rich fabrics and grass-cloth wall coverings. They are air-conditioned and have telephones, refrigerators, coffeemakers, VCRs (on request), and king- or queen-size beds. The Estate House is a posh, secluded two-bedroom villa above the Clubhouse with a large living room, separate dining area, screened porch, and wraparound veranda.

On the beach below the North Sound Suites is a freshwater pool, with bar and lunch service poolside. On "Main Street," other enhancements include major expansion of Bitter End's Pub into a full-service restaurant, featuring a brick pizza oven. In addition to its great pizza, the Pub wins for its flying fish sandwiches and rotis, the West Indian version of a curry wrap. The Pub also serves as a sports venue with five flat-screen television sets, broadcasting sporting events from around the world. It also has a pool table, foosball, and several dart boards, making the Pub a hangout of the yachting crowd which regularly ties up at the marina for dinner and entertainment. The Clubhouse Steak and Seafood Grille, an open-air restaurant, has been a favorite rendezvous for yachties for years. The menu features generous buffets as well as table service for breakfast, lunch, and dinner, and cocktail service on the terrace all day and evening. The meal plan for resort guests includes dining at the Clubhouse or on the Almond Walk, an idyllic setting for numerous events each week, such as Seafood Night and West Indian Night, with dining and dancing under the stars to the resort's own steel band, The Reflections. It is also one of several locations for weddings. The Emporium, a provisioning center catering to yachtsmen for over twenty years, is now housed in a charming new Caribbean-style building. It offers homemade baked goods, fresh fish and meats, and wines, rums and other essentials.

The Spa at Bitter End, added in 2006, is a full-service facility with four treatment rooms and a team of fifteen spa professionals providing manicures and facials to herbal wraps and aromatherapies at the spa or in the privacy of one's room. The spa also offers private and group yoga sessions on the beach. The spa is open twelve hours a day, seven days a week, and uses Decleor spa products, as well as local herb-based ones. Spa packages for bridal parties and wedding day preparations are available.

Even with its expansion, Bitter End remains above all a yachting club. Nautical themes are everywhere, and the flags of yacht clubs from around the world hang in the Clubhouse. The resort's fleet of more than one hundred craft is available to guests for their unlimited use. It includes Boston Whalers, Rhodes 19s, Lasers, Mistral Sailboards, and Sunfish, among others. The resort offers day charters, deep-sea fishing boats, snorkeling, and sightseeing boats.

And if you don't know the difference between a jib and a spinnaker, Bitter End provides free introductory sailing lessons, along with windsurfing and snorkeling instruction. The Bitter End Sailing School holds classes for boaters of all skill levels. The Fall Sailing Festival each November is a month-long, action-packed promotion of Bitter End's sailing facilities and includes Women on the Water Week, Family Thanksgiving Week, and other themed weeks. During the Annual Pro-Am Regatta, guests get to sail with America's Cup–winning skippers and Olympic medalists. It's said to be the only event of its kind in the world. Daily dive classes for beginners and trips for certified divers are also available. A Junior Sailing Program is offered year-round for kids six years old and over. The resort also has a children's program with supervised water sports, crafts, and hikes.

Bitter End's easygoing atmosphere attracts sports enthusiasts of all ages—singles, couples, honeymooners, and families. Most are affluent, active, and somewhat preppie Americans, but there is a sprinkling of Europeans. Life here is so water oriented that those who have no interest in sailing or water sports should look elsewhere. But if you love the sea, this little corner of the Caribbean is paradise.

The Bitter End Yacht Club ***

North Sound, Virgin Gorda, B.V.I.
Phone: (284) 494-2746; Fax: (284) 494-4756; e-mail: binfo@beyc.com; www.beyc.com

Owner: Dana Hokin

General Manager: Mikhail Shamkin

Open: Year-round, except late July–early October

Credit Cards: All major

U.S. Reservations: Bitter End Yacht Club, (800) 872-2392, (312) 506-6205; Fax: (312) 506-6206

Deposit: Three nights

Minimum Stay: None

Arrival/Departure: Transfers cost $70 round-trip

Distance from Airport: (Virgin Gorda Airport) Thirty-minute taxi ride (one-way, $35), plus ten-minute boat ride; or from Beef Island Airport via Bitter End's own North Sound Express high-speed ferry, a thirty-minute scenic trip from the airport directly to the resort, $35 per person ($70 round-trip)

Accommodations: 85 rooms and suites with verandas (45 in beachfront cottages; 38 in North Sound Suites with twin, queen-size, or king-size beds; two-bedroom villa); four live-aboard boats

Amenities: Air-conditioning in North Sound Suites, and ten Beachfront villas, ceiling fans; bath with shower only, hair dryers on request; coffeemaker, refrigerator; television/VCRs in North Sound suites; towels changed daily, nightly turndown service; phones; shops and mini-market; no room service

Electricity: 110 volts/60 cycles

Fitness Facilities/Spa Services: Full service spa

Sports: Sailing, windsurfing, kayaking, water sports (see text); one swimming pool, three beaches; jogging and exercise trail; yoga, aerobics; daily snorkeling excursion; kiteboarding; marina with seventy moorings and twenty-five slips; large complimentary fleet of watercraft; sailing and windsurfing school

Dress Code: Informal

Children: Six years and older; supervised activities; sailing lessons; babysitters

Meetings: Up to one hundred people; conference center; audiovisual equipment

Day Visitors: Welcome

Handicapped Facilities: Limited

Packages: Honeymoon, family, weddings, dive, sailing school, wind-surfing, theme weeks

Rates: Two people, daily, FAP. *High Season* (early January–April 30): $890–$910. *Low Season* (May–late July): $670–$690. *Sailing Season* (early October–mid-December): $650–$670. For Christmas/New Year holiday, rates are almost double those above. For Estate House, inquiry

Service Charge: 11 percent

Government Tax: 7 percent

NECKER ISLAND
Virgin Gorda, Tortola, B.V.I.

For the ultimate escape to the ultimate private-island getaway, there is no better choice: the island haven created by Richard Branson, Britain's boy-wonder entrepreneur (founder of Virgin Records and Virgin Airways), as a holiday retreat for his family and friends.

As laid-back as his resort, Branson is so low-key that it's hard to link the man with the success story—until you see how it all comes together in his Caribbean paradise. Located at the northeastern end of the British Virgin Islands, Necker is a small, dry, rocky island encircled by coral reefs and lapped by the waters that run from cobalt and peacock blue to aquamarine. The island has dramatic scenery at every turn: jutting headlands interspersed with pristine beaches, panoramic hills, and cactus-studded ridges—and, always, that spectacular water.

By his telling, in the 1970s Branson (then still in his twenties) was in New York on business when he heard that some of the B.V.I. were up for sale. He went to have a look, but it took two years before the price was right. An environmental-impact study to help maintain the seventy-four-acre island's ecological balance was carried out, and construction atop Devil's Hill began. Wherever possible, natural materials—including the stone removed from the hilltop—were used in construction.

"I wanted the house designed in an airy Balinese style . . . where the architecture blends so well with the country and culture," Branson says. "I also wanted the house to become the apex of Devil's Hill, as if it grew out of the rock."

He got his wish. As you approach Necker you must look hard to see the Balinese-style villa, it harmonizes so well with the landscape.

The palatial mansion divides into two sections: an enormous living room and dining area in the front, and nine bedrooms on two levels to the back. The huge, open living room with exposed beams of Brazilian hardwood overhead and Yorkshire granite floors underfoot is created around a tropical garden. Large sections of the roof left as natural skylights and a retractable roof allow sunlight to shower the garden, creating a magical effect during the day and a canopy of stars at night.

The enormous room is a combination living-dining-bar area furnished with elephant bamboo chairs and oversize cushions on natural stone banquettes. A giant oak refectory table seating twenty-six people occupies one corner, a snooker table sits in another, and a piano and television and video cabinet with a library of movie cassettes a third. Steps in the center of the room lead up to a gallery lined with books, tapes, CDs, DVDs, video games, and board games.

Surrounding the house on all sides are spacious terraces festooned with brilliant bougainvillea, allamanda, and other tropical flowers. The terraces overlook the sea and drop down to a lower level, where there is a swimming pool and Jacuzzi. There's a telescope for serious stargazers and hammocks for guests who simply want to dream.

A breezeway with tropical greenery leading to the bedroom wing ends in front of a ceiling-to-floor waterfall that tumbles through a chain sculpture. The bedrooms, all with terraces, have views that embrace the sea, sky, sun, and neighboring islands, too.

Named for Indonesian islands, the bed-rooms combine vibrant Balinese fabrics—each with a different color scheme—and elephant bamboo furniture, accented by Haitian paintings. The master suite on the upper level is Branson's Bali—and it was Princess Diana's during her stay. It has a huge terrace and a large wooden deck with its own Jacuzzi and a claw-foot bathub. The villa has nine comfortable bathrooms with stone-grotto showers that cleverly conceal the drainpipes.

Menus feature sophisticated fare as fresh as the chef can make it. You are sum-moned to dinner by a gong and will feel as royal as a princess when you sit at the regal dining table. There are outside dining areas as well.

Both sides of the island are etched with dreamy white-sand beaches. Turtle Beach, on the west, has a fine coral reef only a short snorkel away. Well Bay, a long curve of sand on the southeast, has a raised Bali-nese pavilion with giant bamboo chairs and ottomans. It overlooks the tennis courts and a swimming pool. Alongside the pool is a bar in the shape of a 30-foot crocodile.

Off in the distance on the northwestern tip of Necker is a smaller version of the main house—Bali Hi, and to the center of the island is Bali Lo. They are fully fur-nished in the same manner as the main house. Bali Hi has a plunge pool; Bali Lo, a full-size pool. Bali Cliff, adjacent to Bali Hi, has a rather bizarre layout with a liv-ing room on one level, a bedroom on a higher level that virtually hangs over a cliff, and an open-air bath downstairs—all with expansive views. More recently, two more cottages were added: Bali Beach, near Bali Hi, and Bali Buah, near Bali Lo. Both have interiors similar to their neighbors. Guests in the cottages have a golf cart to use for transportation. Necker's newest addi-tion is a spa facility, Bali Leha, which sits dramatically over a cliff. The spa has a full time therapist; treatments are an additional charge.

Walks around the island are wonderful. A nature trail runs downhill to mangroves and ponds; other paths lead to lookouts. Part of Necker has been designated a bird sanctu-ary, and whales are often sighted offshore in February and March. The island has a full array of water-sports equipment for guests.

Necker is not rented in the conventional way, and the price is prohibitive for most people unless they can round up twenty-five friends—even twelve affluent ones will do. The price includes the entire island and all its facilities; managers and a staff of about sixty; all meals for up to twenty-eight people; an open bar, wine, and champagne. A local calypso band for a party evening is also included. At certain times of the year and twice annually, during Celebration Weeks, the resort takes bookings on an indi-vidual basis.

Necker is very romantic and very glamor-ous, and it would probably appeal to anyone who can afford it. But it helps if you relish unforgettable natural beauty and exquisite man-made comfort.

Necker Island *****
Box 1091, Virgin Gorda, Tortola, B.V.I.
Phone: (284) 494-2757; Fax: (284) 494-4396; www.necker.com; email: pr@virgin limitededition.com

Owner: Sir Richard Branson

General Managers: Natalie and Gordon Overing

Open: Year-round

Credit Cards: None

U.S. Reservations: Sanctuare, (877) 577-8777, (212) 994-3070; Fax: (212) 497-9051

Deposit: 20 percent at booking, 40 percent nine months prior to arrival, balance three months prior. Inquire regarding refund policy.

Minimum Stay: Inquire; mostly five nights year-round

Arrival/Departure: Transfers included by boat from Virgin Gorda (fifteen minutes) or Beef Island (forty minutes)

Distance from Other Islands: Virgin Gorda, 1 mile; Tortola, 8 miles

Accommodations: One master with king-size bed and eight king- or twin-bedded rooms, each with bathroom and terrace; five Balinese cottages for two guests, each with king-size bed

Amenities: Ceiling fans; satellite television, VCR; bath with shower only, hair dryer, toiletry amenities, bathrobe; business facilities; helicopter landing pad; video, book, and music libraries

Electricity: 110 volts

Sports: Three freshwater swimming pools, two Jacuzzis; snorkeling, waterskiing, sailing, sea kayaking, windsurfing; two lighted tennis courts and equipment; gym with exercise equipment; Lasers, Sunfish, catamaran, light tackle, fishing equipment; snooker table; children's books and games

Children: All ages

Dress Code: None

Meetings: Up to twenty-eight people

Day Visitors: No

Handicapped Facilities: No

Packages: All-inclusive

Rates: Daily, All-inclusive. Start from $47,000, depending on the number of guests and time of year. Celebration Weeks start at $23,500

Service Charge: 2.5 percent

Government Tax: Included

ROSEWOOD LITTLE DIX BAY
Virgin Gorda, B.V.I.

Opened in 1964, RockResorts—exclusive enclaves renowned for their spectacular natural settings, begun by conservationist pioneer Laurance Rockefeller (hence the name)—became the standard against which all other Caribbean resorts were measured.

Understated and environmentally sensitive long before conservation became fashionable, they were a new kind of resort, where less is more. The accommodations were almost spartan in their simplicity: no phones, air-conditioning, radios, television, or room keys. Peace, privacy, and natural beauty—not man-made trappings—were their special appeal.

But times have changed, even at Little Dix, and since 1992 (when the Rosewood group of Dallas took over), Rosewood Little Dix Bay, as it is known today, has been undergoing a renewal that has made it better than ever. The most recent phase added more amenities and facilities, including large, luxurious villas and junior suites, an oceanside swimming pool, and a fabulous spa.

Little Dix is set in a 500-acre garden paradise along a ½-mile white-sand beach on the southwestern side of Virgin Gorda, with the green slopes of Gorda Peak as a backdrop. Still exclusive but not quite as snooty as in its formative years, Little Dix's service and country club atmosphere begin as soon as you step off the plane at the tiny Virgin Gorda Airport (which Rosewood Little Dix Bay owns). There you are met, registered, and driven to the resort's ferry for a twenty-minute ride to the Little Dix dock and taken directly to your beachside room, where you will find fresh flowers, a bottle of rum, and soft drinks.

Camouflaged under dense tropical foliage, Little Dix's spacious guest rooms, each with its own terrace overlooking the sea, are in clusters of cottages—some hexagonal and cone topped, some conventionally shaped—with two to four rooms. Those rooms behind the beachfront cottages are perched on stilts like tree houses to catch the trade winds; they have ground-level patios and hammocks.

The rooms make use of native stone and island hardwoods in their decor, and the results are fabulous. Without changing the tranquil spirit or character of Little Dix, the designers put together an eclectic mix of traditional and contemporary decor in the wonderful manner of understatement that is Little Dix. The rooms are light and elegant yet comfortable and inviting as never before. There are good reading lamps— all the more useful with Little Dix's service, "Hot Type," which enables guests to obtain advance copies of select novels without charge. The junior suites have a large outdoor covered living area, oversize bathrooms with indoor and outdoor showers, soaking tubs, and walk-in closets.

Perhaps even more telling about changing times are Little Dix's luxurious villa suites, each with three bedrooms and a private pool. They are located at the west side of the resort on a small beach. Five of the three- and four-bedroom hilltop villas have been added. Each has an oversize living area, spacious bathrooms with outdoor showers, a private pool, and dining pavilion/barbecue area.

The exotic spa treatment rooms are in simple, thatched huts. It has my vote for the most beautiful spa in the Caribbean. The spa treatments that use local ingredients are right up there, too. Both the villas and spa were designed by Roger Downing, whose firm is based in the British Virgin Islands and who has a keen sense of harmonizing the structures with their natural environment and maximizing their setting. The spa sits at the edge of a bluff that commands a spectacular, wide-angle view of the Caribbean, the resort, and Virgin Gorda. It is centered by an open-air pavilion beside a vanishing-edge pool. From here rock-lined paths wind through tropical gardens bright with exotic flowers to a series of individual, thatched roof cottages housing treatment rooms.

Daytime activities—most included in the room rate—can be as strenuous as lazing on a bright blue float on smooth azure water (a protective reef keeps it that way) or more demanding: Sunfish sailing, waterskiing (extra charge), and scuba lessons. A water taxi will take you to one of seven pristine beaches to snorkel, sunbathe, and picnic. Most fun of all may be a tennis challenge, with six or more people kept in constant motion by the Peter Burwash–trained pro.

The center of life at Rosewood Little Dix Bay is the Pavilion, a terrace with four interconnected dining and lounge areas topped with a soaring, four-point shingled roof where lavish breakfasts and lunch buffets, afternoon tea, and candlelight dinners are served. For Thursday lunch guests are taken by Boston Whalers to Spring Bay for a beach party. The resort can also arrange private dinners on the beach with full service, tiki lights, and steel pan music, at an extra cost.

A special private dining room for twelve has its own china and decor and personalized menus. The room, situated off to the side of the Pavilion, is equipped for meetings.

Cuisine under Rosewood's executive chef has been upgraded and greatly improved with lighter, more imaginative and sophisticated fare.

The Sugar Mill Restaurant and Bar, adjacent to the main terrace, is a dinner alternative, and the service is first-class all the way.

Indeed, service is one of Little Dix Bay's strengths. Most employees are Virgin Gorda natives who have been at Little Dix for more than two decades, giving the resort a sense of family. As with so many other exclusive resorts, the need to attract a younger market and cater to the ever-increasing family market led Little Dix to add a children's facility, the Children's Grove, which operates year-round. Children are divided into three age groups.

Rosewood Little Dix Bay *****
P.O. Box 70, Virgin Gorda, B.V.I.
Phone: (284) 495-5555, (888) 767-3966;
Fax: (284) 495-5661; e-mail: littledixbay@rosewoodhotels.com; www.littledixbay.com

Owner/Management: Rosewood Hotels and Resorts

Managing Director: Martein van Wagenberg

Open: Year-round

Credit Cards: All major

U.S. Reservations: Rosewood Hotels and Resorts, (888) ROSEWOOD; Fax: (214) 871-5444

Deposit: Three nights; twenty-eight days cancellation

Minimum Stay: Applies in high season; inquire in advance.

Arrival/Departure: Upon arrival at Tortola airport (EIS), Little Dix rep takes guests to private boat for twenty-minute ride to the resort. Welcome drinks are served while guests register. Cost: $95 per person, round-trip (50 percent off for children five to twelve; four and under, free). Fly BVI air taxi to Virgin Gorda is available from St. Thomas, $250 per person, one-way.

Distance from Airport: (Virgin Gorda Airport) About 1 mile

Distance from Spanish Town: 2 miles

Accommodations: 100 double rooms, one two-bedroom and two three-bedroom villas; 16 junior suites

Amenities: Ceiling fans, air-conditioning; bath with double sinks, tub and shower, bathrobes, slippers, toiletries, hair dryers; telephones; CD player; minibars; safes; nightly turndown service, towels changed and ice service two times daily; room service

Electricity: 110 volts/60 cycles

Fitness Facilities/Spa Services: Fitness center with cardiovascular equipment; spa (see text)

Sports: Swimming pool; seven tennis courts (two lighted), clinics, resident pro; hiking trails; dive trips for fee

Dress Code: Gracious informality; trousers, collared shirts, and closed-toe shoes (no beach attire) required after 6:30 p.m.; jackets and ties not required

Children: All ages; year-round program (see text); nanny service

Meetings: Up to twenty people

Day Visitors: Individuals welcome with reservations

Handicapped Facilities: No

Packages: Honeymoon, wedding, spa

Rates: Two people, daily, EP. *High Season* (mid-December–March 31): $650–$1,900.

Shoulder Season (April 1–31 and mid-November–mid-December): $525–$1,300.
Low Season: $375–$1,000. Villa rates: inquire

Service Charge: 18 percent on meals

Government Tax: 7 percent

Daily Surcharge: 10 percent resort fee

CAYMAN ISLANDS

Known as the Mount Everest of diving, the Cayman Islands are a British Crown Colony tucked under the western end of Cuba. The group is comprised of three low-lying islands almost completely surrounded by reefs: Grand Cayman, the resort and commercial center; Cayman Brac, a string bean of untamed wilderness, 89 miles to the northeast; and Little Cayman, the smallest, 5 miles west of Cayman Brac.

One of the most prosperous places in the Caribbean, the islands have excellent communications and their own airline and currency—and a population of only 25,000. Early in their history they were a favorite hiding place for pirates, and Pirates' Week, held in October, is a frolicking annual commemoration of the islands' history.

Grand Cayman, with the capital at George Town, is the largest of the trio. Seven Mile Beach, where the majority of the hotels are located, is a magnificent crest of powdery white sand just north of George Town. The 22-mile-long island rises only 60 feet above sea level and is made up largely of lagoons and mangroves rich in bird life.

Across one of these areas, North Sound, lies a barrier reef, and just inside the mouth is one of the Caribbean's most unusual sites. Dubbed Stingray City, it offers divers and snorkelers a thrilling opportunity to touch, feed, and photograph a dozen or more friendly stingrays in only 12 feet of water.

Grand Cayman also has the world's only sea turtle farm, where you can see turtles at various stages of development in their breeding pans. For a nominal fee you can sponsor a turtle for release to the ocean.

Under the sea the Caymans are surrounded by extensive cliffs, slopes, and valleys of submerged mountains, collectively known as the Cayman Wall, and densely encrusted with forests of corals, giant sponges, and other marine life. Nondivers can see the Caymans' underwater splendors thanks to recreational submarines.

Cayman Brac is 12 square miles of untamed tropics yet to be discovered by nature buffs for its hiking, fishing, birding, and caving. Little Cayman is even less developed. The 10-mile-long island has large expanses of mangroves and lagoons and is surrounded by long stretches of white-sand beaches, extensive reefs, and spectacular walls that some experts consider make up the finest diving in the Western Hemisphere.

Information
Cayman Islands Department of Tourism, 6100 Blue Lagoon Drive,
Miami, FL 33126; (305) 266-2300; www.caymanislands.ky
Offices are in Chicago, Houston, New York, and Toronto.

THE RITZ-CARLTON, GRAND CAYMAN

Seven Mile Beach, Grand Cayman

The Ritz-Carlton, Grand Cayman, which opened in December 2005, raised the bar for all resorts in the Cayman Islands. Ideally situated on Grand Cayman's famous Seven Mile Beach, the resort's 144 acres stretch from sea to sea, from the Caribbean-washed beaches across the island to the world-renowned dive waters of the North Sound. Designed in classic British-colonial architecture and surrounded by tropical gardens, the $500 million Ritz-Carlton is twenty minutes from the airport and only sixty-six minutes by air from Miami.

The resort offers a wide choice of deluxe accommodations; two restaurants by highly regarded chef Eric Ripert of New York's Le Bernardin; a shopping arcade with premium brand boutiques and a bridal retail store; a full-service La Prairie Spa—the first in the Caribbean; a Ritz Kids/Ambassadors of the Environment program by Jean-Michel Cousteau; a Nick Bollettieri tennis center with clay courts lighted for evening play and a small tennis stadium court with professional instruction; and Blue Tip, an unusual nine-hole golf course, designed and built by the PGA legend Greg Norman that is open only to hotel guest and residence owners.

In 2007, the Ritz-Carlton Grand Cayman owner purchased the Safe Haven golf course which lies adjacent to the hotel and renamed it, The North Sound Club. It operates as an independent eighteen-hole course; however, the plan is to redevelop the course with Greg Norman to make the Ritz-Carlton course an eighteen-hole one. Neither a groundbreaking nor a completion date for the project has been announced.

The resort's 365 guest rooms include forty-nine suites and the premier Ritz-Carlton Suite. The beautifully appointed rooms offer a choice of king-size or double beds, a large desk, stocked honor bar, marble baths, deluxe toiletries, sewing kit, lighted makeup mirror, hair dryer, and bathroom scales. Oceanfront rooms have views of the Caribbean, beach, and pool; Waterway rooms, located on the North Sound side of the property, overlook the golf course and the waterway pool. Club level rooms have the option of either views. The resort provides concierge service, twenty-four-hour room service, twice-daily housekeeping, overnight laundry service, and morning newspaper.

Guests on the Ritz-Carlton Club level have elevator key access, an exclusive lounge, a private Club Concierge, and five food presentations daily. The elegant Ritz-Carlton Suite, with panoramic ocean-view rooms, has a master bedroom, one and one-half baths, living room, dining areas and butler's pantry, and seafront balcony.

The Ritz Kids program has been combined with the Ambassadors of the Environment by Jean Michel Cousteau's Ocean Futures Society to provide a supervised program of children's activities, centered on multifaceted learning and recreational experiences designed to immerse children in the natural aspects of the Cayman Islands.

The resort has six dining and entertainment choices. Blue by Eric Ripert is the resort's gourmet restaurant in a formal setting with a poolside alfresco bar and grill overlooking the lagoon. Other dining options include 7, an oceanfront cafe, offering open-air all-day dining overlooking the Caribbean Sea and Periwinkle, a more casual alfresco bistro with a Mediterranean focus. In the evening, 7 Prime Cuts & Sunsets specializes in high quality steaks. Cocktails, a wine bar, and light fare, including traditional tea on weekends, are served at Silver Palma. The lively beachfront pool bar, Bar Jack, is a popular sunset gathering place. There's also twenty-four-hour in-room dining service.Silver Raid, the 20,000-square-foot La Prairie Spa, has seventeen treatment rooms and a full range of pampering and relaxation treatments and spa services. There also is a full-service beauty salon and state-of-the-art fitness center.

The resort's large meeting facilities brought another new dimension to Grand Cayman with the ability to cater to corporate executive meetings at the luxury level. The flexible facilities include the largest ballroom in the Cayman Islands, an elegant boardroom, and five meeting rooms. The resort's grounds and terraces provide options for outdoor functions.

The Ritz-Carlton, Grand Cayman ****
P.O. Box 32319, Seven Mile Beach, Grand Cayman, Cayman Islands
Phone: (345) 945-7489; Fax: (345) 945-2210; www.ritzcarlton.com

Owner: Michael Ryan

Management: The Ritz-Carlton Hotel Company, Atlanta, Georgia

General Manager: Jean Cohen

Open: Year-round

Credit Cards: Most major

U.S. Reservations: Ritz-Carlton, (800) 241-3333

Deposit: Three nights; seven days cancellation

Minimum Stay: Varies by season; inquire

Arrival/Departure: Transfer service; inquire

Distance from Airport: (Owen Roberts International) 4.3 miles

Accommodations: 365 guest rooms, including 49 suites with king-size or two doubles; one Ritz-Carlton oceanfront suite; 44 Ritz-Carlton Club level rooms; 24 two- and three-bedroom oceanfront condominiums

Amenities: Air-conditioning; safe; stocked bar; marble bathrooms; cable television, digital clock/alarm radio, CD player; dual-line phones and dataports, high-speed and wireless Internet; bathrobes and slippers; twice-daily housekeeping, twenty-four-hour room service; Ritz-Carlton Suite: living room/dining area, pantry, master bathroom, one-and-one-half bathrooms

Electricity: 110 volts

Fitness Facilities/Spa Services: Fitness center; La Prairie Spa (see text)

Sport: Swimming pool, snorkeling, diving, fishing, boating; tennis; golf (see text)

Dress Code: Casually elegant

Children: All ages; Ritz Kids/Cousteau program; babysitting

Meetings: Up to 1,000 people

Day Visitors: Yes

Handicapped Facilities: Special rooms

Packages: Golf, wedding, spa

Rates: Per room, double, per day, EP. *High Season* (mid-December–April 30): $759–$1,149. *Low Season:* $349–$499. Inquire for suite rates.

Service Charge: 10 percent

Government Tax: 10 percent

PIRATES POINT RESORT

Little Cayman, Cayman Islands, B.W.I.

Unusual if not unique, Pirates Point is a diver's resort owned and operated by Gladys Howard from Tyler, Texas.

What's unusual about that?

Gladys also happens to be an award-winning cookbook author and a Cordon Bleu chef who has studied with Julia Child, James Beard, and Lucy Lo. And she operated an international cooking school and gourmet catering service in East Texas for twenty years.

When you arrive at the Edward Bodden Airstrip, Gladys meets you in her van for the ½-mile ride to the resort. The airport strip was recently tarmaced, but the terminal is still a wooden shack; Little Cayman has a total population of one hundred people.

Pirates Point consists of a central pavilion that includes the front desk, lounge and bar, dining room and outdoor barbecue, and five cottages constructed of cut stone and wood. They're only twenty steps from the beach. Three of the cottages have two units each, one has four units, and one is reserved for single guests. Two cottages have large verandas.

The little inn is immaculate. Rooms are spacious and surprisingly pleasant and comfortable, given their rustic setting. They have white stucco and wood-paneled walls and high wood-beamed ceilings. Furnished in wicker, they have either two twin beds or one king. In the bathroom you'll find fluffy towels, terry robes, and a shower with hot and cold water. Pirates Point has its own reverse-osmosis plant, which helps ensure a freshwater supply. The resort has a guest telephone and VCR and DVD players in the lounge. DVD movies and videos are available.

Each year Gladys repaints all guest rooms and buildings as well as overhauls

and refits the *Yellow Rose III,* the resort's 42-foot custom dive boat. For her tenth anniversary in 1996, she built a new kitchen and added a large freshwater pool and a ten-person Jacuzzi surrounded by an 8-foot deck. She also added a second 1,200-gallon reverse-osmosis plant and 24,000-gallon cistern. She enlarged and air-conditioned the bar and added wireless Internet service for guests at a charge of $15 per week. There is a dedicated computer for guest use in the clubhouse, or guests can use their own laptops within about a 50-yard radius of the clubhouse.

The complex is shaded by large almond, sea grape, and coconut palm trees. Along the path by the cactus garden leading to the reception area, you will notice some sculptures made from coconuts, driftwood, and other natural material. What started as a pastime has developed into a wacky tradition, and now these "works of art" by guests decorate the bar and add character to the inn. Since 1988, Gladys has run an annual contest for the most original creation; the prize is a week's vacation at the resort.

You can count on the food to be good. Gladys uses whatever she can get and works miracles in her kitchen. It is difficult to get products locally, except fish. Her supplies come by boat from Grand Cayman, and she flies in fresh fruits and vegetables.

For this caterer and gourmet chef, dining is serious business. There's no roughing it here: You'll dine with crystal stemware and linen napkins even at picnics. Lunch, an outdoor buffet under the sea grape trees, is in your swimsuit, and dinner offers a buffet and table service in the dining room. There is a barbecue on Thursday and sunset wine and cheese evenings at Gladys's house—and this lady is the ultimate hostess. If you are a hotel guest during Pirate Week (in late October or early November), the Cayman Islands's annual carnival bash, you will surely get involved in helping to construct the resort's float and join the party and the parade. It's great fun.

A coral atoll 10 miles long and 1 mile wide, Little Cayman is one of diving's last frontiers. Its Bloody Bay Wall is one of life's great diving experiences. Rising to within 20 feet of the surface and plunging in sheer cliffs more than a mile deep, these pristine formations offer marine life found nowhere else. There are giant sponges, trees of black coral, elaborate sea fans, and eagle rays, to name a few. The late Philippe Cousteau called it one of the three finest dive areas in the world.

Pirates Point is located only 2 miles or a short boat ride from the wall and with its fast boat can easily reach the most dramatic dive sites. The resort has a full scuba operation with six instructors on staff who handle everything from a short resort course to full certification and advanced training. The resort offers two dives daily and night dives by request. The two dives do not have time limits and are done safely, opting for longer quality dives, rather than quantity dives.

Good snorkeling (gear costs extra) can be enjoyed directly in front of the resort about 10 feet from shore. You can have an underwater video of your dives shot for an additional charge.

The resort has a sandy beach, but the entrance into the water from shore is rocky and better made from its small pier, which puts you into about 3 feet of water. Pirates Point often takes all the guests for a picnic lunch on nearby cays and can arrange fishing and group-dive programs on request.

Gladys, as avid an environmentalist as she is a gourmet chef, chairs the Little Cayman National Trust, which has created trails for hiking and bird-watching. The Caymans are a flyover for North American birds, and Little Cayman is a sanctuary for the red-footed booby and frigate bird. It also has its own island lake for tarpon fishing, with an endemic subspecies.

Pirates Point operates as an all-inclusive resort. The certified dive package includes accommodations with private bath, three meals daily with wine, an open bar with unlimited drinks, two boat dives daily, tanks, weights, belt, guide, transfer to and from the airport, and the use of bicycles, beach towels, and terry robes. Add the experience of diving at Little Cayman and Gladys's food, and Pirates Point tallies up as one of the best buys in the Caribbean.

Pirates Point Resort ** 🏝

Box 43LC, Little Cayman, Cayman Islands, B.W.I.

Phone: (345) 948-1010; Fax: (345) 948-1011; e-mail: piratept@candw.ky; www.piratespointresort.com

Owner/Manager: Gladys B. Howard

Open: Year-round except early September–late October

Credit Cards: Visa, MasterCard; personal checks accepted

U.S. Reservations: Direct to hotel

Deposit: Half total package rate within ten days of booking; thirty days cancellation, refund half of deposit; fewer than thirty days, deposit forfeited

Minimum Stay: Three nights

Arrival/Departure: Complimentary transfer service

Distance from Airport: (Boden Airport) ½ mile; no taxi service (Little Cayman is 90 miles northeast of Grand Cayman; Cayman

Airways, [800] 4-229-626, provides daily flights from George Town.)

Distance from South Town: ¾ mile

Accommodations: 11 rooms in bungalows (seven air-conditioned; six oceanfront); doubles have twins or king; maximum of twenty divers

Amenities: Ceiling fans, floor fans; seven rooms with air-conditioning; baths with shower only; custom 42-foot Newton dive boat; daily maid service, no room service

Electricity: 110 volts

Sports: See text

Dress Code: Very casual

Children: Over five years of age, but must be over twelve to dive

Meetings: Up to twenty people

Day Visitors: Welcome, with reservations

Handicapped Facilities: Limited

Packages: All-inclusive, dive, honeymoon

Rates: Per person, double, weekly package, AP. *High Season* (mid-December–mid-April): $1,895 diver; $1,495 nondiver. *Low Season:* $1,695 diver; $1,395 nondiver. Single supplement, $80 per day or request single room.

Service Charge: 15 percent

Government Tax: $8.00 per room daily

CURAÇAO

Only 39 miles off the coast of Venezuela, the cosmopolitan capital of the Netherlands Antilles is noted for its commerce, diversity of restaurants, and fashionable shops with goods from around the world. These features are found side by side with the colorful colonial harbor of Willemstad, making it easy and fun to explore on foot.

At the heart of the compact historic old city are Fort Amsterdam, the Governor's Palace, the eighteenth-century Dutch Reform Church, and, nearby, Mikve Israel-Emanuel Synagogue, the oldest synagogue in the Americas (founded in 1654).

Juxtaposed against the sophisticated city center is the little-known landscape of windswept shores, chalky mountains, and rugged terrain, as well as two of the best nature parks in the Caribbean. In the 3,500-acre Christoffel National Park, the cactus grow as tall as trees. Dominated by the rocky peak of 1,238-foot Mount Christoffel, the park has 20 miles of roads with color-coded routes for self-guided tours and hiking trails.

Curaçao is completely surrounded by reefs with an extraordinary variety of coral and fish that are only now being discovered by divers. The 1,500-acre Curaçao Underwater Park, stretching for 12½ miles from the SuperClubs' Breezes Resort to the eastern tip of the island, protects some of Curaçao's finest reefs. Many areas can be enjoyed by snorkelers as well as divers. East of the marine park is the Curaçao Aquarium, a private facility where 400 species of marine life native to Curaçao waters are displayed.

Quiet seas wash Curaçao's western shores, but wild surf crashes against the windward north. The coast has many small coves with beaches and large bays or lagoons with very narrow entrances and wide basins. These waterways are among Curaçao's most distinctive features. Some lagoons are used for commerce, others for sport.

On the east, Spanish Water is one of the island's largest, prettiest lagoons with a long, narrow opening to the sea. It has hilly green fingers and coves, islands, and beaches, and is the boating and fishing center with marinas and water-sports facilities. Santa Barbara, on its eastern side, is a popular public beach with changing facilities.

The constant northeastern trade winds that cool the island have made windsurfing one of Curaçao's most popular sports, with international recognition and an Olympic champion. Annually in June the Curaçao Open International Pro-Am Windsurf Championship attracts world masters. The most popular windsurfing area is on the southern coast between Willemstad and Spanish Water, also the site of the island's main hotels and water-sports centers.

Information

Curaçao Tourism Corporation, One Gateway Center, Suite 2600, Newark, NJ 07102; (973) 353-6200; Fax: (973) 353-6201; email: northamerica@curacao.com; www.curacao.com (Also see Renaissance Curaçao Resort and Casino on p. 303 in On the Horizon.)

CURAÇAO MARRIOTT BEACH RESORT & EMERALD CASINO

Curaçao, N.A.

Curaçao's first large, deluxe beach resort in more than twenty years when it opened in 1992, the Curaçao Marriott Beach Resort & Emerald Casino is something of a monument to the island's architecture and rich history. From the magnificent facade of the hotel in deep ochre stucco and white gabled trim to the traditional red tile roof and colonnaded promenades, you can pick up echoes of the island's past.

More so than other former colonies, Curaçao's Dutch heritage is evident throughout the island in its architecture. The colorful stucco buildings that line the harbor and streets of Willemstad, the capital; the historic landhuis, or manor houses, that dot the countryside; the homes in the Scharloo area, during the nineteenth century a lively neighborhood of wealthy merchants—all are relics of the colonial era. In addition to the Dutch touch, the architecture was shaped by the spirited colors and exuberant flair of Spanish, Latin American, and African influences.

All served as the inspiration for original designers Mary Jane Rosa and John Olson, who spent days combing neighborhoods, noting details, getting ideas, and even collecting paint chips to re-create authentic colors. The results are subtle and sophisticated—a modern interpretation of historical tradition.

Set on Piscadera Bay, the tropically elegant three-story resort stretches along a white-sand beach on the southern end of the island, ten minutes from the airport and from downtown Willemstad and next door to the World Trade Center Curaçao.

A circular driveway fronted by a massive gabled roof, a fountain, a garden driveway, and pith-helmeted bellhops make for a grand entrance. As you walk up a set of steps into the hotel, you can look through the open-air lobby to a fabulous view of the white sandy beach and the turquoise Caribbean waters.

On the periphery of the hotel, a shaded promenade of bellied columns, symmetrically bowed in the typical fashion of Curaçao, frames the marvelous ocean views and blurs the line between indoor and outdoor living. The lobby, with its rich wooden ceiling and weathered brass fixtures, is meant to recall the Curaçao of the eighteenth and nineteenth centuries, when it was a major hub for trade ships cruising between Europe and South America. The result was the Curaçao style, an eclectic blend of decorative themes and products from all over the world.

The lobby's front desk is made entirely of wood panels crisscrossed with carved, rope-style moldings. Sturdy unfinished wooden furniture with carved detailing and textured upholstery in deep colors lends a Dutch flavor to the sitting areas.

A modern accent is added by a large metal abstract wall sculpture by local Curaçaoan artist Yubi Kirindongo, which hangs near the concierge desk. Two fiber wall hangings by Alexander Calder and a commissioned floral painting by Lucio Pozzi are just across the way.

Matching pieces of furniture or one singular design style were rare in Curaçaoan households. The Emerald Bar and Grille reflects this pleasing melting pot of styles.

Recalling the elegant Scharloo courtyards, tiled pathways—lined with more white columns and flaming bougainvillea—lead to the turquoise doors of the plush guest rooms. The large, air-conditioned rooms, with furnished balconies or terraces and full or partial ocean views, have been renovated with new decor in contemporary colors.

The immense pool and beach area, graced with fountains and lush tropical greenery, is the center of the hotel—and the action. Comfy chaise lounges ring the free-form pool, which has a swim-up bar, a wading pool, and two large whirlpools. A shack dispenses beach towels, and an outdoor grill serves up burgers and barbecued chicken. A beach hut for resort activities is also available for special events and groups of up to a hundred.

The man-made beach—the largest of any Curaçao resort—is wide, long, and studded with thatched shelters under which you can escape the hot sun. Caribbean Sea Sports, which operates directly on the beach, offers snorkeling, waterskiing, windsurfing, sailing, kayaking, and scuba diving lessons and equipment rentals. It also has a new lobby shop.

For dinner, Portofino, a glass-enclosed restaurant with high ceilings and palm-frond fans, provides an elegant setting for enjoying outstanding northern Italian cuisine and a selection of fresh pasta prepared by the resort's Italian chef. It offers alfresco dining on the patio adjacent to the restaurant. The Emerald Lounge, an upscale martini bar, serves seafood and features light jazz music nightly.

Across from it the Emerald Casino—fashioned after the patios or courtyards at the center of Scharloo homes—glitters with elegance and sophistication. An opulent French crystal chandelier 8 feet in diameter sparkles overhead against a white-clouds-on-blue-sky mural. In front of the casino, the Voila Delicatessen is a relaxing sitting area.

In addition to water sports, the resort's sports and fitness facilities include two lighted tennis courts, a health club with a gym, two saunas, two steam rooms, and a massage room. There are aerobics classes, Universal machines, exercise bikes, stair climbers, and free weights. The fitness center provides exercise and strength-training equipment. The spa area is scheduled to be renovated to enhance its natural surroundings. The resort has a beauty salon, shopping arcade, and a state-of-the-art, twenty-four-hour business center offering fax, copying, computer and high-speed Internet access, and business services. The hotel offers shuttle service to town.

Meeting facilities are centered on the Queen's Ballroom, which has a distinctly Spanish flavor and Old World, formal atmosphere. It takes its cue from the Scharloo salas, rooms saved for special celebrations filled with music and dancing.

The Marriott was a welcome addition to Curaçao; it rejuvenated the island's lackluster hotel scene and helped raise the standard of service and luxury on the island. The resort has received the coveted Four Diamond rating from the AAA for several years running.

On a clear night—and every night in Curaçao is clear—there's a touch of Caribbean magic when you sink your body into the bubbling waters of an outdoor Jacuzzi and watch moon shadows dance upon the yellow gables, white columns, and crimson tiles of this most modern yet delightfully traditional resort.

Curaçao Marriott Beach Resort & Emerald Casino ★★★★
Piscadera Bay, P.O. Box 6003, Curaçao, N.A.
Phone: (599) 9-736-8800; Fax: (599) 9-462-7502; www.paradisebymarriott.com

Owner: Reef Resorts

General Manager: John Toti

Open: Year-round

Credit Cards: Most major

U.S. Reservations: (800) 223-6388

Deposit: One night with credit card; three days cancellation in high season

Minimum Stay: Christmas/New Year's

Arrival/Departure: Transfers not available

Distance from Airport: 10 miles; taxi one-way, $20

Distance from Town: 5 miles; taxi one-way, $20

Accommodations: 247 rooms and ten suites, with balconies or patios (eight terrace suites and two Presidential Suites with ocean view; 124 rooms with king, 123 with queens)

Amenities: Air-conditioning; bath with tub, shower, toiletries, hair dryer; remote control television with cable; radio; fridge; telephone; safe; iron and ironing board; casino; turndown service on request, room service 6:00 a.m.–midnight

Electricity: 110 volts and 220 volts

Fitness Facilities/Spa Services: Fitness center with aerobics classes, Universal equip-ment, steam rooms, massages, saunas; beauty salon

Sports: Freshwater swimming pool, two outdoor whirlpools; two free, lighted tennis courts; water-sports center for snorkeling, waterskiing, windsurfing, sailing, kayaking, and diving lessons and equipment rentals

Dress Code: Casual by day; casually elegant in evening; jackets and ties not required

Children: Up to two children under twelve years old free in parents' room, including meals; cribs, high chairs; babysitters

Meetings: Up to 400 people; hotel adjacent to the World Trade Center Curaçao

Day Visitors: May use pool, beach, fitness center, tennis courts, and other facilities for $95 per person; limited if hotel is busy

Handicapped Facilities: Available on request

Packages: Family, romance, sand dollar

Rates: Per room, EP. *High Season* (early January–March): $259–$299. *Low Season* (June–mid-December): $149–$169. Meal plans available

Service Charge: 12.84 percent

Government Tax: 7 percent

HOTEL KURA HULANDA SPA AND CASINO AND LODGE KURA HULANDA AND BEACH CLUB
Willemstad, Curaçao

Kura Hulanda means "Dutch courtyard" in Papiamentu, the native language of Curaçao. Given that the island is the architectural crown jewel of the Netherlands Antilles, this simple term perfectly denotes the distinctive, charming environment of the Hotel Kura Hulanda Spa and Casino, an extraordinary fusion of "urban renewal," Caribbean style, and one man's vision.

Opened in late 2001, the hotel is the centerpiece of Project Kura Hulanda, which includes sixty-five historic buildings, mostly former private homes, in an 8-block complex. Project Kura Hulanda showcases meticulously restored eighteenth- and nineteenth-century Dutch colonial architecture and includes an internationally recognized cultural museum, as well as a conference center, casino, spa, and retail shops.

Dutch millionaire Jacob Gelt Dekker, along with his longtime partner John R. Padget, made his fortune in rental-car and one-hour-photo businesses in Europe. On a trip to Curaçao after he and Padget had sold off their major business interests at huge profits, Dekker fell in love with the island's extraordinary architecture. Almost overnight, he drew up plans for Project Kura Hulanda. In a run-down neighborhood of dilapidated houses and broken streets, Dekker and his team carved out, quite literally, an architectural and cultural oasis.

Hotel Kura Hulanda is conveniently located in the center of the Otrabanda section of Willemstad, Curaçao's capital, only fifteen minutes from the airport. The brightly colored compound, located above St. Anna Bay near the Queen Emma Bridge, is within easy walking distance of Punda, Willemstad's major downtown district across the retractable pontoon bridge.

The hotel gives the impression of a peaceful village, with tree-lined lanes carefully crafted of imported stone and a tour-book facade with some interesting architectural flourishes, such as perfect replicas of historic houses Dekker saw on his travels to Suriname and a charming central courtyard between the lobby and the restaurants and shops. Elsewhere around the property there is a series of intimate courtyards that include an African sculpture garden and an herb and fruit garden.

Kura Hulanda's spacious, nicely appointed accommodations include double rooms and suites. Because the units are adapted from renovated private homes, no two are the same. As a decorative motif, each room displays a wall with a hand-painted design by a local artisan. Custom-made furniture, including a four-poster bed, is handcarved from the finest mahogany and old teak; the handwoven linens are from India; bathrooms are of Indian marble.

Two signature suites are a 996-square-foot, two-story, one-bedroom presidential suite that includes an entertainment center with big-screen television and a fully equipped kitchen; and a sexy yet sophisticated bridal suite with handcrafted furniture made of hammered sterling silver, including a canopied, handcarved bed worthy of Cleopatra. A pair of duplex luxury spa loft suites have huge bathrooms suitable for in-room treatments.

Amenities include air-conditioning, ceiling fans, waffle-weave bathrobes, hair dryers, cooler, cable television, portable CD system, high-speed Internet, and teak butler stands for clothing and comforter. The hotel's international appeal is reflected in its telephone system with modem and voice mail available in English, Dutch, French, and Spanish.

Kura Hulanda has two swimming pools, including the "eco-pool," a grotto surrounded by natural rock formations and fed by a waterfall, and a more traditional pool near a sculpture garden. Hotel guests enjoy access to a private beach club and preferential golf privileges at a golf club nearby. Kura Hulanda offers complimentary transportation to these clubs, which are approximately fifteen minutes from the hotel. An air-conditioned and fully equipped fitness center has free weights and the latest machines and a sauna and steam room.

Next to the fitness center is the hotel's spa, where guests can enjoy facials, massages, manicures, and pedicures for an additional charge. In-room services are also available. The hotel has a business center, and among its most important facilities in today's post–September 11 world is an unobtrusive state-of-the-art security system that monitors the grounds around the clock from eighty discreetly placed video cameras.

For dining, Kura Hulanda offers a number of options, from casual to classy. The hotel's Indian influence is carried through at Jaipur, its signature restaurant serving tandoori oven specialties from traditional chicken and naan breads to shrimp and lamb. The restaurant, set by the rock grotto eco-pool, also has a cozy, alfresco bar. The AstroLab Observatory restaurant, with a courtyard filled with museum-quality maritime navigational instruments, serves breakfast and dinner. For dinner, the specialties are meat and seafood in a pristine, white-tablecloth ambience. Jacob's Bar offers tapas and cocktails in a Spanish setting with an outdoor dining terrace overlooking the central courtyard.

In 2007, the hotel added the Mansion Executive Lounge, to serve as the Executive floor found in upscale city hotels. Situated in a house overlooking the Kura Hulanda Museum Square and enjoying a private entrance, the Lounge is furnished with items from a private collection including artwork. It offers wireless Internet, two computers and a printer, and wide-screen HD television. Complimentary coffee, tea, and fresh fruits are provided in the morning; wine, coffee, and snacks in the late afternoon. For rates, inquire from the hotel.

The Kura Hulanda Museum houses the largest African collection in the Caribbean and a stunning, eye-opening exhibit that chronicles the history of slavery.

For travelers more interested in history and culture than beaches and who like being within easy walking distance of Curaçao's main attractions, Hotel Kura Hulanda is an ideal option. To say that Kura Hulanda is charming—which it is—would be an understatement. It's truly a rare jewel and like no other hotel in the Caribbean.

Now Kura Hulanda offers another option. The Lodge Kura Hulanda and Beach Club, a beachfront resort on the island's west end. Located about thirty minutes from the airport, the beachfront haven offers pleasantly appointed villas, suites and guest rooms—all with balconies or patios overlooking the ocean or gardens. The lodge, facing a natural reef off of its beach, has an on-site dive shop offering snorkeling, diving courses, and daily excursions. Scuba gear, snorkeling equipment, Sunfish, and kayaks are available for rental, as are bikes and helmets. Price per bike is $6.50 for a half day, $10.00 full day. Town and country packages combining the hotel and the lodge are available. Daily complimentary scheduled transportation between the two is available.

The lodge proved to be so popular it is already being expanded with eighteen new villas that are expected to be ready by December 2008. Set atop a stone bluff, each of the 2,300-square-foot, three-bedroom, three-bath villas offer sea views, a two-story great room, marble floors, granite countertops, top-of-the-line appliances and furnishings, and a plunge pool. The master suite has a waterfront patio, walk-in closets, and a Jacuzzi tub. Available for purchase, starting at $850,000 per villa, buyers have the option of placing their villa in the hotel rental program (lodge@kurahulanda.com; www.kurahulanda.com).

Hotel Kura Hulanda Spa and Casino and Lodge Kura Hulanda and Beach Club ***
🌿

Langestraat 8, Willemstad, Curaçao
Phone: 011-5999-434-7700; Fax: 011-599-9-434-7701; e-mail: hotal@kura hulanda.com; www.kurahulanda.com

Owners: Dr. Jacob Gelt Dekker and John R. Padget

President/Managing Director: Peter Heinen

Resident Manager: Michael Molema

Open: Year-round

Credit Cards: Most major

U.S. Reservations: (877) 264-3106; e-mail: reservations@Kurahulanda.com

Deposit: Only credit-card guarantee required; cancellation up to seventy-two hours in advance

Minimum Stay: None

Arrival/Departure: Transportation available by taxi; Kura Hulanda can arrange transfers to/from the airport for fee.

Distance from Airport: (Hato International Airport) 8 miles. Taxi one-way from airport to hotel, $25; to Lodge $65

Accommodations: Hotel, 80 rooms and suites (17 deluxe, 12 superior, 14 standard rooms; 14 junior, three one-bedroom, five deluxe one-bedroom suites; one presidential, one bridal, one executive, and two spa loft suites). Lodge, 74 villas, suites and rooms

Amenities: Air-conditioning, ceiling fans (in some rooms); marble bathroom, hair dryer, bathrobes; stocked cooler; cable television; teak clothing and comforter butler stand; portable in-room CD player/stereo; 110-outlet by desk, multilingual telephone system with modem and voice mail; high-speed Internet; safe; room service (7:00 a.m.–11:00 p.m.); nightly turndown service

Electricity: 110/220 volts

Fitness Facilities/Spa Service: Fitness center, spa (see text)

Sports: Two swimming pools; transportation to and from private beach club and golf club. Lodge: Tennis, diving, snorkeling, bicycles, water sports

Dress Code: Casual; shorts and T-shirts not allowed at dinner

Children: All ages

Day Visitors: Yes

Handicapped Facilities: Inquire

Meetings: Two conference rooms for up to fifty people; auditorium for 160; executive boardroom for twenty with adjacent dining room; closed-circuit television; audiovisual equipment; interpreter/translator system for Dutch, English, French, and Spanish. Lodge: room for up to forty-five people and with state-of-the-art audiovisual equipment.

Packages: Spa, golf, dive, museum, honeymoon, hotel/lodge combinations

Rates: Per person, double, per day, EP. *High Season* (late December–mid-April): $199–$1,200. *Low Season* (mid-April–late December): $180–$1,000. Third adult, children, and MAP rates available. Lodge: *High Season* $180–$1,055; *Low Season* $165–$810

Service Charge: 12 percent

Government Tax: 7 percent

DOMINICAN
REPUBLIC

The Dominican Republic is a land of superlatives: the oldest country of the Caribbean, with the tallest mountains and the lowest lake. Historic Santo Domingo was the first Spanish settlement in the New World. Here the Spaniards built their first cathedral, first hospital, first university, and first fortress.

The Old City has been beautifully restored and is alive with restaurants, shops, art galleries, and museums. Columbus Square boasts the oldest cathedral in the Americas.

Modern Santo Domingo, the fun-loving, sophisticated capital with Old-World charm, has more than one million people and about the lowest prices in the Caribbean. The modern Plaza de la Cultura is the heart of the capital's cultural life. It includes the National Theatre, where plays, concerts by the National Symphony Orchestra and jazz ensembles, and performances by visiting artists are held.

But Santo Domingo is far more than history and culture. Dominicans are warm and friendly and love to have a good time, and their city bounces with every sort of entertainment, from piano bars and smart supper clubs to brassy cabarets. One of the city's most unusual attractions, Los Tres Ojos (the three eyes) Park, is a subterranean cave with three lagoons, each with different water: sweet, salt, and sulfur.

From the rolling terrain of the east and south, the land rises toward the island's center in two tree-covered spines where two national parks contain the country's highest peaks—three that are more than 10,000 feet high and several rising to almost 9,000 feet—with trails.

In the northeastern corner Samana Peninsula and Bay is one of the most beautiful and least developed areas. From December to March whales play at the mouth of the bay. On the Rio Limon, in the center of the peninsula, a footpath leads to a magnificent waterfall, all but hidden amid the savage beauty of the thickly forested mountains. On the southern side of the bay, Los Haitises National Park is a 100-mile karst region with dense mangroves, estuaries, and tiny cays that are rookeries for seabirds.

Over the last three decades, the Dominican Republic has been developing its coastal areas, first along the north coast from Puerto Plata east and along the east coast where resort development at Punta Cana continues nonstop. Most of the new resorts have been large all-inclusives catering to the mass market. But recently, both areas have welcomed their first small, boutique resorts, three of which appear in this edition.

Information

Dominican Republic Tourist Office, 136 East 57th Street, Suite 803, New York, NY 10022; (888) 374-6361 or (212) 588-1012; Fax: (212) 588-1015; 848 Brickell Ave, Suite 405, Miami, FL 33131; (888) 358-9594, (305) 358-2899; Fax: (305) 358-4185; www.dominicana.com.do

(Also see The Westin Roco Ki Beach and Golf Resort on p. 304 in On the Horizon.)

CASA DE CAMPO
La Romana, Dominican Republic

Think big. Three golf courses, thirteen tennis courts, a dozen restaurants, three polo fields and 150 polo ponies, a hundred-station sporting clays center, fitness and water-sports centers, a fleet of sport-fishing boats, a marina and yacht club, a 5,000-seat amphitheater, a museum, an art school, a replica of a sixteenth-century Mediterranean village, an international airport, a cruise port, a new spa, 267 guest rooms, and 150 villas on 7,000 acres.

Yes, it's big. But Casa de Campo is never overwhelming or noisy or crowded, as megaresorts often are. On the contrary, it's tranquil and very private. *Casa de Campo* means "a house in the country" in Spanish, and despite its size, Casa actually has that feeling to it.

Set in pretty rolling countryside in the southeastern corner of the Dominican Republic near the sugar-producing town of La Romana, Casa de Campo began in the early 1970s as a private retreat for local sugar barons, who played polo and golf on a preserve owned by Gulf & Western, whose founder, the late Charles Bluhdorn, developed the property into a sprawling resort. Later Gulf & Western sold it to the present owners, brothers Jose Alfonso and Jose "Pepe" Fanjul, who developed it further. Today it is something of a sophisticated amusement park and a posh country club with Caribbean attractions and Spanish charm, appealing to families, honeymooners, sportsmen, incentive winners, and just about anyone who wants a vacation with lots of choices at affordable prices.

The lobby of the main building holds the guest services area, Excel Concierge-VIP lounge, transportation center, La Cana Bar, Tropicana Restaurant, Sports Bar, and Business Center—designed by Dominican designer Patricia Reid, who combined the textures and colors of fine fabrics and plantation-style furniture with island craftsmanship, local coral rock, rich woods, and woven palms to integrate Dominican cultural elements into the decor throughout the resort.

The hotel rooms come in two categories: superior, and luxury. All are spacious and furnished with two double beds or a king and have a private balcony or terrace with views of the golf courses or gardens. Each room is equipped with a minibar, a coffee-maker, cable television, air-conditioning, a Bose Wave radio, a refrigerator bar, direct-dial telephones with voice mail and data-port, a separate vanity and dressing area, a hair dryer, a walk-in closet with a safe, an iron and ironing board, and a terrace. Luxury rooms have extra amenities such as Serta pillowtop mattresses, a cozy seating area, bathrobes, a dressing area with a marble-topped vanity, a lighted makeup mirror, three phones, and a writing desk.

The resort's private villas, located throughout the resort—near the tennis club and the Equestrian center, around the golf courses, and in the countryside—have two to four bedrooms, each with air-conditioning and private bath. Each villa has cable television, a pool or whirlpool, a comfortable living room, a dining room, a fully equipped kitchen, and a screened terrace. Guests can add a supplement for a maid and butler services and other amenities. The villas are particularly popular with families and friends and golfing buddies traveling together. Of the group, some thirty sumptuous, commodious Exclusive Villas have three and four bedrooms and an array of high-end features and amenities.

Recently the resort added the Cygalle Healing Spa, an eco-friendly sanctuary that offers indoor and outdoor spa services, using natural body-treatment products made in small batches at the on-site from indigenous ingredients. Guests can receive treatments in a lush Zen garden, a spacious spa suite, an outdoor private gazebo on the beach, or in their private villa. Designed by Dominican Myra Gonzalez, the spa is located in the main area of the resort.

Perched on a cliff overlooking the Chavon River, several miles from the main hotel, Altos de Chavon is a replica of a sixteenth-century Mediterranean village conceived by Bluhdorn and created by Italian cinematographer Roberto Copa to foster the culture of the Dominican Republic. Begun in 1976, with local artisans building the village of stone, wood, and iron by hand, it was completed and officially inaugurated with a concert by Frank Sinatra in its 5,000-plus-seat amphitheater in 1982.

At the heart of the village in a cobblestone square stands the Church of St. Stanislaus. Nearby, the Regional Museum of Archaeology houses a comprehensive collection of artifacts of the Taino Indians (the island's inhabitants at the time of Christopher Columbus's arrival). Three art galleries showcase the works of Dominican, European, and American artists. Altos de Chavon School of Design, in affiliation with New York's prestigious Parsons School of Design, offers degrees in various design fields and the arts. The amphitheater is home to the school's performing arts department and has hosted Julio Iglesias and Gloria Estefan, among others. Along the narrow streets, local shops sell handmade jewelry, pottery, and Dominican crafts.

The variety and quality of sports are among Casa de Campo's prime attractions.

Its four eighteen-hole championship Pete Dye–designed courses (one for private membership only) attract players from around the world and regularly host international tournaments. The Teeth of the Dog course, with seven holes skirting the Caribbean, is one of the most beautiful in the world and has been named the top course in the Caribbean by *Golf* magazine. The open-air Lago Grill, which sits under a tall thatched roof and overlooks the famous golf course, is the most popular restaurant for breakfast and lunch with all-you-can-eat buffets. The Links is an inland, rolling course with water coming into play on five holes. Both are dedicated resort courses, with no public access.

Casa de Campo's fourth and newest golf course (third resort course), also by Pete Dye, opened in 2003. Laid out around Altos de Chavon with fabulous views of the Chavon River, the surrounding countryside, and the Caribbean, it has a distinctive feature that is bound to make history. Known as Dye Fore, it is planted with two new strains of grass, or paspalum, that thrive on saltwater and can be watered directly from the ocean. Some predict it will change the face of golf in the Caribbean. The 19th Hole Bar, with a fabulous view overlooking the golf course, the Chavon River, and surrounding countryside, serves light fare and is an ideal watering hole after a round of golf.

La Terraza Tennis Center offers thirteen Har-Tru tennis courts, ten lighted for night play. Ballboys are available, and games are guaranteed at all times for all levels of expertise. Clinics and private lessons are offered.

Casa de Campo's equestrian and polo facilities are without rival. The Equestrian Center offers guided rides along trails and the beach, along with jumping and riding lessons for beginners and experienced riders; it is the venue for authentic rodeos. The facility has more than 150 trained polo ponies and equipment for players of any level.

For skeet or trapshooting, the 245-acre Sporting Clays Center is outstanding. Shaun Snell, a famed British marksman, is a sought-after instructor.

Casa de Campo has plenty of water toys—three swimming pools, including a children's pool, dot the resort. Water sports are featured at the resort's private Minitas Beach, and there are trips to the offshore islands of Saona and Catalina. The new Beach Club by Le Cirque at Minitas Beach is an upscale, breezy outdoor restaurant specializing in the cuisine of the famous New York eatery with local variations. Another major feature of the resort is the Marina and Yacht Club, a boating and residential community at the mouth of the Chavon River where it empties into the Caribbean Sea. Designed by Italian architect Gianfranco Fini to resemble an Italian seaside village, the development consists of a private yacht club and marina with 350 slips for yachts up to 280 feet in length. It has a residential community, shops, galleries, restaurants, and a movie theatre with first-run movies in English.

The heart of the complex is the Italian Plaza, an oceanfront two-story structure with restaurants, a bakery, delicatessen, pizzeria, ice-cream shop, and piano bar on the first floor and two- and three-bedroom apartments on the upper floor. Behind the plaza on a single level are a drugstore, bank, travel agency, art gallery, beauty parlor, gift shops, and boutiques—all open to Casa de Campo resort guests.

The other residential areas in the Matina area are Ensenada with two- and three-bedroom apartments with boat slips in front; and the even more luxurious Darsena

with fourteen villas in three-, four-, and five-bedroom configurations and forty-one boat slips (30 feet to 50 feet). Each villa has its own pool.

The marina has a fleet of 31-foot Bertram sport-fishing boats for deep-sea fishing, and others for river fishing and sailing. Marlin is the main catch on the ocean, while you can fish for snook in the Chavon River with a local guide.

Casa de Campo's children's program, Kidz 'n Casa, is a day camp offered daily year-round from 9:00 a.m. to 4:00 p.m. for children ages three to eight. There is a separate program for children ages nine to twelve, teens thirteen to eighteen, and a new program for toddlers, one to three with nannies, day and night.

Casa de Campo offers many dining choices. In the main hotel area, Tropicana is a steak house specializing in imported beef and seafood for dinner. The Upper Deck, above the main pool, serves sandwiches and snacks. La Cana Bar, a thatched-roof lounge, features merengue bands, a folkloric ballet, and different international artists nightly.

The Safari Club at the shooting center is dressed in African decor with carved wood furnishings and hand-painted ceilings under a 30-foot thatched roof. The club and bar are open for lunch and dinner during high season.

Some of the resort's best restaurants are located at Altos de Chavon, where nighttime offers floodlit views over the ravine several hundred feet below. La Piazetta is an Italian restaurant with strolling musicians, and Cafe del Sol, an open-air pizza parlor, has daily specialties, ice cream, and desserts. El Somrero offers authentic Mexican cuisine; the Sports Bar is in the main area of the resort.

Casa de Campo is the Good Life—a fun-filled destination, especially for families, providing options, privacy, security, and the kind of friendly service usually associated with smaller resorts.

Casa de Campo ★★★★

P.O. Box 140, La Romana, Dominican Republic

Phone: (809) 523-3333; Fax: (809) 523-0000; e-mail: reserva@ccampo.com.do; www.casadecampo.com.do

Management: Premier Resorts and Hotels, Claudio A. Silvestri, President and CEO

General Manager: Alberto Grau

Open: Year-round

Credit Cards: All major

U.S. Reservations: Premier World Marketing, 2600 Southwest Third Avenue, Miami, FL 33129; (800) 877-3643, (305) 856-7083, (305) 856-5405; Fax (305) 858-4677; e-mail: reserva@ccampo.com.do

Deposit: Two nights within seven days of booking; balance fourteen days prior to arrival

Minimum Stay: Seven nights Christmas/ New Year

Arrival/Departure: Direct flights daily from Miami to Casa de Campo's international airport of La Romana (LRM) via American Airlines; American Eagle daily from San Juan

Distance from Airport: From La Romana: ten minutes; from Santo Domingo: one hour and fifteen minutes

Distance from Santo Domingo: One and a half hours

Accommodations: 267 superior and luxury hotel rooms in two-story buildings with balcony or terrace; 150 two- to four-bedroom classic and exclusive villas—all with pool or whirlpool and some with both

Amenities: Hotel rooms: Air-conditioning, ceiling fan; minibar, coffeemaker; cable television, Bose Wave clock-radio, direct-dial telephones with voice mail and dataport; hair dryer, separate vanity and dressing area; baths; walk-in closet, safe, iron and ironing board; golf cart. Supplemental option: maid and butler, concierge from 8:00 a.m.–10:00 p.m.

Electricity: 110 volts

Fitness Facilities/Spa Services: Fitness center, free weights, exercise equipment. New spa (see text)

Sports: Four championship eighteen-hole golf courses (one private membership); thirteen Har-Tru tennis courts (ten lighted); shooting center; equestrian center, polo; marina, water sports, river fishing, boating

Dress Code: Smartly casual

Children: All ages

Meetings: Up to 500 people

Day Visitors: Yes with reservations

Handicapped Facilities: Limited

Packages: Golf, villa, inclusive meals

Rates: Per person, double, per night, EP. *High Season* (January–April): $280–$527. *Low Season:* $178–$345

Service Charge: 16 per cent

Government Tax: 10 per cent

CASA COLONIAL BEACH & SPA

Puerto Plata, Dominican Republic

Old world grace and contemporary elegance were combined to create Casa Colonial Beach & Spa, the first luxury boutique hotel on the Dominican Republic's north coast, previously known for large, all-inclusive resorts.

Located a few miles east of Puerto Plata on the beach at Playa Dorada, the elegant all-suite hotel, opened in late 2004, was designed in colonial architectural style by Sarah García, a noted Dominican architect and interior designer and daughter of Isidro García, who owns VH Hotels & Resorts, which operates Casa Colonial as well as two adjacent resorts.

Casa Colonial's white colonnaded buildings, set in magnificent tropical gardens that add to its gracious ambience, reflect the area's Spanish-colonial past. The design, enriched with Dominican historical and cultural elements, gives the hotel its special character and enhances the guests' experience.

The front of the "Casa," or home, resembles a classic Dominican plantation estate. But upon entering, you are greeted by a cool, modern lobby made all the more elegant by very high ceilings, Italian marble floors, and rich wood accents against white walls. Local materials such as Dominican coral stone and mahogany are incorporated into the decor. Quality and attention to detail are evident throughout.

Upon arrival, you are welcomed by a friendly staff and given a refreshing, cold, scented towel. Instead of the traditional reception, there is a sophisticated, contemporary lobby-lounge and a concierge desk, whose attendant handles check-in and just about any other need a guest may have. A few steps farther on in the center of the next lounge area is a large glass bar, which is illuminated in the evening (another bar is located at the beach). To one side is Lucia, the gourmet restaurant, named for another daughter.

Beyond the bar is a second building—all but hidden in the hotel's lush gardens—that houses the resort's oceanfront guest rooms and suites. Along the hallways leading to the guest rooms are displays of handsome old clay jars once used on the Garcia family's farm to keep water cold. Room numbers on guest room doors are embroidered on linen and framed, in the manner of an old Dominican tradition.

The fifty spacious accommodations range from junior and one-bedroom suites to a presidential suite. They have generous balconies with views of the ocean or gardens and are furnished with table and chairs and lounger. The bedroom is fitted with a four-poster king or two queen-size beds with custom-made Serta mattresses, which the resort calls the "best sleep in the Caribbean." They are very comfortable, indeed.

Junior suites extend to a comfortable sitting area and balcony (some with an additional sofa bed and/or dining area). Deluxe suites have a separate living room and dining alcove. With the addition of an adjoining suite, three deluxe oceanfront suites and two garden ones can be made into two-bedroom master suites with a private entrance. The rooms have custom-designed, Caribbean-inspired furnishings and fine linens.

All accommodations have air-conditioning and marble floors, ceiling fans, high-speed Internet (a laptop is available for rent), flat-screen cable television (most channels in

Spanish), Bose radio/alarm clock/CD-player, original art, three phones with international direct dialing and voice mail, and twenty-four-hour room service. Each floor of the three-story building and the rooftop are accessible by elevator.

Rooms are equipped with a minibar, coffeemaker, hair dryer, bathrobe and slippers, iron and ironing board, umbrella, and in-room safe (large enough for a laptop). The large marble bathrooms have double sinks, walk-in shower, separate toilet, and a big bathtub alongside a louvered window that looks into the bedroom and, in some cases, the gardens and ocean. The Penthouse and Presidential Suites each have a crow-foot bathtub on a tree-shaded, open-air terrace off the bathroom.

Casa Colonial's gourmet (read expensive) restaurant, Lucia, is open for dinner only. Adjoining it is the wine cellar and small dining room that is used for private parties and wine tastings. The Veranda, an inside/outside restaurant overlooking the beach, offers three meals daily, and also services the rooftop snack bar, where light fare is available at lunch. The bar is beside the hotel's pretty rooftop infinity pool and four hot tubs that overlook the beach.

The Bagua Spa is a beautiful space of gleaming white marble and offers indoor treatment rooms including two private couples therapy rooms with a Jacuzzi, and outdoor treatment pavilions set over a tropical pond with waterfalls. Treatments include massages, wraps, aromatherapy, and facials. The spa also has a sauna, steam room, and an ocean-view fitness center with cybex equipment. Special classes and a personal trainer are available.

The hotel has a meeting room, a wedding pavilion on the beach, and provides private transfer to the eighteen-hole Robert Trent Jones championship golf course nearby. It provides valet parking, golf-club

storage, newspapers via Internet, and laundry service. Casa Colonial is a member of the Small Luxury Hotels of the World.

Named by a leading travel magazine as one of the year's twelve hot spots in 2006, Casa Colonial was apparently to the liking of fashion jetsetter Donatella Versace, enough for her to spend two weeks with her two children there.

Casa Colonial Beach & Spa ***

P.O. Box 22, Puerto Plata, Dominican Republic
Phone: (809) 320-3232; Fax: (809) 320-3131; e-mail: reservascc@vhhr.com; www.casacolonialhotel.com

Owner: VH Hotels & Resorts

General Manager: Luigi Di Ciaccio

Open: Year-round

Credit Cards: All major

U.S. Reservations: (866) 376-7831

Deposit: Secured with credit card

Minimum Stay: Seven nights from December 24–January 7

Arrival/Departure: Airport transfer provided for fee

Distance from Airport: 15 minutes from Puerto Plata Airport; 45 miles from Santiago

Distance from Santo Domingo: 110 miles

Accommodations: 50 suites (42 junior, two one-bedroom, four deluxe, one penthouse, and one presidential)

Amenities: Balconies, Frette linens, bathrooms with double sinks, Kohler tubs, walk-in showers; stocked minibar, high-speed Internet, in-room safe; flat-screen television; wireless Internet access in lobby and rooftop

Electricity: 110 and 220 volts

Fitness Facilities/Spa Services: Spa with ten treatment rooms and three oceanfront pavilions, sauna, steam room; rooftop pool and four ocean-view hot tubs; fully equipped gym, classes, personal trainer

Sports: Pool; nearby Playa Dorada Golf Course and Playa Grande Golf Course; Ocean World Aquatic Park; windsurfing

Dress Code: Casually elegant

Children: All ages, but no facilities

Meetings: Up to fifty people, audio/visual equipment; wireless Internet; private dining room

Day Visitors: Yes

Handicapped Facilities: Yes

Packages: Weddings, honeymoon, golf, spa, romantic, extreme sports

Rates: Per room double, **High Season:** from $350; Christmas/New Year, from $450; **Low Season:** from $286

Service Charge: 10 percent

Government Tax: 16 percent

SIVORY PUNTA CANA
Uvero Alto/Punta Cana, Dominican Republic

Situated on a long, secluded, private beach, Sivory Punta Cana is the first boutique hotel in the area immediately north of Punta Cana and a welcome addition to a coast saturated with mass-market, all-inclusive resorts. The luxury resort, a member of the Small Luxury Hotels of the World, has fifty-five spacious, beautifully appointed suites, most with ocean views, some with plunge pools.

Located one hour's drive from the Punta Cana International Airport, the all-suite Sivory (pronounced see-vory), which opened on the Dominican Republic's eastern shores in December 2005, has a wonderfully care-free ambience, yet is elegant and sophisticated. Guest services and amenities are tailored to upscale, discerning clientele, starting with a two-to-one staff-to-guest ratio.

The fine service at Sivory Punta Cana begins when you arrive at the resort and are greeted with a chilled towel, a cool drink, and broad smiles by a staff that embodies the friendly Dominican nature. The check-in desk is situated in an open-air lobby. Across

the way, you can't help but notice the seventeenth-century, hand-carved wooden frame around the hotel's boutique door and wonderful Dominican sculpture displayed in the shop's windows. The resort is replete with interesting art and antiques, from modern paintings on the walls and heads of Buddha in the garden to concrete bed slabs in the swimming pool. That's some of what makes Sivory so appealing.

The overall style and design of this upscale oasis combines native Dominican elements with refined European and Asian traditions. Most of the furnishings in the guest rooms, restaurants, bars, lobby, and meetings rooms were specially selected and imported from Spain and Indonesia. A great deal of thought has gone into the design and decor; everything throughout the resort harmonizes, nothing jars.

From the lobby a wood-paneled walkway edged by two small ponds with water lilies and sea turtles leads to the resort's center— a pretty infinity-edge pool bordered by a sundeck with handsome lounges of finely woven rope. On one side of the pool, walkways lead to the accommodations; on the other are several thatch-roofed structures housing a bar, the spa, and two restaurants. Beyond the pool are the putting green, the beach, and water-sports center.

The exterior of the two-story accommodations, staggered along three rows, is not particularly interesting architecturally, but the interiors make up for it. All rooms have ocean views but some are much better than others. Dominican and Asian influences continue in the decor of the suites, which are furnished with handcrafted rich mahogany and finely woven rattan. They have a separate sitting area and a private balcony or terrace with built-in chaise lounges, or, in the case of the Luxury Oceanfront Junior Suites, a private plunge pool set in teak wood decking, outdoor shower, a chaise lounge, and coral stone divider for privacy.

Everything in the room speaks of quality and an attention to detail. The bedroom is furnished with a four-poster canopied king-size bed in dark mahogany dressed in white. The decor is minimalist, understated, and refined, but with a touch of color in the throw on white bed linens, pillows on the sofa, and art on the walls. Finely woven windows shades allow light in but keep out the glare of the strong Dominican sun. The owner's European tradition echoes in such touches as a white linen towel on the floor on which to alight when leaving your bed.

Each suite has a plasma screen television with satellite channels, CD/DVD player, coffeemaker, air-conditioning; ceiling fan, writing desk, safe, high-speed Internet connection, and three phones with international direct dial/voice mail. The complimentary mini-bar is stocked with beverages and a wine cooler has vintages from the resort's wine cellar for purchase. All guest rooms are air-conditioned and have a separate dressing area with mahogany vanity and porcelain basin. The spacious marble bathroom has an oversize tub and a floor-to-ceiling glass and coral stone shower with double heads. A hair dryer, makeup mirror, bathrobes and slippers, and generous toiletries by ETRO are also provided.

Nonsmoking rooms are available on request, and there's twenty-four-hour room service. In the morning, a daily "open eye" of freshly squeezed orange juice, strong Dominican coffee, and breakfast pastries, along with a fax version of the morning paper will be on your doorstep at the time you specify.

For guests seeking ultimate privacy, The Ysla Club is situated in a secluded section, slightly away from the resort. There are seven lavish oceanfront suites, a private beach club, an exclusive beach area, and private butler service.

Sivory Punta Cana's guest services include pool and beach valets who attend to guests' food and beverages requests poolside or on the beach. They also dispense cooling water spray or sunscreen upon request.

The resort has three restaurants with very attentive staffs and fine French, Asian fusion, and international cuisine. LaVeranda, an indoor/outdoor restaurant overlooking the pool and beach, serves international cuisine with a Mediterranean twist. It opens daily for breakfast, lunch, and dinner. It's hard to imagine anything more pleasant than lunching on the terrace shaded by a timber overhang, looking out across the blue-tiled swimming pool to the palm-shaded villas in one direction and the Atlantic Ocean waves breaking on the reef in the distance, the golden sands in the foreground, with tall palms swaying in the gentle breeze that keeps the air cool and balmy.

Gourmond Restaurant, upstairs from LaVeranda, is the resort's most elegant restaurant with a wine cellar housing 8,000 vintages from around the world. It specializes in fine French cuisine and is open for dinner only. To one side is a small cigar lounge. Tau, an attractive small restaurant in Asian decor located off the lobby, serves Asian fusion fare. It, too, is open for dinner only.

The 4,300-square-feet Aquarea Spa and Wellness Center, housed in a thatched cottage, has two treatment rooms, a steam room, a Vichy bath, thermal pool, saunas, beauty salon, and Jacuzzis. It offers manicures and/or pedicures and an extensive treatment menu, including signature massages and body treatments such as a caviar facial. The spa also has packages for couples, wedding parties, and others specially designed for men.

The resort has a library, a computer with Internet access for guests' use, and Wi-Fi in the conference and pool areas. Helicopter service can be arranged and private butler service is available for $150 per day plus tax.

Sivory Punta Cana is a resort for romantics to spend quality time together. It has distinguished itself from the big Punta Cana resorts by being small and personal. Children are accepted but the resort does not have special facilities for them.

Sivory Punta Cana
Uvero Alto (Punta Cana), Dominican Republic
Phone: (809) 468-0005; Fax: (809) 552-8686; e-mail: sales@sivorypuntacana.com; www.sivorypuntacana.com

Owner: Manel Vallet

General Manager: O'Neiel Espinal

Open: Year-round

Credit Cards: Most major

U.S. Reservations: reservations@sivory puntacana.com

Deposit: Guaranteed with credit card

Minimum Stay: Seven nights Christmas/New Year

Arrival/Departure: Airport transfers arranged by car, $80 + tax, one-way; by helicopter (10 to 25 minutes with sightseeing) minimum two/maximum three persons $398 (for two persons) including tax

Distance from Airport: (Punta Cana International Airport) 60 minutes by car; 10 minutes flight by helicopter

Distance from Santo Domingo: Three-and-a-half-hour drive

Accommodations: 48 junior suites and 7 Ysla suites (28 deluxe and 10 premium oceanfront with private balcony or terrace; 10 luxury oceanfront with plunge pool. Ysla Club: 3 honeymoon, 3 Ysla Bonita, 1 Sivory Grand

Amenities: See text

Electricity: 110 volts

Fitness Facilities/Spa Services: Spa, gym

Sports: Swimming pool, water sports, putting green

Dress Code: Casual elegant

Children: Age seventeen and older

Meetings: Two rooms for 30 and 150 persons; state-of-the-art facilities

Day Visitors: With reservations

Handicapped Facilities: Yes

Packages: Romance, honeymoon, Good Life

Rates: Per room, single or double, per night, EP. *High Season* (December 22–March 31): $490–$2,400. *Low Season* (April 1–December 1–20): $290–$1,100. Rates include Ysla Club suites.

Service Charge: 10 percent

Government Tax/VAT: 16 percent

TORTUGA BAY AT PUNTACANA RESORT & CLUB

Punta Cana, Dominican Republic

Simple elegance is simply the best way to describe Tortuga Bay, the new boutique hotel that opened in December 2005 on the eastern shores of the Dominican Republic.

Located at the heart of the PUNTACANA Resort & Club, a 15,000-acre Caribbean resort where Julio Iglesias and other international celebrities keep vacation homes, Tortuga Bay is a private enclave of fourteen luxurious two-story villas with one- and two-bedroom suites. All the interiors—which are fabulous—were designed by renowned fashion designer Oscar de la Renta, who, too, is one of the resort's owners.

The gracious and spacious villas—custard yellow with white trim—are set on a 1,200-foot-long beach (a segment of the PUNTACANA Resort & Club's 5-mile stretch) and are very practically, as well as prettily, designed. You can book the entire villa or only the ground level, which has a two-bedroom apartment; or one of the very large junior suites on the second floor. The junior suites have large verandas facing the beach and on the side, bathing it in sunlight.

De la Renta's decor takes full advantage of the space with four-poster canopied beds (king or two doubles), a large comfortable easy chair and ottoman, desk, and chest of drawers. Most of the furniture is in dark wood set against white walls and bed covers with just the right touch of color in decorative throws and throw pillows. The result: simple but elegant, or as one might say in Spanish, *muy simpatico*.

Suites have ceiling fan, minibar, flat-screen plasma television, CD/DVD player, Internet connection, laptop rental, direct-dial phone/voice mail, microwave, coffee/tea maker, fully stocked bar, walk-in closet, safe, pillow menu, and laundry service. The large bathrooms are fitted with twin sink vanities, whirlpool bathtubs, separate showers, bathrobe and slippers, hair dryer, deluxe toiletries, makeup mirror, iron/ironing board, daily newspaper, and room service.

Upon check-in guests get their own golf cart to use during their stay. They also meet their Villa Manager (butler by another name)—a personable young Dominican (one for every two villas) who attends to all your requests from check-in to departure. The Villa Manager accompanies you to your villa, familiarizes you with its gadgets and gives you a cell phone and number to call when you need him. He will book your dinner or spa reservations, tee-times, horseback riding excursions or lessons, and take care of your shoe shine or ironing.

Tortuga Bay has its own private reception area, which also houses the bar and restaurant, Bamboo, also decorated by De la Renta, a cozy place with an elegant touch. Bamboo serves three meals—either in the pretty air-conditioned interior or outside on a terrace by the swimming pool. The menu is international; a Dominican menu is available from room service from 7:00 a.m. to 11:00 p.m. Afternoon tea (or excellent Dominican coffee) is served on the restaurant/bar patio. The Bar is also the place to try one of the famous Dominican rums and a good Dominican cigar.

On one side of the patio in the garden is a whirlpool and just beyond, the well-equipped Fitness Center. Other amenities include wireless Internet access in the lobby and the restaurant, bar, and pool areas. For those who prefer not to travel with their computers, the resort rents laptops. The resort also has full-time nanny service for an additional fee.

In addition to Bamboo, Tortuga Bay guests may dine at any of PUNTACANA Resort's eight restaurants and bars using an electronic key card programmed for their exclusive use, avoiding the need for cash or signatures. They also have access to PUNTACANA Resort's sports and recreational facilities that include La Cana golf course designed by Peter Dye, a full-service marina and water-sports center, a horse ranch, a private nature reserve, and International Biodiversity Center. The nature reserve has eleven hiking trails, several leading to spring-fed natural pools that are great for a refreshing swim.

Another of the shared facilities is the Six Senses Spa, located in the handsome Clubhouse about a mile north of Tortuga Bay's reception center. The full-service spa offers a wide range of treatments, administered by therapists, mostly from Thailand, as well as yoga, Reiki, and tai chi classes.

Personalized service begins for Tortuga Bay guests upon arrival at the Punta Cana International Airport, which the Resort also owns. (Indeed, it was the opening of the international airport two decades ago that launched Punta Cana's incredible resort development where now more than three million visitors vacation annually.) Tortuga Bay's guests are met, whisked through immigration by the resort's staff, and driven in an air-conditioned minivan to the resort, 5 miles away. On departure, guests get preferred use of the airport's VIP lounge. A VIP terminal is available for those who arrive by private aircraft.

Tortuga Bay at PUNTACANA Resort & Club
Phone: (888) 442-2262, (809) 959-2262, ext. 7237; Fax: (809) 959-3951; e-mail: reservationstb@puntacana.com; www .puntacana.com

Owner: Green Diamond Inc.

General Manager: Alberto Abreu

Open: November to September

Credit Cards: All major cards

U.S. Reservations: (888) 442-2262

Deposit: Christmas and Easter, one night secured with credit card

Minimum Stay: Four nights, President's Week and Easter; ten nights Christmas/New Year's

Arrival/Departure: Airport meet/assist services and resort transfers; use of VIP airport lounge on departure included in rate.

Distance from Airport: (Punta Cana International Airport) 5 miles

Distance from Santo Domingo: 3½-hour drive

Accommodations: 14 Villas/32 suites (can be configured as 10 three-, 4 four-bedroom or 14 two- or 18 one-bedroom suites)

Amenities: See text

Electricity: 110 volts

Fitness Facilities/Spa Services: Fitness center, outdoor whirlpool; spa, yoga, Reiki, and tai chi classes

Sports: Swimming pool, bicycles, kayaks, tennis; use of Punta Cana water sports, Ecological Reserve; La Cana golf and access to Clubhouse

Dress Code: Smart casual

Children: Complimentary program, children's pool, cots and cribs; full-time nanny service (for fee)

Meetings: Yes

Day Visitors: No

Handicapped Facilities: No

Packages: Golf, honeymoon, spa

Rates: Per room, per night, FAP. *High Season* (January 7–early April): $670–$870. *Low Season* (mid-April–December 23):

$580–$755. Easter: $790–$975. For two- to four-bedroom villa, inquire. Rates include airport transfers, meet/assist and use of airport VIP lounge, and golf cart for complete villa.

Service Charge and Government Tax: 26 percent mandatory

RENAISSANCE JARAGUA HOTEL & CASINO
Santo Domingo, Dominican Republic

Robert Redford once spent weeks here while filming *Havana*. So what else do you need to know? Yes, it's big, brassy, and painted in colors that will make you reach for your sunglasses. But it's also wonderfully Dominican.

Located on the Malecon, Santo Domingo's popular seashore boulevard overlooking the Caribbean, the Jaragua (pronounced Ha-RAG-wa) offers the best of two worlds: a resort set in fourteen acres of tropical gardens in the heart of the capital and a city full of history, culture, and fun.

The Jaragua doesn't have a beach (there are no beaches in Santo Domingo), but it has lagoons spilling into a huge swimming pool, a health club and spa, a tennis complex, several restaurants and bars, a nightclub, a disco, a casino, shops, and beautiful rooms. And it's all within easy reach of any of Santo Domingo's many attractions.

Opened in 1987 on the site of the first Jaragua, a popular Havana-in-the-old-days hotel with outdoor gardens and a splashy nightclub, this Jaragua is today. A modern high-rise of ten floors combined with garden low-rise buildings, its design is sleek and the decor sophisticated, with stylish art deco details throughout. You

will be impressed by the quality and high standards. Marble floors and satiny, hard-finished fixtures are kept polished to such a shine, you'll think they're mirrors. And the luster on the floor isn't one bit more impressive than the polish of the service. The Jaragua puts the city's other hotels to shame and demonstrates what Dominicans can do with a hotel when they set their mind to it.

You arrive at the hotel by way of a grand driveway graced with fountains and gardens and step from a large portico directly into the lobby. Prepare yourself for the experience. On your left is the huge, wide-open casino, brimming with action and bouncing with merengue music most of the time. To your right is the quiet, elegant reception area with soft indirect lighting that highlights the lobby's art deco features. The contrast of the two sides is amazing. But it works.

The guest rooms are in two areas: the majority in the main ten-story tower, with the others in two-story garden buildings on the western side of the main building. All are large, luxurious, and attractive, and the penthouse suites with their own Jacuzzis are small palazzos. The stylish appointments of contemporary design include plush upholstery, draperies, and bedspreads.

The rooms, designed as much with business travelers in mind as tourists, each have a desk and three phones, including one in the marbled bathroom. The tower rooms, most with views of the sea, are for those who want to be at the center of the action. Being more removed, the garden rooms provide greater privacy and quiet and are particularly popular with guests enrolled in the fitness center program. Directly in front of the guest-room tower is the fitness center, which offers saunas, massage, and more. The hotel has packages for a full beauty program.

Beyond the lagoon and gardens is the swimming pool, which is likely to be crowded, particularly on weekends. It can also be noisy with kids and music. To the rear is the tennis complex with four lighted clay courts, a viewing stand, and a pro shop.

The Jaragua has several dining outlets: Coffee Corner is a venue with music in the evening. Quisqueya Restaurant is located in a corner on the main floor. It is the main venue for breakfast and lunch and offers American entrees along with their Spanish counterparts. Las Cascadas, overlooking the waterfalls and lagoon, is used for private functions. Champions Sports Bar offers good food, good sports, and good times, day into night. The grill and bar by the pool serves lunch and snacks.

The Jaragua jumps in the evening, and there's plenty of opportunity to be part of the action. In addition to the casino and the casino bar, the 1,600-seat La Fiesta Room often has headline entertainers. Merengue Bar is the place for cocktails, live music, and dancing; and the disco.

The Jaragua indeed has glamour and style—not so much Caribbean as Latin— and is as popular with Latin Americans as it is with gringos. This hotel is not for the traveler who wants a laid-back Caribbean retreat on a beach. If you prefer having the facilities and services of a large luxury hotel, thrive on a glittering, lively nightlife, and like to be in the center of the action, though, you'll love the Jaragua.

Renaissance Jaragua Hotel & Casino ***
367 George Washington Avenue, Apartado Postal 769-2, Santo Domingo, Dominican Republic
Phone: (809) 221-2222; Fax: (809) 686-0528; www.marriott.com/sdqgw

Owner/Management Company: Marriott International

General Manager: Eduardo Reple

Open: Year-round

Credit Cards: Most major

U.S. Reservations: Renaissance Worldwide, (800) 468-3571; or direct to hotel, (800) 331–3542; Fax: (809) 221-8271

Deposit: One night

Minimum Stay: None

Arrival/Departure: Transfer service arranged for charge

Distance from Airport: (Santo Domingo Las Americas International Airport) 20 miles (forty minutes); taxi one-way, $40

Distance from Old City: 1 mile; taxi one-way, $10

Accommodations: 300 rooms and suites with double or king-size beds (200 deluxe rooms, including nine suites, in ten-story tower; 100 in two-story garden buildings)

Amenities: Air-conditioning, bath with tub and shower, hair dryer, makeup mirror, basket of toiletries, bathrobe; cable television, radio, direct-dial telephone, high-speed Internet access; minibar and refrigerator, ice service; nightly turndown service; concierge; twenty-four-hour room service;

Jacuzzis in penthouse suites; business center with Internet access

Electricity: 110 volts

Fitness Facilities/Spa Services: See text

Sports: Freshwater swimming pool; free use of tennis courts; tennis rental equipment and lessons for fee; golf, horseback riding, water sports, fishing arranged through concierge

Dress Code: Casual

Children: All ages; cribs, high chairs; babysitters; up to two children under eighteen stay free in garden room with parents

Meetings: Up to 1,000 people

Day Visitors: Yes, for casino and restaurants

Handicapped Facilities: Yes

Packages: Spa, honeymoon, merengue, golf, adventure, all-inclusive, other Renaissance standards

Rates: Per room, single or double, daily, EP. Year-round: $95–$429

Service Charge: 10 percent

Government Tax: 16 percent

GRENADA

Known as the Spice Island, Grenada is a tapestry of tropical splendor where banana trees by the side of the road grow as tall as the palm trees fringing the powdery beaches, and trade winds nourish the lush mountainous interior.

St. George's, the capital and one of the Caribbean's prettiest ports, is set on a deep horseshoe-shaped bay. Clinging to green hillsides behind it are yellow, blue, and pink houses topped with red roofs and historic buildings climbing to a series of colonial forts built to protect the strategic harbor.

Grand Anse Beach, south of St. George's, is a lovely 2-mile crescent of white sand bathed by calm Caribbean waters. It is the island's main resort and water-sports center, with snorkeling, sailing, diving, and windsurfing. Bay Gardens, a hillside botanic oasis, has trails covered with nutmeg shells that wind through woods of an estimated 3,000 species of tropical flora.

The main cross-island highway from the capital winds up the mountains to the Grand Etang Forest Reserve, crossing it at 1,910 feet within a few hundred yards of Grand Etang, an extinct volcano whose crater is filled with a lake.

The Grand Etang National Park, part of Grenada's national park system protecting most of the interior mountains, has hiking trails around the lake, through surrounding rain forests, and up to mountain peaks that showcase the island's exotic vegetation, birds, and wildlife.

North of St. George's, the road hugs the leeward coast, passing fishing villages and winding along the edge of magnificent tropical scenery on mountains that drop almost straight into the sea and hide little coves with black-sand beaches.

Grenada is one of the world's largest producers of nutmeg and just about every fruit known in the Tropics. In Gouyave you can visit the country's major nutmeg processing station. The staff at nearby Dougaldston Estates, a nutmeg plantation, have a wealth of information on the cultivation of spices and tropical fruits.

In the same vicinity Concord Falls, a triple-stage cascade set deep in the central mountains, is about an hour's hike; it requires some rock hopping, but your reward is a lovely waterfall that drops through jungle-thick vegetation to a pool where you can enjoy a refreshing swim.

Information
Grenada Tourist Board, Grenada Board of Tourism, P.O. Box 1668,
Lake Worth, FL 33460; (800) 927-9554, (561) 588-8176;
Fax: (561) 588-7267; www.grenadagrenadines.com
(Also see Mount Cinnamon on p. 305 in On the Horizon.)

THE CALABASH HOTEL

St. George's, Grenada, W.I.

Having a private maid prepare your breakfast isn't a bad way to start a vacation—and she'll serve it to you in bed, if you like.

Since it opened in 1961, the Calabash has been the last word in British gentility, attracting lords and ladies and an occasional prince or princess, who fly in on their private planes. Once they've checked in, though, no one (except the staff, of course) will know who they are or see them being treated differently from you or me. This is true though times and owners have changed.

In 1989, when the new, young British owner, Leo Garbutt, took over, he updated, upgraded, and expanded the rather staid resort, making it much better (would you believe exciting?), but without diluting any of its grace. Among the improvements were more units with private pools and the addition of a keyhole-shaped swimming pool in a quiet area near the main building, which has men's and women's restrooms and showers. The tennis court was lighted, and the beach bar moved to a more convenient location at the center of the beach.

The resort has regular live entertainment and a full range of water sports, which are included in the room rates. Telephones have been installed in all rooms but—as the management is quick to tell you—you may have yours removed if you consider it a nuisance. Now that's gentility. Television has been added, too, but you can close the cabinet door and never look at it, if you prefer. A computer with Internet is available for guests' use at no charge.

The Calabash is spread over eight landscaped acres overlooking a quiet bay.

Accommodations, each named for a tropical flower that grows in the gardens, are in one- and two-story cottages arranged in a half moon around a broad, open green with the main building at the center. Each of the spacious, airy units has a bedroom and a bathroom, sitting area, and patio or balcony. In the older, cozier units, where the decor has been updated in soft green and aqua decor, retaining a Caribbean feeling, the bedrooms and sitting rooms are separate. In the newer units they are combined in one spacious room and sport a contemporary look.

Adjacent to or, in some cases, within each unit is a small pantry where the maid appointed to your room prepares your breakfast each morning.

In the newer two-story units, six on the ground floor have small, private pools; those on the second floor have whirlpools. They also have pitched roofs, which make them seem all the larger and airier. Two units with pools were specially designed to accommodate handicapped guests.

Each unit has a garden view leading down to the sandy beach, where you will find lounge chairs and lots of shade trees as well as a beach bar and a casual restaurant where lunch is available.

The most spacious accommodation is the Thorneycroft Suite, named for Lord Peter and Lady Carla Thorneycroft, who have spent many holidays at the Calabash. The suite, which has more than 2,000 square feet, has a large master bedroom leading out to a balcony, a huge marble-tiled bathroom with double shower and large double whirlpool bath, a walk-in closet, and a dressing area. A large and well-appointed lounge leads to a sundeck beside the private pool. The suite's luxurious interiors were created by Penny Barnard, a well-known designer from St. Lucia. For families that need more than one bedroom, the Thorneycroft Suite has a spiral staircase that can connect with the Calabash Suite below; the two suites can be booked as one family unit.

The Calabash has embarked on its largest venture yet, Amber Belair, a luxurious villa community next to the resort on a peninsula that marks Grenada's most southerly point. Several of the initial homes, which have set the style for the new development, were designed by the late Arne Hasselqvist, who created most of the famous posh homes on the island of Mustique. Plans for the complex include a clubhouse, tennis court, fitness center, and meeting place. Owners have access to all of the facilities of the Calabash. Some of the villas are available for rent.

Rhodes restaurant, named for the award-winning chef who designed its kitchen to his specification, created menus that favor the use of local products, and trained the staff for a year under the direction of a top Rhodes chef based at the resort.

The hotel manager invites all the guests to cocktails at the beach bar on Wednesday, and there is live entertainment on different nights. Despite the assorted royalty that drops in, do not get the idea that the Calabash is a posh pleasure palace. Heaven forbid. It's anything but.

The Calabash is unpretentious and understated. It appeals to a wide range of visitors: couples, honeymooners, families with children, and nature lovers. Most come from the United States and Britain, but you'll find a sprinkling of Germans and other Europeans. All appreciate the quality that has long made the Calabash one of the best in the Caribbean.

The Calabash Hotel ***

P.O. Box 382, L'Anse Aux Epines Beach, St. George's, Grenada, W.I.
Phone: (473) 444-4334, (800) 528-5835; Fax: (473) 444-5050; e-mail: calabash@caribsurf.com

Owner: Leo Garbutt

General Manager: Clive Barnes

Open: Year-round

Credit Cards: All major

U.S. Reservations: Direct to hotel

Deposit: Three nights; twenty-one days cancellation

Minimum Stay: Seven nights during Christmas and February

Arrival/Departure: Upon request, hotel can send transportation to airport to pick up guests

Distance from Airport: (Point Salines Airport) 3 miles; taxi one-way, $16

Distance from St. George's: 5 miles; taxi one-way, $17

Accommodations: 30 suites, all suites have whirlpool baths (1 Thorneycroft suite with private pool; 7 private plunge pool suites; 10 superior suites; 6 West side suites; 6 Whirlpool suites)

Amenities: Air-conditioning, ceiling fans; most baths with tub and shower, hair dryer, toiletries; telephone; safe; minibar, CD player; tea/coffeemaker; iron/ironing board; nightly turndown, room service 11:00 a.m.–8:30 p.m.; concierge; boutique; repeat guests greeted with fruit basket and bottle of wine; television, CD player; small library; Internet

Electricity: 220 volts

Fitness Facilities/Spa Services: Fitness center with exercise equipment; aromatherapy, and other spa treatments available for fee

Sports: Freshwater swimming pool; free use of lighted tennis court, racquets, balls; snooker and billiards room; shuffleboard and beach boules; snorkeling equipment, Sunfish, kayaks, windsurfing, and other water sports from beach concessionaire for charge; fishing, diving, yacht charters, and hiking with guide in national park arranged; free green fees at Grenada Golf Club

Dress Code: Casual

Children: Over twelve years old in February, all ages other times; cribs, high chairs; babysitters

Meetings: No

Day Visitors: With reservations

Handicapped Facilities: Yes

Packages: Honeymoon, wedding, romantic escapes, gourmet getaways

Rates: Per person, daily, MAP. *High Season* (mid December–early April): $415–$625. *Low Season:* $250–$335

Service Charge: 10 percent

Government Tax: 8 percent

LA SOURCE
Pink Gin Beach, St. George's, Grenada, W.I.

Located on the southeast corner of the island on forty hillside acres overlooking Pink Gin Beach, La Source was all but blown away during a hurricane in 2004. After extensive rebuilding, refurbishing, and upgrading, this all-inclusive resort reopened in February 2008. La Source, which combines the facilities for an active beach vacation with pampering of body and mind, has developed a loyal following over the years and while the same welcoming atmosphere will greet returning guests, a completely new look awaits.

Designed by Miami-based architect and interior designer Lane Pettigrew, the resort reflects Grenada's British and French heritage with West Indian and Victorian–inspired architecture and colonial-style interior decor upgraded and modernized by the resort owners. The French connection is in the name, inspired by *La Source,* a painting by the nineteenth-century neoclassic French artist Jean Ingres, known for his portraits and nudes. The resort's signature image—a female figure similar to that of a woman bathing in Ingres's painting, is incorporated into the design of the outdoor tiles and elsewhere throughout the resort.

The layout, set around a central courtyard with fountains and sculpture, is meant to suggest a West Indian colonial village; the main building would have been the governor's residence, complete with a clock tower permanently set at 5:10 p.m., the traditional time of the governor's cocktail hour in colonial days. The resort's one hundred guest rooms were renovated extensively and all now have large, contemporary marble bathrooms and new air-conditioning units, among other upgrades.

Four restaurants provide guests with a variety of dining options. Oscar's is a new open-air beach restaurant and tropical lounge serving lunch and dinner with a la carte choices. Guests can also enjoy breakfast, lunch, and dinner at the Garden Restaurant and dinner and a la carte options at the Great House. The Café Deli offers soups, salads, sandwiches, and other lunch choices. Room service for continental breakfast is available. Also, as part of the rebuilding, three new state-of-the-art kitchens were installed.

La Source rates include three meals plus afternoon tea, red and white wines at lunch and dinner, and all beverages (except for champagne and wines ordered from the wine list), as well as taxes and gratuities. Tipping is not allowed.

The Oasis Spa, a focal point of the La Source experience, has been completely transformed and now includes seventeen treatment rooms, including three wet rooms, two Vichy shower rooms, and one hydro-tub, in addition to a new salon with cushy manicure and pedicure chairs. Prior to the spa's reopening, thirty new spa technicians completed an intensive training program. The resort's rates include one prearranged spa treatment per day, following the day of arrival. These body and beauty treatments from the "Mind, Body, and Spirit" program range from facials and massages to body wraps and exfoliating polishes. You can also take more unconventional treatments such as reflexology, Reiki, and Vichy shower at an additional cost.

La Source's all-inclusive program includes a dive each day for certified divers, an introductory dive course for first timers, and a variety of sports, such as tennis, par-three golf, volleyball, fencing, archery, windsurfing, sailing, and more. The new Dive and Watersports Center has a new boat for diving and waterskiing. A regular schedule of yoga and tai chi classes, as well as special ones taught by masters in these fields, are available during designated weeks throughout the year.

An expanded deck and boardwalk surround the swimming pool and whirlpool, providing additional room for sunbathers. The pool and beach area look out at a spectacular view of Grenada's coast—all the way to St. George's, the capital. A larger, redesigned fitness center and a new retail boutique round out the updates.

La Source is almost within walking distance of Point Salines International Airport; guests are met on arrival.

La Source

Pink Gin Beach, P.O. Box 852, St. George's, Grenada, W.I.

Phone: (473) 444-2556, (800) 544-2883; Fax: (473) 444-2561; www .theamazingholiday.com; email: lasource@ theamazingholiday.com

Owner/Management: Liberty Club Limited

General Manager: Adolf Fratton

Open: Year-round

Credit Cards: All major

U.S. Reservations: La Source Vacations, 10 West Broadway,#5E, Long Beach, NY 11561; (888) 527-0044, (516) 432-5388; Fax: (516) 432-5488; email: LaSourceVacations@hotmail.com

UK Reservations: Advantage Management Group, Suite 200 Parkway House, Sheen Lane, London SW148LS; 0870-220-2341, 20-8487-9881; Fax: 20-8878-9124; e-mail lasource@amgltd.biz

Deposit: 30 percent, forty-two to thirty-one days cancellation; 60 percent, thirty to sixteen days; 75 percent, fifteen to six days; 100 percent, five to zero days.

Minimum Stay: None

Arrival/Departure: Transfer included

Distance from Airport: Five minutes from Point Salines International Airport, taxi one-way, $8

Distance from St. George's: 7 miles; taxi one-way, $20

Accommodations: 90 rooms and 10 suites, all with terrace, most with ocean views, in three buildings of three and four stories; furnished with two double or king-size beds

Amenities: Air-conditioning, ceiling fan, telephone, clock radio, minifridge, walk-in closets, marble bath with tub and shower, hair dryer, makeup mirror, bathrobe, basket of toiletries; room service for continental breakfast; nightly turndown service; boutique, hair salon. No television.

Electricity: 220 volts; rooms have one 110 volt outlet

Fitness Facilities/Spa Services: Weight training, jogging, hikes, aerobics, stretch and dance classes, yoga, tai chi, stress management—all with instruction; personal trainer. Oasis Spa: Loofah rubs, body and foot massage, seaweed wraps, facials, reflexology, and aromatherapy. Beauty salon extra charge.

Sports: Free-form pool, large whirlpool; two lighted tennis courts; fencing; croquet; ping-pong; archery; volleyball; golf (nine-hole, nonregulation, par three); snorkeling, waterskiing, windsurfing, sailing—all with instruction; complimentary introductory dive course; PADI certification additional cost

Dress Code: Sports/beachwear by daytime; casually elegant in evenings

Children: Minimum age sixteen except June 20–September 8, when minimum age is ten years. Children age ten to twelve pay 50 percent of rate, if sharing room with parents.

Meetings: None

Day Visitors: Day pass for 10:30 a.m.–6:30 p.m., $100 includes lunch, drinks, and scheduled activities. Spa treatments subject to availability and priced separately. Dinner Pass: $100 includes dinner, drinks, and scheduled nightly entertainment

Packages: Weddings complimentary for guests staying seven nights minimum. Honeymooners receive a couple's massage, complimentary bottle of sparkling wine, and fresh flowers.

Handicapped Facilities: No

Rates: Per person, daily, all-inclusive. *High Season* (December 27–early January; late January–mid-March): $320–$420. (January 3–20): $290–$370. *Low Season* (mid-March–mid-December): $200–$390

Service Charge: Included

Government/Hotel Tax: Included

SPICE ISLAND BEACH RESORT
St. George's, Grenada, W.I.

In 2004, after a hurricane devastated the island of Grenada, leaving most of its homes and hotels badly damaged, Spice Island Beach Resort closed for sixteen months to rebuild. It reopened in December 2005, after a $12 million reconstruction, as practically a new resort and better than ever. In the process, all the accommodations and facilities were upgraded and updated, starting with the elegant new entrance, which sets the upscale tone for the resort.

Spice Island operates as an all-inclusive resort with rates covering accommodations, three meals and afternoon tea, bar service, and more. A landscaped swimming pool near the beach was enhanced, and there's a new, expanded full-service spa housed in its own separate building, a Cybex fitness center, a children's center, and a business center with Internet access. The upscale boutiques—one for women's fashion and one for men—were also enlarged. The central building housing the dining room, bar, open-air terrace, reception area, lounge, and kitchen was completely redesigned and rebuilt and is now open from the entrance to the sea.

Spice opened in 1961 as a rustic, laid-back inn that defined the very notion of a Caribbean escape. In 1988 it was bought by some local businessmen headed by managing director Sir Royston Hopkin, K.C.M.G., who was the 1991 Caribbean Hotelier of the Year and honored by Queen Elizabeth II in 1995. Spice, now a Hopkin family enterprise, is more than triple its original size.

The Spice welcome begins at the front door, where you are greeted upon arrival with a cooling tropical fruit drink or a Grenada-style rum punch. It comes with a generous sprinkling of nutmeg—Spice's friendly reminder that Grenada, the Spice Island, is the world's second largest producer of nutmeg.

Spice has seven types of guest rooms, ranging from 620 to 1,500 square feet. Stretching along the beach on both sides of the main building and the pool are one-story cottages, which were rebuilt from the ground up and are fabulous. Each houses four Sea Grape junior suites; two also have one master suite. The master and junior can be combined into a two-bedroom suite. The junior suites, with handsome contemporary Caribbean decor, have a large bedroom with a king bed (and the most comfortable pillows I've ever had in a hotel). The room extends to a sizeable

seating area furnished with a day bed-style sofa that turns into a double bed. The room opens onto a patio, only a few steps from the beach. The huge marble bathroom has a double sink, large whirlpool tub, and a louvered window that looks out to the bedroom and the beach. Behind them are the honeymooners' favorites: suites with private pools a step away from a bedroom with a king-size bed. To the left of the main building and also set back from the beach are two-story bungalows whose ground-level suites have plunge pools. All accommodations are air-conditioned and have ceiling fans, flat-screen cable television, DVD players, CD-clock radio, minibar, hair dryer, iron and ironing board, direct-dial phone with Internet access, safe, and coffee/tea maker. Further enhancing the luxury, guests in all suites sleep on fine Frette linens and enjoy Molton Brown toiletries.

The pool suites, spacious and airy with marble floors and glass doors, are furnished in more regal decor than the beachfront ones. All rooms have whirlpools big enough for two, found either in a tiny garden atrium open to the sky or in a corner of a large bathroom with a skylight. Four are ultraposh Royal Collection Pool suites have pools, which are surrounded by high walls and large enough for laps—albeit short laps—and secluded enough for skinny-dipping.

The Royal Collection suites, thought to be the only ones with a large, redwood cedar in-room sauna at a Caribbean resort, have another unusual feature—a canopied fitness area, set in the gardens, with an exercise bike. Each has a sundeck with chaise lounges and patio table, along with a flower garden. Each suite, measuring 1,500 square feet, has a separate living room, a bedroom with a king-size bed, and a marble tile bathroom with double sinks and double whirlpools. They also have a stocked minibar, flat-screen television, music center, phone, coffeemaker, hair dryer, safe, ceiling fan, and iron and ironing board. Breakfast and lunch are served in the open-air beachside restaurant or from room service, which is available from 7:45 a.m. to 10:00 p.m. Dinner in Oliver's Restaurant is a five-course menu with two or three choices of continental and local dishes. On Friday night a steel band livens up the evening and a Caribbean buffet highlights the most popular native dishes. On Sunday, guests enjoy a barbecue lunch buffet. During the winter season there is music for dancing several nights of the week.

Guests at Spice spend lazy days on the 1,200 feet of beach, occasionally cooling off in the languid waters or reading and dozing under leafy sea grape trees. Or they can luxuriate in Janissa's Spa, where they will find a full range of face, hair, and body treatments. If they are a bit more ambitious, they can try the Cybex equipment in the fitness center, or enjoy tennis, water sports, a game of golf, or a bicycle ride.

To maintain the setting's serenity, motorized water sports are not available in this section of Grand Anse Beach.

The Nutmeg Pod is the children's center, open daily from 9:00 a.m. to 5:00 p.m. for kids age three to twelve and up. It has a weekly schedule of organized activities.

In keeping with the resort's impressive environmentally conscious stewardship, Spice Island becomes a completely non-smoking resort in December 2008. Already, its accommodations are nonsmoking; the new move will include the restaurant, bar, and all indoor/outdoor facilities.

Spice's inclusive rates cover accommodations; breakfast, lunch, and dinner daily; afternoon tea; house wine at dinner; non-motorized water sports such as snorkeling, kayaking, and Hobie Cat sailing; tennis; golf greens fees at the Grenada Golf Club; and concierge and room service.

I have always enjoyed my stays at Spice and found the service eager to please but running on Caribbean time, that is, at a stroll. With the latest rebuilding and upgrading, especially of the beachfront suites, you will not find a more comfortable, attractive, and delightfully serene place in the Caribbean to enjoy a vacation.

Spice Island Beach Resort **** 🌿
Grand Anse, P.O. Box 6, St. George's, Grenada, W.I.
Phone: (473) 444-4258; Fax: (473) 444-4807; e-mail: spiceisl@spiceisle.com; www.spiceislandbeachresort.com

Owner/Managing Director: Sir Royston O. Hopkin, K.C.M.G.

Resort Manager: Brian Hardy

Open: Year-round

Credit Cards: All major

U.S. Reservations: (800) 44-UTELL

Deposit: Three nights in winter; one night in summer; thirty days cancellation prior to arrival, mid-December–mid-April, except during Christmas holidays and February when it is forty-five days, fourteen days in summer

Minimum Stay: Seven nights Christmas holidays and February; none in summer (mid-April–mid-December)

Arrival/Departure: Transfer service not available due to Taxi Association regulations

Distance from Airport: (Pointe Salines Airport) 4 miles; taxi one-way, $16 day; $20 after 6:00 p.m.

Distance from St. George's: 6 miles; taxi one-way, $20

Accommodations: 64 rooms and suites, most beachfront and ocean view, all with whirlpools; 17 suites with private swimming pools (six luxury pool suites, seven private-pool suites, four royal private-pool suites), each with king-size beds

Amenities: Air-conditioning, ceiling fans; whirlpool tub, shower, hair dryer, basket of toiletries; television, telephone with Internet access; clock-radio; stocked minibar, coffeemaker; iron and ironing board; safe; nightly turndown service; room service for meals and beverages; boutique; Internet access

Electricity: 220 volts

Sports: Tennis court, balls, racquets; snorkeling gear, Hobie Cats, kayaks, windsurfers provided; boating, diving, fishing, hiking arranged

Fitness Facilities/Spa Services: See text

Dress Code: Casual by day; elegantly casual in evening

Children: All ages; none in pool suites year-round. Children's center for age three and older; cribs; babysitters

Meetings: Up to sixty-five people; business center with Internet access and business equipment

Day Visitors: Yes

Handicapped Facilities: Limited

Packages: Honeymoon, wedding, renewal of vows

Rates: Two people, daily, All-inclusive. **High Season** (mid-December–mid-April): $750–$1,990. **Low Season:** $600–$1,265. Children and single rates are available.

Service Charge: 10 percent

Government Tax: 8 percent

TWELVE DEGREES NORTH
St. George's, Grenada, W.I.

Joe Gaylord, who has lived in Grenada since 1967, gave up the real estate business in New York for his patch of paradise. He created Twelve Degrees North—which takes its name from Grenada's latitude—out of the frustration of not finding the resort he wanted for his vacation. His nest is the most unhotel hotel you are ever likely to find. Joe believes it is unique in the Caribbean, and perhaps it is. It's also one of the Caribbean's best bargains.

The small complex has only eight units of one and two bedrooms. They are situated in four two-story buildings that are interconnected by steps. The rooms have terra-cotta floors and are decorated with rattan furniture.

The bedrooms have a king or two twin beds joined by a king-size headboard. The two-bedroom suites have two baths and large living rooms. The suites on the second floor have pitched ceilings, which make them seem more spacious. All the units have kitchens and terraces with picture-postcard views of the Caribbean; all face west, making your terrace the ideal perch at sunset for enjoying the rum punch you will find in your refrigerator upon arrival. And that's not all you'll find in it.

Your refrigerator and pantry will be fully stocked with beverages and food—chicken, fish, fruit, vegetables, bread, and other staples— for your stay. The reason for this horn of plenty is one of the features that make Twelve Degrees so unusual: Namely, for your entire stay you will have a personal attendant (a combination maid, cook, and housekeeper) assigned exclusively to your suite.

Joe has devised a system that seems to work like magic for them, the women attendants, and their guests. Each attendant's sole job is to care for the occupants of her unit and her unit only, year in and year out. She is available from 8:00 a.m. to 3:00 p.m. daily and will keep your room immaculate, change the linens, do your personal laundry, and cook and serve your breakfast and lunch.

If you don't want her to come as early as 8:00 a.m., it's no problem; just say so. If you don't need her to hang around to serve you lunch, just tell her. She can make your lunch and leave. For the evening you are on your own, but if you would like her to prepare your dinner in advance, she will do that too. If you don't care to bother with making dinner, there are restaurants nearby.

You pay for the provisions that are stocked for you in advance of your arrival. If you do not intend to use certain items, you can tell Joe or your attendant, and they will be deducted from your bill.

You will find that these women are good cooks and are pleased to introduce you to Grenadian cuisine, but if you prefer your own style of cooking, they will prepare meals as you request.

Joe's care in selecting his location and staff extends to getting the right kind of guests—namely, ones who are suited to the quiet, intimate ambience of this resort. He does not welcome children, for example, simply because his guests do not want them around. Most people come for the tranquillity; anyone who needs activity or entertainment would definitely be in the wrong place.

Twelve Degrees North—the 12th degree north line actually runs through the property—is about as low-key and laid-back as

the Caribbean gets. It is set in a little cove on a hillside of tropical woods and gardens that slope to a small beach. A stone path leads from the cottages downhill to the beach. There you find an ample-size L-shaped freshwater pool, three hammocks, lounging chairs, a built-in gas barbecue, and a thatched hut with a self-service bar and library of well-read books. Pick a spot and spend the day. You might converse with some of the other guests around the pool or by the beach. Most will be from the States—professionals, a university professor, a stockbroker, a television producer—and most are good company.

They usually are experienced travelers who have tried many of the better-known, ritzier places in the Caribbean. They probably heard about Joe's place from a friend or their own research. They are not likely to learn about it from their travel agent, unless they have a very knowledgeable one.

To the right of the beach is a 100-foot pier with a gazebo and benches. It juts out into the sea where the water is deep enough to swim (by the beach the water is very shallow), and there's a reef for snorkeling. The use of snorkeling gear, Sunfish, and kayaks, as well as the tennis court, is included in the rate. Scuba diving and waterskiing can be arranged for a fee.

There's a 720-square-foot over-the-water sundeck. When you look up from the beach or pier, you will see Joe's home. If you think you have a wonderful view, wait until you see his. And you are likely to do so: Joe often invites guests to join him for cocktails. Most consider it the highlight of their visit. The house sits out on a point; the entire front is open to the view.

Oh, I forgot to mention: Twelve Degrees North has no office; it's in Joe's house. But if he knows you are coming, he will be standing by the driveway to greet you when you arrive. You can count on it.

Twelve Degrees North **

P.O. Box 241, St. George's, Grenada, W.I.
Phone: (473) 444-4580; Fax: same as
phone; e-mail: 12degrsn@caribsurf.com;
www.twelvedegreesnorth.com

Owner/Manager: Joe Gaylord

Open: Year-round

Credit Cards: Mastercard, Visa

U.S. Reservations: Direct to hotel

Deposit: Three nights

Minimum Stay: Seven–ten nights during
Christmas and February

Arrival/Departure: No transfer service

Distance from Airport: (Pointe Salines International Airport) 3 miles; taxi one-way, $16

Distance from St. George's: 5 miles, taxi
one-way, $18; from Grand Anse, 2 miles,
taxi one-way, $8

Accommodations: Six one-bedroom suites;
two two-bedroom suites, all with terrace,
kitchen, and twin beds or king

Amenities: Ceiling fan; kitchen; bath with
shower, basket of toiletries, hair dryer,
shampoo and conditioner dispenser; complimentary rum punch; personal maid-cook

Electricity: 220 volts

Sports: Freshwater swimming pool; use of
tennis court, snorkeling gear, kayaks, Sunfish included; scuba, fishing, waterskiing
for fee; trail hiking, birding arranged

Dress Code: Casual

Children: None under fifteen years old,
year-round

Meetings: No

Day Visitors: Not suitable

Handicapped Facilities: No

Packages: No

Rates: Two people, daily, FAP. *High Season*
(mid-December–mid-April): $250. *Low
Season:* $165. Four people in two-bedroom
unit, $425 and $275, respectively

Service Charge: 10 percent

Government Tax: 8 percent

JAMAICA

From the 7,400-foot peaks of the Blue Mountains, where the famous coffee is grown, Jamaica's terrain drops to foothills of banana groves and sugarcane fields and orchards of mangos and limes. Brilliant flowers, vivid birds, exotic fruit, gentle people whose voices lilt as though they are singing—these are the charms with which this Caribbean beauty seduces her admirers.

Jamaica, the land of reggae, is the quintessence of the Caribbean and offers diversity—in landscape and lifestyle, culture and cuisine, sports and attractions—that few islands can match. There are waterfalls to climb, mountains to hike, trails to ride, golf, tennis, polo, diving, fishing, plus attractions that are unique to Jamaica, such as rafting on the Rio Grande and trips into the mountainous Cockpit country that once sheltered the Maroons, runaway slaves who defied British rule.

Jamaica, 144 miles long and 49 miles wide, is located 90 miles south of Cuba. The third largest Caribbean island, Jamaica was called Xaymaca, meaning "land of wood and water," by the Arawaks who populated the island when Columbus arrived in 1494.

The British took Jamaica in 1655 and stayed for the next 300 years. Although the colonial trappings disappeared on the road to nationhood since independence in 1962, vestiges of the British, such as cricket and croquet, tea parties and polo, are still very much a part of the Jamaican fabric, incongruous as they may seem.

If its British past was the stock for the Jamaican bouillabaisse, the traders, slaves, and settlers who came to the island were the ingredients that created a culture as diverse as its scenery. Jamaica's influence in art, dance, and music extends far beyond the Caribbean.

Jamaica's diversity enables every visitor to find a niche. From the laid-back beaches of Negril on the west to the quiet coves and busy resorts along the 100-mile northern coast to Port Antonio on the east, there are resorts to suit most travelers, regardless of interest and budget.

Information
Jamaica Tourist Board, 5201 Blue Lagoon Drive, FL 33126;
(800) 233-4582, (305) 665-0557; www.visitjamaica.com

STRAWBERRY HILL

Kingston, Jamaica, W.I.

One of the most enchanting Caribbean havens is not on a beach but rather, it is perched high in the Blue Mountains of eastern Jamaica, where eco-green must have been invented.

Strawberry Hill is the dream-come-true of Island Records mogul Chris Blackwell, who launched Bob Marley, U2, and others to superstardom and helped create the hip image of Miami's South Beach with his art deco hotels. Set amid gardens and wooded hills at an elevation of 3,000 feet near Irish Town, Strawberry Hill is a former coffee plantation whose manor house commands one of the island's most enviable views, with the mountains over 7,000 feet as the background and the sea at your feet.

The great house, renovated to serve as the centerpiece of the hotel, has a lounge and restaurant. Its decor is designed around Island Records memorabilia dating from the company's beginning in 1962 and including its many gold records and awards as well as items from its stable of recording stars. There's a library and a small conference room for up to thirty people. Wi-Fi service is available for no charge in the common areas of the resort.

Most accommodations are found in twelve veranda-encircled one- and two-story cottages. Designed by Jamaican architect Ann Hodges in a modified gingerbread-trimmed West Indian style and painted in neutral colors, they have one- and two-bedroom cottages with beautifully finished, local wood interiors.

Rooms are furnished in country-casual fashion by Tanya Melich, a British-by-way-of-the-Bahamas designer. They feature four-poster beds and antiqued, handmade island furniture.

The cottages are positioned to take maximum advantage of their heart-stopping views. Each has a terra-cotta bathroom with recessed lights and a small kitchen nook—intended as a convenience for an early-morning or late-evening repast rather than serious cooking. If you have a hammock on your veranda, it will be hard to resist for an afternoon nap or a cocktail-hour perch to watch the sun drop into the sea and Kingston light up for the evening show.

Each accommodation can be equipped with a state-of-the-art entertainment center for enjoying videos and recordings from a stocked library. Electronic gear enables you to stay plugged into the outside world, should you need to disrupt the serenity of this very private escape. There is a television in your room and a selection of DVDs is available. You will also find a cordless phone with answering machine, a CD player with a selection of CDs, a coffeemaker, a minibar, a large writing desk (that's to lay a guilt number on writers who goof off), and heated mattress pads (can you believe it actually gets cold at night in Jamaica!) on the huge four-poster beds. These pads are set on low to prevent mildew as well as to warm guests. Huge white pillows, down-filled comforters, and sheer mosquito netting—not necessary but aesthetically pleasing—make the beds very inviting.

Wooden walkways connecting the cottages wind their way up to the manor house and its crowning glory—a 60-foot swimming pool set in gardens on the highest point of the forty-five-acre property with vistas to infinity.

The Strawberry Spa provides a wide range of treatments and services that encourage wellness. Designed by the same

Jamaican architect (Ann Hodges) as the resort, the facility is the perfect complement to the resort's idyllic setting. It utilizes natural ingredients in a variety of services, including hydrotherapy, facials, and body care, as well as Aveda massage treatments based on Ayruyedic philosophies. The first step is to determine your unique "aroma identity" and formulate a personal aroma blend, which is used in all of your treatments. In addition to massage and skin- and stress-relieving treatments, the spa has a full-service hair salon that offers manicure, pedicure, facials, and body waxing. It also organizes hiking, mountain biking, and other outdoor activities in the Blue Mountains.

Chef Kingsley McGregor creates truly unique and outstanding dishes that combine nouvelle cuisine techniques with traditional spicy Jamaican cooking; many praise it as the best food in Jamaica. Chef Kingsley's signature dishes include grilled snapper, jerk-style lamb rack, and homemade ice creams. Herbs and spices grown in the resort's vegetable garden include spearmint, lemongrass, dill, and cilantro, and a newly planted tropical orchard yields mangoes, Otaheite apples, naseberry, pomegranate, jack fruit, and sweet sop.

Meals can be enjoyed in the sun-dappled, high-ceilinged main dining room, which manages to be formal yet casual and relaxing all at the same time. Continental breakfasts (huge plates of fresh fruit, toast, and Blue Mountain coffee) are served, weather permitting, on the covered veranda that's just a few steps away. The restaurant, open from 7:00 a.m. until 10:00 p.m., serves all three meals, as well as high tea and Jamaican Sunday brunch. Room service is available from 7:00 a.m. to midnight. The grounds at Strawberry Hill are interesting and historic as the property was a coffee farm since around 1890. To date, the resort has catalogued 350 endemic and exotic plant species. The main canopy is of Juniper (*Juniperus barbadea*) lining the old driveway with specimens of Cedar (*Cedrela odoratissma*), Eucalyptus (*Eucalyptus nicolae*) and Mango (*Mangifera indica*). The gardens are an ongoing process as only four acres out of a possible ten acres of terraced land have been defined, along with a further 35 acres of slopes.

Strawberry Hill is an all-inclusive resort and includes all meals, beverages, and a customized minibar stocked daily with juices, bottled water, and herbal waters; taxes and service charges are additional.

Although Strawberry Hill is 5 miles from Kingston, the drive can take thirty minutes or more because of the narrow mountain roads. From the Kingston Airport on the far side of the city, you need to allow for at least a fifty-minute drive, depending on the traffic. Those who do not care to make the drive can arrive by helicopter (a seven-minute ride)—if cost is no object.

If you fall in love with Strawberry Hill and can't bear to leave, ask about monthly rates—particularly if you're a writer.

Strawberry Hill *** 🍃
Irish Town, Jamaica, W.I.
Phone: (876) 944-8400; Fax: (876) 944-8408; e-mail: reservations@islandoutpost .com; www.islandoutpost.com

Owner: Island Outpost

General Managers: Paula and Jonathan Surtees

Open: Year-round

Credit Cards: All major

U.S. Reservations: (800) OUTPOST

Deposit: Determined by length of stay

Minimum Stay: Three nights

Arrival/Departure: Upon request, hotel can arrange transfers by car for a fee; helicopter service available (seven-minute flight) for fee (very costly)

Distance from Airport: (Kingston Airport) 15 miles (fifty-minute drive on mountain roads)

Distance from Kingston: 5 miles (thirty or more minutes on mountain roads)

Accommodations: 12 villas with 16 rooms (four studio suites; four one- and two-bedroom villas); five kings, nine queens, two twins; all with balcony or veranda; some with kitchen

Amenities: Bath with tub and multihead shower; coffeemaker, minibar; nightly turn-down service, room service; telephone, hair dryer, television, CD player/DVD

Electricity: 110 volts

Fitness Facilities/Spa Services: See text

Sports: Hiking; mountain biking in Blue Mountains; sightseeing excursions, coffee plantation tours; swimming pool

Dress Code: Casual

Children: Allowed but no programs or facilities

Meetings: Small conference room for up to thirty people; state-of-the-art audiovisual equipment

Day Visitors: Welcome for lunch and dinner with reservations. Visitors may tour property; see manager at front desk upon arrival.

Handicapped Facilities: Not recommended for handicapped persons

Packages: Honeymoon, wedding, spa

Rates: Per room, for two people, per night, seasonal, starting at: $790 for one bedroom; $1,190 for deluxe villa. Monthly rates available; inquire

Service Charge and Government Tax: 18.25 percent

HALF MOON
Montego Bay, Jamaica, W.I.

The entrance leading to the porte cochere is a long, flower-festooned driveway, a wedding cake of arches and filigree wrapped in bouquets of exuberant tropical flowers. It's so pretty that you barely notice you've passed security gates. Walls are camouflaged with flowered hedges to protect this fairyland of snow-white villas and gazebos.

From the porte cochere you are greeted by a large marble-paved lobby open all the way to the sea. This elegant lobby, furnished with Queen Anne–style mahogany chairs and other pieces, has a front desk with computerized check-in facilities and

a private check-in lounge for VIP guests. Beyond is a lobby bar and open-air lounge next to the Seagrape Terrace, the main indoor-outdoor restaurant by the sea.

Set in carefully tended lawns and gardens at the edge of a 2-mile stretch of white-sand beach, Half Moon is one of the most complete resorts in the Caribbean. Since it opened in 1954, it has grown from a cluster of cottages around Half Moon Bay—truly a perfect crescent—to a vast resort spread over 400 acres. It boasts a wide range of accommodations and extensive sports facilities, including a championship golf course, tennis and squash complex, and fitness center, along with an array of activities and services.

Half Moon marked its fiftieth anniversary with a multimillion-dollar renovation, demolishing the sixty-six-room Hibiscus Wing to make way for sixty-eight brand-new luxury rooms and suites. Its plantation-style buildings house spacious guest rooms, most with sitting areas, large suites, and baronial one- and two-story villas with patios and balconies. The newest accommodations are furnished with a contemporary Caribbean theme and have large, modern bathrooms, large verandahs, dataport/Internet access, minibar, television/VCR, and electronic safe, among other signature amenities. The villas have kitchens, large tiled bathrooms, and separate dressing areas; some have private or semiprivate pools. Each of the thirty-two Royal Villas, the most luxurious of the accommodations, has a private pool. They offer privacy, but they are quite a distance from the main restaurant and bar. Two golf carts come with each villa, making it easy to cover the distance. The villas also come with a cook, butler, and housekeeper. There is a grocery shop in the hotel's shopping arcade.

Throughout, from the lobby to the guest rooms and air-conditioned meeting rooms, British colonial architecture harmonizes with English country house interiors, using furniture made in Jamaica. Most rooms have four-poster beds.

The large, tree-shaded Seagrape Terrace restaurant and its breezy bar directly by the beach are the center of activity throughout the day. In the evening the setting, especially pretty for candlelit dining under the stars, offers a wide selection of continental and Caribbean-Jamaican cuisine. Next to the Terrace is Il Giardino, serving Italian cuisine.

The Sugar Mill, on the hillside above Half Moon, has an enchanting garden setting next to a 200-year-old waterwheel. This gourmet restaurant offers its own original Caribbean haute cuisine.

Half Moon's beach is not deep, but it is long. Swimmers also have a choice of four large freshwater pools; as part of the renovations, the main pool by the new Hibiscus wing was extended. Guests in some villas enjoy one of the seventeen private or semi-private pools. Snorkeling, scuba diving, sailing, windsurfing, and deep-sea fishing (all at additional charge) are available from the water-sports center. The resort, long a popular venue for weddings, has added a new open-air interdenominational wedding chapel on Sunrise Beach.

Half Moon's beautiful eighteen-hole championship golf course, designed by Robert Trent Jones, is one of Jamaica's best. Built on undulating terrain in the foothills and by the sea, the 7,115-yard, par-seventy-two course is made difficult by the tricky breezes that blow in off the ocean. The last renovations encompassed the golf pro shop and created a custom-built teaching academy.

In 2007 the Fern Tree Spa at Half Moon, housed in the luxury villa for which it is named, opened. The $4 million project also included converting other accommodations into six beachfront spa suites. Each suite has a large bedroom, sitting area, and oversize bathroom, along with a seaview patio with an outdoor soaking tub and shower and a studio for en-suite treatments or yoga.

The spa introduced a Spa Elder versed in the art of holistic healing, who created a treatment menu that reflects traditional remedies and current spa techniques. Treatment rooms are set in tropical gardens and can be enclosed or open to a private garden terrace. A couples massage room has a private patio with dipping pool. The spa will have a relaxing lounge, hydrotherapy swimming pool, yoga pavilion, and several water features.

Half Moon's fitness center has been upgraded and expanded with the latest exercise equipment; a personal trainer is available. Yoga and aerobics classes are offered daily. A championship tennis pavilion adjoins the tennis complex, which has squash and tennis courts. There are jogging and biking paths and horseback-riding trails.

The newly built children's center, called the Anancy Children's Village at Half Moon, is centered around the Jamaican folk hero, Anancy. It is attended by a staff of trained counselors and is open daily. Each of four age groups has its own playhouse and a center facility has a kitchen where kids learn to make cookies and other items. It offers arts and crafts, nature walks, and other activities. It has a swimming pool, swings, tennis courts, playhouses, sandboxes, and a duck pond.

Half Moon is the very definition of barefoot elegance, combining a certain glamour and style with a laid-back Caribbean ambience. Guests are the most international you'll find at any of Jamaica's resorts: British and European princes and princesses—not to mention Hollywood ones—captains of industry, and sportsmen as well as business-meeting participants and Japanese honeymooners. Somehow it all seems to fit together.

Half Moon ****
P.O. Box 80, Rose Hall, Jamaica, W.I.
Phone: (876) 953-2211; Fax: (876) 953-2731; e-mail: reservations@halfmoon.com; www.halfmoon.com

Owner: Half Moon Bay Ltd.

Managing Director: Richard Whitfield

Open: Year-round

Credit Cards: All major

U.S. Reservations: Direct to hotel (twenty-four-hour service), (800) 626-0592

Deposit: Three nights

Minimum Stay: Fourteen nights during Christmas/New Year's

Arrival/Departure: Transfer service arranged for fee

Distance from Airport: (Montego Bay Airport) 5 miles; taxi one-way, $20

Distance from Montego Bay: 7 miles; taxi one-way, $30

Accommodations: 398 units (34 superior rooms; 119 deluxe, junior, and imperial suites; 60 royal suites with private pools; 32 five- to seven-bedroom villas, all with private pool and terrace); all doubles with two double beds or kings

Amenities: Air-conditioning, ceiling fans; direct-dial telephone, television; safe; bath with tub and shower (some with bidet, too), hair dryer, basket of toiletries; bathrobe in royal suites; minibar or refrigerator, kitchen in villas; nightly turndown service, room service 7:00 a.m.–midnight

Electricity: 110/220 volts

Fitness Facilities/Spa Services: Fitness center and spa (see text)

Sports: Three large freshwater swimming pools, forty-nine private or semiprivate pools, children's pool; four squash courts (lighted), thirteen Laykold tennis courts (all lighted), free use, lessons, equipment for fee; windsurfing, Sunfish, diving, snorkeling, guided horseback riding for fee; 50 percent discount on golf for hotel guests; pro, pro shop, equipment, caddies, carts for fee; bikes for rent

Dress Code: Casual by day, but long-sleeved shirts after 6:00 p.m. in winter; informal in summer, but shorts, T-shirts, jeans not allowed at dinner

Children: All ages; cribs, high chairs; Children's Center with playground and supervised activities; babysitters; children's menus and discounts

Meetings: Up to 1,000 people

Day Visitors: Welcome

Handicapped Facilities: Yes

Packages: Golf, honeymoon, wedding; Platinum (all-inclusive)

Rates: Per person, daily, EP. *High Season* (mid-December–mid-April): $400–$1,650. *Low Season:* $250–$1,100. For Royal Villa rates, inquire

Service Charge: Included

Government Tax: Included

THE RITZ-CARLTON GOLF & SPA RESORT, ROSE HALL, JAMAICA
Montego Bay, Jamaica, W.I.

Located east of Montego Bay in the Rose Hall plantation area on Jamaica's north coast, the Ritz-Carlton Golf & Spa Resort, Rose Hall, Jamaica opened in late 2000. The beachfront resort, owned by an affiliate of the Rollins Group of Wilmington, Delaware, is fifteen minutes from Sangster International Airport in Montego Bay and within easy reach of the Shoppes at Rose Hall and Half Moon Shopping Village.

The layout, which fronts 1,500 feet of prime beach, includes the main building with a spacious lobby, looking out to the gardens and sea, and four separate wings with guest rooms overlooking the gardens or sea. The off-white stucco buildings with rust-colored roofs frame the swimming pool and the resort's tropical gardens and fountains. Arched doorways, vaulted ceilings, tall columns, and open-air spaces are architectural features throughout the hotel, which together with the British-colonial interior decor reflect the style of Jamaica's historic plantation homes. Over two years in two phases, the resort got a multimillion-dollar renovation to all guest

rooms, meeting rooms, lobby and lounges, and spa and fitness center.

All guest rooms and suites have private, covered balconies with balustrade fronts. Tropical floral prints, mahogany bedposts, and rattan furniture are elements in the casually elegant decor. All rooms are equipped with complimentary Internet access and have flat-screen plasma television, DVD/CD player, gourmet coffeemaker, and minibar. Bathrooms with white marble floors and walls have double sinks in a long white marble counter with the usual array of Ritz-Carlton toiletries, hair dryer, and separate shower stall, tub, and toilet.

The Ritz-Carlton Club, accessed by elevator key only, has a dedicated concierge and elegant, private lounge where complimentary food and beverages are offered five times daily along with personalized concierge service. It has thirty-three rooms, including two for handicapped, three suites, and the Presidential Suite.

The resort's eighteen-hole, 6,800-yard championship golf course, White Witch, is named after the famed storybook, *The*

White Witch of Rose Hall, by Herbert G. de Lesser. Designed by Robert Von Hagge and Associates, the course is situated across more than 200 acres of lush green mountainsides and rolling country with sixteen holes embracing dramatic views of the Caribbean Sea and several holes with water hazards. The clubhouse has an open-air restaurant with a 1,700-square-foot veranda and takes in views of the golf course, the ocean, and the mountains. White Witch has a resident pro, pro shop, and separate men's and ladies' locker rooms.

The Ritz-Carlton's outdoor swimming pool area, located between the central gardens and the beach, is crowded with lounge chairs. There is a small Jacuzzi hidden in the foliage near the pool. A walkway from the pool area leads to the beach where a variety of water sports is available. In another area of the grounds, you find two tennis courts and a tennis pavilion with a juice bar and a tennis pro available for group or individual lessons.

The spa and fitness center, one of the resort's most popular amenities, has eleven treatment rooms, newly adorned with beautifully painted murals of the blue sky on the ceiling. The spa offers a new menu of island-inspired treatments featuring local ingredients, plant extracts, and essential oils, such as Jamaican Coffee Scrub and Sugarcane Body Polish. It also offers the full array of body treatments including deep-tissue massage, reflexology, shiatsu, and Ritz-Carlton's signature facials and facials for men.

The spa's wet rooms offer a rain-forest bath as well as scrub, seaweed, and mud therapies and wraps. Massages, facials, and wet treatments are also given in rooms designed specifically for two—couples, mothers and daughters, and siblings. Therapists are on hand to train spa guests to perform massage techniques on each other

at home. The salon offers hair and nail services for men and women.

A fitness center, which overlooks the lush tropical gardens of the West Wing, has state-of-the-art cardiovascular and weight-training equipment and new E Series treadmills and cross trainers with made-for-iPod and USB port connectors. Ladies' and men's relaxation lounges are outfitted with new wood furniture and soft plush recliners. A steam and sauna and cold plunge area, shower facilities, and full-sized lockers are also provided.

The Ritz-Carlton's dining options include Horizon for breakfast and dinner indoors in air-conditioning or on an outdoor patio, located on the lower level of the lobby overlooking the gardens. Adjacent to it is Jasmine, an adults-only restaurant, serving outstanding (but expensive), creative Asian-Jamaican fusion cuisine, an innovative concept, new to Jamaica when it was introduced; and Mangos, the casual poolside bar and restaurant with a wide selection of local and international choices for lunch and dinner. For a taste of Jamaica, The Reggae Jerk Centre offers barefoot casual dining for lunch with island specialties on the hotel's west beach, while the White Witch Restaurant takes you into the hills of the golf course to enjoy sunset cocktails, lunch, or dinner on the terrace. Cohoba, the lobby lounge and outdoor terrace, has a rustic coffee station, where morning guests can enjoy Jamaica's famous Blue Mountain coffee. During the day, the Lounge becomes a "Kiddies Candy Corner" with goodies for young guests; and in the evening, it is transformed into a tapas bar with live local entertainment. Off the lobby are the main bar, a boutique, and the signature shop.

Revamped too, were the hotel's extensive meeting and banquet facilities, which cover 16,745 square feet and include a 10,800-square-foot ballroom and four meeting rooms. The area for outdoor functions can accommodate up to 800 people.

The hotel also manages the famous Rose Hall Great House, one of Jamaica's prime attractions, which won the Phoenix Award, the highly coveted recognition for historic preservation and conservation given annually by the Society of American Travel Writers. The lower level of the house has a bar and the manor house is available for weddings and special events.

The Ritz-Carlton brought to Jamaica a high level of service, associated heretofore in Jamaica with such top small hotels as Jamaica Inn and Round Hill, and which is apparent throughout the resort.

The Ritz-Carlton Golf & Spa Resort, Rose Hall, Jamaica ****

One Ritz-Carlton Drive, Rose Hall, St. James, Jamaica, W.I.

Phone: (876) 953-2800; www.ritzcarlton.com

Management: The Ritz-Carlton Hotel Company, L.L.C., Washington, D.C.

General Manager: Bernd Kuhlen

U.S. Reservations: Ritz-Carlton, (800) 241-3333

Deposit: Three nights; seven days cancellation

Credit Cards: Most major

Minimum Stay: Seven nights Christmas/New Year's with forty-five days full, nonrefundable prepayment

Arrival/Departure: Transfer service by Jamaica Tours Ltd., for $40 shuttle and $175 for exclusive town car round-trip

Distance from Airport: (Montego Bay) 7 miles

Accommodations: 427 guest rooms and suites with private balconies (260 king; 118 double-doubles; 51 executive suites; one Ritz-Carlton suite) with garden, pool, mountains, and partial or full ocean views; 33 Ritz-Carlton Club rooms and three suites and private lounge

Amenities: Air-conditioning; safe; stocked bar; marble bathrooms with separate shower and tub and dual sinks; cable television, digital clock/alarm radio, three telephones with dual lines and data ports, computer and fax hookups; terry bathrobes and slippers, goose-down pillows; twenty-four-hour room service; Ritz-Carlton Suite: living room/dining area, pantry, foyer with powder room, master bathroom, dressing area, walk-in closet, twice-daily maid service

Electricity: 120 volts

Fitness Facilities/Spa Services: See text

Sports: Swimming pool, water sports, tennis; golf, see text

Dress Code: Casually elegant

Day Visitors: Yes

Handicapped Facilities: Special rooms

Children: All ages; Ritz Kids program; babysitting

Meetings: Up to 800 people

Packages: Golf, wedding, spa, honeymoon, weekend, special occasion, and meal plan

Rates: Per person, double, per day, EP. *High Season* (January 4–May 15): $429–$695. *Low Season* (May 16–late November): $195–$375. Call for rates for late November–January 3. Ritz-Carlton Club rooms: inquire

Service Charge: 13 percent

Government Tax: 8.25 percent

ROUND HILL
HOTEL AND VILLAS

Montego Bay, Jamaica, W.I.

If you like the idea of sunset cocktails around the same piano Cole Porter once played, or dining on the terrace next to Ralph Lauren or the queen of Norway, Round Hill may be just the place for you.

Nothing is guaranteed, of course, but for more than five decades this hillside enclave has been one of the Caribbean's most cherished retreats for the rich and famous. It's still not a bad place to hang out, if you think Paul McCartney—a recent guest—makes good company.

You can't mistake the roadside entrance to Round Hill: white pillars with round (what else?) tops. The road along the 110-acre peninsula rounds the hill at the crest before descending quickly to the main building by the sea. Housed in a replica of the Good Hope carriage house, the reception with its white-and-black checkerboard tile floor and mahogany furnishings looks through to the gardens and sea, setting a gracious tone for arriving guests.

Round Hill was opened in 1953 by John Pringle, a prominent Jamaican who purchased the property. After selling land to some titled Europeans and affluent Americans, he created a deluxe resort by getting his celebrity friends to become shareholders and build houses there. Noël Coward, Adele Astaire, the William Paleys, and the Oscar Hammersteins were among those who flocked here in the 1950s and came to regard Round Hill as their club.

Set amid acres of marvelous gardens, the villas cascade from the hilltop to the beach. Practical as well as pretty, villas are made up of two to five separate suites. Each has a private entrance, but they share the kitchen. You can rent the entire villa or a suite and still have your privacy, along with the services of the villa staff: a cook, maid, and gardener. Twenty-three of the twenty-seven villas have private swimming pools.

The exteriors are similar in design: All are one-story stone and white clapboard structures with shingled roofs and louvered shutters and doors opening onto terraces and seaward views. Inside, no two villas are alike, but most merit a spread in *House Beautiful*. Your housekeeper prepares and serves breakfast on your private terrace, from which you can feast on Jamaica's beauty framed by the flowering gardens that surround you.

Pringle's original hotel is now the beach-front Pineapple House, a white two-story building at the water's edge. All rooms have been completely reconstructed and redesigned into large junior suites. Those on the ground floor now have screened louvered doors that open onto wooden balconies furnished with a table and two chairs. Rooms on the second floor do not have balconies but they have high-pitched roofs, making the rooms seem larger and airier and they enjoy unobstructed views of the sea and coastline. With handsome decor by Round Hill homeowner Ralph Lauren, the rooms are now all white from ceiling to their white Brazilian mat-tile floors. They are comfortably furnished with a desk and new four-poster beds (king or two doubles) made in Jamaica from big bamboo painted black and dressed in white woven spreads. A touch of color is added in bright blue or fuchsia pillows and throws. The sitting area has a coffee table and overstuffed chair and a Lauren-designed chaise longue, also in black bamboo; both are covered in sturdy white canvas. Television with VCR or DVD is available for $30 rental per night.

Pineapple House takes its name from Round Hill's logo, a Caribbean sign of welcome and a reminder that this was once a pineapple plantation. The emblem is everywhere: embossed on menu covers, shaped into lamps, and printed on all stationery. Pineapple House guests can breakfast in their rooms or at the seaside dining terrace.

Lunch for all is served alfresco on the hotel's tree-shaded dining terrace overlooking the bay. Round Hill, which recently acquired award-winning Chef Martin Maginley, one of the Caribbean's most creative chefs, can boast some of the best cuisine of any hotel in Jamaica.

Evenings at the resort begin with cocktails in the piano bar, which was decorated by Ralph Lauren. Dinner settings change from Monday night's barefoot picnic on the beach to Saturday night's dinner dance in the Georgian Pavilion. Four nights a week, dinner in the dining terrace is followed by entertainment from the resident band and local artists, with dancing under the stars. Friday is Jamaica Night, featuring a folklore group and reggae band, while a steel band livens up the Monday scene.

The Restaurant at Round Hill is an elegant new dining venue housed on a spacious terrace above the main dinning area and features creative contemporary Caribbean cuisine for which Chef Martin is known. The restaurant is open five nights a week and brunch on Sunday during the winter season. Advanced reservations are recommended.

The beautiful, large new infinity pool by Pineapple House compensates somewhat for Round Hill's small beach. A coral reef lies within swimming distance of shore, and use of snorkel gear is included in the rates

(as are use of the tennis courts and transfers to nearby golf at Tryall). The air-conditioned business center has computers with high-speed Internet access and laptop dataports.

Welcome Wharf, the resort's full-service spa, is housed in a restored eighteenth-century plantation house on ten waterfront acres. It has ten air-conditioned treatment rooms, an indoor/outdoor fitness center, and a beauty salon. The spa offers a comprehensive program of face and body treatments, using Elemis aromatherapy products. Among the services are stress-reduction aromatherapy massage; Reiki; reflexology; and body wraps.

Round Hill also has a children's program called Pineapple's Kids' Club, open daily from 9:00 a.m. to 5:00 p.m., with a full daily schedule of activities for all ages. Childen under three years old must be accompanied by a nanny anywhere else.

Times have changed, and so have the owners of the villas, but Round Hill is still glamorous in a way that's hard to find.

Round Hill Hotel and Villas ★★★★
P.O. Box 64, Montego Bay, Jamaica, W.I.
Phone: (800) 972-2159, (876) 956-7050;
Fax: (876) 956-7505; e-mail: reservations@ roundhilljamaica.com; www.roundhill jamaica.com

Owner: Round Hill Developments Ltd.

General Manager: Josef F. Forstmayr

Open: Year-round

Credit Cards: All major

U.S. Reservations: Direct to hotel, (800) 972-2159; Elegant Resorts of Jamaica, (800) 237-3237

Deposit: Three nights

Minimum Stay: Christmas/New Year, President's Weekend, Easter, and Thanksgiving holidays, inquire

Arrival/Departure: Transfer service arranged for fee

Distance from Airport: (Montego Bay Airport) 10 miles; taxi one-way, $35; free daily shuttle to town once daily.

Accommodations: 110 rooms (36 in Pineapple House, 13 with two double beds, 23 king; 74 rooms and suites in 27 private villas with twins and kings; all villas staffed, 23 with private pools)

Amenities: Air-conditioning, ceiling fans; bath with tub and shower, bathrobes, basket of Elemis toiletries; telephone; kitchen in villas; ice service; nightly turndown service, room service 7:30 a.m.–9:30 p.m., (additional charge); beauty salon; Pineapple House rental with VCR or DVD, $30 per day; radio; boutiques; afternoon tea in cocktail bar; Internet access service for a fee

Electricity: 110 volts

Fitness Facilities/Spa Services: Fitness room with exercise equipment; aerobic, exercise, yoga classes; jogging trail, weekly nature walk; beauty salon, spa (see text)

Sports: Remodeled double infinity-edge swimming pool, twenty-three private pools for villas; five Laykold tennis courts (two lighted), equipment free, proper tennis attire required; snorkeling gear; golf

arranged at four Montego Bay courses; free transfers to Tryall for golf daily at 9:00 a.m.; a shopping bus weekdays at 10:00 a.m.; water sports for fee; deep-sea fishing, horseback riding arranged

Dress Code: Casual during day. In dining areas, long trousers and collared shirt for gentlemen, no shorts after 7:00 p.m., except Monday

Children: All ages; cribs, high chairs; babysitters; children's dinner served from 6:00 p.m. May 1–October 31; half price meal plans for children under twelve; Kids Club (see text) and more

Meetings: Up to 120 people for weddings

Day Visitors: Welcome; reservations for lunch or dinner required

Handicapped Facilities: No

Packages: Honeymoon, wedding, family packages, Platinum (all-inclusive)

Rates: Two people, daily, EP. *High Season* (mid-December–mid-April): $620-$1,240. *Low Season* $410-$1,000. Two- to five-bedroom villas, including full American breakfast daily, $1,240-$4,300 and $820-$3380, respectively.

Service Charge and Government Tax: Included

TRYALL CLUB
Montego Bay, Jamaica, W.I.

To take afternoon tea on the terrace of the Great House at tradition-rich Tryall is to glimpse the grand style of colonial life in bygone days. (No wonder the British didn't want to give up the Empire!)

To spend a week in a villa at Tryall is to peek at the lifestyle of the rich, more than

the famous—and today more American than British.

To play golf on Tryall's famous eighteen-hole championship course, one of the best in Jamaica, is to experience the island's beauty while being humbled by the difficulty of these benign-looking greens. And to travel the 2,200 acres of this former sugar and coconut plantation is to understand why its aficionados say, "There will never be another Tryall."

In recent years Tryall seemed to be suffering an identity crisis—a parade of managers and name changes. However, since the owners brought in hotel and food and beverage veterans and undertook a major upgrade of facilities including the golf course, the enterprise has taken on new life.

Located on the northern shores of Jamaica, Tryall is an exclusive luxury suite and villa resort of great distinction. Its vast acres flow from forested mountainsides through manicured gardens to the sea. At the center the restored nineteenth-century manor house sits high on the hillside with gardens sloping down to the beach. The site catches a constant breeze and commands breathtaking, wide-angle views.

The gracious Great House, with its antiques-filled parlors, dining room, and broad terraces, is the hub of the resort's social life. A long one- and two-story wing perpendicular to the Great House houses the hotel's spacious, elegant one- and two-bedroom guest suites, which are among the finest in the Caribbean. Some of the region's most palatial vacation homes, belonging to Tryall's owners, are in the hills framing the Great House and by the sea.

There are two categories of rooms, based on their view. All overlook the gardens and the fairways, with magnificent, expansive views stretching to Montego Bay. Some are duplex suites, others are on one level; all have living and dining areas and fully equipped kitchens. The upper floors of the duplexes have small balconies; those below have terraces.

The guest rooms are individually furnished in British-colonial style, accented with a museum collection of antiques and art belonging to individual owners. Recently all the rooms and suites were refurbished with handsome new fabrics and posh marble bathrooms, several with Jacuzzi baths.

You can take breakfast in your room (your housekeeper will cook breakfast and lunch for you at no additional charge; an excellent food shop is on the property) or in the Great House. A casual lunch can be taken in the delightful setting of the Beach Cafe or by the pretty pool with a swim-up bar.

The villas are Tryall's crown jewels. All in harmonious, traditional design, the privately owned mansions, with names like Linger Longer, Tranquillity, and No Problem, are exquisitely furnished and fully staffed. They are set in spacious lawns and gardens, providing greater privacy than the Great House suites. Each villa has its own pool and staff: cook, chambermaid, laundress, and gardener. The four- to seven-bedroom villas have a larger staff. You may choose to dine in your villa or at the Great House.

On Wednesday down by the beach, an early-evening barbecue features Jamaican dishes, entertainment by a Jamaican folklore group, and a crafts fair. The setting for dinner—weather permitting, on the lamplit terrace—may be more spectacular than the food, although new menus, by the new chef, are changed daily, now relying more on fresh ingredients, and have improved the fare noticeably. The service is exemplary. Dinner might be followed by light entertainment. Guests usually adjourn to the popular, newly enlarged bar.

A spacious and well-equipped center houses Tryall's recently added Kids Club, where the nature walks, craft lessons, and sessions on Jamaican folklore have scored high with young families.

Tryall's tennis center, recently rated among top resort facilities worldwide in an Internet poll, has a resident pro, Biah Maragh, who organizes weekly tournaments and helps put together foursomes. He also oversees the resort's popular Junior Tennis Camps.

The golf course, familiar to television audiences as the host of the Johnnie Walker Championships, tops the list of Tryall's sports facilities. The attractive course runs along Tryall's 1½ miles of seafront and through palm groves and rolling terrain, with fairways bordered by fruit and flowering trees, and rises to forested hills before returning to the sea. There is a jogging track near the Great House and a range of water sports by the beach. At the beauty salon and massage center, a variety of spa treatments are available, and for fitness enthusiasts Tryall has a new activities coordinator who starts them on their day with a one-hour power walk, gives aerobics and dance lessons in reggae and soca, and leads nature walks. And for those who had something less strenuous in mind, Tryall is an official bird sanctuary.

Tryall is tony, gracious living at its best with the facilities of a modern resort. Honeymooners and romantics of all ages will not find a more beautiful place, and families are among the most dedicated fans. But Tryall is a resort with a clubby ambience. If you are a part of the club, you will love it. If not, come with friends.

Tryall Club ***
P.O. Box 1206, Montego Bay, Jamaica, W.I.
Phone: (876) 956-5660; Fax: (876) 956-5673; www.tryallclub.com

Owner: Privately owned units

Managing Director: Delwin Rochester

Open: Year-round

Credit Cards: All major

U.S. Reservations: Karen Bull Associates, (800) 238-5290; Fax: (404) 237-1841; karenbull@mindspring.com

Deposit: 25 percent; sixty days cancellation in winter, thirty days in summer

Minimum Stay: Fourteen nights at Christmas; seven nights in villas; applicable at other times, inquire

Arrival/Departure: Transfer service on request

Distance from Airport: (Montego Bay Airport) 14 miles; taxi one-way, $35 for one to four passengers

Distance from Montego Bay: 12 miles; taxi one-way, $30 for one to four passengers

Accommodations: 13 one- and two-bedroom Great House villa suites; 59 estate villas with two to seven bedrooms

Amenities: Great House: air-conditioning, ceiling fans; telephones; bath with tub and shower, hair dryer, basket of toiletries, bathrobe; beauty and massage salon, gift shop, cigar shop, art/craft gallery, convenience store; room with computer/Internet connection and fax for guest's use. For villas, inquire.

Electricity: 110 volts

Fitness Facilities/Services: See text

Sports: Freshwater swimming pool; nine Nova cushion tennis courts (five lighted), equipment, resident pro; golf, caddies required, pro, pro shop; jogging trail; Sunfish, windsurfing, paddle boats, snorkeling; scuba diving, fishing, waterskiing, sailing, horseback riding arranged

Dress Code: Casual by day; elegantly casual for evening with long trousers and collared shirts for men year-round

Children: All ages; cribs, babysitters; Kids Club daily program

Meetings: Up to one hundred people

Day Visitors: Welcome

Handicapped Facilities: Limited

Packages: All-inclusive, golf, tennis, and others available

Rates: Great House, two persons, daily, EP. *High Season* (early January–April 16):

$440–$550. *Low Season*: $275–$395. Inquire for villa prices.

Service Charge: Included

Government Tax: Included

COUPLES SWEPT AWAY
Negril, Jamaica, W.I.

If ten tennis courts, a fully equipped gym, two racquet courts, a squash court, an aerobics center, an Olympic-size swimming pool, unlimited golf, and yoga sessions hit the right buttons, you'll think you're in heaven when you arrive at this spiffy resort, which sweeps around the white sands of Negril Beach. And these marvels are part of an all-inclusive package: You pay nothing extra for meals, beverages, use of sports facilities, or even transfers and gratuities.

Couples Swept Away has found a niche within the niche of Jamaica's all-inclusive resorts. Not as frenetic or glitzy as the rest, but more romantic than some of its neighbors down the beach, Couples Swept Away enjoys a laid-back, serene ambience geared to people interested in keeping fit even when on vacation.

You don't really have to be a health and fitness nut to enjoy Couples Swept Away— mildly interested will do. No one will push you to rise at 7:00 a.m. and hit the courts before the sun gets too hot (besides, the courts are lit for night play) or if you don't show up for aerobics. The marvelous sports facilities are right here, on the premises, when—or if—you want to work out and use them.

Here you vacation in sync with nature. Wind chimes fill the air; flowers and tropical foliage dress the grounds. The Veggie Bar serves up incredible fresh fruit and

vegetable drinks that look more like works of art than beverages.

The architecture and decor throughout show a sense of style. Low-key and in stellar good taste, the guest rooms as well as public areas make use of the best examples of Jamaica's superior-quality furniture, crafts, and art. Earth-toned fabrics, natural woods and ceramics, and rattan pieces contrast well with the terra-cotta floors, which are practical as well as attractive.

The guest rooms, clustered tightly between the road and the beach, are in villa-style buildings of cream stucco trimmed with rich, dark hardwood and linked by a labyrinth of garden walkways. Floor-to-ceiling louvered doors and windows, helped by ceiling fans, encourage sea breezes to cool your suite. Spacious verandas with built-in divans and comfy rattan lounges lure you to laze away the hours gazing out to sea.

There are three categories of accommodations in the original section of the resort, comprising 140 suites. Garden Suites are the farthest from the beach. Atrium Suites, on or close to the beach, are in groups of four rooms that share a central garden. These can be a bit noisy if your neighbors have loud voices. Both the garden and atrium suites have huge verandas. The third type are villas directly on the beach. Each has two rooms upstairs with a separate veranda, and one suite on the ground floor, also with a private veranda.

A major expansion costing $36 million was completed in 2006, adding 172 new suites, all with king beds, television, and minibar. The expansion also includes the addition of a large conference room, a full-service spa, a disco/piano bar, Internet cafe, wine bar, logo shop, pool with swim-up bar, two Jacuzzis, a beach grill, and a large open-air restaurant with a show kitchen.

Directly across the road from the resort's front entrance is the ten-acre Sports and Fitness Complex, the most comprehensive facility of its kind in Jamaica—if not the Caribbean. In addition to the air-conditioned racquetball and squash courts and the lighted tennis courts (hard and clay), the fully staffed facilities include a 25-meter lap pool, a complete gym with Cybex, an aerobics center with an ExerFlex floor (it gives when you bounce), a basketball court, aquacise, saunas, steam rooms, whirlpools, bicycles, a jogging track, and a pro shop. The complex hosts trendy fitness workout classes including "butts, guts, and thighs"; boxing and instruction; superabdominals, basketball clinics and games, Step 101; stretch classes; and a circuit cardio routine. All these are in addition to a mind-boggling daily schedule of exercise sessions and clinics, from aerobics and power walks to tennis and yoga. The center offers fitness assessments and evaluations and has personal trainers available by appointment.

Water sports include Sunfish sailing, windsurfing, waterskiing, snorkeling, and scuba diving—all with instruction. A dive resort course is included; PADI certification is extra. A free-form pool and a whirlpool are alongside a great beach. Unlimited golf at the Negril Hills Golf Club, a few miles from Couples Swept Away, is included; transportation is provided.

The Oasis spa offers a full array of beauty and body services at an additional charge. Treatments include aromatherapy facials and massages, prenatal massages, and couple baths. Wedding spa packages are also available.

Buffets feature international fare with a Jamaican flair, and table service is available. Pizza lovers might easily get swept away with the fresh renderings in the Sports Lounge, which has a big-screen television. Feathers, the resort's top restaurant, is open in the evening, offering sophisticated international and Caribbean selections with French influences. The Seagrape Cafe in a romantic, open-air setting by the beach features grilled fare with Jamaican flavors. The newest restaurants include a twenty-four-hour grill, and Lemongrass, a Thai specialty restaurant.

The piano bar is lively in the early evening, and a resident band plays nightly for dancing. Varied entertainment—a native floor show or a Jamaican band with a cabaret singer—is scheduled throughout the week. You'll find a game room with billiards and cable television.

Most guests come from the United States and Canada, but the number coming from Europe, other Caribbean islands, and Latin America is growing. In addition to its obvious appeal to fitness-oriented couples, Couples Swept Away has great charm for honeymooners and romantics of all ages.

Couples Swept Away ***
Norman Manley Boulevard, Box 3077, Negril, Jamaica, W.I.
Phone: (876) 957-4061, (876) 957-4040; Fax: (876) 957-4061; e-mail: inquiry@ couples.com; www.couples.com

Owner: Issa Hotels and Resorts

General Manager: Ricardo Bowleg

Open: Year-round

Credit Cards: All major

U.S. Reservations: (800) COUPLES (268-7537); online booking available at www.couples.com

Deposit: $400, thirty days cancellation

Minimum Stay: Three nights

Arrival/Departure: Transfer included in all-inclusive package

Distance from Airport: (Montego Bay Airport) 60 miles, one-and-a-half hours by car

Distance from Negril: 3 miles; taxi one-way, about $8

Accommodations: 312 rooms in two sections. Original 26 two-story villas (no television) all suites with king beds and verandas; 64 garden; 56 atrium; 20 beachfront. New section are all suites with king bed, television, and minibar (48 Garden Verandah; 48 Ocean Verandah; 48 Beachfront Verandah; 24 Great House Verandah; 4 Great House Jacuzzi)

Amenities: Air-conditioning, ceiling fans; bath with shower only, hair dryer, basket of toiletries; telephone, CD player, coffee-maker; iron and ironing board; room service for continental breakfast, ice service, nightly turndown service; spa (extra charge for treatments)

Electricity: 120 volts

Fitness Facilities/Spa Services: See text

Sports: See text

Dress Code: Casual by day; casually elegant in evening

Children: No

Day Visitors: $75 per day provides access to Sports Complex and Resort

Meetings: Up to 200 people

Handicapped Facilities: No

Packages: All-inclusive, honeymoon, wedding ceremony complimentary ($200 government license & processing fee extra)

Rates: Per couple, per night, All inclusive. *High Season* (mid-December–mid-April): from $530. *Low Season:* from $385

Service Charge: Included

Government Tax: Included

GRAND LIDO NEGRIL RESORT & SPA
Negril, Jamaica, W.I.

Do you want it all on a vacation? Leave your worries on the doorstep? Then Grand Lido Negril might be the answer. It guarantees everything under the sun. In fact, it even guarantees the sun.

Grand Lido Negril is the SuperClub flagship and top category of its sixteen resorts, which the group calls "Super-Inclusive" for all the extra features that are included in its all-inclusive price.

Set in twenty-two acres of tropical gardens just north of Negril on Jamaica's southwest shore, the resort curves around a 2-mile crescent of white-sand beach on Bloody Bay and is made up of several components, each with different architectural details.

You enter under a modern, glass-topped porte cochere to a pink stone and marble passageway with ponds and fountains and a colonnaded courtyard with a gigantic floral display at the center. Its pink stone walls are enlivened with paintings by local artists from Kingston-based Chelsea Galleries. From here, you step into a large lobby with the check-in desk in one corner, a concierge desk in another and, as incongruous as it may seem, a huge water-wheel turning slowly and spilling water into nearby pools. Here you will be greeted by a staffer with a glass of champagne to enjoy while the concierge completes your check-in.

Farther along, a sidewalk opens onto the large open-air, main restaurant, bar, and the main swimming pool to one side and a series of specialty restaurants on the other. Parts of these areas are faced with glass brick walls, an art deco feature from the 1930s. Tucked under the lobby on the ground floor are slot machines, a game room, and a business center with Internet access.

Cupping the crescent-shaped beach, almost from one end to the other, are the Mediterranean-style two-story semidetached cottages housing the all-suite accommodations. They include spacious junior suites, one-bedroom suites, luxury and royal suites, two presidential suites, and eight luxury beachfront Jacuzzi suites. All offer comfortable living areas furnished in mahogany and private terraces with a view of the beach, ocean, or manicured gardens. Some fifty-two rooms are reserved for the clothes-optional beach tucked discreetly at the southwestern end of the resort.

The majority are beachfront split-level junior suites with king-size or twin beds and a step-down living room area with sofa, coffee table, desk, and patio or balcony. All are air-conditioned and have satellite television, CD player, small refrigerator (stocked with water and soft drinks daily), safe, direct-dial telephone, hair dryer, iron and ironing board, tile and dark green marble

bathroom with Jacuzzi bathtub or multihead Euro-flux shower.

In addition to accommodations, all meals, airport transfers, taxes and gratuities (no tipping allowed), the special amenities that enables a Superclub to boast it's "Super-Inclusive" are a full menu, twenty-four-hour in-room dining service, complimentary manicure and pedicure, complimentary laundry, valet and dry cleaning services, premium brand cocktails, instruction and equipment for most water and land sports, daily recreational activities and nightly entertainment, and complimentary weddings (see below for details). A registered nurse is also on the premises.

The resort's seven restaurants provide a broad selection that includes the open-air Gran Terrazza serving breakfast and lunch buffets and afternoon tea, plus two dinner events—the Beach Party on Monday and Grand Gala Buffet on Friday. La Pasta, an inside/outside "sidewalk" cafe, complete with the colors of the Italian flag—white tables, red and green chairs—offers Italian fare; and next door, Cafe Lido serves continental dishes at dinner in a casually elegant atmosphere (no shorts).

Open for dinner only are Reggae Café, a Jamaican eatery, specializing in jerk chicken and pork, roast fish, and other local delicacies; Piacere, the gourmet restaurant that offers French and Italian nouvelle cuisine (jackets required); and best of all, Munasan, a Japanese restaurant with teppanyaki stations and sushi bar. Reservations are required for the latter two.

If you're a foodie, you'll do no better than go for the annual Epicurean Weekend when Chef Martin and a host of well-known chefs, mostly from the United States, (for example, Lynn Crawford, executive chef of the Four Seasons New York) strut their stuff. Usually held in midsummer (contact SuperClubs for the exact dates), it's a hands-on four-day culinary exchange with hotel guests helping and learning at cooking demonstrations, pastry classes, wine seminars, and a final day cook-off and eight-course gala dinner. It's great fun.

After dark the beat goes on at Amici, the piano bar, and Atlantis, the disco, as well as themed parties in the Gran Terrazza.

Tucked away in the gardens under the shade of a gigantic, beautiful old cotton tree is Timber House, a tree-house snack bar at the center of the property and one of the resort's seven bars. It is open 24/7 and serves light fare. Up in the trees with it is one of the resort's three large, outdoor Jacuzzis.

Nearby, too, is the Blue Mahoe Spa and fitness center. The spa has three air-conditioned treatment rooms and steam and sauna rooms, encircling a plunge pool for cool, post-sauna dips. There are also four cliff-side gazebos for open-air massages by the sea. Treatments include facials, hand and foot paraffin treatments, a variety of massages, body wraps, and body scrubs.

The gym, open 24/7, has two air-conditioned exercise rooms with Cybex equipment including free weights and Olympic barbells, treadmills, Stairmasters, semi-bikes, and stationary bikes. There is also a padded aerobic platform overlooking Bloody Bay. The gym offers daily classes for power walking, aerobics, aquacise, body sculpting, weights, and stretch. Aerobics sessions include soca and reggae dancing. The facility has licensed resident and visiting instructors and certified personal trainers.

At the beach, the water-sports shop offers diving, Sunfish sailing, snorkeling, water-skiing, windsurfing, kayaking, beach volleyball, indoor games room, and glass-bottom boat rides. Tennis lessons and tournaments are arranged by the resident pro;

scuba with resort certification is available for a $70 charge.

Grand Lido Negril is big on weddings and even has a wedding coordinator to attend to the details. Its complimentary wedding package for a minimum three-nights' stay includes marriage license, minister, witnesses, bouquet of tropical flowers and boutonniere, champagne and traditional Jamaican wedding cake, and arrangements for the ceremony. All a bride and groom need to do is pick a location in the gardens, on the beach, or at a cliff-top gazebo. A photographer can be arranged at an additional cost, and couples are responsible for the necessary legal fees. The resort has specials for honeymooners or couples celebrating an anniversary or renewing their vows—for a minimum of six nights, they get a seventh night free, as well as the legal fees.

Grand Lido Negril is designed for couples, singles, and families with children sixteen years and older.

Oh, and about those guarantees—it's something like having year-round weather insurance. The Sunshine Guarantee: For every day the sun doesn't show its face during your stay, SuperClubs will give you a credit voucher equal to that day's Super-Inclusive room value, good for one year toward another SuperClubs vacation. No Hurricane Guarantee: Should a hurricane strike the resort, guests will receive reimbursement for the value of disrupted nights and a voucher for a future stay for the same number of disrupted nights.

There's also a Satisfaction Guarantee. If you are not 100 percent satisfied with your holiday at the resort, and if, after notifying the general manager of the problem, he is unable to rectify the situation by the second night of your stay, SuperClubs will issue you a credit voucher for the value of the unused portion of your stay, good for up to one year at a SuperClubs resort.

Grand Lido Negril Resort & Spa
Norman Manley Boulevard, P.O. Box 88,
Negril, Jamaica, W.I.
Phone: (876) 957-5010; Fax: (876) 518-
5147, (876) 957-5517, (800) 467-8737;
e-mail: info@superclubs.com; www.grand
lidonegril.com

Management: SuperClubs

General Manager: Roberto Pellicia

Open: Year-round

Credit Cards: All major

U.S. Reservations: (800) GO-SUPER, (800)
467-8737

Deposit: Secure with credit card

Minimum Stay: Three nights; five nights
Christmas/New Year

Arrival/Departure: Airport transfers included
in rate

Distance from Montego Bay: 55 miles;
ninety-minute drive from Sangster International Airport in Montego Bay.

Distance from Kingston: Three and one half
hours drive

Accommodations: 210 suites private patio
or balcony (two presidential suites, eight
luxury beachfront Jacuzzi suites; 200
beachfront, ocean view, or garden split-level
junior suites and one bedroom, with king or
twin beds)

Amenities: Business center with Internet
access; private terraces, air-conditioning,
satellite television, CD players, room refrigerators, safes, hair dryers; complimentary
laundry; spa services; valet and dry cleaning
services; fitness center; sauna, Jacuzzis;

Sunshine, No Hurricane, and Satisfaction
guarantees

Electricity: 110 volts/50 cycles

Fitness Facilities/Spa Services: Spa with
massage, body treatments, facials, complimentary manicure/ pedicure (specialty one
for added cost); Cybex gym; power walks,
aquacise, and aerobics classes; reggae and
soca dance classes; five Jacuzzis

Sports: Two pools (one in main beach area,
one at au naturel beach); four tennis courts
(two night lit) with lessons and tournaments; golf with transfers and green fees
included, scuba resort certification ($70
charge), snorkeling, waterskiing, windsurfing, Sunfish sailing, kayaking, beach volleyball, indoor games room, five Jacuzzis,
glass-bottom boat rides

Dress Code: Resort casual; cover-up for
Gran Terrazza; jacket for Piacere

Children: None under sixteen years of age

Meetings: Meeting facilities for up to 800
people

Day Visitors: Yes, must be booked in
advance; day pass $79, 10:00 a.m.–6:00
p.m.; night pass $99, 6:00 p.m.–2:00 a.m.

Handicapped Facilities: Yes

Packages: Wedding, honeymoon, golf, Epicurean weekend

Rates: Per person, per night double, *High
Season* (January 1–mid-April): $239–$546.
Shoulder Season (mid-April–June 30):
$229–$536. *Low Season:* $220–$501.

Service Charge: Included

Government Tax: Included

ROCKHOUSE HOTEL AND RESTAURANT

Negril, Jamaica, W.I.

Rockhouse was one of Negril's first hotels. Flower children put this then-undiscovered hideaway on the map in the early 1970s. But in 1995 Inhouse Hotels, owned by three enterprising young Aussies, purchased the old Rockhouse and renovated and upgraded it to such a degree that it became a new hotel.

Situated in the rocky area of the western coast on four acres at the top of a cliff that drops precipitously to the sea, Rockhouse is comprised of twenty thatched-roof, octagonal cottages of rock and wood in a jungle of exotic gardens. It reminds some people of a South Seas island and others of an African village.

Two particularly welcome amenities that the new owners added were a restaurant (the old hotel never had one) and a cliffside, freshwater swimming pool (which replaced a small, saltwater tidal pool).

The restaurant, built of stone with a thatched roof, has a cantilevered balcony suspended over the cove. It serves three meals daily and features local specialties, as well as a broad wine list. There is also a full room-service menu; after the installation of a phone system, guests can order from the restaurant to have food served in their room or anywhere on the property. The pool bar is open from 10:00 a.m. to sunset.

The new pool, carved from rock at the edge of the cliff, pleases former guests who might not have cherished diving into the sea from the rocks, although the water here—aptly named Pristine Cove—is perhaps the cleanest and clearest in Negril. Ladders and stairs carved into the rock provide easy access to the water for swimming

and snorkeling on the nearby reef. There is no beach but many sunning places. These cozy corners, built out over the rocks, have two lounge chairs and an umbrella and provide greater privacy and direct access to the sea. They also make a fine perch for watching dolphins or sunsets. Also near the pool, an outside pavilion is used for yoga and special events.

Even with all the changes, the resort maintains its seclusion and Jamaican flavor as a rustic escape with a primitive charm, light-years away from the action of Negril.

Regardless of how rustic the accommodations may look from outside, they are quite comfortable inside. The stone and wood, peaked-roof cottages have sliding glass doors that provide great vistas and lead outside to a terrace. They have an indoor toilet and sink and an enclosed outdoor shower open to the skies. The cottages are set far enough apart to offer privacy, too. Most are situated directly over the water so that you can fall asleep to the sound of the surf.

The original cottages are furnished with comfortable beds, and electricity runs the air-conditioning, ceiling fans, and minibars. All cottages have queen-size beds. Four cottages have a sleeping loft with one double and a twin bed. Some of the cottages have stone facing on the outside and inside. The modern bathrooms are separated from the sleeping area by an attractive stone partition. Other cottages have brightly painted exteriors, and terraces are paved with cut stone. But perhaps the biggest change came when air-conditioning was added to all the accommodations along with safes and CD players. Free wireless Internet access is available 24/7.

Rockhouse also has fourteen rooms in two two-story cement-block buildings (well disguised with colorful exteriors and wooden slat doors under thatched roofs). Less expensive rooms in the block farthest from the sea have small indoor bathrooms; more deluxe rooms are found in the building near the pool. The latter has eight rooms with tiled baths and large patios at the front and back, each separated from the others by an outdoor shower and tropical garden. The rooms are outfitted with furniture designed for Rockhouse and made from local woods. Recently, eight premium villas, larger than the existing ones, were built over the water on the cliff's edge, facing west with sunset views. Each thatch-roofed villa has an enclosed outdoor shower open to the skies and a spacious, wraparound private terrace and sliding glass doors providing great vistas of Pristine Cove. All rooms have ceiling fans, safes, and minibars.

Rockhouse also has a pressurized water system with master tank storage, while power from backup generators ensures continuous service. The entire property runs on solar-heated water with electrical backup. There's a Rockhouse Shop, and a sunset bar.

The Rockhouse Spa works with spa consultant Linda Hall and Jamaican-based Starfish Oils to develop new local spa wraps, scrubs, and oils. Spa treatments are undertaken "on-the-rocks" in the cliff-edge massage cabana, at the Caribbean drench hut (which feels like a warm Jamaica rainfall), inside the eight room garden spa, or in one's room. Yoga classes are offered daily in the recently built yoga room.

A commendable effort of the resort is Rockhouse Foundation, a U.S.–chartered nonprofit organization established in 2003, primarily focused on support for education and poverty prevention in childhood. The foundation's first project with generous supporters invested more than $300,000 to improve Negril schools after seeing that students were sitting in overcrowded classrooms under leaky roofs, with poor wiring and other problems, adding up to an inadequate learning environment. The current project is a complete renovation and expansion of the Negril Community Library, a resource for children of all ages.

Rockhouse has built a reservoir of loyal fans, particularly behind-the-scenes people from the movie and music world, such as producers and directors. But now, with the greater amenities, almost anyone who wants a close-to-nature experience, without giving up comfort and still be at the heart of the action in Negril, could be happy here.

Rockhouse Hotel and Restaurant *
P.O. Box 3024, West End Road, Negril, Jamaica, W.I.
Phone: (876) 957-4373; Fax: (876) 957-0557; e-mail: info@rockhousehotel.com; www.rockhouse.com

Owner: Inhouse Hotel, Ltd.

General Manager: Matthew Marzouca

Open: Year-round

Credit Cards: Most major

U.S. Reservations: Direct to hotel

Deposit: Three nights

Minimum Stay: Three nights during U.S. public holidays

Arrival/Departure: Transfer by car $80 for up to four people, by bus $20, one-way

Distance from Airport: (Montego Bay Airport) 56 miles (two-hour drive); bus one-way, $80 up to four people

Distance from Negril: 2½ miles; taxi one-way, $5–$8

Accommodations: 34 rooms (eight premium villas; 12 cottages, five studios of which two have bunk beds, nine standard rooms), all with terrace or balcony and queen-size four-poster bed; four cottages with additional sleeping loft with double bed and twin

Amenities: Ceiling fan, stand fan, air-conditioning; safe, CD player in villas; minibar; telephone; bath with shower, hair dryer and iron available; room service; video monitor

Electricity: 110 volts

Sports: Swimming pool; horseback riding, tennis, golf, sailing, snorkeling, diving, and other water sports arranged

Dress Code: Informal

Children: Twelve years and older; charged at third-person rate

Meetings: None

Day Visitors: Welcome

Handicapped Facilities: No

Packages: No

Rates: Per room, double, EP. *High Season* (mid-December–mid-April): $175 (studio), $325 (villa). *Low Season* (mid-April–mid-December): $150 and $295

Service Charge: 10 percent

Government Tax: 6.25 percent

TENSING PEN
Negril, Jamaica, W.I.

"It's my idea of Paradise," the New Yorker poet and librettist told me when I asked her why she kept coming back to Tensing Pen. "And I really enjoy the people who come here. My husband and I always meet such interesting people here," she explained.

For a long time Tensing Pen has attracted writers, artists, musicians, and executives with high-stress jobs looking for a place to cool out. They have come to the right place.

It is set atop the cliff on Negril's West End, only one hundred yards from Rick's, the town's most famous bar/restaurant, if not Jamaica's, and a mecca for visitors at sunset. But those at Tensing Pen don't need to move: They have their own front-row perch for sunset watching.

Sixteen cottages are hidden in a jungle of lush foliage, far enough apart to provide the ultimate privacy and connected by pebble and stone paths that meander through the dense tropical setting edged by the blue Caribbean Sea.

Four cottages called "Pillars" cottages rest on a high stone base, giving the effect of treehouses. The upper level has a bedroom, bath, and terrace that captures the view and the breezes; below on the ground level is an enclosed outdoor shower.

All the cottages are topped with high, pointed, thatched roofs that from a distance resemble an African village hidden in the jungle. But their rustic exteriors belie their comfortable interiors. Inside, the handsome, airy rooms of white stucco walls are surrounded on three sides by wooden louvers of Jamaican cedar. The dark wood furniture includes a four-poster bed, either queen- or king-size, with mosquito netting (you'll be happy to have it after a rainy spell) draped from the top. The rooms have a basic clean and easy-to-live-with look. All cottages have roomy baths with either a marble or tiled deep shower.

One of the cottages, rather grandly called the Greathouse, has three bedrooms, a large living room and dining room, and is particularly suited for a family or group of friends traveling together. South House, a two-story cottage, is somewhat different from the others. The lower floor has two day beds and bath; the upper floor is a large bedroom with a king bed, bath, and large furnished balcony with fabulous views. Both levels have a refrigerator. Red Birch Cottage, a villa acquired in 2004, is located on the north side of the property and has two bedrooms and two baths.

Gradually, Tensing Pen has added dining options (the lack of which in the past under the previous owner was a frequent guest complaint and one of the reasons I had not included the resort in earlier editions of this book). Breakfast (included in the rate) is always a casual affair. Lunch and dinner are available daily in The Lodge, an open-sided dining room/lounge. They are also informal. The resort also offers moderately priced massage and other spa treatments in a new "massage hut" on the far north side of the property. Yoga sessions are offered there on Tuesday and Thursday; private yoga lessons are also available. Tensing Pen added a freshwater pool in 2007.

Tensing Pen is the essence of laid-back Negril. Relaxed, comfortable, friendly, being here is like visiting a friend. It's no wonder that its devotees think it is Paradise.

Tensing Pen **
P.O. Box 3013, West End Road, Negril, Jamaica, W.I.
Phone: (876) 957-0387; Fax: (876) 957-0161; e-mail: tensingpen@cwjamaica.com; www.tensingpen.com

Owners: Karin and Richard Murray; Sam and Anne-Marie Petros

General Manager: Courtney Miller

Open: Year-round

Credit Cards: MasterCard, Visa, American Express

U.S. Reservations: Direct to hotel

Deposit: 50 percent of total stay

Minimum stay: Three nights during U.S. public holidays

Arrival/Departure: Transfer by van for one to three people, $60 one-way; add $20 for each additional person

Distance from Airport: (Montego Bay Airport), 58 miles (one-and-one-half hour drive); Negril Airport, 9 miles, fifteen-minute drive (taxi one-way, $15)

Distance from Negril: 3 miles; taxi one-way, $5 to $10

Accommodations: 15 cottage rooms, a two-bedroom/two-bath villa, and one three-bedroom cottage; most rooms double occupancy with queen- or king-size beds; one room with one queen and two singles; one room with one queen, one single; Great House: two queen suites, one single, two and one-half baths, full kitchen with housekeeper

Amenities: Ceiling fan, stand fan; private baths with shower; refrigerator in all rooms; hair dryer available; safe in office, CD player in Great House, Red Birch Cottage, and main dining area; hammock huts overlooking the sea; sea floats; boutique with beverages; no telephones or televisions in rooms; telephone and Internet service available in boutique

Electricity: 110 volts

Fitness Facilities/Spa Services: Spa services and yoga on property

Sports: Snorkeling on property, other water sports; horseback riding, tennis, gym, golf; fishing, diving, and tours arranged

Dress code: Casual

Children: Great House and another cottage suitable for families with young children; children over twelve accommodated in other rooms

Meetings: Open-air facility at SeaSong Hut for ten to twelve people

Day visitors: Guests of Intimate Negril, a group of small Negril hotels, are welcome

for dinners, yoga, and spa services with twenty-four-hour advance reservations

Handicapped Facilities: No

Packages: Wedding

Rates: Per room, daily, AP; *High Season* (mid-December–mid-April): $183–$629 (Great House). *Low Season:* $116–$416 (Great House). Discounts on weekly stay.

Service charge: 10 percent

Government tax: 8.25 percent

COUPLES SANS SOUCI
Ocho Rios, Jamaica, W.I.

Romance *toujours*. It's always in the air at Couples Sans Souci. Is it the gorgeous setting or the mellow air of tradition? Or is it the ambience of sans souci?

In French *sans souci* means "without a care," and you will not have many in this pink palazzo by the sea. One of Jamaica's oldest resorts, Couples Sans Souci is nestled tightly between the mountains and sea on a bluff in terraced gardens. Enormous African tulip trees form umbrellas beside a mineral spring that spills down the rock-bound cove to the sea. The springs, the centerpiece of the resort's spa, were known for their curative powers as far back as the 1700s. Recent tests found them to be on a par with the most famous spa waters in Europe.

The current resort was born in the 1960s when a Jamaican company created a luxurious beachside residential complex to replace an earlier spa on the site. Stanhope Joel, one of Britain's wealthiest men, teamed up with well-known Caribbean architect Robertson "Happy" Ward to

design Sans Souci with a charming blend of Georgian colonial and Italian Renaissance styles. At Ward's request Berger Paints created an exclusive color—Sans Souci Pink—for the hotel, which is still used.

Ward's plans, advanced for the times, put electrical and phone wires underground; an outdoor elevator from the lobby level to the mineral pool below for easy access; and an oversize outdoor chessboard on the terrace with 2-foot-high pieces (carved by a local Rastafarian who had never seen a chess set!). In all, forty-three apartments were built and sold to wealthy and titled British travelers.

The complex changed ownership several times over the years, but the major transformation came in 1984, when a Jamaican businessman formed the Sans Souci Hotel and Club. His wife, an interior designer, renovated the entire complex, dividing the apartments into deluxe rooms and one-bedroom suites. Her signature, the charming Balloon Bar with its tiny papier-mâché figures of famous balloonists, remains.

Jamaica-based Issa Hotels and Resorts, which owns the all-inclusive Couples group, purchased Sans Souci in 2005 and in early 2008, a multimillion-dollar refurbishing of the resort was completed.

Between 1991 and 1998, the previous owners expanded Sans Souci by adding a complex of seventy-two beachfront Jacuzzi suites, divorced from the older hotel, on a 400-foot private white-sand beach at the western end of the property. Its suites are a vision of pinks and corals with buff ceramic tiles and walls. They have folding French doors that separate the bedroom from the sitting room; other doors open onto the terra-cotta tile terrace. The bathroom, marbled from top to bottom, has twin sinks, a Jacuzzi tub, and a separate shower.

The units are convenient to the tennis courts, the pool, and Ristorante Palazzina, a casual air-conditioned indoor restaurant with covered terrace where buffet breakfast and lunch are served. The informal setting is convenient for sunbathers (often topless Europeans, who need only add a top for lunch). In the evening Palazzina serves Italian cuisine, with reserved seating from 6:30 to 9:30 p.m. Other options include the Beach Grill for snacks and traditional Jamaican specialties; the Terrace for afternoon tea; Bella Vista, where Jamaican cuisine is served in a casual setting under the stars less than 10 feet from the water's edge (no reservations required); and Casanova, serving gourmet cuisine in a sophisticated atmosphere (reservations required). The resort has a separate, private au naturel beach where there's a pool with swim-up bar and a grill.

Accommodations in the older wings include veranda suites and one- and two-bedroom suites with large bedrooms and living rooms, most in vibrant blue decor with custom-designed fabrics. Twenty-four-hour food service, including in-suite dining (6:00 a.m. to 11:00 p.m.), is available.

The main lobby has elegant carved-wood furniture. A game room by the lobby has a pool table, backgammon, chess games, and various board games. From the lobby several terraces (one for dining, another with a freshwater pool) shaded by pink-and-white-striped umbrellas and huge tulip trees step down to quiet lanes that wind through the gardens. They lead to the mineral pool, spa, and beachside pavilion with a gym and exercise room. Charlie's Spa, named for a giant green sea turtle that lives in the mineral springs, is professionally staffed and offers massage, body scrubs, facials, reflexology, saunas, as well as manicures and pedicures in the beauty salon at additional charge.

Live nightly entertainment showcases some of Jamaica's finest cabaret artists, musicians, and cultural shows. Weekly themed galas are also on the entertainment roster. And with a restaurant named Casanova offering candlelight-and-wine dinner and music for dancing under the stars, what else is there but romance in the air "without a care"?

Couples Sans Souci ★★★★
P.O. Box 103, Ocho Rios, Jamaica, W.I.
Phone: (876) 994-1206; Fax: (876) 994-1408; www.couples.com

Owner: Issa Hotels and Resorts

General Manager: Pierre Battaglia

Open: Year-round

Credit Cards: All major

U.S. Reservations: (800) COUPLES (268-7537)

Deposit: $400 to confirm the reservation. Full payment required thirty days prior to arrival.

Minimum Stay: Three nights

Arrival/Departure: Transfers by air-conditioned bus from Montego Bay included. Intra-island flight transfer arrangement from Montego Bay Airport to Ocho Rios (Boscobel Airport) for one-way, $85 per person, which can be booked with your hotel reservations.

Distance from Airport: (Montego Bay Airport) 60 miles; taxi one-way, $120; $30 round-trip in an air-conditioned minibus. Boscobel Airport: 10 miles; taxi one-way, $20

Distance from Ocho Rios: 2 miles; taxi one-way, $10

Accommodations: 150 suites, most with balconies, in seven two- and three-story buildings (23 veranda suites, 8 ocean suites, 35 one-bedroom ocean balcony suites, 72 one-bedroom beachfront Jacuzzi suites; 10 penthouses, and one stand-alone Hibiscus Cottage—all kings)

Amenities: Air-conditioning, ceiling fans; bath with tub and shower, hair dryer, basket of toiletries, bathrobe, slippers; radio, CD player, telephone, television; minibar, tea and coffeemakers; iron and ironing board, ice service, nightly turndown service, twenty-four-hour food service

Electricity: 110 volts/50 cycles

Fitness Facilities/Spa Services: Charlie's Spa and gym with Universal equipment (see text); hair salon

Sports: Four swimming pools (three fresh-water, one mineral water); three whirlpools; two lighted tennis courts; Sunfloats, snorkel gear, kayaks, windsurfing; diving, fishing arranged; complimentary green fees at Upton Golf and Country Club; Jacuzzi; au naturel beach

Dress Code: Casual by day, but cover-up and shoes required in Ristorante Palazzina for breakfast and lunch, and more elegantly casual in evening

Children: None under eighteen years of age (adult couples only)

Meetings: Up to 140 people theatre style; multimedia capability

Day Visitors: Day pass includes food, water sports, tennis, beach, and more (but not the spa): $75 from 10:00 a.m. to 6:00 p.m. and $150 to 11:00 p.m.

Handicapped Facilities: No

Packages: Honeymoon, wedding, all-inclusive

Rates: Per couple, per night, All inclusive. *High Season* (late December–late March): from $520. *Low Season:* from $415, double occupancy

Service Charge and Gratuities: Included

Government Tax: Included

JAMAICA INN
Ocho Rios, Jamaica, W.I.

Located by a pretty beach on Jamaica's northern coast, this unpretentious inn has an elegance and timeless grace that can only be acquired through years of not trying to be anything more than it is—simply the best.

Set on a six-acre rise, it overlooks a cove with a crest of golden sand anchored by rocky fingers at each end. A reef, within swimming distance of shore, protects the waters and the beach, and a gentle breeze cools the air.

Built originally in 1950 as a four-room inn, Jamaica Inn is owned and operated by the second generation of Morrows from New England, Peter and Eric, who grew up here and consider it their home. They have inherited a fine tradition along with a fine inn, and their pride shows in every minute detail.

The staff, as polished as the silver with which you dine, is part of the attraction. Most have been here at least ten years and underscore the inn's continuity. When you have breakfast on your terrace—and don't even think of doing anything else—a courtly waiter will lay out a starched white damask cloth, set the table, and provide fresh fruit and home-baked bread.

The inn's exterior is painted a distinctive blue—deeper than Wedgwood—mixed specially for the hotel. It's trimmed with snow-white balustrades and louvered windows. Guest rooms are located in wings that extend from each side of the house to embrace the lawn, pool, and beach.

The hotel's crowning glory is its accommodations. Your bedroom opens onto a large balustraded veranda with a beautiful view. No hotel in the Caribbean has verandas quite like these. Fully furnished as a living room, each balcony has a sofa, wingback chair, breakfast table, antique writing desk, drying rack, and large beach towels. It's like living in a villa. The bedrooms are tastefully furnished with Jamaican antiques and period pieces. You can request king or twin beds.

Room categories—premier, deluxe, superior—are determined by location: on the beach, on the water, or viewing the beach and sea. Each location has something going for it, but the rooms in the one-story West Wing (Rooms 16 to 20) are very special. They are right at the edge of the sea, with the water lapping the rocks at the foot of your veranda. The water is so clear that you can see to the bottom.

In the last two years all guest rooms have been renovated completely down to the last detail, including for example, new window frames, and all bathrooms renovated, modernized, and upgraded.

The inn's special suites include the Blue Cottage, directly on the beach, and the stylish Cowdray Suite on the second floor. Then there's the legendary White Suite, on a promontory with its own pool; over the years it has served as the haunt of European royalty, an occasional prime minister, a famous poet, a best-selling novelist, and a galaxy of media stars.

And, there are more choices. Six airy and stylish cottages, which the inn acquired in 2002, were completely rebuilt and refurbished, with decor that combines Jamaican tradition with Indonesian touches. Situated near the spa, the cottages are set in gardens of Jamaican fruit trees and flowering shrubs. Two have two bedrooms and terraces overlooking the sea or beach, while Cottage Three and Cottage Four were made into large, luxurious one-bedroom suites. Sitting at the edge of the bluff, the freestanding suites with wide French doors opening onto spectacular views of the Caribbean Sea, are furnished with a king-size mahogany bed and a bamboo chaise, positioned to take advantage of the view. White covers contrast with the dark furnishings and flooring; gold and beige pillows add earth tones; and flowers and plants bring a fresh note. Most of the furniture was made in Jamaica. The oversize bath with marble floor and a gold and coral mosaic tile wall has a separate shower and tub. Each suite has an outdoor shower, and Cottages One to Five have small infinity pools just off the bedroom.

If you can pull yourself away from your comfortable room, you will find the beach to be one of Jamaica's finest. You can take up residence under a thatched umbrella;

the pretty oval pool and sea are only steps away.

If you are more energetic, there's a croquet lawn, tennis next door, and terrific snorkeling off the beach. Sunfish, sea kayaks, and snorkeling equipment are available without charge, as is the expanded gym with new equipment. Anthony, the beachman, will take you sailing, or if you had something less strenuous in mind, the resort's KiYara Ocean Spa offers an eclectic menu of treatments from around the globe. The spa is housed in thatched-roofed huts with hand-carved wooden pillars overlooking the sea. And for the e-mail addicted, there's a computer in the library, as well as wireless there and on the terrace.

Dining at Jamaica Inn is a special experience, whether in the romantic ambience of evening or breakfast on your veranda. The resort's young chef has added lighter contemporary fare and Jamaican specialties to the traditional repertoire.

Guests gather for cocktails at 7:00 p.m. on the front terrace and dine at 7:30 p.m. on the lamplit lower terrace, where the soft music of the resident band sets the mood. The palms sway gently overhead, and the band serenades with quiet tunes for dancing under the stars. It's straight out of a Dick Powell or Myrna Loy late-night movie: the romance of the Tropics. It's pure schmaltz. And it's wonderful.

While some might find Jamaica Inn a bit old-fashioned, most guests want it no other way. The Morrows frequently ask their guests—most of whom come from the United States—if they want less formality. The answer is always, "Don't change a thing." I agree.

Jamaica Inn *****
P.O. Box 1, Main Street, Ocho Rios, St. Ann, Jamaica, W.I.

Phone: (876) 974-2514, -2516; Fax: (876) 974-2449; e-mail: jaminn@cwjamaica.com; www.jamaicainn.com

Owners: Eric and Peter Morrow

General Manager: Mary Phillips

Open: Year-round

Credit Cards: All major

U.S. Reservations: (877) 470-6975, (800) 837-4608; Fax: (876) 974-2449

Deposit: Three nights; 50 percent on booking and balance forty-five days in advance for Christmas/New Year's. Full stay deposit for February, thirty days in advance

Minimum Stay: Ten nights Christmas/New Year. Five nights, midweeks in February; four nights, Thanksgiving Week. Cancellation, thirty days winter, fourteen days summer; forty-five days Christmas/New Year and February

Arrival/Departure: Transfer service arranged for charge

Distance from Airport: (Montego Bay Airport) One-and-a-half-hour drive by private car, with refreshments, one-way, $115; by shuttle bus, $25 per person

Distance from Ocho Rios: 2 miles; taxi one-way, $10

Accommodations: 47 rooms and suites in one- and two-story wings with terrace; king beds convertible to twins; four two-bedroom cottages

Amenities: Air-conditioning, ceiling fans; bath with tub and shower, hair dryer; direct-dial phone with Internet access; nightly turndown service, ice service; room service with $5 charge 7:30 a.m.–11:00 p.m.

Electricity: 110 volts

Fitness Facilities/Spa Services: Fitness room with exercise equipment; beautician and masseur or masseuse on call

Sports: Freshwater swimming pool; free tennis nearby; water sports; special rates for golf at Sandals Golf and Country Club; horseback riding arranged

Dress Code: Informal during day. After 7:00 p.m., shirt with collar required (jacket optional). In February men wear black tie for dinner; women, long dresses; neither required

Children: No children under twelve years old in winter; none under ten in summer.

Meetings: Off season, may book entire hotel

Day Visitors: Yes, with charge, based on availability

Handicapped Facilities: No

Packages: Honeymoon, weddings; Jamaica Inn/Round Hill combination

Rates: Two people, daily. *High Season* (mid-December–mid-April): $550–$825. *Low Season:* $300–$430. White Suite and Cottage Three: $760 winter, $830 summer. Inquire for other suites and cottages.

Service Charge: Included

Government Tax: Included

ROYAL PLANTATION
Ocho Rios, Jamaica, W.I.

What's old is new and what's new is old—that could be the tagline for the Royal Plantation.

Quietly elegant and stylish, the Royal Plantation is a beach hideaway set on seventeen acres of manicured tropical gardens on two private white-sand beaches overlooking the Caribbean Sea. Built almost five decades ago in classic British colonial style, the historic resort, formerly Plantation Inn, was acquired in 2001 by Butch Stewart, who is best known for his all-inclusive Sandals group. Stewart renovated and reopened the resort as the Royal Plantation, to be the flagship of a new group of luxury resorts aimed at recapturing the grace of days gone by, with less formality, modern amenities, and activities not imagined fifty years ago.

Situated on the north coast a few miles east of Ocho Rios, the Royal Plantation is ninety minutes by car from Sangster International Airport in Montego Bay. Guest transfers by private taxi are included in the rate.

From the entrance, you step into a checkerboard, marble foyer and bar and a large game room decorated with fine Jamaican antique mahogany furniture and a large-screen television. The game room opens onto a big balcony with a large dining terrace and lounge area with views of the sea. The resort has a spa, dining options from casual to white-glove service, and a variety of sports and recreation.

Royal Plantation's accommodations include spacious, very comfortable suites with ocean views and most with balconies, and a three-bedroom villa. There are seven categories of suites. The well-appointed rooms have custom-crafted mahogany furniture, king-size beds, air-conditioning, ceiling fans, dataports, safes large enough for laptops, and satellite television, VCR and CD players, and large bathrooms faced with colorful tiles. The posh three-bedroom Villa Plantana has a private pool and comes with a personal butler and chef.

Royal Plantation's top accommodations are the two-bedroom Prime Minister Suite (2,100 square feet), situated atop the west wing overlooking the property's west beach; and the one-bedroom Governor General Suite (1,500 square feet), which is almost identical but without a second bedroom. The spacious master bedroom has its own patio and is furnished with a grand four-poster mahogany bed and large-screen television. In the marble bathroom there is a deep Jacuzzi tub and separate mosaic shower. The second bedroom with its own private entrance may be booked separately.

Other top category suites are the one-bedroom Honeymoon Plantation and Honeymoon Grand-Luxe (600 square feet) located on the first to third floors of the east wing, others in the west wing. All have king beds and large balconies, separate living area with large television and VCR, marbled bathroom, and walk-in closet. A special feature is a romantic Roman Spa room outfitted with a marble bar, Cleopatra chaise longue, a whirlpool tub, and wall-to-wall French windows looking out to the sea.

Other suites—luxury, premium, and deluxe—vary by location but all have a king or two double beds (pillow menu is available), sitting area, walk-in closet, spacious bathroom with marble double vanities, whirlpool bath, and separate marble shower. Some have balconies; others have French balconies and all have ocean views.

The Red Lane Spa offers an array of body treatments including an outdoor moonlight couples massage, four-handed massage, aromatherapy, and reflexology. Facials, waxing, hairstyling, manicures, and pedicures are also available. The facility has steam rooms and a relaxation room. The Fitness Center schedules a variety of classes such as evening yoga classes on the Gazebo Pier overlooking the sea.

The resort has a freshwater swimming pool, two whirlpools, and two private beaches where beach butlers provide food and beverage service right to your beach chair. The resort also offers equipment and instruction for tennis on floodlit courts and for canoeing, kayaking, sailing, windsurfing, snorkeling, and diving.

A daily program of inviting events includes such activities as learning to cook the Jamaican way, watching hand-rolled cigars being made, enjoying Jamaican hot chocolate on the beach, and classical concerts in the elegant drawing room with its Steinway grand piano. Nightly entertainment might be as varied as a jazz trio, pianist, calypso band, or cultural show.

Royal Plantation has three restaurants, all overlooking the sea and with well-developed wine list, as well as twenty-four-hour-room service. Le Papillon, which boasts a Five-Star Diamond Award, specializes in fresh seafood. It offers white-gloved service in a formal setting. Reservations are required, as are jackets for gentlemen. The C-Bar, a champagne and caviar bar, is situated within Le Papillon.

La Terrace features a la carte outdoor dining. The Royal Cafe serves grilled items, fresh salads, open-faced sandwiches, ice cream.

For meetings, the Plantation Room accommodates up to 212 people theater style and can be divided into two rooms.

Royal Plantation offers personalized butlers who become the "manager" of your suite during your stay, coordinating and supervising any service that you want for $200 per day.

Royal Plantation is a smoke-free resort. The lobby, all of the indoor common areas, and dining venues are nonsmoking. Smoking is permitted outdoors and in designated rooms. The popular Jamaican cigar-rolling classes led by Royal Plantation's in-house expert continue to be offered on Friday afternoons.

Royal Plantation appeals most to romantics and those who appreciate its "grand tradition" in ambience and service together complemented by modern amenities and creative activities.

Royal Plantation
P.O. Box 2, Main Street, Ocho Rios, Jamaica, W.I.
Phone: (876) 974-5601; Fax: (876) 974-5912; e-mail: rpmail@jm.royalplantation.com; www.royalplantation.com

Owner: Ocho Rios Management Company

General Manager: Peter Fraser

Open: Year-round

Credit Cards: Most major

U.S. Reservations: (888) 487-6925

Deposit: Secure with credit card

Minimum Stay: Seven nights, Christmas/New Year's

Arrival/Departure: Private car transfer

Distance from Airport: (Montego Bay) 1.5-hour drive

Distance from Kingston: Two-hour drive

Accommodations: 74 suites in six categories

Amenities: See text

Electricity: 110 volts

Fitness Facilities/Spa Services: The Royal Spa; gym

Sports: Swimming pool, water sports with instruction; golf with greens fees and transfers

Dress Code: Casual elegance; no jeans, hats, tank tops, shorts, sneakers, or bare feet permitted

Children: Age eighteen and older

Meetings: Up to 212 people

Day Visitors: Yes

Handicapped Facilities: No

Packages: Honeymoon, wedding, Fourth Night, others

Rates: Per room double, per night. *High Season:* from $900 (EP) to $2,800 (all-inclusive). *Low Season:* from $545 (EP) to $1,690 (all-inclusive); all rates include airport transfers

Service Charge: Included

Government Tax: Included

SANDALS DUNN'S RIVER VILLAGGIO GOLF RESORT & SPA

Ocho Rios, Jamaica, W.I.

If you have never been to a Sandals resort, you need to understand what it is before you think of spending a week at one. Essentially, Sandals is a well-orchestrated, twenty-four-hour beach party for couples only.

More than two decades ago, Jamaican businessman Gordon "Butch" Stewart (Sandals's founder, owner, and number one asset) took a dying hotel, applied the all-inclusive Club Med concept (but with a Jamaican spin), limited the resort to couples only, and launched one of the Caribbean's biggest success stories. Sandals Dunn's River Villaggio, which opened in 1991, is one of twelve resorts in the Sandals group.

The beachfront hotel, only seven minutes from Ocho Rios's famous Dunn's River Falls, typifies the Sandals experience and reflects Stewart's bounce and boyish enthusiasm. Here, as in all Sandals resorts, you have already paid for all your accommodations, meals, snacks, beverages (alcoholic included), sports (including equipment and instruction), entertainment, gratuities, taxes, and airport transfers in one package at one price. Now just dive in and enjoy it.

Should you tire of this Sandals—which is unlikely—you can take advantage of the Sandals special "stay at one, play at seven" feature: Guests staying at any Sandals resort have access to all other Sandals in Jamaica at no additional cost. There is a free shuttle to Sandals Grande in Ocho Rios, but transfers to Montego Bay or Negril are not included.

Set on twenty-five tropical acres, the multistory Sandals Dunn's River is a complex of impressive structures in Italian Mediterranean style with Jamaican touches. You enter from a long garden driveway into an open colonnaded lobby furnished with rather grand divans; a welcoming-arms staircase with iron-filigree banisters leads to a mezzanine. The lobby opens onto Piazza del Campo, a large tree-shaded terrace newly renamed in keeping with the Italian focus that the resort initiated following a $25 million renovation. At the east end of the piazza is one of two free-form swimming pools. It has a waterfall cascading over rocks, meant to resemble the resort's namesake, and a swim-up bar; it attracts activity throughout the day. The second pool, more sedate and intended to be a quiet zone, is at the western end of the piazza. It has a

wooden deck and a sunken bar on one side. The whirlpool at the water's edge is big enough to accommodate the neighborhood; two smaller ones are located elsewhere.

Guest rooms, in two midrise buildings and low-rise lanais, come in seven categories based on location: deluxe, premium, luxury, ocean view, grand luxe, grand-luxe ocean view, penthouse honeymoon, and one-bedroom oceanfront suites. Essentially, the eastern wings are intended for those who want an active holiday, and the low-rise lanais are for those who prefer a quiet one.

The spacious rooms were recently renovated and given more regal decor with mahogany furniture and four-poster beds. An arched doorway bordered with pretty tiles leads into a dressing area and the tiled bathroom. French doors open onto balconies with views of the sea and gardens or mountains.

The resort has six restaurants. The main one, Ristorante Colombo, serves breakfast and lunch buffets but with an army of waiters on hand. Caffe Arno offers quick snacks such as hamburgers, hot dogs, popcorn, and fresh fruit. Pizzeria del Campo offers fresh, made-to-order pizzas straight from a wood-fired pizza oven set right on the piazza. The outdoor trattoria also serves fine Italian pastries. Bar del Campo's specialty is flavored coffees and there's ice cream at Gelateria Luigi and praline/cotton candy at "Mondorle e Zucchero Filato." In the evening dinner at candlelit tables in the Ristorante Marco Polo features white-glove service and an a la carte menu, which is changed daily.

You can also enjoy gourmet dining in three specialty restaurants: Colombo, serving Jamaican cuisine; Kimonos serving Teppanyaki–style Asian dishes; and Il Capitano, an inside/outside eatery featuring Italian fare. Reservations are required only in Kimonos.

Sandals's staff of young men and women, known as Playmakers, schedule activities on the beach and in and around the pool, as well as entertainment and special events throughout the day and evening. It's their job to make sure you don't have an idle moment—unless you want one, of course.

In addition to the white-sand beach and offshore reef, good for snorkeling, you'll find tennis courts (lit for night play), basketball, a nine-hole pitch-and-putt golf course, billiards, shuffleboard, and complete water-sports facilities: diving, sailing, snorkeling, waterskiing, and more.

If you're into fitness, you'll enjoy the bilevel health center with exercise and weight rooms, aerobics classes, two steam rooms, wet- and dry-heat saunas, and hot and cool Japanese tubs. The Red Lane Spa is a full-fledged facility with Swedish massage, aromatherapy, reflexology, body wraps, facials, and other treatments. All carry an extra charge. A personal trainer is also available.

Other activities include croquet, billiards, horseshoes, table tennis, and outdoor chess; there's an indoor game room, movies, slot machines, a television room, a library, and a weekly crafts show. An excursion to Dunn's River Falls and round-trip transportation to Sandals Grande Ocho Rios are available. Sandals's Golf and Country Club green fees are included, but rental of equipment is additional. A free shuttle is provided from Sandals Dunn's River Villaggio.

Nightly entertainment features appearances by Jamaica's premier performers, theme parties, particularly Italian accented ones, and staff-produced shows. There is dancing every evening and informal social gatherings at the poolside piano bar.

Most guests are from the United States. While Sandals is for couples, don't think that means only young couples. Every time I have been to a Sandals resort, I have seen couples of all ages. For anyone who wants a fun-filled, active vacation in a casual, friendly atmosphere, Sandals is a great deal.

Note: Beaches Resorts is Stewart's answer for the many Sandals couples who now have children and want to bring them on vacation. Beaches Negril Resort and Spa; Beaches Boscobel Resort & Golf Club, Ocho Rios; and Beaches Turks and Caicos were the first of the chain, but you can look for others in the future. In May 2006 Sandals Resorts and Beaches Resorts went smoke-free in all enclosed areas—bars, nightclubs, restaurants, lobbies, conference rooms, and retail shops. Smoking is allowed outdoors and in designated rooms.

Sandals Dunn's River Villaggio Golf Resort & Spa ★★★★

Box 51, Ocho Rios, Jamaica, W.I.
Phone: (876) 972-1610, (800) SANDALS; Fax: (876) 972-2300; e-mail: sdrmail@grp.sandals.com; www.sandals.com

Owner: Gordon "Butch" Stewart

General Manager: Louis Grant

Open: Year-round

Credit Cards: All major

U.S. Reservations: Unique Vacations, (305) 284-1300, (800) SANDALS; Fax: (305) 667-8996

Deposit: $400 seven days after reservations; full payment forty-five days prior to arrival; forty-five days cancellation

Minimum Stay: Three nights

Arrival/Departure: Transfer from Montego Bay included

Distance from Airport: (Montego Bay Airport) 56 miles (one-and-a-half-hour drive)

Distance from Ocho Rios: 5 miles; taxi one-way, $15

Accommodations: 256 rooms, including ten suites in five- and six-story buildings, two-story lanais; all with terrace and king beds

Amenities: Air-conditioning; television, clock radio, telephone; safe; bath with tub and shower, iron and ironing board, coffee/tea maker, hair dryer, basket of toiletries; minibar in five suites; ice stations; nightly turndown service. Room and suite concierge service includes preferred check-in, in-room bar, robes, *New York Times* fax, escorted shopping tour, and twenty-four-hour butler service in top category suites. Personal butler service is available for top-category suites.

Electricity: 110 volts

Fitness Facilities/Spa Services: Fitness center and spa (see text)

Sports: Two freshwater swimming pools with swim-up bar; three Jacuzzis; hammocks; four lighted tennis courts and equipment; boating, snorkeling, diving (two-day resort course), windsurfing; horseback riding, deep-sea fishing, and golf arranged

Dress Code: Casual

Children: No

Meetings: Up to one hundred people

Day Visitors: Day pass, $85

Handicapped Facilities: Limited

Packages: All-inclusive, three to seven nights; honeymoon, wedding ($750 charge or free with minimum five-night stay)

Rates: Per person, per night, All-inclusive. *High Season* (December 26–early April): $525–$1,400. *Shoulder Season* (early April–August; November–December 25): $436–$1,230. *Low Season* (September–October): $364–$1,034

Service Charge and Government Tax: Included

SUPERCLUBS BREEZES RUNAWAY BAY

Runaway Bay, St. Ann, Jamaica, W.I.

The flagship of SuperClubs' Breezes group, this resort got such a thorough renovation, redesign, and expansion in 2007, it's practically a new resort. Among the major additions were two freshwater swimming pools for a total of three; two new restaurants for a total of six; an expanded spa, a new water-sports center, and new rooms and suites with plunge pools.

But the resort's Number One asset did not change—its golf program. It sets Breezes Runaway Bay apart from its Super-Clubs cousins and all-inclusive competitors.

Located next to the resort, the eighteen-hole golf course, which SuperClubs owns, is available to guests staying at this Breezes to enjoy free, unlimited greens fees. Better yet, Breezes offers the Golf Academy, supervised by a PGA pro. When it was inaugurated in 1990, it was the first year-round golf school in the Caribbean. It is available to Breezes guests for free; non-Breezes guests pay $45 for half-hour instruction, $90 for one hour.

You can have up to forty-two hours of golf instruction weekly, and the school has a lecture room with video equipment and analysis facilities, ten practice bays, a practice sand bunker, and a chipping green. Golf clubs and carts are available for rent at the pro shop. On the western side of the resort's entrance is a nine-hole putting green; to the east is the golf clubhouse.

Travelers who don't know a wood from a five-iron need not fear: Breezes has a lot more going for it. The resort, set on twenty-seven acres, fronts a wide 2-mile stretch of golden sand on Jamaica's northern shore in Runaway Bay. In addition to the Olympic-size main pool, one of the new freshwater swimming pools serves the new group of rooms on the western beach, while the other with a swim-up bar and misting pool is set along the eastern shore. There are three Jacuzzis and a secluded corner of the beach set aside for sunning in the buff.

Other sports facilities include four lighted tennis courts—and instruction; a full water-sports program including snorkeling, windsurfing, sailing, kayaking, and scuba for certified divers, plus a resort course for beginners with certification for a $70 fee. The water-sports center has new Nitrox equipment, which divers can test on the Jamaica's Canyon wall, located just beyond the beach. The gym has Nautilus equipment and a daily aerobics and exercise program. There is a jogging track, cricket, volleyball, bicycles and bicycle tours, and a nature walk. The resort has a game room, a croquet lawn, billiards, and table tennis, and there are enough scheduled activities daily to keep you busy into the night, even if you never get near a fairway. You might try your hand at arts and crafts or the Circus Workshop featuring flying and swinging trapeze and trampoline

clinics. There are horse-and-carriage rides, glass-bottom boat rides,. themed nights, and beach parties. And when you want to take a break from all the activity, you'll find plenty of hammocks strung throughout the property.

The week starts on Sunday with an orientation, the introduction of the young, cheerful staff, and the manager's cocktail party. The new dining options include the casually elegant Munasan with a sushi bar and Teppanyaki stations, where chefs cook dinner to order; reservations are required; and the casual Reggae Café, serving Jamaican specialties for lunch and dinner near the beach. Buffet meals are served in the Beach Terrace, a large open-air pavilion conveniently located at the center of the resort by the beach and the Beach Grill for snacks throughout the day, and afternoon tea. Pastafari is an air-conditioned, casually elegant Italian restaurant for dinner; reservations are required; and the Starlight Grill serves Asian fusion cuisine for dinner and midnight snacks from 11:30 p.m. to 1:30 a.m.

The piano bar opens for cocktails, and different entertainment is presented every evening: beach on one night; nightclub or folklore show on another; staff and guest talent night on another; and a cabaret featuring Jamaican performers on intervening nights. The Club Hurricane disco opens at 11:00 p.m. and goes until the last person leaves.

Guest rooms are located in several two-story buildings on both sides of the main building and the expansive gardens, connected by "Breezeways." On the western beach is the new block of rooms introducing thirty oceanfront rooms and suites, including seven one-bedroom suites and eight veranda suites with private plunge pools. On the eastern courtyard, thirty garden-view rooms were expanded and transformed into forty veranda suites, each with plunge pools.

The original guest rooms—all comfortable and with private balconies overlooking gardens and beach—were spruced up with new mahogany furnishings, LCD flat-screen televisions, and high-speed wireless Internet access. Bathrooms sport a fresh new look with new countertops and polished hardware and faucets. The resort's attractive gardens have their own "rain forest." The Blue Mahoe Spa was revamped into a full-service facility as part of a new Blue Mahoe Spa signature line at SuperClubs Resorts and offers a wide range of treatments at additional cost. For example, massages start at: $58, half-hour; $90, for ninety minutes. The fitness center is in an air-conditioned pavilion.

Breezes is one of the few all-inclusive resorts that welcomes singles. The resort is popular with honeymooners (weddings are offered without additional charge, but there's a mandatory government tax of $225), and it's a bargain for any sports enthusiast. There are other Breezes resorts in Montego Bay, Curaçao, Brazil, Cuba, and Nassau, Bahamas. As in the other resorts, SuperClubs backs up its claims of a Super vacation here with guarantees for credit or money back in case of a hurricane, days without sunshine, and other considerations. Rates include accommodations, all meals, snacks, premium brand drinks, wine with lunch and dinner; sports with instruction and equipment; golf greens fees; entertainment; full-service weddings; and airport transfers. No tipping is allowed. Airfare is not included.

SuperClubs Breezes Runaway Bay ***
P.O. Box 58, Runaway Bay, St. Ann, Jamaica, W.I.
Phone: (876) 973-6099; Fax: (876) 973-2352; e-mail: breezesgolf@superclubs .com; www.superclubs.com

Owner: Innovative Resorts, Ltd.

General Manager: Kevin Levee

Open: Year-round

Credit Cards: All major

U.S. Reservations: SuperClubs, (800) 467-8737 (1-800-GO-SUPER); Fax: (954) 925-0334

Deposit: $250 per person within seven days of reservation; balance due thirty days prior to arrival or on arrival

Minimum Stay: Two nights; five nights during Presidents' Week, Easter, and Christmas

Arrival/Departure: Complimentary transfer service from Montego Bay Airport

Distance from Airport: (Montego Bay Airport) 42 miles (one hour by car)

Distance from Ocho Rios: 17 miles

Accommodations: 266 guest rooms and suites (four ocean-view and four pool-view suites; 30 new ocean-view of which seven are one-bedroom suites and eight veranda suites with plunge pools; 40 revamped garden rooms with plunge pools), all with terraces; twin or king-size beds

Amenities: Air-conditioning; bath with tub and shower, hair dryer, toiletries; telephone, television, radio, CD player; wireless Internet connection; coffeemaker; iron and ironing board; room service for continental breakfast

Electricity: 110 volts/50 cycles

Fitness Facilities/Spa Services: Blue Mahoe Spa and gym (see text)

Sports: See text

Dress Code: Casual; beachwear on Beach Terrace; no shorts or T-shirts in Pastafari's

Children: Fourteen years and older

Meetings: Up to 400 people

Day Visitors: Day pass, $49; evening pass, $69

Handicapped Facilities: Yes

Packages: All-inclusive, including greens fees

Rates: Per person, per night, All-inclusive. *High Season* (early January–early April):

$175–$320. *Shoulder Season* (mid-April–late June): $165–$270. *Low Season* (early July–late December): $145–$255

Service Charge: Included

Government Tax: Included

MARTINIQUE

As French as France and equally stylish, Martinique, the island of flowers, is a seductive beauty of savage mountain scenery and sophisticated resorts. From the north the land drops from razorback peaks covered with rain forests and an active volcano to flowing meadows and pastureland, to bone-dry desert. Whitecapped Atlantic waves crash against eastern shores; quiet, dreamy beaches hide in coves on the west. And it's all within a day's drive.

Fort-de-France, the pretty capital, is a shopper's favorite for French perfumes and designer fashions. La Savanne, the central square overlooking Fort-de-France Bay, is bordered by historic buildings and eighteenth-century town houses. South of Fort-de-France the Caribbean coast is scalloped with white-sand beaches. Pointe-du-Bout, a finger in Fort-de-France Bay, is the island's main tourist center, with hotels, marinas, a Robert Trent Jones golf course, restaurants, bistros, and a casino. The two sides of the bay are connected by frequent ferries.

On the southern shore overlooking Diamond Rock, a 2-mile stretch of palm-shaded beach is popular for windsurfing. Sainte-Anne, an idyllic colonial village around a tree-shaded square, is known for its seafood restaurants. Grande Anse des Salines at the southern tip has the island's most idyllic beaches.

Dominating the northern profile of Martinique is 4,584-foot Mont Pelée, usually crowned with swirling clouds. Its eruption in 1902 was one of the most devastating ever recorded. A north-country tour often returns via the extraordinary memorial of St. Pierre, the town buried in seconds under Mont Pelée's ashes.

Route de la Trace, a central highland road between Fort-de-France and Mont Pelée, winds northward through rain forests; each hairpin turn looks across sweeping views of the capital and coast. On a hillside at 1,475 feet is Le Jardin de Balata, a private botanic garden with more than 1,000 varieties of tropical plants.

On the northern skirt of Mont Pelée, Grand' Rivière, an old fishing village of spectacular scenery, is reminiscent of a Gauguin painting. Big volcanic rocks from Mont Pelée rest at the edge of black-sand beaches where vertical cliffs carpeted with wind-sheared foliage drop to the sea and huge whitecaps roll in from the Atlantic.

Information

Martinique Promotion Bureau/CMT USA
825 Third Avenue, 29th Floor, New York, NY 10022; (212) 838-6887;
Fax: (212) 838-7855; www.martinique.org; email: info@martinique.org

LE CAP EST LAGOON RESORT AND SPA

Francois/Vauclin, Martinique

One of the best kept secrets in the Caribbean is a resort in Martinique that opened several years ago to very little fanfare, yet it not only set a new standard for Martinique but is on par with the leading contenders in the Caribbean.

Located on the east coast of Martinique between the towns of Francois and Vauclin, Le Cap Est Lagoon Resort and Spa is an elegant, all-suite resort situated on its own peninsula about a 30-minute drive from the International Airport in Lamentin.

The seaside member of Relais & Chateaux overlooks a lagoon created by protective coral reefs that turn Atlantic waves into gentle waters. The long driveway into the resort, bordered by sugar cane and stately palms, is a comely invitation to what lies ahead. At the open-air reception, you are greeted by one of the hostesses (rather than a concierge) elegantly clad in long beige tunics, who serves you a cool refreshment and a soothing cold towel. While you relax, she completes your registration and accompanies you to your suite.

The resort's fifty suites are housed in eighteen villas designed to resemble a Creole-style cottage with gingerbread trim and set in a profusion of tropical gardens along the seafront and aside the large swimming pool at the center and walkways leading to the boat dock and the beach.

Cap Est, which got a four diamond award from AAA in 2008, has three types of suites: garden- or ocean-view; De Luxe with private pool and ocean view; and Executive suites, with private pool and ocean view. All are very large, measuring 2,400 feet or more. All suites are air-conditioned with overhead fans and have a bathroom with bathtub, separate shower and toilet, and a terrace.

The De Luxe and Executive suite bedrooms are furnished with king-size bed, desk, telephone, and have a shower outside in a small enclosed garden. The bathrooms have dual sinks, hair dryer, mirror, scales, and telephone. Executive suites have a dressing room. The living room is furnished with a sofa and loveseat, a plasma-screen television with satellite access, DVD player, cordless phone, safe, Internet access, and fax machine. Its maxibar is equipped with a fridge, espresso machine, and ice cube maker.

Guests at Cap Est have a choice of two restaurants—the casual, beachside Le Campeche for light fare, fresh grilled fish, and lobster, fresh from the lobster tank on site; and Le Belem, which serves a buffet breakfast and offers elegant gourmet dining in the evening. At the center of the room is the wine cellar contained in a huge drum meant to represent the tanks used for aging rum, Martinique's century-old industry. It holds 8,000 bottles of more than 120 varieties of wines from the main wine regions of France. Guests also have the option of room service from 6:30 a.m. to 11:00 p.m. with a charge.

Le Cohi-bar, near the lobby and Le Campeche restaurant, is the evening's rendezvous spot before dinner for cocktails and after dinner for entertainment when it becomes a piano bar or features performances by one of the local music groups several times during the week. The bar also has a large choice of rums (more than one hundred brands) including old rums from Martinique and a cigar cellar.

The resort's has an executive meeting room.

The interior decor throughout the resort is colorful but quiet, and emphasizes natural materials, textures, and exotic woods, with a touch of Asian influence and sense of tranquillity.

The Spa, built with fine marble, is operated in collaboration with Guerlain, the famous French cosmetic and perfume company. It is possibly the most exclusive spa in the Caribbean—only two people are scheduled at any one time. The facility has two individual massage rooms, steam room, and offers seaweed treatments, mud therapy, and hydrotherapy as well as manicures, pedicures, and facials. Guerlain cosmetics are on sale at the Spa.

Cap Est's other amenities include a library of books and DVDs, a well-equipped fitness room, and one lit tennis court. The swimming pool has a counter-current swimming lane and its private beach provides beach service. Windsurfing, sea kayaking, snorkeling, and kite surfing (with qualified instructor) are available, as is a small catamaran and a motorboat (no license needed) for guests' use for lagoon and sea outings. The resort can arrange for deep-sea fishing, excursions to nearby islets, golf at the eighteen-hole Robert Trent Jones golf course in Trois Ilets; helicopter excursions from the hotel's helistation; and car or 4X4 rental from Hertz. A hairdresser and limousine service are available on request.

Cap Est will appeal to anyone who appreciates a refine, sophisticated setting of tropical elegance, sumptuous yet understated accommodations, fine food, and service in an European ambience.

Le Cap Est Lagoon Resort and Spa
Francois/Vauclin, Martinique, F.W.I.

Phone: +0596 (596) 54-80-80; Fax: +0596 (596) 54-96-00; info@capest.com; www.capest.com

Owner: Geoffroy Marraud des Grottes

General Manager: Stephane Baras

Open: Year-round except from September 1 to October 15

Credit Cards: All major

U.S. Reservations: Relais & Chateaux, (800) 735-2478, 212-319-4880, or direct to the hotel

Deposit: None

Cancellation fees: Twenty-one days before date of arrival, 25 percent; fourteen days, 50 percent; seven days 100 percent. No show, full-stay payment

Minimum Stay: None except Christmas/New Year minimum seven nights

Arrival/Departure: Inquire from hotel re meeting service at airport

Distance from Airport: (Lamentin Airport) 10 miles; Private Airport transfer and return: €130 one to three persons; €160 4 to 6 persons

Distance from Fort-de-France: 16 miles

Accommodations: 50 suites (19 garden, 24 deluxe, and 7 Executive) in one- and two-story villa, all with balconies or patios; king-size or twin beds

Amenities: Air-conditioning; direct-dial telephone, cable television, DVD, VCR, radio; safe; bath with tub and shower, radio, hair dryer, makeup mirror, basket of toiletries; minibar; room service; concierge; boutique

Electricity: 220 volts

Fitness Facilities/Spa Services: Fitness center, full-service spa with six treatment rooms

Sports: Freshwater swimming pool; one lit tennis courts; windsurfing, kayaks. Diving, waterskiing, sailing trips, deep-sea fishing, golf, horseback riding, hiking arranged

Dress Code: Casual during day; resort elegant for evening

Children: All ages; cribs; babysitters

Meetings: Up to forty-five people

Day Visitors: Yes

Handicapped Facilities: Two suites

Packages: Summer

Rates: Per room, single or double, daily, including breakfast buffet. **High Season** (January 5–mid-April 3) €600–€1,125; **Low Season** (April 4–August 31; October 10–December 18) €450–€1,100

Service Charge: Included

Government Tax: Included

SOFITEL BAKOUA MARTINIQUE
Martinique, F.W.I.

The first time I visited Martinique, more than three decades ago, the Bakoua was the only hotel of any size or merit in the area of Pointe-du-Bout—all thirty rooms of it. Today the Bakoua has more than quadrupled in size, and Pointe-du-Bout has mushroomed into the center of Martinique's tourism industry, with many hotels, restaurants, cafes, shops, marinas, and water-sports centers.

Of course, the ambience of the hotel and its environs has changed completely. If you like to be at the heart of the action rather than sequestered in a quiet retreat, and if you prefer the conveniences of a large resort to the intimacy of a small inn, you will be happy at the Bakoua.

The lobby captures a panoramic view of the Bay of Fort-de-France. The dining room, with its open-air Creole architecture, embraces the tropical setting that faces the cove of Anse Mitan. You can watch the yachts at breakfast and have a romantic view of the distant lights of Fort-de-France in the evening.

Accommodations are located in three large, long white stucco buildings topped by red roofs, all with balconies, overlooking either the gardens or the sea. Three of the buildings are in the gardens on a rise above the bay; the fourth is a two-story block directly on the hotel's small beach, with the upper-story balconies shaded by coral-and-white-striped awnings.

All the guest rooms were recently renovated and upgraded. The deluxe rooms were refitted with the Sofitel "MyBed"— a soft, feather over-mattress, duvet, and four pillows treatment (MyBed bedding is hypoallergenic). If you fall in love with MyBed, you can buy one online at www.soboutique.com.

The guest rooms and suites have modern, minimalist decor while retaining their rich mahogany colonial-style furniture—including some carved headboards on four-poster beds and cane-backed chairs.

In addition to its pretty, oval-shaped swimming pool perched on a terrace overlooking the beach and the bay, the Bakoua offers tennis, windsurfing, an introductory dive lesson, and exercise equipment and aerobics classes in the fitness center. Water sports such as sailing, diving, and waterskiing are available from a nearby dive shop for a fee.

The Bakou provides thrice-daily shuttle service to the nearby eighteen-hole golf course designed by Robert Trent Jones (the island's only golf course). Sailing excursions on the hotel's own boat, jeep excursions, hiking, deep-sea fishing, and horseback riding can be arranged. The Bakoua has its own dock where visiting yachts tie up and from which you can take an odyssey of a day or longer.

From the lobby and dining level at the top of the rise, steps lead down to the beach and water sports. Le Coco is the beach bar at the water's edge; La Sirène, a casual but not inexpensive beachside restaurant, serves snacks and a light lunch of salads, fish, and grilled meats. Le Châteaubriand, the main restaurant, offers a buffet breakfast and gourmet dining in the evening, featuring French Creole and international cuisine, as well as nightly musical entertainment. Guests can enjoy steel bands on one night, the Ballet de la Martinique on another, a salsa parade or a fashion parade on others.

Le Gommier, the open-air cocktail lounge off the lobby, offers a ringside seat for sunset along with music for listening. The cozy lounge, with its circular sunken bar, is something of the hotel's social center. The balmy tropical air, the convivial ambience, and the wonderful views of the sailboats in the bay impart the warmth and friendliness of the old Bakoua.

The Bakoua is essentially low-key. Its biggest attraction is its location at the center of Pointe-du-Bout resort life, yet quietly secluded in its own gardens. It's connected by frequent ferries to the heart of the capital directly across the bay and offers the services of a modern resort hotel in the French milieu of Martinique. You might want to brush up on your French.

Sofitel Bakoua Martinique ***
La Pointe-du-Bout, 97229 Les Trois Îlets, Martinique, F.W.I.

Phone: (596) 66-02-02; Fax: (596) 66-00-41

Owner: Accor/Resort Hotels

General Manager: Hugues Lefevre

Open: Year-round

Credit Cards: All major

U.S. Reservations: (800) SOFITEL (763-4835); Fax: (914) 472-0451; www.sofitel.com/sofitel/fichehotel/gb/sof/0968

Deposit: Ten nights at Christmas; three nights in winter, one night in summer, thirty days in advance; twenty-one days cancellation in winter, seven days in summer

Minimum Stay: None

Arrival/Departure: Meeting service at the airport

Distance from Airport: (Lamentin Airport) 10 miles; taxi one-way, approximately €40 day, €60 night

Distance from Fort-de-France: 20 miles (forty-five minutes by road; twenty minutes by ferry); ferry one-way, €7.00 round-trip

Accommodations: 139 rooms and suites (including 39 beachside, 53 ocean view, 39 garden view) in three three-story buildings and one two-story block, all with balconies or patios; king-size or twin beds

Amenities: Air-conditioning; direct-dial telephone, cable television, VCR, radio, safe; bath with tub and shower, radio, hair dryer, makeup mirror, basket of toiletries; minibar; room service when restaurants operating; concierge; shop

Electricity: 220 volts

Fitness Facilities/Spa Services: Fitness center with equipment and exercise sessions

Sports: Freshwater swimming pool; two lighted tennis courts (night-play charge); windsurfing, kayaks; putting green, table tennis; diving, waterskiing, sailing trips, deep-sea fishing, Sunfish, fishing dock;

golf, horseback riding, biking, hiking arranged

Dress Code: Casual

Children: All ages; cribs; babysitters; one child under twelve years old can stay in garden room with parents free

Meetings: Up to fifty people

Day Visitors: Yes

Handicapped Facilities: No

Packages: Summer, spa, romance, others

Rates: Per room, single or double, daily, FAB. *High Season* (early January–May 31): €410–€644. *Low Season:* €360–€585

Service Charge: Included

Government Tax: Included

NEVIS

The lovely island of Nevis still typifies the Caribbean as many would like it to remain: gracious, innocent, and charming. Separated from St. Kitts by a 2-mile channel, Nevis rises in almost perfect symmetry from the sea to a dark green cone more than 3,000 feet high at its cloud-capped peak. Stretches of golden beach protected by coral reefs outline the coast.

Nevis was discovered by Christopher Columbus in 1493, and the first settlers came here from St. Kitts in 1628. Tobacco was their first export. By the eighteenth century sugar had replaced tobacco as the main crop, bringing with it large plantations and great wealth. Soon Nevis became the social hub of the Caribbean and developed an international reputation as the "Queen of the Caribbees."

Charlestown, on the western side of the island, is a West Indian colonial village lined with a medley of colorful old buildings so perfectly caught in time that the place could almost be a movie set. The Hamilton Museum was the home of Nevis's most famous native son, Alexander Hamilton, the first U.S. secretary of the treasury, who was born here in 1755.

North of Charlestown, Pinney's Beach is a 4-mile stretch of palm-fringed sands, where the Four Seasons Resort—the island's first large modern hotel and golf course—opened in January 1991, bringing with it jobs and a tourist boomlet.

Nevis and its sister island of St. Kitts have something of a monopoly on charming historic inns set in old sugar plantations, much as the plantations themselves cornered the market on sugar in their heyday. Morning Star, known locally as Gingerland, has several plantation inns located at about 1,000 feet in elevation on the southern slopes of Mount Nevis. Lanes and footpaths, ideal for hikers, run from one estate to the other.

Organized tours of Nevis with particular emphasis on the historical and natural attractions are available through Top to Bottom, (869) 469-9080; e-mail: walknevis@caribsurf.com.

Information

St. Kitts and Nevis Tourist Board, 414 East 75th Street, New York, NY 10021; (212) 535-1234, (800) 582-6208; Fax: (212) 734-6511; www.stkitts-nevis.com
Nevis Tourism Authority, Main St., Charlestown, Nevis; (869) 469-7550, (866) 55NEVIS; Fax: (869) 469-7551; e-mail: info@nevisisland.com; www.nevisisland.com

FOUR SEASONS RESORT NEVIS

Charlestown, Nevis, W.I.

When the resort first opened, before the wood of the cottages had weathered and the vegetation had grown tall, I was not happy to see the twelve long, two-story buildings—devoid of any architectural merit—strung out along the beach. Given the hotel's fabulous location at the foot of Mount Nevis and on the island's most beautiful, palm-studded beach, I thought Four Seasons had missed a golden opportunity.

I am pleased to report that time has been kind to Four Seasons Nevis. After being all but blown away by a hurricane in 1999, the resort took the opportunity to correct some of its worst mistakes. It helps, too, that the buildings I had described previously as looking like army barracks are now weathered and well-hidden behind thick tropical foliage. More recent renovations added a fourth restaurant and a third pool, while guest rooms and Nelson and Hamilton suites were refurbished.

Located on Nevis's leeward coast, Four Seasons enjoys a glorious setting along a 2,000-foot stretch of golden sand on Pinney's Beach, where hundreds of stately palms grace the property from the sand to the foothills of lofty Nevis Peak. Arriving by boat from St. Kitts, you see the resort in the distance after twenty minutes at sea.

The resort maintains the high standards for which Four Seasons is known, and its facilities are outstanding. Others think so, too: The resort was the first in the Caribbean to receive the highly coveted AAA Five Diamond rating. The resort's commitment to hire and train local people is another plus.

The modern Great House with lounges, bars, and restaurants anchors the complex. Its lobby rises high to a mahogany-beamed ceiling and opens onto flower-filled terraces that lead down to the swimming pools and beach. To one side is a mahogany-paneled library-bar; on the other side is the reception center.

Four restaurants offer a choice of casual or elegant dining. They highlight local fresh fruits, vegetables, and seafood, including lobster. The casual Neve, specializing in Italian cuisine for dinner, is a large, indoor/outdoor restaurant with an open kitchen and a wraparound, screened porch for outdoor eating. Beyond, the more formal Dining Room is set with candlelit tables, flowers, and linens. A children's menu is available. The poolside Cabana restaurant is open for lunch, cocktails, and dinner, and there's a separate beach bar. Mango, a casual seaside restaurant serving grilled specialties and West Indian cuisine, is located on the north side of the resort, just past the eighteenth green, from where diners can enjoy a great view of St. Kitts across the narrows.

The large, luxurious guest rooms are actually junior suites. Their decor is enhanced with stone tiles and a Caribbean color scheme. But the huge bathrooms (with telephones)—marbled from top to bottom—are the real showstoppers.

All rooms have large verandas where you can dine. They are furnished with a teak dining table and chairs. Other nice touches include genuine down pillows, individual reading lights that clip onto books, and free laundry room facilities in each building. Dual-line phones are available in all guest rooms.

The resort also has a group of forty-three luxury two- to six-bedroom villas (some with private swimming pools) available for rent.

All are equipped with a kitchen, washer and dryer, multiple televisions, DVD and CD players. These villas enjoy panoramic views of the sea, golf course, and nearby islands; they have fully equipped kitchens and spacious living and dining areas, along with full access to the resort and its services, including room service and catering.

Four Seasons' spectacular eighteen-hole championship course designed by Robert Trent Jones II, put Nevis on the map as a golf destination. The 6,682-yard course climbs from sea level up the volcanic slopes of Mount Nevis to an altitude of about 400 feet at the signature fifteenth hole: an awesome 240-yard par five across a deep ravine.

The resort has three swimming pools, including one for adult's only, and a large tennis complex, managed by Peter Burwash International. Five courts are lit; four are clay and six are hard courts. The resort offers extensive water sports (use of nonmotorized equipment is free) and a health club with Lifecycles, Stairmasters, and other equipment; locker rooms; a steam room, weight training, studio classes, and trainers. Exercise, aqua-aerobics, walks, and other fitness activities are offered daily.

There's a variety of hiking tours that can be tailored to individual preferences as well as diving excursions. The resort has several dive programs with a local dive master including one in which a day of diving is followed by a private beach dinner prepared by a Four Seasons chef; in another participants are challenged to lasso their own lobsters and help prepare their catch at a beach barbecue.

Among the latest additions are four free-standing, 200-square-foot beachside cabanas, available for rent. The cost begins at $350 per day per cabana in low season and provides an attendant and array of amenities.

The resort's spa is one of the most attractive in the Caribbean. It has twelve treatment rooms, most found in small West Indian–style gingerbread cottages, set in gardens around a large hot, rock-bound bath to one side and a long, cold-water pool on the far side of an outdoor lounge.

"Kids for All Seasons" is Four Seasons's program (free year-round) for children ages three to nine; it has a playroom with supervised activities and an outdoor playground. The resort provides children's beach toys, a bottle- and food-warming service, and supervised lunch, which is optional, as is early dinner. The program operates from 8:30 a.m. to 5:30 p.m. Several times weekly there are beach activities and a snorkeling program for children ages eight to twelve. An entertainment center for teens and preteens has video games, billiards, and other activities. A sea turtle education program developed in conjunction with the nonprofit Caribbean Conservation Corporation teaches children about Nevis' three species of endangered turtles. The Adopt-a-Turtle program involves a group of turtles that have been satellite-tagged with transmitters for scientific research purposes, and which can be followed through an Internet-based program at home or at school.

Reminiscent of a Florida golf resort, the hotel is designed to attract groups: small meetings, golfers, and honeymooners. Guests, mainly from North America, range from tots to seniors, but most are active couples eager to enjoy the resort's spa and sporting facilities.

Four Seasons Resort Nevis ★★★★
Box 565, Piney's Beach, Charlestown, Nevis, W.I.
Phone: (869) 469-1111; Fax: (869) 469-1040; www.fourseasons.com

Owner: Maritz Wolf & Company

General Manager and regional vice president: Andrew Humphries

Open: Year-round

Credit Cards: All major

U.S. Reservations: Four Seasons Resort Nevis, (800) 332-3442, (869) 469-6234

Deposit: Three nights; thirty days cancellation

Minimum Stay: Ten nights during Christmas

Arrival/Departure: American Eagle has nonstop service from San Juan directly to Nevis where guests are met and escorted to the resort. Alternatively, guests arrive by air in St. Kitts, where Four Seasons representatives meet and drive them to dockside lounge in Basse-Terre to board deluxe launch for thirty-minute zoom across channel to hotel. En route, staff completes check-in.

Distance from Airport: (Vance Amory International Airport) 6 miles; $50 per room round-trip transfer. From St. Kitts airport, transfer via twenty-five-minute boat ride, $115 round-trip for adults; $58 children (ages 5–11)

Distance from Charlestown: 1 mile; taxi one-way, $10

Accommodations: 196 rooms and suites (41 with two double beds, 138 with king-size beds; 17 suites) all with verandas; 43 two- to six-bedroom villas, some with pools

Amenities: Air-conditioning, ceiling fan; telephone, clock-radio, television, VCR; baths with tub and shower, hair dryer, bathrobes, scales, lavish toiletries; stocked minibar; coffeemaker, icemaker; safe; no-smoking rooms; room service; hair salon

Electricity: 110 volts

Fitness Facilities/Spa Services: Health club and spa (see text)

Sports: Golf (see text); ten tennis courts (five lighted), racquet rental; jogging, hiking, volleyball, croquet; three freshwater pools; snorkeling gear; abundant complimentary nonmotorized water sports; dive excursions

Dress Code: Casual by day; cover-up and footwear in Great House but no swimwear after sunset. For dining room, collared shirts, trousers, closed footwear for men; jacket and tie not required. Dress shorts permitted elsewhere.

Children: See text. Children's pool; babysitting; no charge for children under eighteen years old in same room with parents

Meetings: Up to 200 people

Day Visitors: Welcome with reservations

Handicapped Facilities: Yes

Packages: Romance, golf, honeymoon, wedding, villa

Rates: Two people, daily, EP. *High Season* (January–mid-April): $695–$3,950. *Shoulder Season* (mid-April–May 31; November 1–mid-December): $490–$3,200. *Low Season* (May-October): $335–$2,830. Prices include nonmotorized water sports. Villas: inquire

Service Charge: 10 percent

Government Tax: 9 percent, plus $10 per day Coastal Protection Levy

GOLDEN ROCK INN
St. Georges Parish, Nevis, W.I.

High on the side of Mount Nevis, in an area known as Gingerland, is an unusual, small inn 1,000 feet above the sea. It's on the grounds of an eighteenth-century sugar plantation operated by a direct descendant of the plantation's original owner.

Pam Barry, a Philadelphia native, came to Nevis on a visit in 1965 and stayed. She eventually became the owner-manager of Golden Rock and runs the inn as though she has invited you to her home. Recently, she took on partners—artists Helen and Brice Marden, whose abstract works are in the Museum of Modern Art in New York— and together, they are refurbishing and undertaking extensive renovations through-out the property. The tireless innkeeper dines with her guests, organizes garden walks, hikes, and tours, shuttles them back and forth from town and the beach, and takes them to interesting folklore shows and other activities around the island. If you prefer to go off on your own, she can arrange car rentals at a very good rate.

Set in twenty-five acres of flower-filled gardens and surrounded by another seventy-five acres of tropical beauty, Golden Rock was built in the early 1800s by Pam's great-great-great-grandfather, Edward Huggins. As soon as you start up the nar-row lane from the main road to the inn, you know you've arrived at a special place. Rooms with walls of century-old stone masonry, barely visible under curtains of brightly colored tropical flowers, have been converted into the living and dining spaces, with practical additions made only where needed.

The Long House, formerly the estate's kitchen and storeroom, contains the dining room, bar, and library and is the center of social activity. The rustic bar has a vaulted ceiling exposing the building's old walls. From it hang two large wicker baskets— lobster traps used by local fishermen— woven in a typical West Indian design that originated with the Carib Indians, who once inhabited the island. The congenial atmosphere at cocktails and after dinner makes it easy to be part of the family of new friends. The Courtyard, a flower-graced terrace with the bougainvillea-laden stone walls of the Long House as its backdrop, is the setting for lunch, afternoon tea, and cocktails, enjoyed to the musical accompa-niment of birds and crickets.

The Sugar Mill, the original stone wind-mill tower pictured in the hotel's literature, was built in 1815 to supply power to the plantation. Today it houses the honeymoon suite but is large enough for a family of four or five. It has two floors connected by a winding wooden stairway and is furnished upstairs with a larger-than-king antique four-poster mahogany bed for romantics and three beds downstairs. The rooms, dec-orated in blue and white, have wide window seats for reading or enjoying distance ocean views over the treetop.

Other accommodations are in brightly colored cottages on the mountainside above the Long House, the new, vivid colors coming from some of Mardens' paintings. Inside, the cottages are serene with white walls and white ceramic tile floors covered with colorful antique Moroccan rugs. Each has a private bathroom, and a front porch with a grandstand view. The rooms are basic but comfortable, with island-made furnish-ings. The most noteworthy are the cano-pied four-poster bamboo and mahogany beds made by the multitalented operations manager Rolston, who is also acclaimed for his rum punches. Amenities—shampoo, cream rinse, deluxe soaps, hair dryer, coffee and tea makers, ice buckets, and ceiling fans—are found in all rooms. Rolston and David (the head gardener, whose old-time string band plays on Saturday night) are typical of Golden Rock's gracious, friendly staff, most of whom come from the area and have been with the inn for a decade or more.

Dinner is served family-style in the Long House with a high arched ceiling (tables for two are also available), which has gotten a new, more elegant look with new red teak chairs and tapestry table cloths. You will dine on homemade soups and other specialties prepared with herbs grown in the estate's own gardens, fresh produce from village farmers, and fresh seafood caught by local fishermen. The new small dining room with lovely old stone on four sides is in use while a new dining room and kitchen are being constructed. The new dining room will have a barrel vaulted roof of glass through which diners will be able to view the stars.

In the gardens between the Long House and the cottages is a large spring-fed pool with a shaded terrace and comfortable chaise longues from which you'll find wonderful views across the southern part of the island and the sea. The estate has a strand of sand on 4-mile Piney's Beach for its guests' use. The beach bar, open December to July, prepares a daily lunch of fresh seafood, cheeseburgers, and its famous lobster sandwiches. Golden Rock owns another sandy surf-washed beach on the windward side, where the snorkeling (gear provided) is good and the beachcombing excellent. When you go off on your own, the hotel will pack you a picnic lunch.

Conservationists will appreciate Pam's strong commitment to protecting the local environment. Golden Rock is a natural for nature lovers, with trails and unpaved roads in the immediate area for hiking. The Rain Forest Trail, beginning from Golden Rock, leads up the mountain past several hamlets to the rain forest on the side of Mount Nevis. Pam has a map for her guests to use. The trail is an easy hike. Keep a watchful eye and you are likely to see some wild monkeys observing you from behind the trees. Hikes that explore other areas of Nevis with excellent local guides are also available.

A stay at Golden Rock is an unusual experience. The inn has a loyal clientele: an intellectually curious, well-traveled, eclectic group as likely to come from Europe as from the United States and Canada. Its historic setting is relished by romantics and history buffs alike. Its cozy, homey atmosphere makes everyone feel welcome, particularly someone traveling alone. There's also a special feature: Anyone can join the captain's table with the proprietor and enjoy good company, along with the good food. Now, Pam Barry's new American artist partners have brought a new dimension to the Rock, including an artist studio and the many artists who find their way to this little Caribbean oasis.

**Golden Rock Inn ** ** 🐚

Box 493, St. Georges Parish, Nevis, W.I. Phone: (869) 469-3346; Fax: (869) 469-2113; e-mail: goldenrockhotel@sisterisles .kn; www.golden-rock.com

Owner/Manager: Pam Barry

Open: Year-round except mid-August to mid-October

Credit Cards: Most major

U.S. Reservations: Direct to hotel or the resort's Web site

Deposit: Three nights; twenty-one days cancellation in winter; two nights deposit, fourteen days cancellation in off season

Minimum Stay: None except Christmas–New Year holidays

Arrival/Departure: Transfer from St. Kitts via ferry boat costs $8 per person and takes thirty to forty-five minutes. Contact hotel for schedule. American Eagle offers daily service from San Juan.

Distance from Airport: 7 miles; taxi one-way, $20

Distance from Charlestown: 5 miles; taxi one-way, $16

Accommodations: 13 hillside bedroom cottages with porches; all rooms with twin or king-size beds; Sugar Mill tower for up to five people

Amenities: Bath with shower, toiletries, hair dryer; coffee and tea makers, ice buckets; ceiling fans; no air-conditioning

Electricity: 110 volts

Sports: Freshwater pool, transport to two private beaches; mountain bikes, mountain hiking; tennis nearby; waterskiing, scuba diving, sailing, windsurfing, sport fishing, kayaking, golf, horseback riding arranged

Dress Code: Smartly casual at night; informal in day

Children: All ages; babysitters available

Meetings: Small groups and wedding parties, up to 26 people

Day Visitors: Welcome

Handicapped Facilities: No

Packages: Honeymoon, wedding

Rates: Per room, double, daily, EP. *High Season* (mid-December–mid-April): $220–$310. *Low Season:* $165–$185

Service Charge: 10 percent

Government Tax: 9 percent

THE HERMITAGE
Gingerland, Nevis, W.I.

Hugging the forested southern slopes of Nevis Peak, 800 feet above sea level, this one-of-a-kind resort resembles a Lilliputian village of dollhouses tucked into acres of tropical gardens. Its centerpiece is a small, 250-year-old great house, said to be the oldest all-wood house standing in Nevis. It is surrounded by traditional West Indian cottages with gingerbread trim, brought here from various locations around the island and reconstructed to serve as guest quarters.

The house was probably built about 1740—perhaps as early as 1680—by a family from Wales. Its longevity is attributed to the termite-resistant wood used for its heavy timbers, lignum vitae, which is highly prized for its strength and was perhaps taken from the original forest of Nevis.

The house remained in the same family until 1971, when it was bought by Maureen and Richard Lupinacci, then newly arrived from Quakertown, Pennsylvania. The couple made extensive renovations and added the cottages before they opened the inn in 1985. Maureen runs the daily operation and oversees the kitchen; Richard, one of Nevis's most active hoteliers, is a director of the Bank of Nevis.

The great house is small (less than 2,000 square feet) even by Caribbean standards and built in the shape of a cross aligned to the points of the compass. The drawing room has a high, beamed ceiling constructed in the old style with dovetailed corners to strengthen the frame.

The northern and southern extensions have two stories, each with lounges on the first level and bedrooms above. The great house has a formal dining room, a bar, and, to one side, a small music room/library walled with books and DVDs—all comfortably furnished in antiques and Victoriana like your grandmother's parlor. The music room opens onto a pretty veranda, and the drawing room steps down onto a covered terrace with garden tables and chairs in a romantic setting with latticework and arches draped with flowering shrubs. The terrace is used for breakfast and lunch. An enchanting intimate dining room furnished with walnut and mahogany antiques from Nevis's original Nelson Museum (there is a new museum near town) was added.

Guests stay in picturesque cottages—some old and some made to look old. The charming old ones have been carefully restored using original construction methods when possible. They are surrounded by tropical gardens brimming with flowers and exotic fruit trees. The guest rooms are furnished with romantic four-poster canopy beds with colonial-print coverlets; they have small bathrooms and private porches. All the rooms were refurbished and upgraded and most of the bathrooms were also redone and now have tubs and showers and pretty Victorian pedestal sinks.

Another three cottages by the swimming pool are newer and more deluxe. They have large, airy rooms with a bath and dressing area and a patio or balcony with a hammock for taking in distant views of the sea. Seven of the fifteen cottages have been upgraded to luxury level. Each has a sitting room,

kitchen, private porch, cable television, and telephone.

The Yellow Manor House, a replica of a Nevis manor house, sits in private gardens at the top of the hill. It has two large master bedrooms with large baths and dressing rooms, a living room, a dining room, and a full kitchen with laundry as well as its own private pool. Cook and daily maid service can be arranged.

Among the Hermitage's most unusual features is the riding stables made up of rescued horses for a breeding program. The hotel arranges weekday trips through the countryside.

In the evening guests and island friends congregate in the parlor for cocktails and congenial conversation. Dinner, announced by ringing bells, is a family affair served in the dining room or on the cozy veranda, depending on the number of guests and the ambience they desire. If you prefer, you can dine romantically on your private balcony.

The Lupinaccis, known for their warm hospitality, usually dine with guests at a communal table. The couple has a reputation for serving some of the finest cuisine and wines on the island. A set menu, changed nightly, offers four courses of French, Italian, or Caribbean specialties stressing fresh local fish, vegetables, and fruit. On Wednesday evening there is a West Indian buffet. Your companions are as likely to be English or European as American, and most will be in their midforties.

The Hermitage recently acquired two boats with which to entertain guests: A 34-foot trawler named *Intermezzo,* which the hotel can use to pick up guests arriving into St. Kitts; and *Gremlin,* a 27-foot sailboat. The hotel will also organize outings, prepare picnic baskets, and arrange car rentals. But the Hermitage is a homey, easygoing sort of place. You need not stir farther than the gracious gardens for afternoon tea or to a hammock strung between the breadfruit and mango trees, where gentle breezes will rock you to sleep.

Families are still important in Nevis, the Lupinaccis say. "We invite you to join ours at the Hermitage, a place where the cool breeze off the mountains meets the warm breezes from the sea . . . a special place where you make friends forever."

The Hermitage ** 🍃

Figtree Parish, St. John, Nevis, W.I.
Phone: (869) 469-3477, (800) 682-4025; Fax: (869) 469-2481; e-mail: contactus@ HermitageNevis.com; www.hermitagenevis .com

Owners/General Managers: Richard and Maureen Lupinacci

Open: Year-round

Credit Cards: All major

U.S. Reservations: International Travel and Resorts (ITR), (212) 476-9444, (800) 223-9815; Fax: (212) 545-8467

Deposit: Three nights; twenty-one days cancellation in winter, fourteen days in summer

Minimum Stay: Three nights in winter

Arrival/Departure: Transfer service not provided

Distance from Airport: 12 miles; taxi one-way, $25

Distance from Charlestown: 3 miles; taxi one-way, $15

Accommodations: 15 units (six luxury cottages with sitting room, kitchen, private porch, cable television, and telephone; other rooms in cottages with private bath; two guest rooms in stone carriage house, two in manor house); rooms have kings, queens, or twins that can be configured to suit

Amenities: Ceiling fans; most baths have tubs and showers, hair dryers; refrigerator, teakettle; room service 8:00 a.m.–10:00 p.m.

Electricity: 110 volts

Sports: Freshwater pool; tennis; horseback riding; sailing, fishing, hiking with guide arranged

Dress Code: Informal

Children: All ages; cribs; babysitters available

Meetings: Small groups of up to twenty-four people

Day Visitors: Lunch and dinner with reservations

Handicapped Facilities: No

Packages: Honeymoon, wedding

Rates: Per room, double, daily, EP. *High Season* (mid-December–mid-April): $325–$450. *Low Season:* $170–$265

Service Charge: 10 percent

Government Tax: 9 percent

MONTPELIER PLANTATION

Nevis, W.I.

Nestled in lovely gardens and surrounded by thirty acres of rolling terrain, Montpelier Plantation has an air of timeworn grandeur that gives the impression it has been there for three centuries, rather than a mere four decades.

Well, it has, and it hasn't.

The Montpelier Estate, in the interior hills at 750 feet above sea level on the southern side of Mount Nevis, was a prominent sugar plantation in the eighteenth century, belonging to the governor of the Leeward Islands. Here in 1787 the governor's niece, Frances Nisbet, wed Lord Nelson, the famous British admiral.

By the time James Gaskell, the hotel's previous owner, acquired the property in 1964, the original great house was long gone, but remnants of the mill and other structures were enough to provide foundations to build a small inn. By reusing the original stones and retaining the traditional architecture, the inn's authentic appearance—at least in the main buildings—was achieved.

In the summer of 2001, Montpelier Plantation was acquired by the Hoffman family. Lincoln and Muffin Hoffman and the general managers, Tim and Meredith Hoffman, their son and his wife, operate the inn as a family affair as the Gaskells did. The Hoffmans immediately set about upgrading and refurbishing the entire inn, often with interesting and unusual artifacts the family collected during their world travels.

An imposing brimstone structure that appears to be a great house was actually the old sugar boiling room, which was rebuilt into a grand drawing room where evening activities take place. Dinner is served in the Terrace Restaurant on its western terrace.

The attractive room has a high, vaulted ceiling that adds to its grandeur, and its antique furnishings are reminiscent of an English country manor, with portraits and old paintings on the walls and a mahogany bar.

The drawing room opens onto a colonnaded stone terrace on the east, where breakfast is served. It overlooks pretty gardens heavily laced with tropical foliage around a huge eighteenth-century windmill that once powered the sugar factory. The mill has been converted into a specialty restaurant, dubbed the Mill Restaurant, where five nights a week up to eighteen guests can dine on an elegant five-course fixed menu, dining by candlelight with a view of the stars through the Mill's vaulted windows. The gourmet dinner includes a glass of champagne and an intermezzo sorbet. The menu, which changes nightly, can be enhanced with wine pairings or tastings from the Montpelier's extensive wine cellar. Private parties can also be arranged with drinks poolside prior to dinner.

Beyond the mill is a modern spring-fed swimming pool bordered by a masonry wall painted with island murals. The poolside terrace has a bar with tables and chairs where lunch is served.

The hotel's guest rooms are in modest cottages beyond the main hall, all with verandas overlooking Nevis's southern landscape and the sea. The cottage rooms have Italian ceramic tile floors and bathrooms renovated from top to bottom. All have high, beamed ceilings with ceiling fans, making them all the more spacious and airy. They have been refurbished in a modified minimalist style with floral arrangements enlivening the natural white walls. Incidentally, there is power redundancy for water and electricity, thus helping to ensure self-sufficiency in both. All guest rooms have air-conditioning and are furnished with fresh fruit and flowers daily.

Montpelier has a long-established reputation for good cuisine. Breakfast is a treat of local fruits, fresh-squeezed orange juice, and honey and homemade brown bread and johnnycakes. Lunch—a la carte—and tea are served outdoors as well. A continental breakfast can be taken in your room, and the inn will pack you an early bird travel box. The hotel's charming historic setting attracts guests from other hotels for lunch or dinner. It is also a lovely and popular setting for weddings.

In the evening before dinner guests gather in the Great Room for cocktails and canapés in an English weekend-in-the-country atmosphere; new and returning British and other European guests balance out the American ones. The Hoffmans usually join their guests. Dinner, served in The Terrace, a AAA Four-Diamond restaurant, is a candlelight affair with a set three-course menu offering a choice of entrees; menus are changed nightly. You can dine at tables for two, or you may join others. The dining terrace offers views past the floodlit palm trees to the sea and the lights of St. Kitts. Montpelier sponsors entertainment by a local band during the winter season.

The hotel provides free transportation once a day to and from its beach club, Montpelier by the Sea, on the northern end of Pinney's Beach, about twenty-five minutes away. The inn will prepare a picnic lunch for you, and in the winter season, there is a weekly beach barbecue lunch followed by a seaside game of cricket (yes, it's ever so British). There's a gift shop and Internet access, free for guests. There is also a recreation room with television.

A member of the prestigious Relais Châteaux, the informal retreat with a AAA Four-Diamond rating has a wonderful staff who number nearly three times as many as the guests and who have been with the inn for many years. Upon your arrival they will greet you with a rum punch and cool towel, which is always a nice way to start a visit. The inn's timeless, unspoiled quality attracts nature lovers and couples of all ages as well as those traveling alone who appreciate its friendly, homey atmosphere. The guests are likely to be college educated, well-traveled, and in their forties or fifties, perhaps younger in the summer months. Montpelier is like a gracious private house—private enough that when Princess Diana needed to escape from the public eye and the British press, this was the place she chose.

Montpelier Plantation ***
Box 474, Montpelier Estate, Nevis, W.I. Phone: (869) 469-3462; Fax: (869) 469-2932; e-mail: info@montpeliernevis.com; www.montpeliernevis.com

Owners: Hoffman family

General Managers: Tim and Meredith Hoffman

Open: Year-round except mid-August–early October

Credit Cards: MasterCard, Visa, American Express

U.S. Reservations: Direct to hotel

Deposit: 50 percent; twenty-eight days cancellation for a refund of deposit less 5 percent

Minimum Stay: Ten nights during Christmas/New Year's

Arrival/Departure: Transfer service can be arranged

Distance from Airport: 12 miles; taxi one-way, $23

Distance from Charlestown: 4 miles; daily free transport to town and private beach; taxi, $15

Accommodations: 17 rooms in cottages (all with king-size beds; twins available on request), all with inside sitting area and outside verandas, and a new Garden Suite (an adjacent "Plantation" room can be combined with the Garden suite to create a two bedroom suite)

Amenities: Ceiling fans; telephone with international direct dial; safe; tea and coffeemaker; bath with tub and shower, hair dryer; room service for continental breakfast; no radio, television; all with air-conditioning

Electricity: 220/240 volts; 110-volt shavers

Fitness Facilities/Spa Services: Arranged on request

Sports: Tennis, racquets and balls free, professional for extra charge; snorkeling equipment loaned; waterskiing, deep-sea fishing, windsurfing, golf, horseback riding, hiking, eco-rambles arranged

Dress Code: Informal but with style; men wear long trousers in evening; jackets and ties not required

Children: Eight years and older

Meetings: Small executive groups

Day Visitors: Welcome with reservations

Handicapped Facilities: Limited; property has many steps

Packages: Honeymoon, wedding, others

Rates: Two people, daily, AP. *High Season* (mid-December–April 30): $490. *Shoulder Season* (May–early June and November–mid-December): $390. *Low Season:* $290

Service Charge and Tax: 20 percent

Government Tax: See above

NISBET PLANTATION BEACH CLUB
St. James Parish, Nevis, W.I.

The keystone of the Great House indicates that Josiah Nisbet began building the great house of his sugar plantation on the northern shore of Nevis for his young bride, Frances, in 1778. Nisbet died a few years later; soon after, the wealthy widow attracted the attention of the famous British admiral Lord Nelson—and, as they say, the rest is history.

Today Nisbet Plantation, which has an idyllic location at the foot of Mount Nevis on its own beach (most Nevis plantations were on the mountainside), is an antiques-filled plantation inn with a magnificent lawn that flows to the water's edge between double rows of stately palms and flowering gardens. With a little imagination you can easily picture the opulent life here in bygone days.

Nisbet continued as a sugar and coconut plantation until the 1950s, changing hands several times. In 1989 David Dodwell, a well-known Bermuda hotelier, acquired the inn and made extensive renovations, adding deluxe cottages and a handsome beach complex with a freshwater pool, a restaurant, and a bar.

An aura of the past continues to permeate the gracious inn, particularly its eighteenth-century Great House in classic West Indian architecture of gray volcanic stone. The resort's centerpiece, it houses the air-conditioned main dining room furnished with attractive antiques, the lounge with television, DVD, VCR, Internet access, a library, a bar, and a veranda stylishly furnished with rattan sofas and chairs. It makes an inviting setting for afternoon tea and cocktails, when guests gather to socialize before dinner and to listen to a variety of musical entertainment.

Next to the Great House is an open pavilion joining the reception area and the fitness center, a small gingerbread-trimmed cottage.

Accommodations are in pretty, pale yellow Nevis-style cottages generously spaced in the ¼-mile palm grove between the Great House and the beach, assuring ample privacy. The cottages, with louvered windows providing cross ventilation from the ever-present trade winds, are actually duplex suites, some with furnished screened patios serving as sitting rooms.

Other accommodations—three two-story villas near the beach—have four premier units each, more spacious and luxurious than those in the duplexes. Each unit has a king-size bed, a step-down living room, and an open patio with a wet bar and refrigerator. Bathrooms have a tub as well as a shower. All guest rooms are furnished and painted in soft colors with stylish fabrics accented with local paintings, terra-cotta pottery, and fresh flowers.

Nisbet's beautiful palm-studded beach is protected by reefs, but it can be windy, because it faces the Atlantic Ocean. It was the wind, however, that enabled Josiah Nisbet to put the plantation here in the first place. Now, as then, the wind keeps the air cool and relatively insect-free—and gently rocks the hammocks strung between the palm trees.

The resort has a croquet lawn, a large swimming pool with a hot tub, and a tennis court. Complimentary use of the court is limited to one hour at a time, and proper tennis attire is required. The Palms Spa, opened in 2007, has massage treatment rooms and a lounge for manicures and pedicures.

Breakfast is served in an informal setting at Coconuts, the restaurant in the attractive beach pavilion, while lunch is available at Sea Breeze, a beach bar. This is also the venue for the manager's weekly rum punch party and the beach buffet featuring fresh seafood and steak.

Dinner at the Great House, looking out across the avenue of coconut palms to the sea, is the evening's highlight. The romantic candlelit setting in the antiques-filled room, with its original mahogany floors, is ideal for the leisurely dinners of sophisticated European and Caribbean cuisine. During a full moon, when the light shines through the palm trees and reflects on the water, the scene is magical.

Nisbet is the Caribbean as it used to be, appealing to those who appreciate the island's serenity and want their space. In this relaxing setting you can choose privacy or the company of others, who are likely to be an even mix of Americans and British with a sprinkling of Europeans. Families with children are welcome and will appreciate the space. Brides will not find a lovelier wedding setting.

Some people say Nisbet's atmosphere is formal in an English manner, but I find the inn delightful. It's a bit tony, yes, but not stuffy.

Nisbet Plantation Beach Club ***
St. James Parish, Nevis, W.I.
Phone: (869) 469-9325; Fax: (869) 469-9864; e-mail: info@nisbetplantation.com; www.nisbetplantation.com

Owner: David Dodwell

General Managers: Glen and Erin Hurd

Open: Year-round

Credit Cards: Most major

U.S. Reservations: Island Resort Reservations, (800) 742-6008

Deposit: Three nights; twenty-eight days cancellation in high season; fourteen days in low season

Minimum Stay: None, except during Christmas

Arrival/Departure: Airport transfer, $10; transfer package from St. Kitts, $50

Distance from Airport: 1 mile; taxi one-way, $10

Distance from Charlestown: 8 miles; taxi one-way, $15

Accommodations: 36 units with king-size beds in 16 duplex cottages with screened patios; deluxe units have separate living room; twelve suites have living room, terrace, king-size beds, and couch that converts to queen; twin beds available on request

Amenities: Air-conditioning, ceiling fans; telephone; minibar, tea and coffeemaker; bath with tub in deluxe and premier rooms, shower only in superior rooms, hair dryer, bathrobes, basket of toiletries; nightly turndown service, complimentary laundry service, iron and ironing board, room service for continental breakfast

Electricity: 110 volts

Fitness Facilities/Spa Services: Fitness center; spa

Sports: Freshwater pool; free snorkeling gear, tennis; lawn croquet; golf, fishing, kayaking, windsurfing, scuba, horseback riding, and hiking arranged

Dress Code: Informal by day; no beach attire in Great House and no jeans, shorts, or T-shirts after 6:00 p.m.; casually elegant in evening; jackets and ties not required

Children: All ages; children under twelve years old served dinner at 6:00 p.m. or by special arrangement; cribs, high chairs; babysitters

Meetings: Small meetings

Day Visitors: Welcome with reservations

Handicapped Facilities: No

Packages: Honeymoon, anniversary, wedding, adventure, inclusive, spa

Rates: Per room, double, daily, MAP. *High Season* (January–March): $625–$835. *Shoulder Season* (April–May; November–December): $415–$625. *Low Season:* $365–$575

Service Charge: 11 percent

Government Tax: 9 percent

PUERTO RICO

American in tempo, Latin at heart, Puerto Rico is the gateway to the Caribbean. It has big-city action in San Juan and tranquillity in the countryside; glamorous resorts and friendly inns; golf, tennis, fishing, diving, horse racing, and baseball; and more history and scenic wonders than places many times its size.

Puerto Rico's two-year celebration of its 500 years of history in 1992 was centered around the exquisite restoration of Old San Juan, the oldest city under the U.S. flag. Along cobblestone streets, magnificent old mansions are alive with the city's smartest restaurants, shops, art galleries, and museums.

Only thirty minutes from San Juan, the Caribbean National Forest, commonly known as El Yunque, is the only tropical rain forest managed by the U.S. Forest Service. It has recreation areas and trails—and that's only the beginning. Across the center of Puerto Rico, a spine of tall green mountains divides the northern and southern coasts. The 165-mile Panoramic Route winds through the mountains and provides spectacular lookouts, hiking trails, swimming holes, and picnic areas.

Ponce, an architectural gem on the southern coast, is Puerto Rico's second largest town. It undertook a citywide restoration to mark the 300th anniversary of its founding in 1692. West of Ponce on the Caribbean coast, near La Parguera, is one of Puerto Rico's two bioluminescent bays, where microorganisms in the water light up like shooting stars with any movement.

Rio Camuy Caves Park near Hatillo is part of the Camuy River, the world's third largest underground river; you can see caverns as high as a twenty-story building. These are but a few of the attractions that enable Puerto Rico to claim it is the "Complete Island."

Information

Puerto Rico Tourism Company, 135 West 50th Street,
22nd Floor, New York, NY 10020;
(800) 866-7828; www.prtourism.com, www.discoverpuertorico.com
(Also see The Cervantes on p. 306 and La Concha, A Renaissance Resort,
on p. 307 in On the Horizon.)

EL CONQUISTADOR RESORT & GOLDEN DOOR SPA AND LAS CASITAS VILLAGE

Las Croabas, PR

"Hi, there!" the big, muscular waiter with a smile as broad as his shoulders exclaimed, greeting a couple of breakfast patrons, pencil and order pad at the ready. So startled by the robust friendliness were these jaded New Yorkers that it took them a moment to recover their composure. As though on cue, they lifted their shoulders, straightened their travel-weary backs, and responded with smiling faces, "Good morning, buenos dias." Neither could remember when they had been greeted with such enthusiasm by a waiter in the Caribbean, not to mention New York.

Service with a smile is only one of El Conquistador's assets. El Conquistador is a destination in itself. It offers options in accommodations—five separate clusters, each with a different appeal, due to its location and layout; in dining and entertainment—eleven restaurants, several lounges and bars, and a casino; and in diversions—an eighteen-hole golf course, seven tennis courts, six swimming pools, a Golden Door Spa and fitness center, a shopping arcade, a marina, a new water park, an offshore beach-fringed island with water sports, and one of the most beautiful and complete convention centers in the Caribbean. And all of this in a dramatic setting with stunning decor and a multimillion-dollar art collection.

Spread over 500 acres overlooking the fishing village of Las Croabas and Las Cabezas de San Juan National Park on the northeastern tip of Puerto Rico where the Atlantic meets the Caribbean, Puerto Rico's first true megaresort opened in October 1993. It is located 31 miles east of San Juan, about an hour's drive from San Juan International Airport.

Set at the edge of a 300-foot-high bluff and cascading down a heavily wooded cliffside to the shore, the multimillion-dollar resort is a reincarnation of a hotel of the same name built on the site thirty years earlier. El Conquistador, now an LXR Resort, was so thoroughly remodeled and expanded that only those with exceedingly keen memories are likely to recognize anything of its forerunner.

The resort's fifteen-member design team visited megaresorts in Hawaii and elsewhere to study their strengths and shortcomings. The results might be summarized in two words: openness and options.

To avoid the often sterile, homogenized character of megaresorts and to overcome their huge size, interior decorator Jorge Rosello, a master at space planning best known for his renovation of El Convento and La Concha (See La Concha in On the Horizon, page 307.) hotels, drew on Puerto Rico's Spanish heritage to give El Conquistador a distinctive local ambience.

Lounges, lobbies, patios, and plazas lead you from one space to another. Everywhere the eye is greeted with pleasing settings, dramatic vistas, or surprises. Around a corner or by an elevator where most hotels might have a table and mirror, Rosello created a conversation nook; in lounges where guests might idly gaze up to a blank ceiling, he occasionally added an interesting but unobtrusive fresco. Nothing, it seems, escaped Rosello's attention—even the chambermaid's cart is stylish.

Standard guest rooms, most with terraces, are as large as the minisuites of most hotels. They were recently renovated and have the minimalist white walls, furniture, and bedcovers with sunburst yellow and red pillows and throws. Some have two double beds, but most are furnished with a king-size one. Rooms also have a sofa that opens into a bed, handsome rattan chairs, a desk, and three phones, including one in the bathroom, plus a two-line cordless phone. All are air-conditioned and have ceiling fans.

The entertainment unit has a flat-screen television (there's also a small one in the bathroom), DVD, and CD player. All guest rooms have high-speed Internet access.

The bathrooms are a triumph. Unusually large, the dressing rooms—separate from the bathtub or shower and toilet—have a long marble counter with a sink and a large mirror surrounded by theater lights, plus a separate vanity and chair and a small refrigerator.

In the bathroom you will find a hair dryer, bathrobes, and plush towels. The walk-in closet has a safe and an iron and ironing board. Wall-mounted bedside lamps can be turned up brightly for reading or down low for—well, you decide.

El Conquistador's impressive entrance, reminiscent of the courtyard of a grand palazzo, sets the style for the resort. The large, inviting terrace sits under a high ceiling of staggered, peaked red tile roofs, suggesting houses in an Andalusian village. The tile and marble patio with conversation corners tucked in between the lush foliage has as its focus one of the resort's five large bronze sculptures by Angel Botello, the late Spanish-born artist who made Puerto Rico his home for almost forty years. From the sculpture at the edge of the patio, there is an expansive view of the sea, with Palomino Island and other islets in the foreground

and Culebra and Vieques in the distance. Below are bougainvillea-bedecked terraces, fountains, waterfalls, and three swimming pools that connect the main building wings.

Las Brisas, the northern wing, and La Vista, on the south, crown the crest of the bluff, providing most rooms with wonderful ocean views.

The lobby bar near the casino is the late-night hot spot with live entertainment by island bands. The newly renovated Club 21 is a sports bar by the casino. Off the main lobby is Casablanca, a Moroccan-theme nightspot with nightly entertainment; there are also the shops, a Starbucks, and an Internet center for guests to use without charge. The resort also has Wi-Fi. Beyond the casino is an ice cream bar and the coffee shop and family restaurant, and on the second level, accessible by an escalator, are three restaurants: Italian, Asian, and the newest addition, Strip House, the New York City steakhouse.

To one side, the main lobby is connected via a plaza to the newly expanded convention center—gorgeous and glamorous with its handsome carpets, glittering crystal chandeliers, and fine furnishings enhanced by original art and antiques, marble, and rich woods. It is the largest, most beautiful convention facilities in Puerto Rico, if not the Caribbean, with four elegant ballrooms, thirty-seven meeting rooms, terraces, and gardens. The center has a separate entrance and its own activities desk. A helicopter pad is located to its west side.

On the north side the lobby leads to a V-shaped building with five floors of guest rooms. The main floor is actually the fifth floor; guest-room floors are built down the hillside.

Las Brisas Restaurant, with casual indoor and outdoor dining terraces, open from breakfast through late evening, offers continental and American fare, including "fitness first" menus and Domino's pizza. The terrace overlooks the swimming pool complex. Along with three pools—one with a swim-up bar—there are five whirlpools, lanais, lounge chairs with small red flags to signal an attendant, and the Gazebo, an outdoor bar.

La Vista, the hotel's southern wing, is near the golf and tennis facilities. Rooms on the eastern side overlook the pool complex and spectacular sea views; those on the west look out over the golf course.

Additional accommodations are found in three distinct "villages." Each cluster has its own manager. Las Olas, midway down the cliff, has a private setting intended mainly for honeymooners. Built in a half moon around a large swimming pool, the units have large balconies overlooking the marina and coast. Las Olas and La Marina by the shore are reached from the hilltop Las Brisas via a funicular that runs regularly throughout the day and evening.

La Marina, a waterfront village that resembles a Mediterranean fishing village with a boat-filled harbor and waterfront shops, offers accommodations in town houses. It is designed for families and those who want to be near water sports and the new water park. Its restaurants include the Sting Ray Cafe, serving seafood specialties, and the casual Ballyhoo Bar and Grill with pizza, salads, sandwiches, and a raw bar.

From La Marina, where sailing and deep-sea fishing can be arranged, water taxis ferry guests in fifteen minutes to Palomino, the resort's hundred-acre tropical island rimmed with white-sand beaches. The island offers swimming, sunning, snorkeling, sailing, windsurfing, kayaking, horseback riding, and more. All equipment is nonmotorized. Scuba diving can be arranged, and there is a hiking trail. The island's snack bar, Iguana's, serves drinks and tropical dishes.

Next to La Marina is the most significant addition in El Conquistador's recent $120 million renovation: The 2.4-acre Coqui Water Park, the island's first, has something for every member of the family. It's high-tech meets nature in an action-packed 253-foot double innertube slide; high-speed, 40-foot vertical drop; 26-foot serpentine flume body slide; and innertube water rides along an 8,000-square-foot lazy river with wave technology that pushes riders through the river. There is an expansive, 25,554-square-foot sunbathing deck, 8,500-square-foot infinity-edge pool, a kids' pool area with a kids slide, the Oasis Bar & Grill, and an area for events. Park tickets for resort guests cost from $14.95 for children to $19.95 for adults and include tubes, pool chairs, and towels.

Camp Coqui, named for Puerto Rico's indigenous tree frog, the *coqui,* is the resort's daily supervised activities for children age four to twelve and costs $75 per day. The kids are separated into two groups: age four to nine and ten to thirteen. Camp Coqui offers a wide range of educational and fun-filled diversions, from Spanish lessons and nature hikes to a marine biology session before snorkeling. There's specially designed kid-size equipment, such as mini-windsurfers, tennis, and golf gear. Activities are held at Camp Coqui's facilities on Palomino Island daily from 9:00 a.m. to 3:00 p.m. and include lunch and a signature T-shirt. Babysitting services are available. The resort also offers summer camps and special packages.

LAS CASITAS

On the bluff beyond La Vista is Las Casitas, a resort-within-a-resort where exclusivity is the keynote. It combines the privacy and personalized service of a small hotel with the facilities of a large resort. Designed to resemble a colonial village complete with cobblestone streets, a bell tower, fountains, a public plaza, and villas in the style of Old San Juan, it is the most luxurious part of El Conquistador, offering lovely villa accommodations and outstanding personal service—enough to win a AAA Four Diamond rating. The ninety pastel-colored villas, intended for affluent travelers who want privacy and a tony ambience, have one to three bedrooms, a living room, and a fully equipped kitchen. Those poised on the edge of the cliff have balconies that embrace spectacular views.

Concierge service and private butlers are on hand to pamper guests and fill their every request. They will unpack bags, make reservations, arrange parties, and even cook special meals if asked. The service begins before you leave home with a pre-arrival call to determine your preferred drinks, meals, and other details so that your casita can be stocked accordingly. The royal treatment continues on arrival, when each guest is met at the airport by a resort representative who assists with baggage and transfers. Some packages include complimentary private transportation to the resort.

At the resort, Las Casitas guests are personally welcomed by a village host and escorted to their villas, which are fitted with casually elegant, comfortable furniture specially designed for Las Casitas and accented by textured fabrics. All units have entertainment centers in both the living room and bedroom with television, DVD, and CD player and high-speed Internet access. You'll also find a stocked bar, multiline telephones, a safe, a hair dryer, and an iron with ironing board. The kitchen has an oven, a microwave, and a coffeemaker, and it's stocked with dishes and cutlery. Las Casitas guests enjoy housekeeping service twice daily and exclusive use of the village swimming pool, Jacuzzi, terrace, and library lounge.

Las Casitas village is convenient to the golf course and tennis facilities, and next to the resort's fabulous Golden Door Spa. You can begin with a personal trainer who will analyze your needs, discuss your goals, and design a fitness program that you can take home. Then you have a range of treatments—from massage to aromatherapy and hot stones—from which to select. A fitness center with a full range of equipment will help you keep in shape. The spa has outdoor cabanas for treatments in three locations—at the Marina, Palomino Island, and the T'ai Chi lawn.

El Conquistador's eighteen-hole golf course (6,700 yards, par seventy-two), designed by award-winning architect Arthur Hills, is a beautiful spread across hills and valleys with four small lakes, one with a waterfall. Rain-forest-clad El Yunque is in the background; views of the Atlantic are to the north and of the Caribbean to the east. Six holes with water hazards and tight greens of Bermuda grass challenge a player's accuracy rather than strength. There's a practice putting green and free golf clinic daily. El Conquistador is operated by Troon Golf, a leading firm in luxury golf course operations.

The tennis complex has four lighted courts, including a stadium court. A daily clinic is conducted by one of the pros. The clubhouse for the golf and tennis complex has a pro shop, locker rooms, and the Grill, an outdoor terrace where breakfast, lunch, and cocktails are served. Golf Grill is a snack bar on the golf course; a refreshment wagon circles the course during the day.

Make no mistake, El Conquistador is large—very large. You will sense its dimensions upon arrival and when you first walk through the various lounges and levels to your room. But you will quickly forget about its size when you begin to see the details—and that's the beauty of it.

El Conquistador Resort & Golden Door Spa and Las Casitas Village ★★★★

1000 El Conquistador Avenue, P.O. Box 70001, Las Croabas, PR 00738
Phone: (787) 863-1000; Fax: (787) 863-6500
Las Casitas: (787) 863-6746; Fax: (787) 863-6758

Owner: LXR Luxury Resorts

General Manager/El Conquistador: Stan Soroka

Open: Year-round

Credit Cards: All major

U.S. Reservations: (800) 468-5228. Las Casitas: (800) 452-2274

Deposit: One night; seven days cancellation, except thirty days at Christmas

Minimum Stay: Seven nights during Christmas

Arrival/Departure: El Conquistador has a fleet of vehicles to transport guests between San Juan International Airport and the resort. Cost is $66 round-trip, billed to your hotel account. For Las Casitas, see text.

Distance from Airport: (San Juan International Airport) 31 miles

Distance from Fajardo: 2 miles

Accommodations: 983 rooms, suites, and villas with terraces in five locations (750 guest rooms; 17 suites; Las Casitas: 155 casitas (one, two, three bedroom villas). Either two double beds or one king

Amenities: Air-conditioning, ceiling fans; safe; bath with tub and shower, hair dryer, his and hers robes, iron and ironing board; two televisions with movie channels, DVD and CD player, three multiline phones; small refrigerator; desk; nightly turndown service, room service; casino; spa; shopping arcade. Las Casitas: see text

Electricity: 110 volts

Fitness Facilities/Spa Services: See text

Sports: Eight swimming pools; four lighted tennis courts; golf course, clubhouse, pro shop, locker room, bar; thirty-two-slip marina, sailboats, catamarans, yacht charters; deep-sea fishing arranged; Palomino Island with snorkeling, diving, hiking, volleyball, kayaking, windsurfing, horseback riding, new water park, and more

Dress Code: Casual by day; casually elegant in evening

Children: Camp Coqui with supervised activities; cribs, high chairs; babysitters

Meetings: Large convention center with four ballrooms and thirty-seven meeting rooms. Internet, Wi-Fi

Day Visitors: Yes

Handicapped Facilities: Limited

Packages: Adventure, golf, tennis, honeymoon, family, water park

Rates: $459–$769. Christmas rates higher; inquire.

Service Charge: 14 percent

Government Tax: 11 percent

THE GALLERY INN/
GALERIA SAN JUAN

Old San Juan, PR

Artists don't usually have the temperament for managing a hotel, but for Jan D'Esopo, it's only one of several things on her plate—or palette, in this case. This is an art-gallery-cum-inn, as the name implies, and there is nothing quite like it in the Caribbean. But what really sets the Gallery Inn apart is that it occupies five of the oldest buildings in Old San Juan. The last one added after extensive renovations in only 2007.

La Cueva del Indio, as one of the rambling old buildings was known, faces north to the Atlantic Ocean from the topmost crest of the Old City. Strategically located between the two large forts, the structure is the oldest military residence (built about 1750) on the northern side of the old walled city. Historians believe it served as the captain's quarters for the Spanish Artillery.

New York–born Jan and her husband, Manuco Gandia, a native of Puerto Rico, acquired their first building in 1961, and the restoration took two years. Today the complex of adjacent buildings has more than fifty spaces: a maze of rooms, passageways, courtyards, balconies, and gardens. You need a map to find your way around.

The art gallery and its exhibit rooms occupy most of the ground floor and double as the inn's lobby. The entrance is marked only by a street-number sign, but you will know you are in the right place when you see a row of sculpted heads on the windowsill of the silk-screening studio at the front of the house. The gate leads into a small bricked courtyard filled with plants and more sculpture. You may be surprised by the exotic birds—macaws, muluccan cockatoos, and an Amazon parrot peeping down from trees and perches. At dinner time, you may be greeted by a jungle cacophony that can get a bit loud.

The guest rooms are situated in every nook of the three-story white stucco buildings, and you make your way along narrow steps, around tight corners, and under broad arches. You will discover that the old stone, brick, and wood floors are seldom even, and steps go up and back down to reach some rooms. The handsome, beamed ceilings of ausubo wood (a termite-resistant native tree) are high in most places, but occasionally you might need to bend slightly to make your way. And everywhere plants and flowers overflow their bases, some hanging from upper balconies of the inner courtyard to the ground.

Every wall and surface, bookshelf and ledge, is enlivened with sculpture and paintings, either by Jan or a young artist she is helping to get established, or by acclaimed artists who come to give seminars or simply to visit. Special rates are extended to artists—who are often seen painting in a courtyard— and musicians, who may exchange a few days' stay for a concert. Pianists Frederic Chu, Jose Ramos Santana, and Michael Levin are a few of the world artists who vacation and play in the Gallery's handsome Music Room with a 9-foot grand concert Steinway piano. Candlelight chamber music and other concerts, free of charge for the inn's guests, are held frequently throughout the year (schedules available on the inn's Web site). August is its Music Festival Month. The Gallery is equipped with seven studios: painting, sculpture, mold making, cold casting, silk screening, and even a micro foundry for bronze casting. (Inquire in advance if you qualify.)

No two guest rooms are alike in size, decor, or amenities, but all have received a makeover that renovated, refurbished, and upgraded them—some to a deluxe level—with unusual rich fabrics, mahogany four-poster beds, or canopies and Tempur-Pedic mattresses—an unusual extravagance for a small, modest inn. Jan has painted trompe l'oeil in most of the rooms. Artists' rooms are nice and cozy but will not necessarily have a view; those without windows might have a painted balcony with a view. Some have terraces; all guest rooms have air-conditioning, telephone, and their own bath with shower.

Basically, the rooms are furnished in Spanish colonial decor, but the artist in Jan has enabled her to mix contemporary pieces, art, and antiques in an eclectic way without being funky. Well, maybe not too funky. To be honest, the entire house, from workshops to the sundeck on top, has a chaotic order to it, which is not surprising given all that happens here—the sculpting, painting, and music practicing—and that, of course, defines a great deal of its charm. One could say that the Gallery Inn is itself a work of art.

The Gallery offers a buffet breakfast with fresh tropical fruit, which is included in the rate, or a "country breakfast" (sausage, eggs, homemade bread, fresh orange juice, ham, tropical fruits, and Puerto Rican coffee) upon request for an additional $12; and occasionally Jan creates one of her famous dinners. (In addition to being an artist and innkeeper, she is an accomplished chef and caters elegant dinner parties for local businesses and visiting VIPs. She says she can seat as many as ninety

people for dinner, but I haven't figured out where.) With the addition of more restored buildings, a brand-new large kitchen was installed—there's no telling what new wonders Jan will produce now. Then too, within walking distance of the inn are some of San Juan's best restaurants.

Even more exciting, the newly acquired and restored building made possible the creation of a swimming pool with ancient brick walls as its backdrop. In the evening, the pool's indirect lighting creates a magical setting.

The Gallery has a refreshment bar in the main gallery that works on the honor system. You keep tabs and pay upon checkout. A cocktail hour for wine and cheese is also included in the rate. The Wine Deck on the top deck boast being the highest point in Old San Juan with views from San Juan Bay to the Atlantic Ocean and a great perch for sunsets.

The guests who come here—as many from Europe as from the United States—are an interesting group, well traveled, looking for the unusual, and as eclectic as the house. Many, too, are bed-and-breakfast aficionados. If you are exacting or need orderly surroundings to feel comfortable, pass up this one. On the other hand, if being amid art and artists is stimulating for you and you are flexible, undemanding, and willing to forgo some of the usual amenities of a hotel, or might enjoy a heated political discussion with Manuco, the man of the house, or want his opinionated restaurant recommendations, you will enjoy a stay here immensely.

The inn is homey as well as historic, but there's no one to pamper you. The owners and their staff will try to accommodate you, but essentially, you fend for yourself. You are welcome as part of the family and encouraged to explore the six levels of the old house, enjoy the paintings and sculpture, ask questions—even pick up a paintbrush if you feel so inspired.

The Gallery Inn/Galeria San Juan

204 Calle Norzagaray, Old San Juan, PR 00901

Phone: (787) 722-1808, 723-6515; Fax: (787) 977-3929; e-mail: reservations@the galleryinn.com; www.thegalleryinn.com

Owner/Manager: Jan D'Esopo

Open: Year-round

Credit Cards: All major

U.S. Reservations: Direct to hotel

Deposit: One night, payable by credit card

Minimum Stay: Two nights during high season (November–April)

Arrival/Departure: No transfer service

Distance from Airport: 12 miles; taxi one-way, $20

Distance from Condado Beach Area: 3 miles; taxi one-way, $10

Accommodations: 22 rooms and suites, all with air-conditioning, telephone, and private bath. There are four categories: Artist (one double or queen bed, located in the interior with windows onto gardens and patios); Colonial (larger size, one queen or king, opening to interior gardens, patios, balcony, or terrace overlooking San Juan Bay); Vista (more spacious, one queen or king, terrace or balcony overlooking sea or bay); and Top Side Suites (large garden balcony or terrace and Jacuzzi overlooking Atlantic Ocean)

Amenities: Honor bar; room service on request

Electricity: 110 volts

Sports: Horseback riding, tennis, boating, snorkeling, scuba, windsurfing, deep-sea fishing, hiking arranged

Dress Code: Informal

Children: Age nine and older

Meetings: Up to 40 people for meetings, ninety for dinner; 250 for reception; conference room, banquet room

Day Visitors: Yes, by appointment

Handicapped Facilities: No

Packages: Several three-day and off-season packages

Rates: Two people, daily, CP. *Year-Round:* $225–$410. For off-season specials, April 30–November 15, inquire.

Service Charge: 9 percent

Government Tax: 9 percent

HOTEL EL CONVENTO
Old San Juan, PR

This sixteenth-century convent in the heart of Old San Juan was transformed into a lovely, small hotel, with its historic architecture maintained throughout while the facilities behind its imposing facade have been modernized. By the time the present owners acquired the building, it had had so many incarnations, the fact that they could complete the renovations successfully was nothing short of a miracle.

Originally built in 1651 to house the first Carmelite convent in the New World and occupied by them until 1903, the building stood vacant for a decade until it was finally bought by the Church from the Carmelite sisters for $151. Subsequently, the building was rented as a dance hall and a flophouse without electricity, running water, or sanitary facilities. By 1953 it had become a parking lot for garbage trucks.

To save the historic building from the wrecking ball, Robert F. Woolworth (of the Woolworth family) bought it in 1959 from the Catholic Church for $250,000 and, after three years of renovations and restorations, opened it in 1962 as the elegant, hundred-room El Convento Hotel.

The hotel was a triumph socially but couldn't earn back what had been spent on it, and in 1971 the owner gave El Convento as a gift to the Puerto Rican government in lieu of back taxes. Over the next twenty-five years, the hotel deteriorated slowly as a succession of management companies operated it. Finally in 1995 it was sold to a group of San Juan business interests that spent two years and more than $15 million (about $275,000 per room) to create a fifty-seven-room hotel. Several more millions were spent in 2003 to add ten rooms on the second floor.

The renovations, which kept the architectural integrity of the original convent, were done by Jorge Rosello, an enormously talented Puerto Rican interior designer and space planner best known for the handsome interiors he created for El San Juan Hotel.

Partially covered during previous renovations, the spacious interior courtyard of the former convent—its arches and balconies hidden for centuries behind its 30-foot-thick walls—is again open to the sky. The courtyard has three different street entrances. The lower floors of the building house meeting and banquet rooms, along with three informal cafes: Patio Del Nispero, which takes its name from a huge tree whose

spreading arms shade the courtyard, and offers breakfast and Nuevo-Latino lunch menus and also handles the catering functions. CafeCana is a sidewalk cafe, and El Picoteo offers a tapas menu. At Il Perugino, an award-winning Italian restaurant located across the way on Cristo Street, guests who dine here can charge the fare to their room.

The hotel occupies the second to fifth floors and is reached by a private entrance and keyed elevator. Guests enter via the former convent entrance and check in at the ground floor concierge and reception desk. The wide corridors and rooms, decorated with handcrafted furniture from Spain, have retained their ancient tile floors, (previously covered by carpeting), and their mahogany ceiling beams. All rooms are air-conditioned and have a multiline telephone with dataport, flat-screen LCD television, Bose stereo radios, complimentary high-speed Internet access, an iron and ironing board, coffeemaker, refrigerator with bottled water, safe, hair dryer, and robes. The hotel has a junior suite (Room 404), which is an ideal family suite with two double beds in the main bedroom and a pull-out couch in the living room. Located adjacent to the pool terrace, it enjoys great views, too.

The grandest accommodations are the Vanderbilt suite, named for Gloria Vanderbilt, who stayed there, with a large bedroom and sitting room, elegantly furnished with antiques and rich fabrics; and the Casals Suite, named for Pablo Casals, the famous Spanish cellist who made Puerto Rico his home for four decades.

Hotel guests enjoy a complimentary early evening wine and hors d'oeuvres reception on La Veranda Terrace on the third level where the library is also located, offering guests use of computer and Internet access.

The rooftop Mirador Terrace, with wonderful day and night views overlooking Old

San Juan and San Juan Bay, has a small swimming pool and a Jacuzzi. An indoor fitness center with massage facilities is located on the lower level of the hotel. Through a special arrangement, guests also have access to the beach at its sister hotel in Isla Verde. The hotel offers a business and conference center for up to 300 people.

El Convento, an Old San Juan landmark, is located on historic Cristo Street across from San Juan Cathedral, where Ponce de Leon is entombed, and within easy walking distance of the important historic sights, museums, art galleries, shopping, and some of the top restaurants in the city. It is five minutes from the cruise piers, making it convenient for pre- and postcruise stays.

Hotel El Convento ***
100 Cristo Street, P.O. Box 1048, Old San Juan, PR 00902
Phone: (787) 723-9020; Fax: (787) 721-2877; e-mail: info@elconvento.com; www .elconvento.com

Managing Company: International Hospitality Enterprises

General Manager: Efrain Rosa

Open: Year-round

Credit Cards: All major

U.S. Reservations: (800) 468-2779

Deposit: One night; three days cancellation prior to arrival, otherwise one-night penalty will apply

Minimum Stay: Three nights December 27–January 1

Arrival/Departure: No transfer service

Distance from Airport: (San Juan International Airport) 5½ miles

Accommodations: 68 rooms and suites

Amenities: Air-conditioning; flat-screen LCD television, Bose stereo radio; refrigerator; multiline telephones with dataport; complimentary high-speed Internet access; hair dryer; iron and ironing board; safe; nightly turndown service

Electricity: 110 volts

Fitness Facilities/Spa Services: Fitness center

Sports: Plunge pool, Jacuzzi; tennis, golf, water sports arranged; walking tours

Dress Code: Casual by day; smartly casual in evening

Children: All ages; babysitting available; no charge for crib in room; children under thirteen free in room with parents

Meetings: Up to 300 people

Day Visitors: Yes

Handicapped Facilities: Yes

Packages: Romance, Pre-/Postcruise, Town and Country, Walk Through History, and others

Rates: Per room, single/double, EP. *High Season* (December 24–March 31): $365–$440; suites, $750–$1,500. *Low Season* (April–December 23): $210–$295; suites, $600–$1,200

Service Charge: 11 percent

Government Tax: 12 percent

EL SAN JUAN HOTEL & CASINO

Isla Verde, Carolina (San Juan), PR

Stylish, luxurious, and fun, the El San Juan lets you have your cake and eat it, too. It's a complete beachside resort only a few miles from the airport but within easy reach of the city center. It's large enough to offer all the facilities you could possibly want but not so large that it loses its personality.

Indeed, the El San Juan is so distinctive you could never confuse it with another hotel. Walk through its lavish lobby, brimming with art and activity, or stroll over to the poolside veranda and gardens, and you'll know immediately that this is like no other place.

The El San Juan does have its quiet corners, but this hotel is really for people who want to be in the center of the action, day or night. It has seven restaurants (each with a different cuisine), twelve bars and lounges, a casino, a disco, three swimming pools, three tennis courts, water sports, a health club and spa, a daily children's program, an arcade of chic boutiques, and a staff of more than 1,000 who make sure it hums around the clock.

Set in fifteen acres of tropical gardens on the Atlantic northern coast, the El San Juan is located on the eastern edge of the city. The landmark hotel reigned as the grande dame of Caribbean hotels in the 1960s, but by the decade's end, when Puerto Rico's fortunes had tumbled, the El San Juan closed and the Isla Verde area deteriorated. Williams Hospitality bought the hotel in 1984 and reopened it one year and $50 million later, launching Puerto Rico's tourism renaissance. It's now owned by LXR Luxury Resorts, which has just spent $52 million to redesign, renovate, and refurbish the lobby, guest rooms, meeting spaces,

pool and beach areas, and added a new restaurant.

The El San Juan has actually undergone three transformations by three interior designers, with completely different ideas, working more than a decade apart but resulting in remarkable harmony.

In the 1960s New York designer Alan Lanigan traveled through Africa, Asia, and Europe collecting artwork, relics, balustrades, and other decorative and architectural elements to embellish the hotel. He acquired storefronts to design a shopping arcade, and shipped heavy wooden doors, many more than a century old, from North Africa; oil paintings and art deco lamps from Europe. In the 1980s Puerto Rican interior designer Jorge Rosello recognized the uniqueness of Lanigan's work and built on it. He enlivened the interior with a more cheerful environment, creating a more tropical feeling. The top to bottom renovation brought new restaurants and shops and a new beachfront wing with twenty-one deluxe suites and a private pool. The building, set at the edge of the beach and surrounded by tropical gardens, is situated in such a way that the suites—as large as some New York apartments—are furnished in mahogany pieces with colorful fabrics and pillows and a convertible sofa. Each has a minibar, a safe, three multiline telephones, voice mail, fax-modem outlets, and an iron and ironing board. The huge bathrooms have a double-sink vanity, separate shower, and 6-foot-long whirlpool bathtub.

In the latest transformation, the most dramatic new settings are the guest rooms and the gardens. Created by Robert Barry of Barry Design Associates, who was responsible for all interior renovations, the guest rooms have a total new look. Bathed in white with splashes of fuchsia and chartreuse in pillows, throws, and artwork on the walls, one's eye is immediately drawn to the soft and sensual sheers covering the window and door to the veranda with a hint of orange and a tropical pattern that picks up the colors in the room. Subtle textures and tone-on-tone layered elements are seen in the bedcovers and in the flooring of white with a faint gray tint and metal strips between each third tile for contrast. Classic lines are mixed with modern materials in the acrylic desk chair and lamp that are replicas of an antique lamp and chair.

The hotel offers a great variety of guest rooms: poolside, ocean, and garden suites, and moderate, standard, and superior rooms and suites in the tower. A few suites have kitchenettes.

For its outdoor transformation, El San Juan called on New York–based nightlife designer Stephane Dupoux who designed the seductive Encanto Beach Club, meant to create the ultimate outdoor party scene in San Juan's sultry tropical environment. The redesigned deck and poolside areas are now an open-air lounge with twenty-four canopied, double day beds, three private cabanas, twenty-five retro-circular lounging pods, overstuffed chaise lounges and cocoon chairs, hammocks, swings, a swim-up bar, and outside showers. The sexy ambience goes a step further with subtle scents and a state-of-the-art sound system in the entire area.

Early birds can be served "breakfast in bed" poolside that can be ordered the night before, and start their Encanto Beach Club mornings with water chi, an aqua version of tai chi, or yoga classes on the beach. You can sample one of seven varieties of mojito from the Mojito Cart and watch swimsuit fashion shows in the afternoon. You can request conversational Spanish lessons during the day and practice it with salsa dancing lessons in the evening. Programmed iPods with Caribbean music are available to check-out; and you can catch up on your reading with the resort's iBooks (iPods with books from the *New York Times'* Bestsellers List). For an extra level of luxury, one of the three private tiki hut cabanas is yours for $800 for the day where you'll have Wi-Fi, flat-screen television, minibar and safe. The famous, fabulous, action-center lobby, with new decor including a lovely blue-glass sculpture (the famous oval chandelier is still there) is the hub of the hotel and the best people-watching spot in San Juan. To one side is the new Silver Bar, in handsome silver and red. It's the only Cruvinet wine bar in the Caribbean and offers twenty-two champagnes and wines by the glass. To the other side is the Gold Bar and the casino.

Live entertainment in the lobby bars and El Chico nightclub is featured until the wee hours, and at Brava, one of San Juan's "hot" discos and a mecca for the under-twenty-three crowd. The roof has the Tequila Bar and Grill and an outdoor Mexican restaurant where the margaritas are fabulous, and the Agave Ranch, Puerto Rico's first country-western bar and grill, complete with a mechanical bull and the Nashville sound.

Other dining choices include Las Terranzas, a casual outdoor terrace cafe overlooking the pool and gardens; The Palm, a replica of the famous Manhattan steakhouse; La Piccola Fontana, for northern Italian dishes; Yamato, a Japanese restaurant with a sushi bar; Starbucks; and a Pizzeria bar and grill serving open hearth pizzas, located off the lobby.

Koco, a modern Caribbean restaurant, rum bar, and lounge is the newest edition. Its cuisine, as well as its decor, blends Caribbean, Asian, and Latin elements in fun, tropical and relaxed ways. The culinary team is headed by Executive Chef Dustin Atoigue, who has worked with such great chefs as Sam Choy and Wolfgang Puck; and Chef Sylva Senat who studied under Daniel Boulud and worked at Jean Georges and Buddakan in New York City. With its large space situated off the main lobby, Koco easily accommodates private parties and corporate groups. The restaurant is open daily from 5:00 p.m. to 12:00 midnight.

The Edouard de Paris Day Spa, located on the tenth floor, is a full-service spa offering massages, facials, and body treatments. It has five private treatment rooms, a Couples' nook for couples massages, "Vapeur," for a wet steam experience; separate men's and women's locker rooms, and a relaxation lounge.

Kids' Klub, a supervised program for children ages five to twelve offered daily from 10:00 a.m. to 4:00 p.m., costs $40 per day per child, including lunch. Reservations are required twenty-four hours in advance. The program cannot operate if fewer than three children participate.

El San Juan Hotel's sister hotel, the Condado Plaza and Casino in Condado has just completed a multimillion-dollar contemporary redesign of all rooms, meeting, and public spaces, including an impressive new lobby designed by David Rockwell, and the addition of Strip House steakhouse.

El San Juan Hotel & Casino *****
6063 Isla Verde Avenue, #187, Carolina (San Juan), PR 00979
Phone: (787) 791-1000; Fax: (787) 791-6985; www.elsanjuanhotel.com
Owner: LXR Luxury Resorts
General Manager: John Paul Oliver

Open: Year-round

Credit Cards: All major

U.S. Reservations: (866) 317-8935; Fax: (787) 791-0390

Deposit: One night; three days cancellation

Minimum Stay: None

Arrival/Departure: No transfer service

Distance from Airport: (Luis Marin Muñoz International Airport) 5 miles; taxi one-way, $15

Distance from Old San Juan: 10 miles; taxi one-way, about $20

Accommodations: 382 rooms and suites, most with verandas (261 in main building, 128 in gardens and on beach)

Amenities: Air-conditioning, ceiling fan; cable flat-screen television, DVD, clock-radio, CD player; three telephones; safe; iron and ironing board; bath with tub, shower, vanity, bathrobes, toiletry basket, 5-inch television, hair dryer; nightly turndown service on request; ice service, stocked minibar; twenty-four-hour concierge, room service; business services

Electricity: 110 volts

Fitness Facilities/Spa Services: Fully equipped fitness center and spa on tenth floor of main building

Sports: Beach, three freshwater swimming pools, three Jacuzzis, three lighted tennis courts, equipment, daily clinics free; snorkeling, scuba, windsurfing for fee; golf, boating, fishing, horseback riding, hiking arranged

Dress Code: Casual by day; elegantly casual in evening

Children: All ages; Kids' Klub, supervised activities; game room; cribs, high chairs; babysitters

Meetings: Up to 1,200 people

Day Visitors: Welcome

Handicapped Facilities: Limited; wheelchair-accessible; dedicated rooms

Packages: Honeymoon; Caribbean Magic

Rates: Two people, daily, EP. *High Season* (late November–April 30): $229–$1,600. *Low Season:* $169–$1,000

Service Charge: 14 percent

Government Tax: 11 percent

THE RITZ-CARLTON SAN JUAN HOTEL, SPA & CASINO

Isla Verde, Carolina (San Juan), PR

Located in Isla Verde on eight beachfront acres less than ten minutes from the international airport, this hotel is a Ritz-Carlton inside and out, with signature architecture and design. But check the details and you will see that it has a style and character all its own.

First, there is the lobby, whose windows span the first and second floors and look out on the gardens to the swimming pool and the sea. It's very impressive. Here, in the pleasant surroundings of the lobby lounge, a continental breakfast, tea, and cocktails are served, usually with background music. It sets the tone for the hotel. And does this hotel have tone!

From the moment you step into the rosy beige marbled lobby, you see and sense a refinement that no other hotel in San Juan can match. To the right is the front desk—it's marble; to the left is the concierge's desk—it's marble, too. And the floors, here and throughout the hotel, are covered with the most handsome hotel carpets ever to grace a hallway. Wonderful works of art by Puerto Rican artists enliven the walls throughout the hotel.

The building is in the shape of a U around a swimming pool and gardens that stretch to a wide beach and the sea. To one side of the pool is a large Jacuzzi under a pretty gazebo; to the other you'll find the Ocean Bar and Grill (which serves lunch and daytime snacks), a spa and fitness center, and two lighted tennis courts.

Across the gardens in the west wing are the restaurants on the ground level; upstairs is a huge, elegant ballroom that extends to an outdoor terrace overlooking the gardens and the pool. Around the corner from the lobby and tucked out of sight is a large casino—the first for a Ritz-Carlton—with its own separate entrance. Over the last several years, The Ritz-Carlton San Juan has made big and small changes. When the hotel opened a decade ago, only 21 of its 416 rooms had balconies, but now, after frequent guest requests for them, 40 more balconies were added. The hotel is prepared to add more, if demand warrants.

The contemporary-style balconies, designed by a local Puerto Rican architectural/engineering firm, are 15 feet long by 3.5 feet wide with terra-cotta-tiled floors and a wrought-iron frame. Large enough for two chairs and a small table, they overlook the hotel's beautiful gardens and the ocean beyond. The room's air-conditioning automatically shuts off when the balcony door is opened. The balcony rooms will carry a premium of approximately $110 higher per night.

The guest rooms seem a bit small by Ritz-Carlton standards, but they are tastefully appointed and have large marble bathrooms with separate toilets. All guest rooms and suites were refurbished recently with more contemporary decor, Internet access, flat-screen television, Bulgari toiletries, and a new, almost revolutionary (for Ritz-Carlton, that is) amenity—a coffeemaker—has been added. But in true Ritz-Carlton style, it's no ordinary coffee pot. Rather, a sleek, pod-type coffeemaker and an equally stylish pot for brewing tea are encased in a fine mahogany box, reminiscent of a colonial campaign chest. It has compartments for china cups, stirrers, as well as coffee pods (regular and decaf), a selection of teas, small containers of real cream, and packets of sugar. The rooms are air-conditioned and have stocked minibars, three telephones with dual lines and dataport, a clock-radio, a safe, a hair dryer, scales, and signature bathrobes. There is twice-daily maid service and twenty-four-hour room service. Nonsmoking floors are available.

The Ritz-Carlton Club floor, accessible only by a key-activated elevator, has deluxe rooms, a private lounge, and gracious, truly helpful concierge staff and offers complimentary continental breakfast, light lunch, afternoon tea, hors d'oeuvres, cordials, and truffles.

The Caribbean Grill, the main restaurant, has indoor and outdoor seating by the gardens. It seems to have won a big vote of approval from San Juan residents, judging from the crowds at Sunday brunch. By the swimming pool and near the beach is the Ocean Bar and Grill, a moderately priced, open-air eatery, popular for lunch.

In 2007, the rapidly expanding BLT Steak restaurants of French chef Laurent Tourondel opened BLT Steak at the Ritz-Carlton, its first one in the Caribbean. BLT (which stands for Bistro Laurent Tourondel) Steak, is open for dinner only. It has a raw bar and a selection of seafood entries, but the specialty is steak, particularly Kobe beef and Wagyu Skirt, the American version. Both are expensive. There is also a selection of fifteen desserts and a small kid's menu. BLT Steak replaced the former Vintage room and Prime. The well-known New York Italian restaurant, Il Molino, a Tiffany & Company, and Little Switzerland boutiques are other new amenities added in 2006.

Perhaps the hotel's most ambitious project is the building of a new 20,000-square-foot spa, almost double the size of the present spa. The new facility will have sixteen treatment rooms, including ones for couples, and a fitness center. To be built over the hotel's casino, construction is scheduled to begin in late 2008. The present spa and fitness center, which will continue to operate until the new facility opens, is housed in an elegant marble and stone bilevel building, has eleven treatment rooms for facials, massages, manicures, pedicures, hydrotherapy, and body wraps. The fitness center offers yoga, aerobics, and other strength and fitness activities.

The Ritz Kids Club, for ages four to twelve, operates Sunday to Thursday from 9:00 a.m. to 4:00 p.m., Friday and Saturday from 9:00 a.m. to 9:00 p.m. This was the first Ritz-Carlton to offer a Ritz Kids Day at the Spa.

The Ritz-Carlton San Juan Hotel, Spa & Casino ****
6961 Avenue of the Governors, Isla Verde, Carolina, PR 00979
Phone: (787) 253-1700, (800) 241-3333; Fax: (787) 253-0700

Owner: Caribbean Property Group

Management: The Ritz-Carlton Hotel Company, L.L.C.

General Manager: Steve Redkoles

Open: Year-round

Credit Cards: Most major

U.S. Reservations: Direct to hotel, (800) 241-3333

Deposit: One night, fourteen days after booking; three–seven days cancellation in high season, depending on week

Minimum Stay: Four to seven nights in winter

Arrival/Departure: Transfer arranged for fee

Distance from Airport: 1½ miles; taxi one-way, $10

Distance from Old San Juan: 3 miles

Accommodations: 416 guest rooms, six executive suites, 40 pool-view kings, four garden suites

Amenities: Air-conditioning; safe; cable television, three telephones with dual lines and dataport, clock-radio; baths with tubs and showers, hair dryers, bathrobes, scales, deluxe toiletries; honor bar; twice-daily maid service, twenty-four-hour room service; nonsmoking floors available

Electricity: 110 volts

Fitness Facilities/Spa Services: Full-service spa

Sports: Swimming pool, water sports; golf, diving, deep-sea fishing, horse racing, sailing, horseback riding arranged

Dress Code: Casual chic; trousers for men at dinner

Children: All ages

Meetings: Up to 1,300 people

Day Visitors: Yes

Handicapped Facilities: Yes

Packages: Spa, summer, honeymoon

Rates: Per room, EP. *High Season* (December 21–April 30): $399–$1,529. *Low Season:* $209–$899. For Presidential or two-bedroom suites, inquire.

Service Charge: 10 percent

Government Tax: 11 percent on room

ST. BARTS

Tiny St. Barts is an Eden of 8 square miles with green hills and rolling terrain edged with pretty white-sand beaches and ringed by shallow reefs ideal for snorkeling. The darling of sophisticates and others who can afford it, this haven was discovered four decades ago by the Rockefellers and the Rothschilds, who wisely kept it a secret as long as they could.

A ten-minute flight from St. Martin, St.-Barthelémy (as it is properly named) is one of the French West Indies. The language is French, the currency is the euro, and the boutiques are stocked with famous French designer perfumes and accessories. It is also the gastronomic capital of the Caribbean, with sixty gourmet restaurants at last count.

Arawak Indians, Christopher Columbus (who named the island for his brother's patron saint), French settlers from St. Kitts, the Knights of Malta, Carib Indians, Frenchmen from Normandy and Brittany, the British, and the Swedes all were here. Those who left a permanent mark were the Swedes, who named the tiny harbor and capital, Gustavia; and the French from Normandy, from whom most of the population are descended.

At Corossol, the most traditional of the tiny fishing villages, shy elderly women still don the calèche, a stiff-brimmed bonnet derived from a seventeenth-century Breton style, and make handwoven straw hats and other products from the supple straw of latania palms' fan-shaped fronds.

The tiny island is a beguiling beauty on which every turn in the road—and there are many—reveals striking panoramas. It is easy to tour by car on its roller-coaster roads.

Gustavia, the miniature port on the western coast, is a yachting mecca. On the north St. Jean Bay is the center of resort and water-sports activity. Grand Cul-de-Sac, a large reef-protected bay on the northeast, is another resort center. On the north-western end, Colombier is a pretty cove accessible by foot or boat.

Anse des Flamands to the north is one of the island's most beautiful beaches; Governor's Cove and Anse de Grande Saline, to the south, are the most secluded. Signs banning nude bathing abound but are not always obeyed: Teeny monokinis are the fashion.

Information

French West Indies Tourist Board, 825 Third Avenue, 29th Floor,
New York, NY 10022; (212) 745-0950, (800) 391-4909; Fax: (212) 838-7855;
www.stbarthonline.com, www.st-barths.com.
Offices in Chicago, Los Angeles, and Montreal, Canada.
(Also see Le Sereno on p. 308 in On the Horizon.)

EDEN ROCK

St.-Barthelémy, F.W.I.

Perched on a great crag of quartzite splitting the splendid beach of St. Jean Bay, the historic Eden Rock was St. Barts's first hotel—a diamond in the rough now polished and returned to stardom.

Designed and built in 1953 by pioneer-aviator-turned-longtime-mayor Remy de Haenen, who first landed his tiny plane on a grassy field nearby, the stone structure where he made his home sprouts dramatically from a rock base that has long been an island landmark. The property gradually became run-down on an island increasingly chic, until it was sold in 1995 to a British couple armed with the resources and sense of style to set the jewel properly. And did they ever! David and Jane Matthews completely restored and upgraded their tropical stone inn, adding new rooms on the beach, a pool, a water-sports center, and three restaurants.

The Matthews continued to expand by acquiring their next-door neighbor, Filao Beach, and replaced its cottages with new one-bedroom suites and four cottages. Now Eden Rock has thirty-three accommodations of great variety located "on the rock" and along the white-sand beach. Among them are a three-bedroom Big Beach House on the beach with a private swimming pool, Jacuzzi, two bathrooms, and terrace; and two new beachfront villas—the two bedroom ultra-luxe Villa Nina with an art gallery, a private butler, pool, use of a Mini Cooper and more; and Rockstar, scheduled to open in January 2009, with four bedrooms on three levels with spectacular views.

On "top of the rock" the Howard Hughes Loft Suite, the hotel's signature suite, on has 360-degree views of the bay, three terraces, and two bathrooms; and Waterlily,

a one-bedroom beach bungalow with nice stone and woodwork, a private infinity pool, Jacuzzi, and terrace. Michael's Suite on the beach has a private swimming pool and Philippe Starck bathroom. A group of contemporary rooms are found in the newly constructed split-level Plantation houses on the beach. All have terraces with beach views; the ground floor suites have direct access onto the beach. All are furnished with a king bed; two ground floor suites have disabled access and facilities.

Eden Rock's original clifftop rooms, with names such as the Greta Garbo Suite, are the breezy best choices, although every room is different. Some have four-poster beds, mosquito netting, antiques, and panoramic terraces; some are awash in tropical colors with watercolors and gouaches by Jane and her children; others are old-fashioned with whimsical touches such as steamer trunks and family heirlooms from the owners' Surrey estate.

Harbour House has a large balcony overlooking the bay, a private courtyard garden, a plunge pool, a kitchenette, a bath and shower, a sitting area, and a separate children's quarters. The bedroom, decorated in white and gold, is furnished with a hand-carved king-size bed, antiques, and original oil paintings.

All rooms have been individually decorated by Jane Matthews, and all have air-conditioning, direct-dial phone, safe, tea and coffeemaker, bathrobes, Bulgari amenities, hair dryer, minibar, flat-screen satellite television, DVD, high-speed Internet access, nightly turndown service, and twenty-four-hour room service. Concierge and night butler services are also available, as are iPods and daily newspapers.

The Sand Bar, located directly on the beach, is open for breakfast and lunch and busy all day with casual, moderately priced a la carte dining. Adjacent to it is The Pub, which serves drinks and offers board games for guests. On-The-Rocks, open for breakfast and dinner, is literally perched "on the rock." The restaurant was renovated in 2005 and has an open kitchen, tables on two dining levels, a bar, and spectacular views over St. Jean Bay. It serves traditional French-based cuisine with the freshest, local catches (and expensive). The bar is open for pre- and postdinner cocktails.

Eden Rock has a small, open-air spa at the water's edge with seawater pools carved from the rock and an outdoor treatment room; the services of a physiotherapist are available, based on your needs. In-room massage is also available. There's also exercise equipment by the beach.

Eden Rock's beach area is fully serviced with teak beach loungers, umbrellas, bar service, beach towels, and iPods for guests' use. Snorkeling is superb thanks to the coral reef that surrounds the rock. Snorkel gear, rafts, and kayaks are available for guests. Hobie Cats and windsurfing equipment are available for rental on the beach. *Eden Rock–St. Barths,* a new 65-foot yacht, is available for excursions. She has three double cabins and three bathrooms, and can accommodate up to sixteen people. The yacht carries a Jet Ski on its stern Diving and fishing trips can also be arranged.

Jane's Gallery is the art gallery of Eden Rock's owner Jane Spencer Matthews, who studied fine art at Rhodes University South Africa and the Slade Art School in London. It is both a commercial art gallery and a studio where guests can try their hand at painting in any medium. The Rockshop boutique has fashions from around the world for men and women and sells Eden Rock signature label, as well.

The Eden Rock manages to combine elegance and just plain funky fun into a small package on one of St. Barts's prime locations.

Eden Rock ★★★★
Baie de Saint-Jean, 97133 St.-Barthelémy, F.W.I.
Phone: (590) 590-29-79-99; Fax: (590) 590-27-88-37; e-mail: info@edenrockhotel .com; www.edenrockhotel.com

Owners: David and Jane Matthews

General Manager: Sonia Tejero

Open: Year-round except September 1–October 17

Credit Cards: All major

U.S. Reservations: Karen Bull Associates, (888) 576-6677; (877) 563-7105

Deposit: High season, three nights, forty-five days cancellation. Christmas holidays, ten nights, full prepayment, sixty days cancellation. Low season, one night, thirty days cancellation.

Minimum Stay: Ten days during Christmas; five days in February; three days off season

Arrival/Departure: Complimentary transfers included in St. Barts. Direct transfers from St. Maarten or Anguilla to St. Barts on Eden Rock's 65-foot yacht can be arranged.

Distance from Airport: 1 mile; taxi one-way, €10

Accommodations: 33 units (beachfront suites, deluxe rooms, beach cottages) with king, queen, or two single beds; some with four-poster beds

Amenities: Air-conditioning, ceiling fan; direct-dial telephones; safe; minibar; hair dryers; flat-screen satellite television, DVD, high-speed Internet; Bulgari amenities, tea and coffeemaker, bathrobes, nightly turndown service; room service 24/7; concierge. Electricity: 220 volts/60 cycles

Fitness Facilities/Spa Services: Outdoor mini-spa with seawater rock pools; exercise machines on beach

Sports: Swimming pool, water sports

Dress Code: Casual

Children: All ages

Meetings: No

Day Visitors: Yes

Handicapped Facilities: No

Packages: Summer, honeymoon

Rates: Per room, daily: *High Season* (January 4–mid-April) Cottages from €685; beach room from €1,025; classic suites €1,295; ; and premium suites from €1,645; beach houses from €2,025. *Low Season:* from €490; €645; €785; €1,160; €1,400, respectively. Rates include airport transfer, buffet breakfast with champagne, and service charge.

Service Charge: Included

Government Tax: 5 percent

HÔTEL GUANAHANI
St.-Barthelémy, F.W.I.

Gingerbread-trimmed Creole cottages in Easter-egg colors sit in baskets of flowering gardens on sixteen hillside acres sloping down to inviting beaches. Overlooking Grand Cul de Sac to the east and Marigot Bay to the west, Guanahani is an exclusive luxury oasis of refined simplicity.

But this stylish haven has more to it than simply a touch of class. It's *très sympathique.* Friendly, not intimidating, this charmer manages to be classy and cozy at the same time. Since it opened in 1986, Guanahani has been a hit among an international array of celebrities and well-heeled sophisticates in search of privacy and comfort in a quiet setting of tropical luxury.

Guest rooms and suites are situated in colorful one- and two-story cottages, each with one, two, or three units, at various levels of the hillside. Due to their location, some afford a greater sense of privacy and better views than others. They also differ in size, layout, and decor.

For all the exuberant colors of the exterior, Guanahani's guest rooms are marked by the elegance of simplicity: a soft, light, fresh decor in white with pastel accents rendered in the finest of fabrics and linens. All rooms face the sea and have their own covered wooden veranda secluded in a garden.

Most have the high, beamed ceilings typical of Creole architecture, which make them seem spacious, and are furnished with a king-size bed (some four-poster) or twins, a sitting area with a desk, a stocked minibar, and a large tiled bathroom. Some suites have Nespresso coffee machines, some have whirlpools, others splash pools. The landscaping is impeccable and the housekeeping immaculate. Guanahani recently renovated all guest rooms and in so doing, incorporated Zen-inspired design with rich woods and clean lines giving them a trendy elegant look.

Further up the hill from the beach are some deluxe villa rooms and suites—a little funky but elegant in their clean lines—and comfortable and practical at the same time. Adjacent to the spa is a second swimming pool and a reception cottage whose interior resembles the large parlor of a private home, furnished in handsome wicker with stylish fabrics. There's also a small meeting room.

The Garden House, a Prestige suite, is the hotel's newest accommodation. It has a master bedroom and two adjoining rooms, a private pool set in a garden, and as with all its Prestige suites, a personal butler. Other Prestige suites include the loftlike Oceanview Wellness mini-suite which has an outside covered bathroom with shower and a private terrace. Located on the spa's upper level with a 180-degree view of the ocean and hotel grounds, it comes with private access to the spa, one free spa treatment per person per day, and unlimited after-hours use of the spa area. The two-bedroom Pelican Suite, overlooking Grand Cul de Sac Bay, has a master bedroom with king-size bed and second room with king or twin beds—both rooms have bathroom with shower. There is a living room with convertible sofa bed and a private garden with a Jacuzzi. The similar style two-bedroom Beach House is located directly on the beach. La Villa is a three-bedroom pool suite with a living room, private swimming pool in a secluded garden, and private parking.

Early on, Guanahani established a reputation for fine, albeit expensive, cuisine in both of its restaurants. L'Indigo, the informal open-air restaurant, has a delightful setting beside one of the Caribbean's prettiest swimming pools, with a wide wooden deck overlooking the grove of palm trees that lines the beach. Like everything else about Guanahani, it has style. Breakfast is served here, or you can dine on tropical fruit and freshly baked croissants on your terrace. L'Indigo also serves lunch and dinner.

Bartolomeo is a more formal (but only slightly) restaurant serving gourmet French cuisine and Mediterranean specialties at dinner. Actually, the only "formal" elements are the crystal and china glowing in the candlelight and the five-star service.

The resort has a good way of taking care of children. Breakfast and lunch are offered daily with a special menu for children six and under at Indigo at specific hours. A kindergarten for children between ages two and six is provided on the beach from 9:00 a.m. to 5:00 p.m. and offers a taste of French culture and language through various interactive activities and games. For children ages seven to twelve, there is a €100 supplement for a third person in a double room; children under six years old are free of charge. Guanahani has two beaches (neither as inviting for swimming as the pretty freshwater pool or Jacuzzi) and tennis courts, as well as a tennis pro for private instruction. A wide range of water sports is available. Horseback riding and trips by private planes or yachts can be arranged.

You can get your exercise walking between the upper sections and the beach pavilion, reception area, tennis courts, restaurants, boutique; a road barely wide enough for a car winds through the property, connecting the facilities. The fitness center has treadmills, step machines, cycle machines, free weights, and more. Recently. The Guanahani Spa by Clarins was expanded, adding three new treatment rooms for a total of eleven rooms, and more spa services. One of the treatment rooms is housed in the new Marigot Suite, another Prestige suite, built adjacent to the spa and includes a private pool and garden. The full-service spa, built by a local architect, has an open-air design featuring rich woods and natural stone. Cascading water in the entry, gardens, and a lily pond add to the tropical ambience. There is a swimming pool, hammam, herbal tea room, beauty salon, and boutique. Among Paris-based Clarins' signature treatments are safflower or lavender fruit salt body scrub and detoxifying hydrotherapy jet bath. The spa also has exclusive water-based massages and treatments as well as traditional ones. Spa packages with two treatments per day (including a three-day package for couples) are available. Guests have private key access to the spa and pool after hours.

Consider the setting, the style, the panache, then add to these excellent service—and you have what Guanahani is truly about.

Although it's the island's largest hotel, Guanahani doesn't seem big, but that's the secret of St. Barts. Its hotels are on the same scale as the island, the ambience low-key. Gracious and romantic, Guanahani is glamorous in an understated way.

Hôtel Guanahani ★★★★
Anse de Grand Cul de Sac, 97133 St.-Barthelémy, F.W.I.
Phone: (590) 590-27-66-60; Fax: (590) 590-27-70-70; e-mail: guanahani@wanadoo.fr; www.leguanahani.com

Owner: Société Hotelière des Antilles Françaises, a subsidiary of Colony Capital

General Manager: Marc Thézé

Open: Year-round

Credit Cards: All major

U.S. Reservations: Leading Hotels of the World, (800) 223-6800, (212) 515-5600; Fax: (212) 515-5840

Deposit: None; only credit card number; thirty days cancellation in winter, fourteen days in summer

Minimum Stay: Ten nights during Christmas; five nights in February; three nights balance of year

Arrival/Departure: Airport transfers included

Distance from Airport: 3 miles; taxi one-way, €20

Distance from Gustavia: 5 miles; taxi one-way, €25

Accommodations: 68 units (36 of which 15 have pools and 32 double rooms); all suites have sitting room, terrace

Amenities: Air-conditioning, ceiling fans; telephone, cable television, VCR; bath with shower, hair dryer, Frederic Fekkai toiletries, bathrobe; safe; stocked minibar; nightly turndown service, twenty-four-hour room service; boutique, hairdresser; car rental service

Electricity: 220 volts

Fitness Facilities/Spa Services: Fitness center with exercise equipment; full-service spa by Clarins

Sports: Two freshwater swimming pools; private plunge pools; two lighted tennis courts and equipment; free use of snorkeling gear and nonmotorized water-sports equipment; scuba for fee; boating, fishing, horseback riding arranged; two beaches

Dress Code: Casual but chic at all times; no shorts, tank tops, swimsuits, T-shirts, or similar attire in dining room after dark

Children: See text; cribs, high chairs; babysitters

Meetings: Up to twenty-two people

Day Visitors: Welcome

Handicapped Facilities: No

Packages: Five- and seven-nights

Rates: Per room, daily, CP. *High Season* (mid-January–mid-April; November–mid-December): €595–€1,575. *Low Season* (mid-April–October 31): €360–€1,095. For two and three bedroom villas, inquire.

Service Charge: 5 percent

Government Tax: None

HOTEL SAINT-BARTH ISLE DE FRANCE

St.-Barthélémy, F.W.I.

Flanking Anse des Flamands, a wide strand of fine white sand described by Paris Match as "la plus belle" of St. Barts's fourteen beaches, and sprawling into a magnificent latania palm grove across the way, the Isle de France (as it is locally known) is a prime beach resort and elegant retreat.

Opened in 1991, the resort has been extensively redesigned by its new owners over the last eight years resulting in a more contemporary, romantic ambience. The property is divided into two separate areas, each with a large pool and its own charm. On the beach side are a dozen rooms in a large, two-story building: six upstairs, six down, all facing the water and the beautiful beach, and unusually spacious by St. Barts's standards.

The enormous ground-floor junior suites have French doors opening onto patios facing the pool and beach. Huge marble bathrooms have separate shower and tub and dual sinks. Upstairs rooms come with seafront terraces.

The new furnishings follow the fashionable, contemporary minimalist decor with white from floor to ceiling with touches of color in the pillows and throws, lamp shades, draperies, and chairs. Some have splendid handcarved four-poster beds with romantic mosquito netting.

All units have a minifridge, tea and coffeemaker, cable television, and safe. Large, elegant marble baths sport huge tubs (some with whirlpools), separate showers, bidets, double vanities, hair dryers, bathrobes, and other amenities.

The main building has a small reception area, a charming veranda with conversation areas, and a marble breezeway leading to the pool, beach, and restaurant.

On the other side of the road are sixteen woodsy cottages carefully etched into the palm grove in a secluded retreat, quite unlike any other resort on the island. A few of the latania bungalows are designed for family use: Some are suites; some have one entrance to two separate bedrooms, each with its own bath.

Others are intended for couples, particularly those with large oval bathtubs for two beside a blooming planter and a tinted picture window with miniblinds. Some units face the pool directly, but on hot days, the tendency is to close up and turn on the air-conditioning.

The resort has a one-bedroom hillside bungalow, featuring a kitchenette, terrace, and private swimming pool overlooking a spectacular sea view; a two-bedroom Fisherman's cottage with a small sitting area, kitchenette, exterior garden, and courtyard; and a two-bedroom beach suite located directly on Baie des Flamands beach has a private sundeck, living room, and Jacuzzi.

The hillside bungalow, with the best view of the sea and the resort's only accommodation with a private plunge pool, is less expensive than a beach room. It offers lots of privacy. Ah, but there are fifty stairs up or down, no room service, and housekeeping only once a day in the morning—all elements that might deter some people. The room is furnished with a king-size bed and has a bathroom and a terrace with a kitchenette and the private plunge pool.

The resort's spa, housed in its own separate cottage and an al fresco pavilion, offers a wide range of treatments and stocks Molton Brown products for sale. Also tucked among the palms are two lighted tennis courts and an exercise room with treadmill, Stairmaster, Lifecycle, rowing machine, and free weights. The resort's beautiful beach has been made all the more enjoyable with a beach bar, and fresh new lounging chairs under big white canvas umbrellas.

La Case de l'Isle, the hotel's beachfront open-air restaurant and one of the best hotels restaurants in St. Barts, is designed after a traditional island house or case and serves breakfast, lunch, and dinner by candlelight, with light French and island fare.

Service and style both come with smiles under general manager Evelyn Weber, who brings reassurance in English to the hotel's North American patrons and her truly Gallic flair and savoir-faire to the European guests.

Hotel Saint-Barth Isle de France ***
P.O. Box 612, Baie des Flamands, 97098 St.-Barthelémy, F.W.I.
Phone: (800) 810-4691, (590) 590-27-61–81; Fax: (590) 590-27-86-83; e-mail: hotel@isle-de-france.com; www.isle-de-france.com

Owner: Patrick Pilzer

General Manager: Evelyn Weber

Open: Year-round except September–mid-October

Credit Cards: All major

U.S. Reservations: Direct to hotel, (800) 810-4691

Deposit: Three nights; thirty days cancellation; except sixty days December–May

Minimum Stay: None

Arrival/Departure: Round-trip transfers included

Distance from Airport: 3 miles; taxi one-way, €15

Distance from Gustavia: 3 miles; taxi one-way, €15

Accommodations: 35 rooms and suites with terraces or patios (beach, garden, or hillside), all with king or twins, seven with four-poster king. Three garden rooms with shower only.

Amenities: Air-conditioning; telephone, DVD, cable television with remote control; safe; tea and coffeemaker, stocked mini-fridge; marble bath with tub (some with Jacuzzi tub), separate shower, bidet, double vanities, hair dryer, bathrobes, basket of toiletries); room service, nightly turndown service; boutique

Electricity: 220 volts

Fitness Facilities/Spa Services: Fitness room with exercise equipment; full-service spa

Sports: Two freshwater swimming pools; one lighted tennis court. Snorkeling, sailing, windsurfing for fee; deep-sea fishing, boating, scuba, horseback riding arranged

Dress Code: Casual chic

Children: All ages; cribs; babysitters

Meetings: No

Day Visitors: Yes

Handicapped Facilities: No

Packages: Honeymoon; getaway; two-week, three-week packages available May 1–October 31

Rates: Per room, double, daily, CP. *High Season* (January 5–early April): €720–€1,325. *Low Season* (early April–August 31 and mid-October–mid-December): €510–€995. For hillside bungalow, Fisherman's cottage, and two-bedroom beach suite rates, inquire.

Service Charge: At discretion of guests

Government Tax: Included

LE TOINY
St.-Barthelémy, F.W.I.

If you like grand vistas, privacy, and exclusivity; appreciate planning and detail; don't give a whit about beaches; and can handle steep hills and steeper prices—then you are probably a good candidate for Le Toiny.

Perched on a hillside on the windy, rocky southeastern region of St. Barts, the tony cottage complex is the only upscale resort in this corner of the island; in which, heretofore, tourism development had not been seen. Designed in the style of Creole houses, each cottage is a large self-contained deluxe suite with a living room, kitchen, large bedroom, walk-in closet, furnished covered terra-cotta terrace, and 20-by-10-foot private heated pool overlooking the sea, all designed with exquisite attention to detail. The villa suites are staggered along the hillside in tropical flora so as to ensure maximum privacy.

Although the decor evokes the colonial era with mahogany furniture, including four-poster beds, the kitchens have the latest high-tech equipment. The gleaming white tile bathrooms—among the largest in the French West Indies—are ultraposh, with separate tub and shower, double sink, hair dryer, bathrobe, and designer soaps and toiletries. The cottages also have CD and DVD players, wireless Internet, and daily international newspapers.

A main building holds the elegantly decorated reception and a bar-lounge. It opens onto the restaurant, La Gaiac, set on an open-air terrace, which embraces a large swimming pool and overlooks extensive sea views. The restaurant is considered one of the best on the island. Menus can be reviewed on the hotel's Web site.

The hotel has no sports facilities, but water sports can be arranged. A footpath leads down to the shore, but the sea here is generally too rough for swimming.

In November 2007, the resort opened the Serenity Spa Cottage featuring products by Ligne St. Barth, a popular line of locally made skin products. The spa offers facials, wraps, massages, and more in air-conditioned comfort or outdoors on a deck with spectacular views of the sea. The spa also accommodates couples. Spa treatments are available in-suite. Treatments can and should be booked in advance.

In early 2008, Le Toiny acquired new owners, ES Development Company, an American investment group. Until now, they have not announced any major changes.

Le Toiny ✱✱✱
Anse de Toiny, 97133 St.-Barthelémy, F.W.I.
Phone: (590) 590-27-88-88; Fax: (590) 590-27-89-30; e-mail: contact@letoiny .com; www.letoiny.com

Owner: ES Development

General Managers: Guy and Dagmar Lombard

Open: November–August 31

Credit Cards: All major

U.S. Reservations: reservations@letoiny .com

Deposit: Three nights; thirty days cancellation; full prepayment with package

Minimum Stay: Ten nights during Christmas/New Years

Arrival/Departure: Airport transfers included

Distance from Airport: 4 miles (fifteen to twenty minutes); taxi one-way, €20

Distance from Gustavia: 5 miles (fifteen to twenty minutes); taxi one-way, €25

Accommodations: 14 one-bedroom villas with private heated pools (each with central living room/dining room/kitchen, large bathroom, terrace); one villa with three bedrooms

Amenities: Air-conditioning, ceiling fans; three direct-dial telephones, two flat-screen satellite televisions with CD and DVD players, wireless Internet, daily newspapers, fax machine; exercise equipment; hair dryer, bathrobe; safe; stocked minibar; nightly turndown service, concierge, twenty-four-hour room service; boutique; car rental service

Electricity: 110 & 220 volts

Fitness Facilities/Spa Services: Exercise bicycle or Stairmaster in room; New spa; in-room treatments

Sports: Freshwater swimming pool; twelve private pools; water sports, boating, fishing, horseback riding arranged; hiking path; tennis nearby

Dress Code: Casual but chic at all times

Children: Yes

Meetings: No

Day Visitors: Welcome

Handicapped Facilities: One cottage

Packages: Summer (April–August 31); romance, escape

Rates: Per villa, double, daily, CP. *High Season* (January 5–mid-April): €1,680. *Shoulder Season* (mid-April–mid-May; mid-November-mid-December): €830. Airport transfers included.

Service Charge: Included

Government Tax: 5 percent on hotel charge

LE VILLAGE ST. JEAN HOTEL
St.-Barthélemy, F.W.I.

This cluster of hillside cottages is the best-kept secret on St. Barts. Set high on the side of a steep hill overlooking St. Jean Bay at the heart of St. Barts, Le Village St. Jean combines quiet villa living with hotel facilities and amenities. It's all within walking distance of popular restaurants, shops, and the island's liveliest beach.

For years this unpretentious resort has attracted an impressive list of distinguished guests, including the Zabars of New York deli fame; the late well-known food critic Craig Claiborne, who came annually at Christmas, and who kept a set of pots and pans here; an occasional French or American movie star; and an array of smart people from eighteen to eighty who know a good value when they see it.

But even with its great location, grand views, sensible accommodations, and moderate prices, its biggest assets, many habitués will tell you, are the friendliness and care that its savvy family owners convey. Created in 1970 by André and Gaby Charneau, who came to St. Barts from Guadeloupe, the resort is now operated by their daughter Catherine and son Bertrand and his wife, New Jersey–born I.B. Their youthful energy and commitment add that extra sparkle to this hilltop gem. One or all will greet you upon arrival with a welcome drink.

The white stucco cottages trimmed with wood and native stone are designed to resemble a hillside village with a variety of styles and accommodations: hotel rooms, one- and two-bedroom suites with covered sundecks in two-story cottages, a three-bedroom house, and a deluxe villa with a private pool. The units are large for this island, and comfortably furnished with twin or king-size beds and tile floors and baths and newly fitted with flat-screen television with cable. All rooms have sea views, some better than others.

The four hotel rooms are spacious, high-ceilinged bedrooms with a balcony overlooking the sea and furnished with twin beds and a minifridge; continental breakfast is included in the rate for all rooms and cottages. The cottages have kitchens screened behind louvered doors on terraces. Those in the deluxe cottages are larger than the regular ones and have the best views. They have recently been redecorated with designer fabrics. Four units have second bedrooms suitable for children. One suite with a Jacuzzi and kitchenette is actually a tiny villa with a wraparound terrace in a secluded garden with an outdoor shower. Villa Iguana, a two-bedroom, two-bath cottage with a private swimming pool, has a magnificent view of the bay. Designed in contemporary style by Jinnie Kim, a noted Korean-American designer, the deluxe Villa Iguana is a combination of luxury and simplicity as well as practicality with such conveniences as a modern stainless steel kitchen—all at a reasonable price.

At Le Cesar, local fish and Mediterranean cuisine are the specialties. The indoor-outdoor terrace restaurant and bar is opened nightly year-round, except September. The selections are available as takeout if you want to enjoy dinner on your own terrace. Just down the hill is Kiki-é Mo, an Italian gourmet food market offering meals throughout the day in a casual setting as well as takeout and catering.

One level up from Le Cesar is the attractive, newly retiled, freshwater swimming pool with cascading waters on one side and a terrace and Jacuzzi overlooking the bay on the other. Beside the pool is the new Well-Being Cottage where spa treatments are available on the first floor and a gym with exercise equipment is found on the second floor. Private yoga and stretching classes are available on request. Further diversions include a lounge, a reading library, and an Internet cafe with DSL and free wireless connection.

It's about a three-minute spill down the hill to the beach (though a ten-minute steep climb on the return), with restaurants, shops, other hotels, and water-sports centers along St. Jean Bay. You don't need a car, but you might want one for exploring the island, checking out the other beaches, and sampling some of the expensive temples of haute cuisine (with the money you save staying at Le Village).

Le Village St. Jean Hotel *
P.O. Box 623, 97098 St.-Barthelémy, F.W.I.
Phone: (590) 590-27-61-39, (800) 651-8366; Fax: (590) 590-27-77-96; e-mail: vsjhotel@wanadoo.fr; www.villagestjean hotel.com

Owners: The Charneau family

General Manager: Catherine Charneau

Open: Year-round

Credit Cards: Most major

U.S. Reservations: Direct to hotel, 0800 651 8366

Deposit: Three nights, five nights in February; forty-five days cancellation; sixty days for February, thirty days in summer €100 penalty for cancellation year-round; €150 penalty for February cancellation

Minimum Stay: Twelve nights during Christmas

Arrival/Departure: Complimentary airport transfer

Distance from Airport: 1½ miles; taxi one-way, €15

Distance from Gustavia: 3 miles; taxi one-way, €15

Accommodations: 25 units in 14 cottages and three villas (6 hotel rooms, 16 one-bedroom units, one Jacuzzi suite, four one-bedroom units with small guest bed, two two-bedroom villas, and one three-bedroom villa); with twin, queen-size, or king-size beds

Amenities: Air-conditioning, ceiling fans; direct-dial telephone with voice mail, stereo with CD player; bath with shower only, hair dryer; refrigerator; flat-screen cable television; room service for breakfast; in-room massage; Internet cafe, free Wi-Fi, library

Fitness/Spa Facilities: Well-being Cottage for spa treatments and gym with exercise equipment; yoga and stretching classes on request

Electricity: 220 volts/60 cycles

Sports: Freshwater swimming pool, Jacuzzi; tennis, boating, snorkeling, scuba, wind-surfing, deep-sea fishing, horseback riding arranged for charge

Dress Code: Casual

Children: All ages; cribs, high chairs; babysitters

Meetings: None

Day Visitors: Yes

Handicapped Facilities: No

Packages: Summer, honeymoon

Rates: Per room, two people, CP or cottage, daily. *High Season* (January 8–mid-April): €220–€540. *Low Season:* €130–€350

Service Charge: 10 percent

Government Tax: None

ST. KITTS

Located in the heart of the Leeward Islands, St. Kitts has a beauty and grace that enchants visitors, taking them back to another era when life was more genteel. From all the Caribbean islands he saw, Christopher Columbus selected St. Kitts to name for his patron saint, St. Christopher.

It's something of a newcomer to Caribbean tourism, but St. Kitts was the first island settled by the English in 1623, giving England great wealth from the land that produced the highest-yielding sugar crop in the world. From their base in St. Kitts, the English settled Nevis, Antigua, and Montserrat, but not before battling the French, who arrived in 1624 to stake out their claim. St. Kitts remained a British possession until 1983, when full independence was established.

Shaped like a paddle with an area of 65 square miles, St. Kitts rises from intensively cultivated lowlands and foothills to a central spine of mountains covered with rain forests. The northern part of the island is dominated by Mount Liamuiga, known in colonial times as Mount Misery, a dormant volcano that rises to almost 4,000 feet. A coastal road makes it easy to drive—or bike—around the island and provides access to the splendid hiking of the mountainous interior. There are no cross-island roads through the central mountains, but there are footpaths.

The Southeastern Peninsula, a hilly tongue of land different in climate and terrain from the main body of St. Kitts, is covered with dry woodland and salt ponds and scalloped with the island's best white-sand beaches. It has a new magnificently engineered highway of about 7 miles that has made this part of the island accessible by land for the first time.

St. Kitts and its sister island of Nevis are separated on the surface of the sea by a 2-mile-wide strait known as the Narrows, but they're joined below the surface by a subterranean rock base on which their volcanic mountains were formed eons ago. Daily ferry service connects the two islands.

Information

St. Kitts and Nevis Tourist Board, 414 East 75th Street, New York, NY 10021;
(212) 535-1234, (800) 582-6208; Fax: (212) 734-6511;
e-mail: info@stkitts-nevis.com; www.stkitts-nevis.com

THE GOLDEN LEMON INN
AND VILLAS
Dieppe Bay, St. Kitts, W.I.

If you are looking for a definition of style, you will find it at the Golden Lemon, one of the most fashionable small inns in the Caribbean. To be sure, this is style as defined by the resort's owner, Arthur Leaman, but a more practiced arbiter you could not find. One look at this "country inn in the Caribbean" and you might say he invented the word.

On the northern coast of St. Kitts at Dieppe Bay, the Golden Lemon is set in a seventeenth-century stone and wood structure draped in tropical splendor and shaded by a grove of coconut palms. Leaman bought the historic building in 1961 and renovated it to resemble an island plantation house with a second-story balcony where you can enjoy breakfast along with sea views. The ground floor of the gracious old manor—dressed in bright lemon yellow (what else?) with white trim—contains a cozy lounge and bar and the dining room, which has an outside terrace, where lunch is served. To one side is a greenery-cloaked patio and swimming pool.

As he tells the story, Leaman came to St. Kitts by accident on a freighter headed for South America. The ship developed mechanical trouble, and since this was 1950, long before St. Kitts had an international airport, the passengers waited a week or more while repairs were completed. Young and handsome, Leaman soon caught the eye of the island's leading social maven, who took him under her wing.

Leaman had been scouting the Caribbean for a hideaway for himself. Smitten with St. Kitts, he decided there was no need to look farther. He bought the remote

building—with a damaged roof and no water or electricity—and combed the island for antiques and objets d'art to furnish his (then) seven-room inn.

Leaman's friends told him he had bought a lemon, so he named it the Golden Lemon. For more than five decades, it has garnered praise for its stylish accommodations, good food, and fine service, attracting an international set of urbane and sophisticated devotees.

The Golden Lemon has rooms in the historic building and rooms and suites in modern buildings that blend with the old remarkably well. The Lemon Court, a small complex, has spacious superdeluxe one- and two-bedroom villas, each with a pool and private terrace at the water's edge. The Lemon Grove, a cluster of condominiums by the sea, adds ten one- and two-bedroom villas set in walled gardens, giving them a great deal of privacy. Each villa has steps leading from one of the rooms directly into a private swimming pool, a feature first used in the Lemon Court.

The decor throughout the Golden Lemon has the mark of "style by Leaman," a former decorating editor at *House & Garden* magazine. The spacious rooms, always accented with fresh flowers, are extremely comfortable and more like those in a private home than a hotel.

Each room is different but all are decorated with fresh, clean lines—no fuss, no frills—and furnished with Leaman's eclectic collection of antiques, objets d'art, island crafts, original art, wicker, and wrought-iron furniture. Some have high four-poster or canopied beds; others are highlighted with antique chests, armoires, or an unusual piece of furniture or interesting fabrics.

The quiet inn fronts a palm-shaded black-sand beach that might have been a drawback for some; for Leaman, it was just another element to make his resort unique. Good snorkeling can be enjoyed on a reef fronting the beach, and the resort has a tennis court.

Those who enjoy a congenial cocktail hour join Leaman in the front gallery at 7:00 p.m. and dine at 8:00 p.m. Dinner by candlelight in the antiques-filled dining room is the real treat at the Golden Lemon. Leaman seats his guests, sometimes hosting one of the tables, and rotating them so they meet one another, unless they prefer a private table. The dinner menu offers soup and a choice of appetizer, main course—fresh fish or a classic European dish served with local vegetables that you might not recognize—and dessert served with quiet attention and grace.

Rarely is it possible to say that a place is unique, but the Golden Lemon is. Leaman's personal management is omnipresent, down to the last flower and tea biscuit. That the Golden Lemon is not everyone's cup of tea would be good news to Arthur Leaman, since he has worked hard to ensure its singular style.

The inn's distinctive flavor generally appeals to writers, actors, and artists, although a surprising number of young lawyers and doctors seem to have found their way here, too, along with some seasoned sophisticates—some famous, many just with style. Leaman says he designed the Golden Lemon for people who "enjoy being pampered in an ambience of informal elegance . . . people who enjoy doing nothing in grand style."

Golden Lemon Inn and Villas expects to be purchased by the developers of Kittian Hills, a major resort and residence development on St. Kitts' northeast corner. However, after the sale is finalized, the new owners have indicated that the Inn will continue to operate, more or less, as it is now. Stay tuned.

The Golden Lemon Inn and Villas ***

Dieppe Bay, St. Kitts, W.I.
Phone: (869) 465-7260, (800) 633-411;
Fax: (869) 465-4019; e-mail: info@golden lemon.com; www.goldenlemon.com

Owner/Manager: Arthur Leaman

Open: Year-round except September–October 15

Credit Cards: Most major; all subject to 5 percent handling fee.

U.S. Reservations: Caribbean Inns, Ltd., (800) 633-7411; Fax: (843) 686-7411; www.caribbeaninns.com

Deposit: Three nights; twenty-eight days cancellation in high season, fourteen days in low season, and a charge of three nights room rate. Four-nights deposit or 50 percent on booking and balance forty-five days before arrival.

Minimum Stay: Four nights in high season; seven nights Christmas/New Year; villa policy differs

Arrival/Departure: Transfer can be arranged; taxi one-way, $25

Distance from Airport: 14 miles (thirty-minute drive)

Distance from Basseterre: 16 miles; taxi one-way, $30

Accommodations: 32 units with double, twin, and queen-size beds (eight rooms in main building with balcony; six suites in Lemon Court with pool; ten villa condos with private pools and terraces)

Amenities: Ceiling fans; Internet access; bath with shower, hair dryers, basket of toiletries; telephones; room service available for all meals; boutique; no radios, television, air-conditioning

Electricity: 110 volts

Sports: Freshwater pools, tennis, snorkeling on premises; deep-sea fishing, diving, rainforest nature walks, hiking with guide on nearby Mount Liamuiga arranged

Dress Code: Casual but chic

Children: No

Meetings: Small groups

Day Visitors: Welcome for lunch and swim with reservations

Handicapped Facilities: No

Packages: Honeymoon, wedding, all-inclusive; 50 percent on booking and balance due forty-five days before arrival; cancellation sixty days before arrival

Rates: Two people, daily, FAP. *High Season* (mid-December–mid-April): $360; Villas, $545–$904. *Low Season:* $275, Villas, $400–$675. Single: $220 and $360 and $175 and $275, respectively. Inclusive rates available, inquire. Energy surcharge for air-conditioning, $15 per day.

Service Charge: 10 percent

Government Tax: 9 percent

OTTLEY'S PLANTATION INN
Basseterre, St. Kitts, W.I.

Fashion magazines from California to the Champs Elysées have been using this gorgeous Caribbean "Tara" as a backdrop almost from the day it opened. Perched on a hillside overlooking St. Kitts's eastern coast, the elegant inn is built into the historic ruins of a sugar plantation. It is set in fifteen magnificent acres of manicured lawns and gardens, with another twenty acres of rolling sugarcane fields edged by palm trees in the front and a mango grove and rain-forested mountains to the rear.

Established about 1703 after the Ottley family came to the island, it continued to operate as a plantation—under different owners—until the 1960s. In 1988 Americans Art and Ruth Keusch bought Ottley's with their daughter and son-in-law, Martin and Nancy Lowell; they've since been joined by a sister, Karen Keusch. After making extensive renovations and adding

a second floor to the great house, they opened the inn in 1990.

The drive from the main eastern coast road climbs through cane fields and along columns of royal palms to lawns so well tended you'll think they are the fairways of a swank golf course. Upon arrival you will be greeted by a member of the family—all hands-on managers. Marty, a congenial host whose horticultural training is evident everywhere, will offer you a welcome drink and show you to your room.

The great house, dating from 1832, is a majestic brimstone structure with two tiers of wraparound balconies trimmed with white railings, yellow shutters, and Brazilian hardwood doors. On the ground floor is a formal living room, beautifully appointed with antiques and period furniture, and a mahogany bar. It provides an elegant setting for afternoon tea, cocktails, and evening socializing. A small side room has the library, with a television set and DVD player.

The first floor has two guest rooms, and upstairs are six wonderfully spacious ones with high, beamed ceilings—Scarlett O'Hara would have loved them. Each room is different, but all are delightfully furnished with antiques and mahogany and wicker furniture. Plush bedspreads and chair covers are set against pastel walls with island prints and wooden floors. The spacious bathrooms have separate dressing areas, well-lit vanities, tubs, and showers.

Large bedroom windows with dark wood louvers let in the breezes and open onto views of the exquisite gardens and surrounding countryside flowing to the sea. In front of the window are a table and chairs where you can enjoy breakfast and take in the view. And everywhere there are enormous bouquets of fresh tropical flowers.

Near the entrance the English Cottage, once a cotton storehouse, has a large bedroom and a separate sitting room that can be converted into a bedroom; each has its own patio and bathroom—one with a Jacuzzi bath and a plunge pool.

There are five luxury cottages, four with two large guest rooms and one with three guest rooms. These spacious cottages have elegant Italian tile baths, minibars, hardwood doors, and louvered shutters; they are handsomely decorated in Caribbean colonial style. The larger of the two rooms has a king-size bed, a Jacuzzi tub in the bathroom, and a private plunge pool on the ocean-view patio. The slightly smaller second room, furnished with either a king or twin beds, has a romantic corner tub in the bathroom. The second room can be furnished with a sofa and used as a sitting room. Thus, as a private cottage, it has a bedroom and sitting room, two bathrooms, two private patios (one with a plunge pool), and magnificent views.

To one side of the great house is an official-size croquet court and at the back, a tennis court. On the other side is the Mango Orchard Spa, housed in a small attractive West Indian–style cottage at the forest's edge. It offers a wide array of treatments ranging from $30 for a basic manicure to $95 for a fifty-minute aromatherapy massage and $105 for a Shiatsu massage. Treatments need to be booked at least twenty-four hours in advance. A variety of spa packages for a few hours or three days are available. Manicures, pedicures, massages, and other spa services may be had in your room, as well.

On the southern side of the great house, steps lead down to garden terraces and the beautiful stone ruins of the boiling house, now converted into a spring-fed swimming pool with a bar and stone terrace at the far end. One wall of the boiling house, with arched windows opening onto the swimming pool, forms a backdrop for the Royal Palm, the inn's open-air restaurant featuring contemporary Caribbean cuisine, popular with Kittitians and guests from other hotels as well. The Sunday champagne brunch is a particular favorite. Special, too, are the elegant candlelight dinners under balmy, star-filled Kittitian skies.

Next to the great house is the remnant base of the windmill, landscaped with flowers and flowering trees. It is a popular setting for outdoor weddings—a more romantic spot would be hard to imagine. Behind the great house is a mango orchard with wonderful old trees. All of Ottley's fruit- and flower-filled gardens attract birds by the dozens.

Farther on, a bridge leads to footpaths along a gully and stone walls to trails through the property's rain forest. The vegetation is fabulous, with enormous mahogany trees, gigantic elephant ears, and other rain-forest species. Self-guided tours are available, but Marty is a wonderful guide, too.

Ottley's historic, romantic setting, coupled with its informal, friendly atmosphere, will appeal both to singles and couples who seek a quiet vacation in gracious surroundings. The numbers—twenty-four rooms for forty-eight guests, on thirty-five acres, attended by a staff of forty-five—all but guarantee space, grace, and peace.

Ottley's Plantation Inn *** 🍃

Box 345, Basseterre, St. Kitts, W.I.
Phone: (869) 465-7234, (800) 772-3039; Fax: (869) 465-4760; e-mail: info@ottleys.com; www.ottleys.com

Owners/Managers: Art and Ruth/Martin and Nancy Lowell and Karen Keusch

Open: Year-round, except for about one month, September–early October

Credit Cards: All major

U.S. Reservations: Direct to hotel, e-mail: reservations@ottleys.com

Deposit: Full prepayment; thirty days cancellation, except forty-five days for Christmas/New Year's

Minimum Stay: Seven nights during Christmas/New Year's

Arrival/Departure: Airport transfer included for stays of seven nights and longer

Distance from Airport: 6 miles (fifteen minutes); taxi one-way, $20

Distance from Basseterre: 10 miles; taxi one-way, $25; daily free shuttle to town, two beaches, and golf course

Accommodations: 23 rooms (eight in great house; six two-room cottages; one three-room villa), all with verandas; king-or queen-size beds (four with twin or king-size beds, two with two queens); nine with Jacuzzi and plunge pool; villa with full kitchen can accommodate up to eight people

Amenities: Air-conditioning, ceiling fans; telephone; safe; umbrella, flashlight; bath with tub and shower, hair dryers, basket of toiletries; coffeemaker; iron and ironing board; room service on request; minibar; television in some Supreme rooms, if available, by advance request

Electricity: 110 volts

Sports: Tennis court; croquet; daily free shuttle to beach with water sports; hiking on trails adjacent to property; golf, fishing, boating, snorkeling, scuba, windsurfing, horseback riding arranged

Dress Code: Informal; smart casual at dinnertime

Children: Year-round in royal suites and grand villa

Meetings: Up to thirty-five people

Day Visitors: Restaurant open to outside guests; reservations required for dinner and Sunday brunch

Handicapped Facilities: No

Packages: Honeymoon, wedding, golf, diving, five to ten days or longer custom-tailored

Rates: Per room, double, daily, EP. *High Season* (mid-December–mid-April): $318–$778. *Shoulder Season:* $254–$574. *Low Season:* $208–$508

Service Charge: 10 percent

Government Tax: 9 percent

ST. LUCIA

Lush, mountainous St. Lucia, the second largest island in the Windwards, is a nature lover's dream with scenic wonders on a grand scale. Every turn in the road—and there are many—reveals spectacular landscapes of rain-forested mountains and valleys covered with fruit and flowering trees. Mostly volcanic in origin and slightly pear shaped, St. Lucia is only 27 miles in length, but its mountainous terrain rising to more than 3,000 feet makes it seem much larger.

On the northwestern coast Castries, the capital, overlooks a deep natural harbor sheltered by an amphitheater of green hills. On the northern tip Pigeon Point, an island connected to the mainland by a causeway, has been made into a national park. It has a historic fort and museum and is the venue for St. Lucia's annual international jazz festival.

Soufrière, south of the capital, is the oldest settlement on St. Lucia. At its prime in the late eighteenth century, there were as many as one hundred sugar and coffee plantations in the vicinity. The quaint little port has a striking setting at the foot of the magnificent Pitons, sugarloaf twins that rise dramatically at the island's edge.

Soufrière lies amid a wonderland of steep mountain ridges and lush valleys, and it is the gateway to some of St. Lucia's most celebrated natural attractions: a drive-in volcano with gurgling mud and hot springs, pretty waterfalls, sulfur baths with curative powers that were tested by the soldiers of Louis XVI, and a rain forest with a trail across the heart of the island.

St. Lucia has some of the best and the worst roads in the Caribbean. None encircles the island completely, but you can make a loop around the southern half, which has the main sightseeing attractions. A new road along the western coast from Castries to Soufrière has made one of the most scenic drives in the Caribbean a joy to travel again. An alternative is a forty-five-minute motorboat trip available daily between Castries and Soufrière.

Information

St. Lucia Tourist Board, 800 Second Avenue, 9th Floor, New York, NY 10017;
(212) 867-2950, (212) 867-2794, (888) 4-STLUCIA;
e-mail: slutour@candw.lc; www.stlucia.org
(Also see The Landings St. Lucia, A RockResort, on p. 309 in On the Horizon.)

ALMOND MORGAN BAY

Choc Bay, St. Lucia, W.I.

Set on a cove in twenty-two acres of land-scaped gardens, the Almond Morgan Bay is a member of Barbados-based Almond Beach International. Opened in November 2005 on St. Lucia's northwest coast, it is a family-oriented, all-inclusive resort and a cut above the usual.

Formerly the St. James Club Morgan Bay, Almond spent $55 million renovating and redesigning the property beyond recognition of its previous life. From the entrance off the main road, through the open-air lobby to two free-form pools, Almond Morgan Bay has the look of a country club. Its 350 rooms, housed in three-story units, are spread along the beachfront and climb to the hillside. There are plans for a full-service spa; meanwhile, spa treatments are available in rooms.

The rooms come in five categories, some have ocean views, some garden, some both. Four categories accommodate three adults or two adults and two children under age seventeen. The fifth—one-bedroom beach-front suites—have a spacious bedroom and living area and accommodate four adults or two adults and three children. Superior deluxe beachfront rooms are popular for their location and with families because they frequently have connecting rooms.

All rooms are in light tones for the furniture and decor. The addition of full-length windows brightened the rooms and broadened the view; glass doors open to small private balconies. All rooms are air-conditioned and have king or two double beds, satellite television, safe, tea/coffeemaker, hair dryer, and modernized bathrooms.

Almond Morgan Bay has four restaurants. Two casual open-air, seafront restaurants offer a full buffet breakfast, afternoon tea, and a la carte lunch and dinner daily. Two others require reservations and serve dinner only: Morgan's Pier, a rustic over-the-water restaurant for fresh seafood specialties; and Le Jardin, an adults-only, gourmet restaurant featuring French Creole cuisine. The latter becomes a piano bar after dinner. Room service is available for lunch and dinner.

This family resort has a good children's program. The Kids Club is a kids-only activity and play center with an experienced staff that supervises four age-specific programs: a nursery for infants up to twenty-four months; a Mini Kids Club for ages two to four; Kids Club for ages four to seven and eight to twelve; and Teen Center for youngsters thirteen and older. The facilities are housed in colorful cottages near the resort's four tennis courts and next to the poolside Plum Tree Bar and Grill where hot dogs, pizza, sandwiches, and salads are available. All but the very youngest children have a variety of outdoor activities to enjoy and gather in the Slush Hut where machines dispense popcorn, smoothies, drinks, and ice cream—all included in the all-inclusive price.

Almond Morgan Bay has four freshwater swimming pools (two in the Kids Club area) and a variety of water sports. The Fitness Center is fitted with a full line of exercise equipment and offers aerobics, step, West Indian dance, and aquacise classes. A personal trainer is available. Tennis comes with free group instruction, and golf privileges include free transfers to/from the St. Lucia Golf and Country Club. If you stay for a week, you get three golf games at the St. Lucia Golf Club, including transportation and greens fees; carts and club rentals are extra. Tee times reservations are requested twenty-four hours in advance.

Almond Morgan Bay is a very good value for anyone, but particularly for families who appreciate the range and variety of facilities, activities, and services it offers in an all-inclusive environment.

Almond Morgan Bay ***
Choc Bay, Castries, St. Lucia, W.I.
Phone: (758) 451-2500; e-mail: info@almondresorts.com; www.almondresorts.com

Owner: Almond Resorts International

General Manager: Frank King

Open: Year-round

Credit Cards: Most major

U.S. Reservations: (800) 4-ALMOND

Deposit: Prepay in full

Minimum Stay: None

Distance from Airport: (Hewanorra International Airport): 25 miles (ninety minutes); (Castries & George Charles Airport): 3 miles (fifteen minutes)

Accommodations: 350 rooms and suites

Amenities: Air-conditioning, phone/voice mail, minifridge, safe, hair dryer, iron/board, alarm clock, tea/coffeemaker, satellite television; private bath/shower; guest computer in reception ($3 per fifteen minutes); golf cart on call for transport around resort

Electricity: 110 and 220 volts

Fitness Facilities/Spa Services: Fitness center; spa treatments available in rooms

Sports: See text

Dress Code: Strictly maintained in all restaurants: cover-up over swim wear; shoes must be worn; and at dinner, men, shirts with sleeves; no shorts except barbecue nights

Children: Kids Club (see text)

Meetings: Small meetings/groups; private check-in with welcome drink, dedicated hospitality desk, one complimentary room for every twenty rooms booked. Conference center complimentary including coffee breaks and use of audio/visuals. Open bars at private dinners and cocktail parties.

Day Visitors: Day pass, 7:30 a.m.–2:00 a.m., for breakfast, lunch, snacks, drinks, afternoon tea, dinner, use of facilities and entertainment for $120 per adult, $65 per child five to twelve years old; $30 per child from one to four years old. Lunch pass, 12:00 noon–3:00 p.m., for lunch, drinks, use of facilities $50 adult; $25 child, five to twelve years old, $12 child one to four years old. Dinner pass, 6:00 p.m.–2:00 a.m. for drinks, dinner, entertainment $75 adult, $30 child five to twelve years old, $15 child from one to four years old.

Handicapped Facilities: Two ground floor rooms; golf carts available for guest transfer to rooms

Packages: Wedding, honeymoon, renewal of vows

Rates: Per person double daily, All-inclusive, from $235

Service Charge: Included

Government Tax: Included

ANSE CHASTANET RESORT AND JADE MOUNTAIN

Soufrière, St. Lucia, W.I.

On the northern side of Soufrière, facing the twin peaks of the Pitons, is one of the Caribbean's most enchanting resorts. Anse Chastanet, built along a steep hillside of tropical splendor overlooking a secluded cove, has a setting so idyllic that you will forgive (if not forget) the atrocious road leading there. If you prefer, you can also reach this hideaway by boat, arriving directly on Anse Chastanet's golden beach.

There are hillside rooms in octagonal, gazebo-type cottages, all with grandstand views of the Pitons or the sea and the unforgettable St. Lucian sunsets. The rooms are comfortable but not fancy—why compete with nature? They have wood-beamed ceilings and walls of louvered windows and doors leading to wraparound verandas draped in brilliant bougainvillea and hiding under some of the flowering trees for which the cottages are named. Near the beach are three two-story villas, which harmonize so well with their natural setting that they can hardly be seen. The villas house twelve spacious, deluxe suites. Recently, all these account accommodations were renovated.

All Anse Chastanet's rooms have furnishings of tropical hardwood—mahogany, wild breadfruit, and purple heart—designed by owner Nick Troubetzkoy, an architect, and crafted by local woodcarvers. Woven grass rugs (a St. Lucian specialty) are on the earthen tile floors; original art by local and international artists decorates the walls; and bright plaid madras cotton is used for the bed and cushion covers. (Madras is used by St. Lucian women for their traditional dress.)

Troubetzkoy's dazzling creations— eleven huge suites of bold, sensational design—put Anse Chastanet in a league of its own when they were added in 1993. These handsome architectural wonders, perched high above the first cottages, offer luxury and space. Some rooms have atrium gardens; others are built around trees, much like a tree house. Each suite has a different arrangement, and all have breathtaking views. But don't expect them to look like an *Architectural Digest* spread. Rather, they are rustic and sparsely furnished. Six premium suites in Cottage 7, have the Pitons as their centerpiece. The enormous bedroom/sitting room extends to a terrace with no windows or walls; in the upper-story suites, ceilings soar to 20 feet.

More recently, Troubetzkoy has gone himself one better with a new group of rooms even more spectacular than his last ones. Built in harmony with nature on the highest point of the Anse Chastanet mountainside, the "Infinity Pool Sanctuaries," as the resort calls these suites, are grouped together to create a resort within a resort called Jade Mountain. The name comes from Troubetzkoy's love for the Pitons, which led him to collect carved antique jade "mountains," some of which are on display in the club room.

The bedroom and living areas with 15-foot-high ceilings, bathroom, and infinity-edge pool flow into one another. There is no formal separation between the sleeping and living spaces. The rooms have ceiling fans, king-size beds, refrigerators, coffeemakers, irons and ironing boards. The large, spacious suites are open with a fourth wall missing entirely, creating the perfect platform from which to embrace the gorgeous Pitons, sea, and sunset. "Sun" suites, the highest category, also have a small wine cabinet.

Three room-rate categories have been created to reflect the square footage of the suites, pool size, and the scope of the view that changes somewhat with the elevation and location. "Star" suites range from 1,400 to 1,800 square feet with 450-square-foot pools; "Moon" suites are 1,600 to 1,950 square feet with 650-square-foot pools. "Sun" suites, with the most commanding 270-degree panoramic view, have more than 2,000 square feet and pools up to 900 square feet.

All pools have shallow water lounging areas and a swimming area 4½ feet deep. At night they are illuminated with fiber optic lights, the color of which guests can personally control. The pools have been surfaced in one-of-a-kind glass tiles, custom handcrafted and specifically designed for Jade Mountain. These tiles have a sophisticated, textured iridescent surface on one side and a smooth but undulating surface on the other. The pools are lined with the iridescent side facing out, while the suite's bathroom is faced with the smooth, undulating surface. Each pool has its own designed glass tile color scheme that extends to the bathroom, adding to each suite's unique personality.

Bathrooms have tropical hardwood vanities with fine brushed stainless steel European fixtures, polished mirrors, custom light fixtures, and porcelain washbowls, makeup mirrors, and hair dryers. The smooth, cool, coral tile flooring contrasts with the shimmering handmade glass tile shower walls and high-tech stainless steel shower units with powerful massage jets and a gentle rainfall showerhead. Each bathroom has a large whirlpool tub for two

on a raised platform overlooking the room, pool, and the view. The whirlpools are equipped with strategically placed massage jets that can be controlled by the guest. The tub is also equipped with the latest in "chromatherapy"—based on the theory that colors affect bio-rhythms and life equilibrium.

Jade Mountain has its own reception area and concierge service. Like the rest of Anse Chastanet, the new suites are tech-free: no phones, radio, or television in the rooms. Internet access is available at reception. Each suite has a call button to summon room service and housekeeping twenty-four hours a day. There are also five Sky Jacuzzi suites at the lower level of the building that share the same view and Jade Mountain resort privileges but do not have a pool.

Jade Mountain has a small spa, Kai en Ciel, with two treatment suites and a small fitness room for the exclusive use of the Jade Mountain guests. They also enjoy all the facilities of the resort below but exclusive to them is the Jade Mountain Club where they can dine on newly introduced Jade Cuisine, created by Chef Allen Susser of Chef Allen's Restaurant in Miami, who is known for his originality in using fresh fish and locally grown, seasonal fruits, vegetables and herbs. Alternatively, Jade Mountain guests can dine in any of Anse Chastanet's restaurants.

Anse Chastanet requires you to be something of a mountain goat. Nothing but your legs gets you up and down the one hundred or more stone steps that climb from the beach to the topmost rooms (except for Jade Mountain guests, who have shuttle service). But it's worth every heart-pounding breath for the magnificent scenery. There is also an easier way, at least for part of the climb: If you rent a car (as some guests do), you can drive on the service road to the beach. There's also shuttle service.

The main reception pavilion contains an open-air bar, a library, the Treehouse Restaurant and terrace where breakfast and dinner are served. You'll dine in the magical, romantic setting of the Treehouse on cuisine that also makes generous use of fresh seafood, vegetables, and other local ingredients. Trou-au-Diable, the beach restaurant, serves breakfast and features Creole specialties at lunch and the beach bar is open all day. You can also have lunch under your thatched umbrella on the more secluded northern end of the beach. Five or six nights each week the restaurant is transformed into the new and very popular Apsara, specializing in fine Indian cuisine.

By the beach, Anse Chastanet has a tennis court and a spa with several massage therapists who provide an extensive variety of facials, therapeutic massages including reflexology and aromatherapy, and other treatments in the privacy of your room or in the beachside spa center with six treatment rooms. It is open daily from 9:00 a.m. to 8:00 p.m. On the second floor is an art gallery. There are also two boutiques and a water-sports center.

Anse Chastanet fronts some of St. Lucia's best reefs, which are protected as a marine park. They are close enough for snorkelers to reach directly from the beach. Some divers call the stretch between Anse Chastanet and the Pitons the best diving in the Caribbean.

Scuba St. Lucia, the resort's PADI Gold Palm/National Geographic Dive Centre/ SSI (Scuba Schools International) training facility, is directed by a ten-member professional team. Also open to nonhotel guests, it offers beach and boat dives four times daily, night dives, and courses for beginners, certification, and underwater photography. The resort's 37-foot O-Day sailing vessel is available for half- and full-day trips, as well as for introductory lessons.

A more secluded strand of sand is a ten-minute walk (or a few minutes' motorboat ride) north of Anse Chastanet at Anse Mamin, which recently became a fully serviced beach with shelter. Here you can also explore the extensive eighteenth-century ruins of Anse Mamin, one of the earliest sugar plantations on St. Lucia, or if you prefer something less taxing, the resort has palapas on the beach where spa services are available.

Anse Chastanet is close to some of St. Lucia's main natural attractions and offers guided hikes on the property at no charge to guests. Off-property hikes start at $65 per person and include a guide, transportation, and sometimes a picnic lunch. In connection with the St. Lucia National Trust, the inn has developed nature, bird-watching, and botanical tours.

Bike St. Lucia is the resort's mountainbiking facility offering guided excursions on custom-designed rain-forest trails, clearly marked for levels of difficulty and patrolled by Bike St. Lucia staffers. Each rider is issued a Bell helmet, souvenir water bottle, and trail map. The resort has bike rentals: a half day $39, and a full day $69.

The manager's cocktail party starts the week's evening activities. There is live music nightly and a beach barbecue with a reggae band at least twice weekly. But Anse Chastanet is not a place for nightlife; most guests are back in their "tree houses" by 10:00 p.m.

That Anse Chastanet, with its romantic ambience, attracts honeymooners comes as no surprise. It is also the setting for about eight weddings per month. But you don't have to fall into either category to fall in love with this corner of paradise. And yet, Anse Chastanet isn't for everyone. But if you are a sporting enthusiast or something of an escapist, yearn for tranquillity, relish beauty, and are refreshed by remarkable tropical landscapes, you will love every minute at this friendly, unpretentious resort.

Anse Chastanet Resort and Jade Mountain **** 🍃

Box 7000, Soufrière, St. Lucia, W.I.
Phone: (758) 459-7000, (800) 223-1108; Fax: (758) 459-7700; e-mail: ansechasta net@candw.lc; www.ansechastanet.com; www.bikestlucia.com; www.scubastlucia .com; www.jademountainstlucia.com

Owners/Managing Directors: Nick and Karolin Troubetzkoy

Open: Year-round

Credit Cards: All major

U.S. Reservations: Ralph Locke Islands, Inc., (800) 223-1108; Fax: (310) 440-4220

Deposit: Three nights in winter, two nights in low season; thirty days cancellation

Minimum Stay: Three nights in winter, five nights during Christmas/New Year's

Arrival/Departure: Airport transfer arranged for fee; hotel runs scheduled boat to Castries

Distance from Airport: (Hewanorra International Airport) 18 miles (forty-five minutes); taxi one-way, $65. George F. L. Charles Airport: 20 miles (two hours); taxi one-way, $85

Distance from Castries: 20 miles; taxi one-way, $75; private water taxi, $120

Distance from Soufrière: 1½ miles; taxi one-way, $10

Accommodations: 49 units with twin or king-size beds (three standard, four premium, 12 deluxe beachside, and 29 hillside gazebo-cottages; one- and two-bedroom suites), all with verandas

Amenities: Ceiling fans; bath with shower only, hair dryers, basket of toiletries; tea and coffeemakers, minibars with optional provisioning plans; room service for breakfast; no radios, telephones, televisions, air-conditioning

Electricity: 220 volts/50 cycles

Fitness Facilities/Spa Services: See text

Sports: Tennis court (no lights); free snorkeling, Sunfish, windsurfing; no pool; superior dive facilities with full range of equipment, three dive boats and 36-foot tri-hull flattop for up to twenty-four divers, film lab for underwater photography; changing rooms, freshwater showers

Dress Code: Casual; men wear slacks or long-cut Bermuda shorts and shirts in evening

Children: None under ten years of age; babysitters on request

Meetings: Up to seventy-five people

Day Visitors: Individuals with advance notice

Handicapped Facilities: No

Packages: Honeymoon, scuba diving, wedding, spa

Rates: Per room for two people, daily. *High Season,* EP (January 3–mid-April): $450–$860. *Shoulder Season,* EP (mid-April–May 31; November 1–mid-December): $350–$715. *Low Season* (June–October 31): $300–$635. Single and triple rates available, inquire. Jade Mountain EP: *High Season:* $1,100–$1,950. *Shoulder Season:* $950–$1,750. *Low Season* (June–October): $850–$1,650

Service Charge: 10 percent

Government Tax: 8 percent

THE BODY HOLIDAY AT LESPORT

Cariblue Beach, St. Lucia, W.I.

One of the first of its kind in the Caribbean, the Body Holiday at LeSport is a health and well-being resort offering an organized but unregimented vacation. It is designed for today's professionals, striking a middle ground between the rigorous regime of a health spa and a typical beach vacation. For active and fitness-minded people, it's the best buy in the Caribbean and has been recognized with a myriad of awards.

LeSport is the ultimate all-inclusive resort. For one price you get all meals, English tea, and snacks; use of the extensive spa with one treatment per day and an extensive range of sports and fitness facilities with expert instruction; all drinks and beverages; nightly entertainment; and all gratuities and taxes.

Set on secluded Cariblue beach on the northwestern tip of St. Lucia, The Body Holiday spreads over fifteen hillside acres of tropical gardens. It has guest rooms in two-, three-, and four-story buildings. Except for twenty-nine singles with garden views, all have terraces or patios looking west to the sea—and what a treat. Sunsets are magnificent.

Recently, the resort has undergone extensive renovation of guest rooms. The Oceanfront and Oceanview rooms were upgraded with new marble floors and furnished with four-poster, king or two queen beds, minifridge, iPod stations, and bathrooms with double-sink marble vanities.

The Grand Luxury Oceanfront Suites, the most desirable for their size, have large marbled bathrooms with bath and shower, separate marble makeup and double-sink vanities, and generous balconies overlooking the ocean. Those on the top floor of a two-story building by the sea have a separate bedroom and living room, divided by double doors; they adjoin another guest room, providing the option of a two-bedroom suite.

On nearby Morne Soldat, a hill overlooking Cariblue beach and with views across the sea to Martinique, The Body Holiday is building The Villas of LeSport, scheduled to open in 2009. With a choice of two- and three-bedroom luxury villas, each with a private pool, a guest can combine The Body Holiday experience with ultra-luxury accommodations. Also in 2009, The Body Holiday will offer another new concept: Oasis Spa Suites. They are 24 luxurious, 700 square foot rooms with private pool and spa facilities en suite.

The resort has singles' rooms, priced as singles with no supplement, one of the very few hotels in the Caribbean with accommodations for singles. Each is a generous 280 square feet.

The Oasis at LeSport, designed in the Moorish style of Spain's Alhambra Palace, is one of the most comprehensive health and well-being centers in the Americas. A range of new sophisticated "ritual" treatments, including a program for pregnant women, a program of Ayurvedic treatments, a new specialist skin clinic are the latest enhancements. Treatments can be booked in advance on the resort's Web site. What's more, you can customize your entire Body Holiday experience before you come by talking to a staff member directly at the resort.

The Oasis includes a team from Kerala, India, the original source of the art of

Ayurveda, who provides lifestyle counseling and nutritional advice, as well. The Oasis can pamper you with exotic wraps, Balinese massage, facials, as well as acupuncture techniques and Suikodo Chinese Bodywork.

All meals include a wide choice of dishes and are served in a choice of four venues. Cariblue is an open-air, beachside restaurant encased in tropical gardens serving breakfast and lunch with lavish buffets. Dinners in Cariblue are served a la carte, except for a Caribbean buffet one evening each week. Wines at lunch and dinner and all other beverages are included. The Clubhouse is open every evening for an informal barbecue, and the Deli is open throughout the day for snacks and lunch, specializing in smoothies.

Tao, the resort's award-winning, gourmet restaurant, immediately gained a well-deserved reputation for extraordinarily fine East-West fusion dishes. Tao's decor, which blends Asia and the New World, is as handsome as the cuisine is remarkable. And best of all, dining here is included in the resort's basic rates with the exception of a few signature dishes which carry a small supplement.

The air-conditioned piano bar, the gathering spot for cocktails and after-dinner socializing, features music by the resort's pianist nightly from 7:00 p.m. until the last guest retires.

Sports facilities are fabulous. Topping the list of water sports are trips for certified divers. You can also dive and snorkel directly off the beach. Windsurfing, water skiing, and Sunfish and Hobie Cat sailing, including instruction are offered daily. The resort has three pools—one for water volleyball and excercise, one for swimming, and the Oasis spa lap and exercise pool—as well as bicycles, aerobics, yoga, fencing, archery, volleyball, and weight training, all with instruction.

The fitness instructor will adapt a program to your needs. You then get personal, individualized training for the duration of your stay. LeSport has daily tai chi and yoga classes, and a popular "Master Class" program year-round. It includes classes by highly skilled professionals in various physical and mental health and fitness disciplines, all covered by LeSport's all-inclusive rate. There are also daily walking and hiking excursions. Golf is available at a nearby eighteen-hole layout at a special rate including golf cart. The resort has a golf academy with four practice holes, putting green, and two resident professionals; an archery range; and a tennis pavilion with two new tennis courts and club house. Tennis attire is required. Turtle-watching, which might include overnight camping on the beach, is often available from about March through June.

Finally, if all of this wasn't enough, more intrepid guests can opt to "Walk on the Wild Side," an exclusive Body Holiday adventure program that explores St. Lucia's rainforest, climbs the famous Pitons, and more.

The Body Holiday at LeSport ★★★★ 🍃
P.O. Box 437, Cariblue Beach, St. Lucia, W.I.
Phone: (758) 457-7800, (800) 544-2883; Fax: (758) 450-0368; e-mail: reservations @thebodyholiday.com; www.thebodyholiday .com

Owner: Sunswept Resorts, St. Lucia

General Manager: Andrew Barnard

Open: Year-round

Credit Cards: All major

U.S. Reservations: Direct to hotel or (800) 544-2883; e-mail: thebodyholiday@sun sweptresorts.com

Deposit: $300 per person within ten days of booking

Minimum Stay: Six nights during Jazz Festival in May

Arrival/Departure: Transfer not included

Distance from Airport: (George F. L. Charles Airport) 7 miles (twenty minutes); Hewanorra International Airport: 28 miles (ninety minutes)

Distance from Castries: 8 miles; taxi one-way, $20

Accommodations: 154 rooms including 29 singles (most with four-poster king-size beds, terraces, and ocean or garden views)

Amenities: Hotel rooms: Air-conditioning; ceiling fans in some rooms; bathroom with shower, marble vanity with two sinks in Oceanfront rooms; hair dryer, bathrobe, basket of toiletries; minifridge (except single rooms); telephones, Internet access; room service for continental breakfast; boutique; gift shop; no television; iPod docking station in Oceanfront rooms

Electricity: 220/110 volts

Fitness Facilities/Spa Services: See text

Sports: See text

Dress Code: Sports and beachwear during day; cover-up in dining rooms; only slightly dressier in evening

Children: Minimum age, twelve years old during June 16 to September 6 and sixteen at other times

Meetings: None

Day Visitors: Welcome with reservations; packages range from $35 from 12:30–3:00 p.m. with lunch and drinks to $97 full day with lunch, dinner, and drinks; treatments subject to availability and priced separately

Handicapped Facilities: Limited, inquire

Packages: Honeymoon, wedding, occasionally yoga and other specialties, and specially priced ones

Rates: Per person double, daily, All-inclusive. *High Season* (Late December–January 4): $544–$631; (January 4–24; April 14–June 6): $331–$431; (January 25–April 13): $407–$494; *Low Season* (June 7–October 17): $317–$404. *Shoulder Season* (October 18–December 5): $345–$432; (December 6–21): $303–$391. Single rates and Early Booking savings available.

Service Charge: Included

Government Tax: Included

COCO PALM
Rodney Bay, St. Lucia

St. Lucia's first boutique hotel, Coco Palm, is truly one of the best values in the Caribbean, offering services and facilities found in four-star hotels but at moderate prices.

Located in St. Lucia's hip Rodney Bay Village, that is being called St. Lucia's answer to South Beach, the hotel's design is a combination of contemporary and Creole tradition set in gardens overlooking the swimming pool.

All Coco Palm's seventy-one guest rooms and twelve suites are situated in one four-story building. Each room is dressed in island colors of blue, green, and yellow with mahogany furniture reflecting a French Creole style and St. Lucian art on the walls.

Bathrooms have glass-walled, walk-in shower stalls with rain showerheads and a built-in seating area in the shower and granite vanity tops. All rooms are air-conditioned and have ceiling fans, cable television/DVD, cordless phone, international direct dialing, free Wi-Fi, minifridge, safe, coffee/tea maker, hair dryer, iron/ironing board, and dual-voltage outlets.

The thirty Pool View Rooms overlook Coco Palm's free-form swimming pool; some have sliding glass doors that open up to a tiny terrace. The most popular rooms are six ground-level Swim-Up Rooms where guests can literally open the bedroom sliding glass doors and step into the swimming pool.

The suites are located on the top floor, some with pool view, some with garden view. All have a separate bedroom and living room with a window seat, two bathrooms (one with shower and one with double-sink vanity, bathtub, and walk-in shower). They also have iPod/MP3 interface, flat-screen television, and a living room sofa that opens up to a bed. Children under twelve stay for free.

Coco Palm has an innovative "host" system that eliminates the traditional check-in desk. Instead, each floor has an assigned host who serves as a personal guide to assist guests throughout their stay, providing much of the same service as a concierge. To avoid the check-in ordeal, guests upon arrival are taken directly to their rooms; check-in can be done at the guest's leisure. Also each of the floors has two housekeepers who service the rooms on their floor.

The hotel's restaurant. Ti Bananne, is an open-air eatery offering Caribbean Creole fare and on most nights entertainment. It has its own entrance from the street and is popular with local residents. The resort is a five-minute walk from Reduit Beach, one of St. Lucia's nicest beaches, with water sports, beach restaurants, and local bars. Coco Palm will pack a picnic basket and provide a beach bag for guests who want to spend the day there. The hotel offers an array of spa treatments that can be booked in advance. Treatments can be given in-room, near the pool, or on the roof deck of the hotel. Pure Bliss, a Swedish massage, is the signature treatment and the most popular one.

Coco Palm's CYS (Customize Your Stay) program is intended to handle guests' needs—airport transfers, flowers in the room, restaurant reservations, tours, excursions, spa treatments—in advance of their arrival.

Next door to Coco Palm is its sister hotel, the twenty-room Coco Kreole, in a former home renovated into an inexpensive small hotel with its own pool and comfortable rooms that have many of the same amenities as Coco Palm. The poolside corner rooms with king beds and wraparound terraces are truly a bargain.

Coco Palm **

Reduit Beach Avenue, Rodney Bay Village, Gros Islet, St. Lucia, W.I.
Phone: (758) 456-2800; Fax: (758) 452-0713; e-mail: reservations@coco-resorts.com; www.Coco-Resorts.com

Owners: Allen and Feolla Chastanet

General Manager: Jean St. Rose

Open: Year-round

Credit Cards: Most major

U.S. Reservations: 1-866-588-5980 or e-mail: usreservations@coco-resorts.com

Deposit: Secured with credit card

Minimum Stay: Three nights peak seasons

Arrival/Departure: Arrange for fee

Distance from Airport: (George F. L. Charles Airport) 6 miles; (Hewanorra International Airport) 27 miles. Taxi service (with water and cold towels) from Hewanorra, $90 for up to three persons; GFL Charles, $30 up to three; executive taxi: $120 and $40; luxury transfers (with drinks, snacks, and cold towels): $150 and $60 respectively

Distance from Castries: 7 miles

Accommodations: 71 rooms, 12 suites (30 pool view; 35 garden; 6 swim-up; 8 one-bedroom suites; 4 family suites)

Amenities: Air-conditioning, ceiling fans, cable television, cordless phones, international direct dialing, free Wi-Fi, coffee/tea maker, minifridge, hair dryer, iron/ironing board, dual-voltage outlets, safes; walk-in shower stalls with rain showerheads and built-in seat. Suites have additional shower en-suite with roll-top bathtub and walk-in shower; and room service

Electricity: 220/110 volts

Fitness Facilities/Spa Services: Spa treatments in hotel room, near pool, or roof deck

Sports: Swimming pool; short walk to beach with water sports; golf, sailing, waterskiing, diving (for certified divers), snorkeling, kayaking, rainforest hiking, mountain biking arranged.

Dress Code: Resort casual

Children: Day-care and babysitting services available

Meetings: Top floor private room for small meetings, audiovisual equipment, and business services

Day Visitors: In Ti Bananne Restaurant

Handicapped Facilities: Yes

Packages: Wedding, honeymoon, getaway, family, and others

Rates: Per room, CP: *High Season* (January 1–mid-April): $175–$390. *Low Season* (mid-April–mid-December): $145–$343

Service Charge: 10 percent

Government Tax: 8 percent

LADERA
Soufrière, St. Lucia, W.I.

Crowning a ridge directly above the Pitons, the award-winning Ladera is a small resort at 1,100 feet above sea level with unusual accommodations often described as deluxe tree houses. Over the years the privacy and heavenly setting of this enchanting resort have charmed celebrities, such as Oprah Winfrey and Matt Dillon, who have spent almost a week there, and just plain folks—enough apparently that in 2005, readers of a leading travel magazine voted Ladera the "Best Resort in the World."

In the world? That's a tall order, but what is indisputable is Ladera's unique location and the unusual way the resort is designed to take full advantage of the location and its natural surroundings.

All of Ladera's nine villas and eighteen suites have no wall on their west side. They are completely open and front an incredible view of the Pitons and the Caribbean Sea, yet provide complete privacy. Each unit also has a small pool equally as private. With its wooded hillside setting at such height, no one but the birds can see into your room.

Although each of the suites and villas is different in layout and decor, they have many similar features. All are constructed of tropical hardwoods and stone and have wooden beam ceilings. They are furnished with netting-draped mahogany four-poster beds and other furniture made by Ladera's own craftsmen and decorated with colorful prints and local paintings and sculpture.

The Petit Piton, or one-bedroom suites, have grotto-style plunge pools, and two-bedroom villas have slightly larger pools with waterfalls. A one-bedroom suite has an open-air master bedroom with a queen-size bed and a plunge pool. The Gros Piton, or deluxe one-bedroom suite, has a larger open-air master bedroom, a large plunge pool fed by a waterfall, and views of the sea in one direction and the Soufrière Valley in the other.

All accommodations have private bathrooms, refrigerators with a complimentary "welcome stock," and coffee/tea makers, but no telephones or televisions. (Telephone, fax, and computer station in the resort's office are available for guests to use.) Rooms are not air-conditioned and don't need to be due to Ladera's elevation. It's always cooler here than at lower levels in St. Lucia, and trade winds provide constant natural air-conditioning. Flowers from Ladera's beautiful gardens, cut fresh daily, are displayed in guest rooms and throughout the resort. Ladera is a "green" resort; your hot water is solar heated.

The dreamiest of these love nests are the five Hilltop Dream Suites located at the end of the forested ridge at the farthest point from the public areas. These suites have an open bedroom and living area, four-poster king bed, and bathroom. Each suite has a private pool with a waterfall, and fabulous views. Given the resort's dreamy setting, it's no wonder that it has long been a popular wedding and honeymoon destination.

Ladera's restaurant, Dasheene, is as famous as the resort with the same fabulous views from three levels. Headed by award-winning Chef Orlando Satchell from Jamaica and St. Lucian Chef Nigel Mitchel, Dasheene offers an eclectic, innovative cuisine blending Caribbean, Asian, and European traditions and stresses fresh fish and local fruits and vegetables. The no-smoking restaurant serves three meals, afternoon tea, and cocktails. Reservations are recommended. On Saturday the chefs conduct a market tour, followed by a cooking class for hotel guests. The resort also keeps menus from nearby restaurants when guests want to try other places.

Next to the restaurant with full view of the Pitons and the sea is an infinity pool (seen in the movie *Superman II* and rumored to be the first ever built) and deck area where cocktails and snacks are served poolside.

Ladera's Ti Kai Pose Spa (meaning "the little house of rest") has four treatment rooms (in-room massages are also available) and offers a variety of massages, scrubs, wraps, and facials. The most unusual treatment, called Sulphur Mud Wrap, includes both a body scrub and a body wrap. Therapists take spa guests to the nearby Sulphur Springs, where the mineral mud that originates from St. Lucia's famous "drive-in" volcano is used in the treatment. Treatments can and should be booked in advance.

A complimentary shuttle takes guests to/from nearby beaches and provides snorkeling equipment. Ladera can arrange hiking/rainforest walks with local guides, horseback riding, scuba diving, deep-sea fishing, whale watching (seasonal), or a private yacht for a day sail out along the Pitons and St. Lucia's beautiful Caribbean coast.

Ladera is an adult resort and does not accept children under the age of fifteen, except during the Christmas season when families with children four years and older are welcome.

Ladera **
P.O. Box 2225, Soufrière, St. Lucia, W.I.
Phone: (758) 459-7323; Fax: (758) 459-5156; (800) 738-4752; e-mail: reservation@ladera.com; ladera@candw.lc; www.ladera.com

Owner: Tiara Consulting, Inc.

General Manager: Robert Stewart

Open: Year-round except mid-September/early October

Credit Cards: Most major

U.S. Reservations: Direct to hotel, (866) 290-0978 or Karen Bull Assoc., 3355 Lenox Road NE, Suite 750, Atlanta, GA 30326; (800) 738-4752; Fax: (404) 237-1841

Deposit: Two nights; cancellation twenty-one days to avoid forfeiting deposit

Minimum Stay: Seven nights Christmas; four nights New Year; three nights, winter to mid-April

Arrival/Departure: Airport transfer arranged for GFL Charles Airport (SLU) or Hewanorra Airport (UVF) $90 per couple, one way. Transfer included for three- and four-night stays. Both airports allow private jets. Daylight Water Taxi transfer from GFL Charles Airport, $200 per couple one way. Helicopter transfers can also be arranged.

Distance from Airports: (GFL Charles) 25 miles; (Hewanorra) 18 miles

Distance from Castries: 22 miles

Accommodations: 25 units (9 villas, 18 suites) with villa swimming pool or plunge pool

Amenities: Private pool, minibar, coffee/tea maker; hair dryer, iron/ironing board, bathrooms, beach towels; no telephones or television. Safe available. Charge for room service for meals and snacks. Computer/Internet, phone and fax at reception

Electricity: 220 volts, 50 cycles (square, three-prong plug), adapters available.

Fitness Facilities/Spa Services: Ti Kai Pose Spa offers facials, massages, body scrubs, wraps, waxing, manicures, and pedicures. Botanic Gardens mineral baths arranged

Sports: Main pool, private plunge pools; rainforest hiking, bird-watching tours, horseback riding, sailing, diving, snorkeling, sport fishing, and whale-watching (in season) arranged

Dress Code: No official dress code for Dasheene; during day, shorts, T-shirts, dresses, dry bathing suits with cover-ups accepted. For dinner, smart casual to elegant; gentlemen requested to wear sleeved, collared shirts, long pants, and footwear; jackets are not required. No shorts, tank tops, beach footwear, or bare feet.

Children: Ladera does not accept children under the age of fifteen, except at Christmas/New Year when families with children ages four and older welcome

Meetings: No

Day Visitors: At Dasheene with reservations

Handicapped Facilities: No

Packages: Wedding, renewal vows, all-inclusive

Rates: Per night, single/double. *High Season* (January 3–April 30), one-bedroom suite or villa, with pool: $545–$815. *Shoulder Season* (May–June 30; October 1–mid-December): $425–$705. *Low Season* (July–September 30): $340–$620. Two-bedroom, inquire. Rates include breakfast, afternoon tea, beach shuttle, snorkel gear.

Service Charge: 10 percent

Government Tax: 8 percent

ST. MAARTEN/ ST. MARTIN

This small island in the heart of the Caribbean is Dutch on one side and French on the other. How an island of only 37 square miles became divided hardly seems to matter anymore except to history buffs and tax collectors.

Columbus discovered the island in 1493 and claimed it for Spain; several centuries later a young Dutchman, Peter Stuyvesant, lost a limb wresting the island from Spain. Still later the French got into the fray, and somewhere along the way, the Dutch and the French agreed to stop fighting and to divide the island instead.

Today there are no border formalities, because there are no real boundaries. The only way you can tell you are crossing from one country to the other is a welcome sign at the side of the road. A short twenty-minute drive separates Philipsburg, the capital of Dutch St. Maarten, and Marigot, the capital of French St. Martin. The two flags nonetheless give the island an unusual international flair.

Philipsburg is the main port for cruise ships and the commercial center. The international airport is also on the Dutch side. Until recently Marigot was a village, but with new development it has become as busy as its Dutch counterpart. Yet it is unmistakably Gallic.

St. Maarten is intensively developed—overdeveloped is more accurate—for tourists. Still, it remains one of the Caribbean's most popular islands: It has something for everyone, whatever the style, and offers as much to do as places ten times its size.

The island has excellent sports facilities for tennis, golf, horseback riding, sailing, diving, windsurfing, and sport fishing. There's nightlife at discos and casinos. You can shop in trendy boutiques or air-conditioned malls for goods from around the world.

St. Maarten has a well-deserved reputation as a food lover's haven, and you can find restaurants serving Italian, Mexican, Vietnamese, Indonesian, Chinese, French, Dutch, and West Indian cuisine. The truly gourmet ones are in the village of Grand Case, near Marigot, but be prepared when the bill comes: Some of the French restaurants are very expensive.

St. Maarten is a transportation hub for the northeastern Caribbean. Its location makes it an ideal base for exploring nearby Anguilla, Saba, Statia, St. Barts, and St. Kitts/Nevis.

Information

St. Maarten Tourist Office, 675 Third Avenue, New York, NY 10017;
(212) 953-2084, (800) 786-2278; Fax: (212) 953–2145; www.stmaarten.com.
St. Martin Tourist Office, 675 Third Avenue, Suite 1807, New York, N.Y. 10017;
(877) 956-1234; Fax: (212) 260-8481; www.st-martin.org

LA SAMANNA
St. Martin, F.W.I.

Snow-white villas draped in brilliant magenta bougainvillea sit between sea and sky on fifty-five tropical hillside acres stretching along one of the Caribbean's most gorgeous beaches.

Small and exclusive, La Samanna was designed with the international sophisticate in mind, to provide unpretentious luxury far from the real world. Set on the crest of a hill overlooking a 3,500-foot arc of deep white sand on Long Bay, the resort combines striking Mediterranean-Moorish architecture and colorful decor with a sophisticated Riviera ambience. When it opened in 1974, it set a new style in casual elegance in the Caribbean.

La Samanna was conceived by the late James Frankel, a New York businessman who was inspired to bring the flavor of the Mediterranean to the Caribbean. He equated luxury with privacy and asked noted Caribbean architect Robertson "Happy" Ward to design a private oasis that would be more like a collection of villas on a secluded estate than a hotel. La Samanna was named for Frankel's three daughters—Samantha (who's married to tennis great Ivan Lendl), Anouk, and Nathalie.

Today, in contrast to St. Martin's unbridled growth, La Samanna, now owned by Orient-Express Hotels, Trains and Cruises, is an oasis of untrammeled beauty, appreciated even more now than when it first burst onto the scene. Upon entering the gardens, walled from the outside world, you find classic white stucco structures recalling a Greek island village. Stone steps wind down a multilevel sweep of balconies, arches, terraced gardens, and shaded walkways to the beach below.

At the entrance to the main building, you will find a reception desk, a concierge, and a small lounge. They open onto the Restaurant to one side and on the other, step down to La Samanna's signature Bar de Champagne with its colorful Indian wedding-tent canopy and Moorish-style furniture. Below the bar, a flower-encased terrace overlooks a pretty swimming pool smothered in tropical gardens.

In 2007 La Samanna completed a multimillion-dollar renovation with major enhancements that included an infinity-edge freshwater pool by the sea, along with a new beach bar and deck, an expanded fitness center, a special seaview site for weddings, a business center for Internet access and office services, new guest rooms and villas, and a new look for the resort's façade. La Samanna has a surprising variety of accommodations for its size. Over the last several years every guest room, suite, and villa has undergone major renovation with modernized living spaces, expanded bathrooms, new upholstery, bedding, and bath linens. Marble and pastel colors complement the comfortable Provençal-style furniture. Deluxe ocean-view guest rooms are located in the three-story main building and along the beach. Rooms and suites open onto balconies that now have lower balcony walls with ironwork railings to capture the fabulous view of curving Long Bay.

Atop the main building a new 1,200-square-foot Romance suite was added in 2006. It has a large outdoor terrace and plunge pool with grand views of the Caribbean and the beach. The suite has an al fresco dining area and lounging cabana. The outdoor space flows into the interior where the white decor is brightened with the colorful paintings of well-known local artist Roland Richardson. The suite's entertainment center has a plasma television and a DVD collection of romantic films and CDs. Among the mood-setting amenities are a personalized bottle of wine and a pantry stocked with candles and bath salts. Flowers, fruit, and champagne are refreshed daily.

The most recent addition are eight palatial villas perched on the bluff to the west of the main building, bring a new ultra-deluxe level to the resort. Keeping with La Samanna's graceful Mediterranean architecture, the new villas boast over 4,600 square feet of living space with three or four master bedrooms and oversized private terraces, luxuriously furnished with great attention to detail. The villas are air-conditioned and have a sunken living room, wraparound terrace and infinity-edge pool, outdoor shower, indoor/outdoor dining, an office area, large, fully equipped open kitchens with stainless steel appliances, a second floor terrace with breathtaking views of Long Bay, and independent entrances for each floor. Bedrooms are furnished with television, DVD player, large bathrooms, bathrobes, hair dryers, L'Occitane bath amenities, and fresh flowers.

The main accommodation are two-story units and villas with one- to three-bedroom suites that dot the hillsides and spill down to the beach. Most guest rooms and villas have individual entrances and private terraces or patios and are separated by a jungle of flowering hedges and trees that provide maximum privacy. Deluxe suites with bedroom, living room, terrace, and small kitchen also have a rooftop terrace with plunge pool, bistro table and chairs for dining, chaise longues, outdoor showers, and sweeping views of the ocean and beach.

Another recent addition are the six circular beach cabanas with wood flooring. Each is equipped with two iPods with a selection of music, CD/stereo/radio system, DVD player, chilled champagne, sunning products, lounge chairs, and a cabana attendant who brings fresh towels, lunch, and arranges for spa treatments in the privacy of the cabana. Cost per day is $250 in summer, $350 in winter, $500 holidays. The "Midnight Cabana" offers a telescope for stargazing and private dining by the beach.

The pool deck has canopies for shade with a cool misting system, providing a comfort venue for lunch. Beach attendants provide complimentary chilled water, fruit and sorbets, and cold towels during midday. Once weekly, guests can take in a movie under the stars. The resort's array of water sports include sailboats, kayaks, waterskiing, snorkeling, and diving trips, and its own fleet of luxury yachts and cruisers.

The Restaurant, an open-air terrace with an eagle's-nest view of Long Bay, has also had a face-lift with new decor and an additional terrace for alfresco dining, providing a more relaxed, inviting atmosphere. The restaurant has long had a reputation as one of the Caribbean's best and most original— and very expensive. It is headed by award-winning Chef Daniel Echasseriau who has created new menus but retains the resort's tradition of combining innovative French cuisine with Caribbean influences. Once weekly, The Grill becomes a steak and fish house. From time to time the resort offers a celebrity guest chef program. The restaurant has an extensive wine list—a collection begun by Frankel, who was a connoisseur. La Cave, the newly expanded wine cellar, has a private dining room that can handle sixteen guests for private wine tasting and dinners and a total of three rooms for up to forty guests for wine cocktail parties. The Beach Bar features a lobster barbecue for lunch on Wednesday and Sunday and Monday nights.

La Samanna's fitness center has been doubled in space with a dedicated area for cardio equipment and a new wing for free weights and weight training equipment. There also is a Pilates and yoga studio, a certified fitness trainer, and morning aerobics classes. The resort's Elyseé Spa with its indoor/outdoor tropical garden treatment rooms proved to be so popular it had to be expanded in its first year. Also available are three tennis courts with night lights.

Other facilities include a game room with a pool table, table tennis, and board games, including some for children; and a meeting pavilion with state-of-the-art audio-visual equipment, a private dining room, a kitchen, and a lounge. Another new addition is a private beachside facility designed exclusively for weddings. The resort offers wedding packages designed by professional planners. La Samanna has several boutiques that stock designer jewelry, perfume, fine clothing, and the resort's signature line. The boutiques and a helicopter landing pad are built into a coral knoll across from the resort's main building.

La Samanna caters to a sophisticated, affluent clientele. Through the years the privacy and elegant informality have pleased a roster of stars, celebrities, and captains of industry, most from North America, some from Europe. The romantic resort is an ideal honeymoon spot, but its seclusion and villa facilities also make it desirable for couples and families with young children.

La Samanna ★★★★
P.O. Box 4077, Marigot 97064, St. Martin, F.W.I.
Phone: (590) 590-87-64-00; Fax: (590) 590-87-87-86; www.lasamanna.com

Owner: Orient Express Hotels

General Manager: Benard Sarme

Open: Year-round except September–October

Credit Cards: All major

U.S. Reservations: La Samanna, (800) 854-2252; Fax: (212) 832-5390; e-mail: reservations@lasamanna.com

Deposit: Three nights; thirty days cancellation, winter; fifteen days April 2–August 31

Minimum Stay: Fourteen nights during Christmas holidays; five nights over high-season weekends and some holidays

Arrival/Departure: Airport meet-and-assist service. See text

Distance from Airport: 1½ miles; taxi one-way, $18

Distance from Philipsburg: 2½ miles; taxi one-way, $35

Distance from Marigot: 5 miles; taxi one-way, $25

Accommodations: 81 rooms (eight deluxe; four suites in main and hillside buildings; 24 one-bedroom and 16 two-bedroom apartments; six three-bedroom villas), 8 new three- and four-bedroom villas—all with kings or twins, and all with terrance or patio

Amenities: Air-conditioning in bedroom, ceiling fan; telephone; bath with tub and shower, bathrobe, hair dryer, deluxe toiletries; safe, television, DVD; nightly turndown service; refrigerator (stocked on request), twenty-four-hour room service; boutiques. For the new villas, see text.

Electricity: 220 volts

Fitness Facilities/Spa Services: Fitness center; full-service Elysées Spa

Sports: Two freshwater swimming pool; three lighted tennis courts, tennis pro; waterskiing, windsurfing, Sunfish, free snorkel gear; waterskiing lessons available;

golf, horseback riding, fishing, sailing charters arranged

Dress Code: Casual; no jacket or tie required at dinner

Children: All ages; cribs; babysitters; children under age twelve free in room with parents

Meetings: Up to sixty people

Day Visitors: With reservations for lunch or dinner

Handicapped Facilities: No

Packages: Honeymoon; three or seven days

Rates: Per room, daily, FAB. *High Season* (mid-December–mid-April): $995–$2,995. *Low Season:* $495–1,650. For two- and three-bedroom villas, inquire. New villas per night from $3,000 summer (May 1–August 31) to $4,900. *Shoulder Season* (April; November 1–December 19) to $6,500 winter (January 2–March 31) and $8,500 holiday periods

Service Charge: Included

Government Tax: 5 percent

PASANGGRAHAN
ROYAL GUEST HOUSE
Philipsburg, St. Maarten, N.A.

With its back on Front Street and its front on the bay, Pasanggrahan Royal Guest House combines a bit of island beauty and city bustle with a touch of history and a lot of charm—and all at budget prices.

The name (*pasanggrahan* is Indonesian for "guest house") reflects this landmark's history as the former government guest house, after serving as the governor's mansion in the late 1800s. Its distinguished guests included the Dutch queen Juliana (she was Princess Juliana at the time), who stayed here for a time during World War II. (Both Indonesia and St. Maarten were then Dutch colonies.) In 1983 the Pasanggrahan was acquired by Oli de Zela, a native of American Samoa.

Now hidden under tall palms in a tropical garden in the heart of Philipsburg, between the main street and the beach, the Pasanggrahan is a casual and friendly hotel that many would rank as the best bargain in the Caribbean. A wood-frame building

painted white with green trim, it has an antiques-filled reception area and lounge presided over by a portrait of Queen Wilhelmina. A long white veranda extends the length of the front, overlooking the beach and the activity in the harbor.

It's the perfect setting for a Sidney Greenstreet movie. No doubt that's why the bar was given his name. It is located in an area that was once part of the room occupied by the royals. Happy hour here is especially popular with local dignitaries and the business community—and everyone who knows about the great strawberry daiquiris.

There is one guest room on the second floor of the main building; the rest are in a pair of two-story beachfront buildings adjacent to the main building and in one cottage. The most spacious and appealing, the Queen Room—what else?—is directly above the Greenstreet Bar and terrace. It is reached by a private spiral staircase. Pleasantly furnished, the room is cozy rather than queenly. It was once occupied by Juliana, and it does have a queen-size bed, although not the same one Her Highness used.

There are two types of rooms in the annex: standard, which are rather small, and superior, which are larger and deluxe. All rooms have air-conditioning, telephone, and television; superior rooms have small refrigerators.

All rooms are furnished with either twin or king-size beds and have white tile and wood bathrooms. Beachfront rooms have balconies, shared in some cases. The furnishings are simple—basic wood furniture and some wicker. Colorful prints by local artists and Indonesian batik hangings decorate the walls, but they must compete with the colors of the Caribbean and the picturesque sailboats in the harbor outside your window.

Meals are served at the Oceanview Restaurant with seating either on the beachside veranda or in the garden dining area, particularly enjoyable at sunset. The restaurant offers a wide range of choices at moderate prices. The garden area, with a gazebo bar, is also a popular venue for cocktail parties and special events held by the business community. Afternoon tea for guests is served here.

The beach and the new boardwalk in front of the Pasanggrahan stretch the length of the bay. The inn doesn't have a water-sports center, but at either end of the beach you'll find diving, sailing, and water-sports shops where almost anything can be arranged.

Pasanggrahan's owner, Captain Tini, will take you out for a deep-sea fishing trip to try your luck at catching wahoo, mahi mahi, blue marlin, or yellow-fin tuna on the inn's own 32-foot *Prowler,* which is powered by two Perkins Diesel engines. Cost for half day is $450, including bait and drinks; full day $ 900 with bait, drinks, and sandwiches.

The Pasanggrahan expects a major renovation, upgrading, and expansion in mid-2009 that will convert or add twenty-six suites that will be larger and more deluxe than any of the current accommodations, two penthouses, and the addition of a swimming pool with a terrace that can be used for private parties and special groups. They are also negotiating for another property nearby for parking space. The construction will be done in two phases, but the hotel is likely to close for some of the time. Be sure to inquire prior to making plans.

Pasanggrahan Royal Guest House *
19 Front Street, P.O. Box 151, Philipsburg, St. Maarten, N.A.
Phone: (599) 542-3588; Fax: (599) 542-2885; e-mail: info@pasanhotel.com; www.pasanhotel.com

Owners/General Managers: Oli Ale de Zela Tinitali and Tini Tinitali

Open: Year-round except September

Credit Cards: MasterCard, Visa

U.S. Reservations: Direct to hotel

Deposit: Three nights in winter; one night in summer

Minimum Stay: Inquire

Arrival/Departure: No transfer service

Distance from Airport: 5 miles; taxi one-way, $20

Accommodations: 31 rooms, including the Queen Room and cottage (28 have terrace or patio)

Amenities: Air-conditioning, ceiling fans; bath with tub and shower; refrigerators, ice service; nightly turndown service; twenty-four-hour security; telephone, television, radio, clock; no room service

Electricity: 110 volts

Sports: None on premises; tennis, golf, boating, snorkeling, diving, windsurfing, deep-sea fishing, horseback riding arranged

Dress Code: Casual

Children: Off season only, all ages; cribs, high chairs

Meetings: Conference room with facilities; up to 200 people in garden

Day Visitors: Welcome

Handicapped Facilities: Yes

Packages: No

Rates: Per room, daily, EP. *High Season* (mid-December–mid-April): $178–$210. *Low Season:* $105–$150

Service Charge: 15 percent

Government Tax: 5 percent

ST. VINCENT AND THE GRENADINES

Nature's awesome power and exquisite beauty live side by side in this chain of idyllic islands. Mountainous and magnificent, St. Vincent is the largest of the multi-island group. Its lush terrain, thick with tropical forests and banana plantations, rises quickly from the sea to more than 4,000 feet in the smoldering volcanic peaks of La Soufrière in the north.

The Botanic Gardens in Kingstown, the capital, are the oldest in the Western Hemisphere. Among their prized species is a breadfruit tree from the original plant brought from Tahiti by Captain Bligh of the *Bounty*.

St. Vincent has a series of mountain ranges up the center of the island. The Buccament Forest Nature Trail is a signposted loop through the fabulous rain forest where gigantic gommier and other hardwoods make up the thick canopy towering more than 100 feet.

La Soufrière has erupted five times since 1718, most recently in 1979. The crater, about a mile across, smolders and emits clouds of steam and sulfur fumes. The Falls of Baleine tumble 70 feet in one dramatic stage through a steep-sided gorge of volcanic rock at the foot of the Soufrière Mountains. From Kingstown the falls are accessible only by sea; excursions depart almost daily.

The Grenadines, stretching south from St. Vincent more than 65 miles to Grenada, are a chain of three dozen islands and cays often called by yachtsmen the most beautiful sailing waters in the world. Only eight are populated.

Bequia, the largest and most developed of the Grenadines, is known for its skilled sailors and boatbuilders. The island's laid-back lifestyle has made it a favorite of artists, writers, and old salts who never found their way back home.

Young, Palm, and Petit St. Vincent are private island resorts; Mustique is a celebrity mecca. Other islands with resorts are Mayreau, Canouan, and Union, all with remarkable beaches and small resorts with facilities for sailing, diving, fishing, and other water sports. Tobago Cays are four uninhabited islets scalloped with seemingly untouched white-sand beaches and beckoning aquamarine waters.

Dive aficionados call St. Vincent the sleeper of Caribbean diving; reef life normally found at 80 feet in other locations grows here at depths of only 25 feet and includes an extraordinary abundance and variety of tropical reef fish.

Information

St. Vincent and the Grenadines Tourist Office, 801 Second Avenue, New York, NY 10017; (212) 687-4981, (800) 729-1726; Fax: (212) 949-5946; www.svgtourism.com

YOUNG ISLAND

St. Vincent, W.I.

If painter Paul Gauguin had stopped here after leaving Martinique, he might not have pressed on to the South Seas in his search for the totally exotic. The lush, volcanic terrain of undeveloped St. Vincent is a dead ringer for Tahiti fifty years ago, and it's still teeming with mystery.

But there's no mystery about Young Island. This thirty-five-acre private-island resort only 200 yards off St. Vincent's southern shore is luxury amid tropical profusion, a fantasy version of Polynesia in miniature. Your adventure begins when you board a Grenadine version of the *African Queen* for the five-minute ride across the narrow channel to Young Island.

One of Young Island's longtime staff members meets guests at the dock, usually preceded by a waiter carrying a tray of hibiscus-decorated rum punch. (You'll need a drink after the daylong journey—two plane rides, taxi, and boat—it takes to reach Young's tropical shores.) From the dock you will be led along stone paths through a maze of greenery to your island quarters—one of twenty-nine thatched bungalows of Brazilian hardwood and volcanic stone tucked away on the beach or hidden on a hillside. What they lack in television and DVDs, they more than make up for in comfort and lush surroundings.

Guests partial to bird's-eye views and aerobic hikes always choose the hillside aeries. These feel like tree houses but offer great comfort and enchanting island decor as well as unexpected amenities: a huge bowl of local fruits and, for guests on a return visit (often couples who honeymooned here), a bottle of wine. Two of the beachside cottages have plunge pools.

Inside the bungalow you feel as if you are outside. Vertical wooden louvers let in the outdoors, and sliding glass doors open onto a huge balcony suspended above the bush. A seductive hammock for two awaits, along with a splendid view of the mountainous mainland or the Grenadines, dribbling south toward Grenada. Even the shower, cleverly appended to the dressing quarter with its jungle canopy and shoulder-high wooden "curtain," is alfresco. The three original luxury hillside suites (#28, #29, and #30) have plunge pools and the largest accommodation, Duvernette Suite (#26), has a small infinity edge swimming pool. A map on the resort's Web site shows the precise location of each cottage. All cottages have a refrigerator, safe, and private patio. Superior cottages are those nearest the beach and on the shoreline or low on the hillside. Luxury suites are beachside and hillside.

Cottage #15 has been converted into a treatment room of the Spa Kalina, a full-service facility. Guests may pre-book massages, facials, manicures, pedicures, scrubs, reflexology, and waxing. It uses products from Earth Mother Botanicals of Barbados, which are made from natural ingredients and include a Bajan cane sugar body scrub, sea salt body scrub, ylang-ylang hydrating cream, and guava seed foot scrub, among others.

Somewhere down below is a free-form freshwater pool enveloped in a forest of tropical foliage. A tennis court hides amid the breadfruit and banana trees. Water spirits head for the dock to go snorkeling, windsurfing, or sailing. Dive St. Vincent is headquartered directly across Young Island Cut. Young also keeps a couple of yachts at the ready, along with a captain and chef, for day or overnight sailing trips; it offers a year-round package that combines a stay at the resort with a two- or three-day cruise of the Grenadines.

But most guests tend to plop on the beach in hammocks under one of the *bohios,* the thatched-roof gazebos that enhance the island's South Pacific appearance. Occasional thirst may propel some to paddle a few strokes from shore to the Coconut Bar, a swim-up bar in a thatched hut that seems to float atop the Caribbean waters. Breakfast, lunch, and dinner are served in shaded garden nooks, some bounded by a moat, overlooking the beach. In the office nearby, guests can also check out their e-mail free for fifteen minutes at a time.

By night guests gather in the wood-beamed bar and enjoy a variety of local entertainment several times a week. A cocktail party is held by the pool on Friday night with the Bamboo Melodians.

Young offers a proper wine list, and the menu changes daily according to the whim of the chef (and what's available). The results might be such tempting choices as papaya soup laced with garlic or an island-grown avocado brimming with caviar, perhaps followed by just-caught lobster or a fillet of red snapper in cream-and-pepper sauce.

It's only when you hike back into the bush and up the hill that you might regret the many-course dinner, nurtured with spirits of cane and grape.

Young Island ****
Young Island Crossing, P.O. Box 211, St. Vincent, W.I.
Phone: (784) 458-4826; Fax: (784) 457-4567; e-mail: youngisland@vincysurf.com; www.youngisland.com

Owners: Dr. Frederick Ballantyne and Vidal Browne

General Manager: Bianca Porter

Open: Year-round

Credit Cards: All major

U.S. Reservations: Ralph Locke Islands, Inc., (800) 223-1108; Fax: (310) 440-4220

Deposit: Three nights in winter, two nights in summer; $1,500 for packages

Minimum Stay: Seven nights required during Christmas

Arrival/Departure: Transfer service arranged for fee

Distance from Airport: (St. Vincent Airport) 1½ miles; taxi one-way, $10.00

Distance from Kingstown: 3 miles; taxi one-way, $12

Accommodations: 29 cottages, all with patio (19 superior, king bed, beachside, shoreline, or low on hillside; 4 deluxe, larger king bed, with sitting area in bedroom, or large patio; 5 luxury full suites with bedroom, separate sitting room, plunge pool, coffeemaker and CD player. Two beachside suites with king bed, 3 hillside with two queen beds. Hillside Duvernette suite with spacious separate living and dining areas, small infinity-edge pool, furnished deck with chairs, umbrella, hammock, coffeemaker, CD player

Amenities: Ceiling fans; garden shower, hair dryer, basket of toiletries, bathrobe; ice bucket, small refrigerator; safe; nightly turndown service, room service for breakfast

Electricity: 220 volts/60 cycles; some cottages also have 110 volts/50 cycles. 17 cottages have the option of air-conditioning, which must be requested with booking.

Fitness Facilities/Spa Services: Spa Kalina, a full-service facility

Sports: Freshwater swimming pool; one lighted Har-Tru tennis court; free use of pedal boats, snorkeling gear, windsurfing equipment, and kayaks; sailing, deep-sea fishing, diving arranged at additional cost

Dress Code: Casual

Children: All ages; cribs, high chairs; babysitters available at prevailing rates

Meetings: Up to forty people; no equipment

Day Visitors: For meals

Handicapped Facilities: Limited

Packages: Honeymoon; Sailaway, dive, summer family

Rates: Per room, double, daily, MAP. *High Season* (mid-December–March 31): $440–$1,015. *Shoulder Season* (April 1–August; November–mid-December): $390–$775. *Low Season* (September–October): $370–$740

Service Charge: 10 percent

Government Tax: 10 percent on EP portion of rate; 15 percent VAT on all hotel services including meals, bar, spa, etc.

THE FRANGIPANI HOTEL
Bequia, St. Vincent and the Grenadines, W.I.

You've heard it said that if you stand long enough in Times Square, sooner or later you'll see the whole world go by. In its own (decidedly more laid-back) way, the beach bar at the Frangipani Hotel can make a similar claim. Okay, maybe not the whole world—but surely a good slice of its more interesting and eccentric citizens.

Bequia's Admiralty Bay is one of the finest deepwater harbors in the Caribbean, and often the first landfall for yachts cruising from the Mediterranean to these warm waters. The Frangi, as it is known to habitués, is smack in the heart of the waterfront, surrounded by flowering bushes and trees.

Once the family home of the former prime minister of St. Vincent and the Grenadines, Sir James "Son" Mitchell, it has been welcoming yachties and tourists for so many years that it has achieved legendary status throughout the Caribbean.

The Frangi has never tried to be anything other than what it is—a comfortable inn—and there, in its utter lack of pretension,

lies its charm. Mere steps from the yacht-filled bay, the hotel has been described in a novel this way: "Like the white hunter bars in Kenya, it's a pickup place, social headquarters, news central, information booth, post office and telegraph [and now phone, fax, and Wi-Fi] office, in short, the nerve center of the permanently-in-transit charter-boat trade."

Here you can gossip or flirt with serious salts who have circumnavigated the globe often, with boat bums and beach bunnies, Washington lawyers on bare-boat charters, college professors and freelance backpackers, couples with unpublishable biographies, locals and winter residents, dreadlocked Rastafarians in Batman T-shirts, billionaire Arabs on zillion-dollar yachts, minor celebrities, older men with younger women, younger men with older women, and trios and combos of every age, nationality, and color imaginable.

On Thursday night the Frangi holds its weekly jump-up (barbecue and steel band), so called because the music does make it difficult not to jump up and dance. Around the bar, people are generally so chatty (and, as sundown turns the sky mauve, so full of rum) that Attila the Hun could make friends here. Needless to say, solo travelers love it, though most guests are couples.

Breakfast, lunch, and dinner are served in an open-air dining room by the lobby. The food has been upgraded in the last few years and is very good, mostly West Indian fare with international touches cooked in quantities by local women who obviously enjoy their work. A Saturday morning buffet breakfast in the winter months has been added. The drinks along with a new cocktail menu, are good, too. The extensive wine list offers one of the best variety of fine imported wines on the island.

Rooms at the Frangipani also have been updated and upgraded. The rooms are airy and comfortable and have phones and television, and wireless Internet access is available for a fee. The garden and deluxe units are equipped with a safe, fridge, coffeemaker, and the usual amenities such as shampoo. Rooms in the old house that face the water are simple—bed, tabletop fan, cold-water hand basin, mosquito netting. Shared hot-water bathroom facilities are at the end of the corridor, and all share the one balcony overlooking the bay. The view—and the people-watching—make up for it.

The nicer stone units with balconies, two of which now have air-conditioning, are in the back of the main house. The smaller and less expensive garden units overlook the garden, and are furnished with twin or queen-size bed, private bath, separate dressing room, fans, fridge, coffeemaker, and safe. The deluxe units on the hillside have a large, spacious room with a choice of twin or a king- size bed,

private bath, separate dressing room, fans, fridge, coffeemaker, safe, and balcony with lounge chairs. Some rooms have a desk and television/DVD. The air-conditioned rooms are furnished with four-poster king-size bed, private bath, separate dressing room, balcony with lounge chairs, fridge, coffeemaker, safe, desk, flat-screen television with DVD player and have a wonderful view of the bay. Room service breakfast is available in these accommodations.

The marble-tile-floor lobby is small but has maps and a take-one-leave-one paperback library. Anything you need, if it's humanly possible to obtain, will be provided cheerfully by the friendly staff. (In return, satisfied repeat guests happily run a supply train of everything from New York bagels to hard-to-find plumbing supplies.)

Not much happens past 9:00 p.m. on the island, and dinner is nearly impossible to find after 7:00 p.m. But on Thursday, the barbecue, jump-up revelry, and the band (playing the same five amplified songs nearly every night at a different hotel) assault the eardrums till midnight or later.

Pack light; dress is very casual, but swimsuits are frowned upon by the local people except on the beach. Serious resort wear and high heels will cause muffled giggles (if not a sprained ankle). There's some nice shopping, but the island offers no glitz, gambling, or Gucci.

The Frangi has a tennis court and a 45-foot yacht, *Pelangi,* which is available for day charters to other islands or overnight cruises to the Tobago Cays. Full water sports (diving, snorkeling, windsurfing) are available at two dive shops close by; two gorgeous beaches are a half-hour stroll or a short land- or water-taxi ride away.

People stay here for what can honestly be called one of the last few "true

Caribbean experiences" still available. If you're looking for professionally decorated, five-star polish, don't give this one even a thought.

The Frangipani Hotel *

Box 1 BQ, Bequia, St. Vincent & the Grenadines, W.I.

Phone: (784) 458-3255; Fax: (784) 458-3824; e-mail: frangi@caribsurf.com; www.frangipanibequia.com

Owner: Sir James "Son" Mitchell

General Manager: Sabrina Mitchell

Open: Year-round except September–mid-October

Credit Cards: Most major

U.S. Reservations: Direct to hotel

Deposit: Three nights; twenty-one days cancellation less 10 percent

Minimum Stay: None

Arrival/Departure: No transfer service. If arriving by yacht, tie your dinghy to Frangi's dock; if by air, land at airstrip—however, landing could be chancy due to winds on eastern side of island. There's a beautiful twenty-minute roller-coaster drive across southern half of Bequia to hotel. Ferry

daily between St. Vincent's Kingstown and Bequia, one-way, about $8

Distance from Airport: (Bequia) 3 miles; taxi one-way, $12

Accommodations: 15 rooms (five original rooms in main building, ten in garden units, all with balcony)

Amenities: Ceiling fans; bath with shower only; breakfast service in garden units; two units with air-conditioning

Electricity: 220 volts

Sports: Tennis free; boating, snorkeling, diving, windsurfing instruction for fee; hiking, birding; sunset cruises; no pool

Dress Code: Very casual

Children: All ages; cribs; babysitters

Meetings: No

Day Visitors: Welcome

Handicapped Facilities: No

Packages: Dive

Rates: Per room, double, daily, EP, including 10 percent VAT. **High Season** (mid-December–mid-April): $70–$230. **Low Season:** $55–$165. Single rates are available.

Service Charge: 11 percent

Government Tax: 7 percent

RAFFLES RESORT
Canouan Island, St. Vincent and the Grenadines

Raffles is a Hollywood blockbuster of a resort, created, built, and financed by Italian financier Antonio Saladino, who both built the no-expense-spared resort and developed the island's infrastructure, including water system, roads, electricity, and a larger airport with a handsome thatched-roof terminal.

Having already spent a quarter million dollars to create Carenage Bay Resort, the island paradise closed for over a year, spent several more millions to make it even more fabulous, and joined up with the famous Singapore-based chain, Raffles, to manage the resort; the well-known yacht charter, the

Moorings, to manage the marina; and Donald Trump to build a new golf course.

Reopened in July 2004, as Raffles Resort Canouan Island, the resort added a full-fledged spa; several villa buildings, each with beachfront one- and two-bedroom suites; and a spectacular eighteen-hole championship golf course by Jim Fazio. More recently, the Canouan Island airport runway was expanded to handle most private jets; and Grenadines Estate, a gated community of golf and beach villas and estate homes, was added. The resort center, called the Galeria, is a lovely building housing the reception, gourmet restaurant, business center, and fitness center.

The opening of the multimillion-dollar resort heralded a new era for the bucolic island of Canouan, known more for beaches than boutiques.

Until the resort began to take shape, only the Anglican Church, with a crescent beach at its feet, was on this site. And even the stone church is something of a newcomer, having been brought to the island stone by stone from Britain at the end of the nineteenth century. Now, the church rises above the sharp roof lines of paint-washed villas and a free-form freshwater pool that undulates a quarter of a mile parallel to the sea.

Upon arrival, guests are whisked off to the resort by a hotel staff member who arrives with cold water and towel—both needed and appreciated even if you have taken advantage of the resort's flight concierge or private jet service facilitating the transfer from Barbados or St. Lucia to Canouan.

A Raffles flight team meets guests at the airport in Barbados or St. Lucia, handles formalities, and escorts them to a chartered plane for the flight to Canouan (forty-five minutes from Barbados or thirty minutes from St. Lucia). The price, $395 per person, includes round-trip airfare from Barbados, St. Lucia, and/or Martinique to the resort. Raffles also has a private, seven-seat Cessna Citation II that can transfer guests from as far as Miami or other Caribbean locations. Rates vary with location.

After check-in, guests are golf-cart driven to their haven. There, a golf cart waits for guests to use as their transportation around the resort.

Italian designers have a knack for reinterpreting Caribbean clichés with so much style that they are no longer clichés. In the case of Raffles, Italian architects Luigi Vietti, who designed the Aga Khan's villa in Sardinia, freely mixed Caribbean designs with exotic motifs from a range of tropical destinations.

Thus, the villa's unusual multipointed roof lines meant to replicate those of the church's steeple contrast with the Mexican furnishings, Indian fabrics, palapas (thatched-roofed shade pavilions), and original works of art by Italian artists.

The resort occupies only 300 acres (including the golf course) of a 1,200-acre site. The sea and offshore reef, the green hills, and rugged terrain curving around the beach at either end of the resort are constant reminders that this is the Caribbean. That is, until you visit Big Point.

Villa Monte Carlo is Raffles' answer to Monaco. The White House–like edifice atop a steep hill about a fifteen-minute drive from the resort houses the Trump casino. Yes, a casino. Here, the croupiers are better dressed than the guests, the slot machines discreetly tucked in shadows, and the crystal chandeliers outnumber the hidden cameras in the high ceilings. And yes, it's a big Wow, but you will not be the first to wonder why on a sleepy Grenadine island of only 1,500 inhabitants there would need to be so elaborate a gaming house.

On the other hand, you can easily succumb to the spell of La Varenne, the casino's gourmet French restaurant with a selection of thirty-four champagnes, its own Raffles-packaged caviar, and a fabulous view that takes in nearby islands and cays. Dinner is a three-hour event, overseen by a restaurant manager and a maitre d' who know when to hover and when to disappear, when to translate and when to refill.

Raffle's other restaurants include La Piazza, an octagonal-shaped Italian restaurant, framed by tall windows, blue-glazed walls, copper pots, and a walk-through wine cellar. The upstairs of the two-level restaurant is devoted to fine dining in an elegant atmosphere. Bellini's in the lower level is a bar, as well as a venue for more casual family dining in the evening.

The open-air Godahl Beach Bar and Grill, five minutes by golf cart down to Godahl Beach, serves lunch and a casual evening barbecue twice weekly.

Jambu's, comprised of four Balinese-style interconnecting houses, each decorated in its own individual style under a palapa roof and overlooking the pool and beach, rounds out the dining options. (Incidentally, Amazonas Indians were flown to the island to thatch the palapas in the traditional way.) One area houses a bar. Jambu's serves an enormous breakfast buffet and for lunch and dinner offers fish, "trans-ethnic" (their term), and Asian fusion cuisine, and authentic Italian pizzas from the wood-burning oven.

Raffles's accommodations set in amphitheatre style, range from a deluxe, one bedroom of 616 square feet and junior suites to a two-bedroom villa suite with 1,936 square feet and four-bedroom villas, some with private pools. The latest additions are the luxury Grenadines Estates, of which five of the four-bedroom private villas are available for rent.

One of the villas, the luxurious 4,000-square-feet Raffles Villa comes with its own chef, butler, a cutting-edge entertainment set-up with a plasma screen television and Bose sound system, and a two-tiered veranda with an infinity-edge pool. The dining room seats up to twelve guests. The master suite has a walk-in closet and a bathroom with a sun-lit shower that opens to the sky. The other bedrooms are only slightly less opulent, each with a veranda. The villa's fourth bedroom is located in a separate cottage.

My digs were huge. The living room, dining area, and kitchen alone were larger than most New York apartments. And then there's the bedroom, a walk-in closet, and enormous bathroom with a double-sink vanity faced with pretty Mexican tiles, large tub, and separate shower. The kitchen was supplied with china, utensils, a two-burner range, a small refrigerator, an espresso maker, and a selection of coffees and teas.

The living room has an entertainment center, free wireless connection, and flat-screen television, two comfortable couches, an overhead fan, a floor-to-ceiling view of sea and sky, and a sliding door to the spacious patio furnished with an inviting settee and a view over the resort and golf course to the sea. Original works of art by Italian artist Costanzo Rovati depict objects found on Canouan. Rugs are scattered randomly on the tile floors, air-conditioning is controlled by high-tech wall thermostats (familiarity with Celsius temperatures helps), and phones have Internet connection capabilities.

The bedroom is light and airy with gauze curtains, shutters that open and shut easily, two bureaus, and a vaulted ceiling with a fan, another television, and a king-size four-poster bed (or twins) with Frette linens. (Some guest rooms have handcrafted wood bed frames, custom made in India.)

There is twice-daily maid service and a concierge.

The championship golf course, greatly enlarged and completely redesigned by Fazio, runs along the seafront and the flat coastal plain at the Trump International Golf Club center to the hillsides at 500 feet above the sea with more challenging greens and magnificent views. Golf instruction and rental clubs are available.

Raffles's full-service Amrita Spa is the most unusual and one of the most beautiful spa facilities in the Caribbean. Located just beyond the cafe at Godahl Beach, it has eleven treatment rooms of which two (with glass-bottom floors) are situated over the water, and the others are set along a wooded hillside reached by a funicular. All are thatched-roof, open-air cottages, named for the different shades of blue and green seen in the Caribbean waters. Their serenity is enhanced by gentle breezes and views of the sea to infinity. Each has a private deck, Jacuzzi, and Asian day bed where a spa guest can lounge briefly after a treatment. The spa offers a wide range of treatments with names as exotic as the setting. Morning Chi and meditation classes are offered here, too. Spa cuisine is on the beach restaurants' menus.

If you want to bring your kids, the Sugar Palm Club is available for ages four to fourteen. The supervised facility is housed in a well-equipped bi-level cottage, opened daily from 9:00 a.m. to 5:00 p.m., closed for lunch. For tweens and teens, the Teens Club offers a separate meeting point with television, Play Stations, and organized pool games, beach volleyball, and soccer. For other diversions, the resort has four all-weather, lighted tennis courts; Sunfish, snorkel gear, windsurfers, hydro-bikes, and pedalos available on a complimentary basis. You can walk the pretty white-sand beach and take a day trip on the resort's catamaran to nearby Tobago Cays. Scuba diving can be arranged.

And should you decide to get married, the stone church in the heart of the resort, has been lovingly restored with beautiful murals and stained glass windows. A more romantic setting would be hard to find.

Raffles Resort *****
Canouan Island, St. Vincent and the Grenadines, W.I.
Phone: (784) 458-8000; Fax: (784) 458-8885; e-mail: info@raffles-canouanisland.com; www.raffles-canouanisland.com

Owner: Canouan Resort Development Ltd.

General Manager: Gilbert Madhavan

Open: Year-round

U.S. Reservations: (866) 589-2450

Deposit: Three nights, within fourteen days of booking; fourteen days cancellation

Credit Cards: Most major

Minimum Stay: Ten nights Christmas only

Arrival/Departure: Transfer complimentary; see text for information on getting to Canouan

Distance from Airport: Ten minutes

Accommodations: 156 one-to-four bedrooms, suites, junior suites, and villa suites with private patios or balconies (king-size beds; twins, or doubles available). Five Grenadines Estate villas available for rent; more expected to be available in 2009.

Amenities: Air-conditioning, ceiling fans; safe; hair dryer; Frette towels, bathrobes, and bed linen; toiletries; twice-daily maid service, dual-line telephone with wireless computer fax/Internet; television; minibar/refrigerator; fruit basket; concierge; in-room dining; shoe-shine service; business center, Internet center 24/7; florist, boutique

Electricity: 220 volts/50 cycles

Fitness Facilities/Spa Services: Fitness club with locker facilities; personal trainer on request; Raffles Amrita Spa, full-service spa, hair salon

Sports: Swimming pool, beach, tennis courts, mountain bikes, Sunfish, windsurfing, kayaks, snorkeling, included in rate; eighteen-hole championship golf course; pro shop

Dress Code: Casually elegant; appropriate dress required on tennis courts and golf course; jackets required at gourmet restaurant and casino; no shorts or jeans after 7:00 p.m.

Day Visitors: Day golf and beach packages available

Handicapped Facilities: Limited

Children: All ages; Kids Club for ages four to fourteen; babysitting service

Meetings: Six meeting rooms; casino, ballroom

Rates: Per room, per day, single or double, including full American breakfast. **High Season** (Christmas/New Year's): $820–$3,345; (January–April): $850–$2,425. **Shoulder Season** (May 1–mid-October) $495–$1,420. **Low Season** (mid-October–mid-December): $595–$1,685. For two bedroom suites and estate villas, inquire.

Service Charge: 10 percent

Government Tax: 7 percent

THE COTTON HOUSE
Mustique Island, St. Vincent, W.I.

More charming than grand, the Cotton House is neither intimidating nor formal, despite its role as snooty Mustique's only hotel of note. Rather, it has the appeal of an English country inn set on manicured shores, where everything is veddy nice.

Opened in 1977, almost two decades after Colin Tennant bought Mustique and began developing it as a private tropical paradise for his royal and ritzy pals, the Cotton House was created out of the ruins of the stone and coral buildings of an eighteenth-century sugar and cotton plantation. The lovely two-story stone main house, originally the warehouse, was the brainchild of the famous British theater designer Oliver Messel, whose genius created many of the posh houses on Mustique.

The main house, with its refined proportions, is highlighted by cedar shutters and arched louvered doors. It's ringed with wide, breezy verandas where afternoon tea and candlelit dinners are served. A handsome horseshoe-shaped wooden bar is at the entrance to the large salon with high-peaked, wood-beamed ceilings; the salon, or Great Room, is lavished with antiques and amusing accoutrements.

The lounge, bar, and dining veranda have been rejuvenated as part of a major renovation of the entire property. The furnishings were painstakingly preserved, and the original fabric designs by Oliver Messel copied and freshened. It serves as the resort's focal point, where guests meet, mingle, and relax. Afternoon tea is served on the veranda that overlooks the lily pond.

In 2004 the resort added a new pool and a pool bar in the original sugar mill; private plunge pools in eight suites; an expanded reception area in the Great Room; and to the east side of the main house overlooking the Atlantic Ocean, Cotton Hill Residence, a lovely two-bedroom villa with a large sitting room and dining room alongside its own private swimming pool, an outdoor gazebo, and its own butler.

The Cotton House's venue for fine dining is The Veranda Restaurant, which serves breakfast and dinner with a menu of Italian and eclectic international cuisine with Caribbean flavors. For casual dining, The Beach Cafe and Bar offers alfresco dining at the water's edge with a menu that stresses local produce and freshly caught fish, lobster, salads, pizzas, and grill items. In-room dining can be choices from the chef's menu or yours and is meant to be more than plain room service.

A small reception area at the back of the house is flanked by a bulletin board bearing various announcements and ads for charter boats offering day (and longer) sails.

Accommodations are in several Georgian-style buildings. The Grenadine Suites, with two upper and two garden-level deluxe accommodations with private verandas, look out at the ocean and the gardens colored with hibiscus and bougainvillea. They are connected by French doors from the bedroom and living room. The two lower Grenadine suites have private plunge pools. Battowia and Baliccau House, renovated in 2007, both with duplex suites are ideal for families because each has two bathrooms and lots of outdoor space.

Most of the rooms and suites are furnished with a king-size bed draped in mosquito netting and have large marble bathrooms, usually with tub and shower. The attractive and understated interior decor is varied with white and blue, peach and beige and other combinations and white pickled-wood furniture. All guest rooms are equipped with air-conditioning

and ceiling fans, flat-screen television and DVD/CD player, espresso machine, PC connection, minibars, and a pillow menu of ten selections. All have a terrace or patio. In the Great Room, a dedicated computer with broadband Internet access is free for hotel guests' use. Wi-Fi service is available anywhere on the hotel property for a free.

A short way from the main house on the west side and only steps from the Caribbean Sea is the restored Coutinot House with five rooms and suites, adding more variety to the resort's accommodations. The three Seafront rooms (two with plunge pools), and the Seafront Master room and Seafront suite (both with plunge pools), offer the ultimate in privacy and panoramic sea views. They are furnished with writing desks, armoires, full dressing rooms, and wrought-iron, four-poster beds. Their large bathrooms have separate tubs and showers; the landscaped gardens directly outside add privacy and an indoor-outdoor effect. Tubs are strategically positioned for great views of the Caribbean and Grenadine Islands beyond. Each guest room has a wraparound terrace, ideal for watching the fabulous sunsets. Coutinot House has a private path leading to a secluded beach. You can book rooms in Coutinot House individually or book the entire house. Prices include all meals, beverages (including wine, champagne, beer, and house cocktails), afternoon tea, water sports, tennis, and Cotton House amenities and services.

The Cotton House has two tennis courts and is set between two of the white-sand beaches that scallop the island. It has Sunfish, windsurfers, and other water-sports equipment, and the dive shop offers a resort course and PADI certification. Snorkeling within swimming distance from shore at Endeavor Bay Beach is terrific. Deep-sea fishing and sailing excursions to nearby islands can be arranged. Only a short walk from the main house is a bird sanctuary; hiking almost anywhere on Mustique rewards you with outstanding views.

The Cotton House Spa, located on the beach, has four treatment rooms and a relaxation room and offers facials and massage and a selection of body treatments using ESPA and Sundari products. Treatments can be booked online. The ground floor of the bi-level facility houses a fitness center with exercise equipment. A boutique with Cotton House label selections is located on the second floor, along with the spa.

Cotton House guests are greeted by a resort representative in Barbados for their air transfer to Mustique. Upon arrival on the island, they are welcomed by the resort's director of guest relations, who escorts them to the resort and to their rooms. The housekeeping staff will unpack and press all clothing on your day of arrival at no charge. For those traveling with children, nanny service and babysitting is available.

The Cotton House ***

Box 349, Mustique Island, St. Vincent, W.I. Phone: (784) 456-4777, (877) 240-9945; Fax: (784) 456-5887; e-mail: reservations@cottonhouse.net; www.cottonhouse.net

Owner: The Mustique Company

General Manager: Pippa Ona Williamson

Open: Year-round except mid-September—early November

Credit Cards: All major

U.S. Reservations: Direct to hotel, (877) 240-9945; reservations@cottonhouse.net

Deposit: Four nights; twenty-eight days cancellation

Minimum Stay: Seven nights during Christmas with 50 percent deposit upon reservation confirmation; five nights in February

Arrival/Departure: From Barbados, transfer to Mustique for a forty-five-minute flight; or via San Juan to St. Vincent with transfer to Mustique in seven minutes by air, forty-five minutes by boat. Private air transfers available from St. Lucia and Canouan. All transfers are booked by the resort.

Distance from Airport: 1 mile; transfer included in hotel rate

Accommodations: 17 rooms and suites, and cottages (8 with private plunge pools), and including a two-bedroom residence with a large swimming pool, butler, and vehicle

Amenities: Air-conditioning, ceiling fans; telephone; bath with tub and shower, hair dryer, basket of toiletries; ice service, minibar; nightly turndown service, room service, 7:00 a.m.–11:00 p.m.; pillow menu; flat-screen television, DVD players, CD/stereo; safe; wireless Internet connection, iPod docking station; unpacking/pressing service upon arrival. Concierge service from 7.30 a.m.–11.30 p.m.; daily international newspapers, CD/DVD library, boutique

Electricity: 220 volts

Fitness Facilities/Spa Services: Spa with four treatment room; fitness center with cardiovascular equipment

Sports: Freshwater swimming pool, hammocks on beach, free use of two tennis courts and nonmotorized water sports, snorkeling gear, windsurfing, kayaks, biking, hiking, bird-watching. Deep-sea fishing, horseback riding, diving arranged for charge.

Dress Code: Casual by day; casually elegant in evening

Children: All ages; none under eight in dining room after 7:30 p.m.; children's menus; babysitters

Meetings: Up to fifteen people

Day Visitors: No

Handicapped Facilities: No

Rates: Per room, double, daily, MAP including a la carte breakfast and VAT. *High Season* (mid-December–March): $995–$1,520. *Shoulder Season* (April–May; November–mid-December): $795–$1,295.

Low Season (mid-April–mid-December): $700–$1,175. For Cotton Hill Residence rates, inquire.

Service Charge: 10 percent

Government Tax: VAT included

PALM ISLAND BEACH CLUB
Palm Island, St. Vincent, W.I.

In March 1999 Palm Island was purchased by Rob Barrett, the owner of Galley Bay Resort and Spa and other hotels in Antigua, who closed the hotel for renovations. By the time the hotel reopened in January 2000, Palm Island was practically a new resort.

The 135-acre private island, located at the southern end of the Grenadines, was originally turned into a resort by the late John Caldwell, the Johnny Appleseed of the Caribbean. When he came upon the island, it was an uninhabited, mosquito-infested swamp that Caldwell remade as his own private paradise. But then probably anything seemed easy after he had sailed 8,500 miles alone in a small boat from Panama to Australia to find and marry his Mary, separated from him by World War II—a story he described in his book *Desperate Voyage*.

Caldwell obtained the island from the government of St. Vincent for a $1 annual fee and a ninety-nine-year lease and promptly changed the name from Prune (who would believe an island called Prune was paradise?). Over the course of several decades, he planted thousands of coconut palms all over the island (and neighboring islands), earning himself the title of Coconut Johnny. The palms grew into the magnificent specimens that sway in everyone's daydreams and dot the resort's pure white beaches and undulating interior. Caldwell also planted every species of Caribbean tree that blossoms or bears fruit—all attracting an enormous variety of birds and turning Palm Island into a veritable, if not an official, nature preserve and wildlife refuge.

Palm Island, scalloped with five white-sand beaches, has a free-form freshwater swimming pool with waterfalls, two restaurants, two bars, a boutique, and two new wedding gazebos

After recent renovations and expansion, the resort has forty-three guest rooms (up from twenty-eight), four Plantation Suites, five Island lofts; and four new, one-bedroom, air-conditioned rooms with large showers and tubs. There are also two villas: The three-bedroom Seafeathers, the newest addition, sleeps up to six adults and has a patio and a private pool; and Southern Cross, formerly known as The Cave House. It sleeps four adults and has its own 10-foot-by-20-foot infinity edge swimming pool and use of golf cart for duration of stay. The bedrooms have marble bathrooms with large showers. Both villas are surrounded by four decks and are stocked with snacks, coffee, fruit, cereal, and beverages.

The resort has several types of rooms. Palm View rooms, located a few yards from the beach, overlook the tropical gardens.

They have a sitting area, king-size bed (four have canopy beds) and a large bathroom with a deep-soaking tub and separate shower. The Plantation House, a two-story building with wraparound balcony, has four suites (two upstairs and two down). Each has a separate sitting area, a bathroom with a double shower (no bathtub), and is furnished with two queen-size beds plus a pullout couch. These rooms are particularly suited for a small family. The spacious Beach Front rooms have king-size bed, bathroom with shower only, and are only steps from the clearest, purest aqua stretch of Caribbean water ever to lap a beach; mountainous Union Island and other nearby islands float on the horizon.

All have balconies or patios, air-conditioning, ceiling fans, louvered windows, and are outfitted with custom-designed rattan and bamboo furniture and original artwork created by a resident Palm Island artist. The amenities include a safe, minifridge, basket of toiletries, bathrobes, nightly turndown service, and afternoon tea.

Public areas have been upgraded with contemporary furniture in the dining rooms and reception area, library, and the television/Internet room. (There is no charge for the Internet.) The resort has an air-conditioned fitness room with exercise equipment and a massage room for spa treatments. The Royal Palms Restaurant serves breakfast, lunch, and dinner, while the smaller Sunset Grill and Bar offers grills and light fare in a casual beachside setting. Palm Island has long been a popular stop for yachties, who enliven the social scene at the bar and often stay for dinner at the Sunset Grill.

Topping the list of activities is the superb snorkeling for which the island is known. It is surrounded by reefs, most within wading distance or a short swim from shore. A day trip to the nearby Tobago Cays National Marine Park is an absolute must.

These uninhabited islets, surrounded by water so brightly turquoise it almost hurts your eyes, offer some of the best snorkeling in the Western Hemisphere. Palm Island also offers hiking on three nature trails, windsurfing, kayaking, Hobie-style catamarans, reef fishing, tennis court (including balls and rackets), table tennis, bike, and pitch and putt golf course.

Palm Island operates as an all-inclusive resort, one of the few on its own private island in the Caribbean. Breakfast, lunch, dinner, afternoon tea, and all drinks by the glass are included in the rates, as is the use of sports facilities, equipment, and instruction. Scuba excursions, deep-sea fishing, and boat charters can be arranged for an additional charge.

This Palm Island Beach Club is different from its predecessor, but it's still a pristine island in a spectacularly beautiful setting, ideal for a honeymoon or wedding and for travelers who truly want to get away from it all.

By the way, you can leave your cell phone and Blackberry at home. There's no reception for them available here. We said it's tranquil.

Palm Island Beach Club ***
St. Vincent, W.I.
Phone: (784) 458-8824; Fax: (784) 458-8804; e-mail: palm@eliteislandresorts .com; www.eliteislandresorts.com

Mailing address: 1601 30th Avenue, Deerfield Beach, FL 33442

Owner: Rob Barrett

General Manager: Richard Kauper

Open: Year-round

Credit Cards: All major

U.S. Reservations: (800) 345-0356, (954) 481-8787; Fax: (954) 481-1661

Deposit: Three nights; twenty-one days cancellation

Minimum Stay: Three nights, except holidays; inquire

Arrival/Departure: Fifty-minute flight (daily) from Barbados to Union Island (complimentary with seven-night stay); there guests met by Palm Island representative and transferred by golf cart to dock to board *Lady Palm* for ten-minute boat ride to island. Air reservations handled by Palm Island's reservation office.

Distance from Airport: (Union Airport) 1 mile

Accommodations: 43 units (32 rooms, four suites, five lofts) with balconies or patios and king-size beds; two villas.

Amenities: Air-conditioning, ceiling fans; radio; minifridge, coffeemaker; bath with shower only, some with tubs; hair dryer, toiletries. No television in guest rooms; television/library room with satellite television and Internet access.

Electricity: 110 volts

Sports: Five beaches, free-form freshwater swimming pool, tennis, nature trails, non-motorized water sports; minigolf

Fitness/Spa facilities: Air-conditioned room with exercise equipment; massage room for spa treatment and services

Dress Code: Smartly casual

Children: Summer only; all ages

Meetings: None

Day Visitors: No

Handicapped Facilities: No

Packages: Honeymoon, wedding, spa, adventure

Rates: Per room, two people, daily, all-inclusive. *High Season* (mid-December–mid-April): $725–$1,115. *Low Season* (mid-April–mid-December): $690–$915. Single, triple, and quad rates are available.

Service Charge: Included

Government Tax: Included

PETIT ST. VINCENT RESORT
Petit St. Vincent, St. Vincent, W.I.

If you've ever fantasized about owning your own private tropical island—complete with invisible elves to cook, clean, and bring you drinks in your ultracomfy abode—start packing.

The late Haze Richardson was one of those rare individuals who did more than fantasize: He reclaimed what was basically an uninhabited 113-acre speck of land in the middle of nowhere and over twenty years turned it into one of the premier private-isle resorts in the Caribbean. In 2008, the resort marked its fortieth anniversary.

Other resorts may be more stylish and manicured, prettier, and more lush, but only on Petit St. Vincent (pronounced PET-ty St. Vincent, or just PSV to cognoscenti) can you live out your dream of being all alone, in casual luxury, beyond the reach of time and care in the middle of an aqua sea. You and your significant other can easily spend a week on PSV without ever having to see another human being. You can even miss the manager's cocktail party and no one will bat an eye. But you might not want to miss the local string band from

Petit Martinique, or the little band from Carriacou that comes with fiddle, guitars, quatro, and steel pans, or the steel band from Union on Saturday nights.

Then, too, what is paradise to some could drive others to the brink within twenty-four hours. PSV has no town, there's no local bar to repair to, and your fellow guests—while nothing if not well bred and polite—won't be around to socialize. You'll spot other houses, but only in the distance. So be sure you can handle it. PSV is a haven for honeymooners and harried tycoons who expect superior service, security, peace, and privacy—and private beaches outside their widely spaced stone cottages.

The accommodations on PSV aren't suites or even bungalows: They are full-size houses. Built of bluebitch stone with wood-beamed roofs and large windows, each has a spacious living room with two day beds; an oversize bathroom with large vanities, dressing room, and rock showers; big bedroom with two queen-size beds; terra-cotta floors; and patio with hammock. Large windows and sliding doors look out on foliage and sea views. The cottages are furnished with tasteful, very comfortable couches and chairs, upholstered in neutral tones and attractive entryways with patterned brick. All of the accommodations are renovated with new fabrics and furniture from time to time to keep them fresh. Also, greater emphasis has been placed on the gardens, with flowering plants by every cottage and in public areas.

Small, secluded beaches are only steps from the door of most cottages, but be warned: Windy Point is aptly named—the wind gusts can be enough to awaken even heavy sleepers.

Though room rates do not vary by type, there are definite variations among rooms. Those on hills and promontories are more secluded and offer the grandest views, while those on the beach are closer together, but still private. Six cottages are especially suited to families or groups of friends, because they offer larger living rooms separated from bedrooms by patios, with baths off both living rooms and bedrooms.

Meals are served in the Pavilion, the open-air dining and bar area overlooking the dock, or in the smaller pavilion, but many guests prefer room service—and it is room service like no other. You signal your needs by raising the yellow flag outside your door; staff members, who putt-putt continuously around the island in minimokes, take your written or spoken order for food, drink, or whatever else you fancy. Each cottage also has a stocked bar cart.

Guests are the only ones on Caribbean time; service is swift (there is a ratio of two staff members per guest), assuming you haven't raised your red flag mistakenly in the interim. Red flags mean "leave me alone," and PSV personnel have strict orders not to bother you for any reason when they see one.

Should you care to venture beyond your own patch of paradise, there is a lighted tennis court, newly resurfaced with Astroturf, and a jogging and fitness trail that winds around the island. When that becomes too tiring, you'll find hammocks under thatched canopies thoughtfully placed every 100 yards or so along the beach. A day by the beach is so popular with guests that they can order lunch, drinks, and a thermos of cold water to be brought to them. A building with shower and toilet is there for guests' convenience. The thatched canopies on the west beach each have a dining table, two chairs, two chaise longues, and a small cocktail table.

PSV does not have a spa, but it will call in an esthetician from neighboring

Carriacou for facials, massage, and yoga classes upon request.

Water sports? Most—windsurfers, ocean kayaks, "spyaks" for reef viewing, Hobie or Sunfish sailing lessons—are included in the rates. Scuba diving and waterskiing are extra. If island living has gotten into your blood and even a house seems too civilized, you can live out your shipwreck fantasies in style. PSV will arrange a boat to drop you on a tiny island of blinding white sand, in turquoise water even more blinding. It looks unreal, with nothing on it but a thatched umbrella for shade. The islet's official name is Mopion; guests prefer to call it Petit St. Richardson.

Recently, PSV has begun raising turtles which are kept in a temporary turtle pond. The aim is to increase the turtle population in these waters and the number of females that come to the island beaches to lay their eggs.

PSV serves some of the best food in the Caribbean, continental with West Indian flavors. Recently, the resort built an additional dining room, complete with a brick oven as well as outdoor dining venues. The resort grows fruits and vegetables, raises chickens, and imports supplies almost daily from the States (filets mignons, duck, wines, fresh produce), and the chef does wonderful things with them. After dinner, brandy, Scrabble, conversation, or a bit of music on the resident piano, a moke will drive you home. Or you can stroll your way home, flashlight in hand, perhaps accompanied by one of Haze's many yellow Labrador retrievers. Then enjoy a moonlight swim—and don't forget to hoist the red flag, darling, while I open the champagne.

Petit St. Vincent Resort ***
Petit St. Vincent, St. Vincent, W.I.
Phone: (784) 458-8801; Fax: (784) 458-8428; e-mail: psv@fuse.net; www.psvresort.com

Owner/Manager: Lynn Richardson

Open: Year-round except September–October

Credit Cards: All major, but cash, personal checks preferred

U.S. Reservations: Petit St. Vincent, P.O. Box 841338, Pembroke Pines, FL 33084; (954) 963–7401, (800) 654-9326; Fax: (954) 963-7401; e-mail: info@psvresort.com

Deposit: Three nights; thirty days cancellation

Minimum Stay: None

Arrival/Departure: Complimentary transfer arranged by boat only; on Union Island PSV picks up guests who arrive by Grenadine Airways from Barbados or St. Vincent or private charter. In Barbados, PSV representative meets and assists with transfers.

Distance from Airport: (Union Airport) 4 miles

Accommodations: 22 in villas with patios; doubles with two queen-size beds

Amenities: Ceiling fans; bath with shower, hair dryer, basket of toiletries, bathrobe; CD player, safe, minibar; beach bags, umbrellas; flashlights; ice service, nightly turndown service, room service 7:30 a.m.–9:30 p.m.; Internet access available; no air-conditioning, telephone, television

Electricity: 110 volts

Fitness Facilities/Spa Services: Masseuse from nearby Carriacou by appointment for fee, who also gives yoga classes.

Sports: One tennis court; Sunfish and Hobie Cat sailing, snorkeling gear, ocean kayaks, spyaks, windsurfing free; diving, waterskiing, deep-sea fishing, charter boat sailing for charge

Dress Code: Casual by day; elegantly casual in evening

Children: All ages; cribs; high chairs; babysitters

Meetings: No

Day Visitors: No

Handicapped Facilities: Limited

Packages: Summer

Rates: Per room, two people, daily, FAP. *High Season* (mid-December–January 5 and January 25–mid-March): $1,020. *Shoulder Season* (January 6–January 24 and mid-March–mid-April): $860. *Low Season* (November 1–mid-December and mid-April–August 31): $675. Children and single rates available, inquire.

Service Charge: 10 percent

Government Tax: 10 percent

TRINIDAD AND TOBAGO

Different yet similar, this island duet is the ultimate Caribbean kaleidoscope: A mélange of Europeans, Africans, and Asians has woven intricate cultural patterns into a tapestry of fabulous flora and fauna.

The birthplace of calypso and steel bands, Trinidad is the country's banking and trading center; its visitors are more interested in business than beaches. Twenty-two miles to the northeast lies tiny Tobago, an island so lavishly beautiful and serene that it makes even the most severe Caribbean cynic smile.

The mating of Trinidad and Tobago is a bit of a historical irony. Columbus discovered Trinidad on his third voyage and named it for three southern mountain peaks symbolizing to him the Holy Trinity. The Spaniards held the island for three centuries until they were unseated by the British in 1797. But Tobago, because of its strategic location, was so prized by Europeans that it changed hands fourteen times. Finally, in 1889, Tobago asked to become a part of Trinidad; they became independent in 1962.

Trinidad has gone through the oil boom and bust. At the heart of Port-of-Spain, the capital, Victorian architectural relics give it a distinctive character. It has an interesting zoo, botanic gardens, and restaurants featuring local cuisine that reflects the country's West Indian, East Indian, and Chinese components.

Trinidad explodes once a year in Carnival, the granddaddy of all Caribbean Carnivals. The balance of the year, it offers tennis, golf, art galleries, and museums in historic buildings, antiques in offbeat shops, and a music- and dance-filled nightlife.

The most southerly of the Caribbean island states, Trinidad is 7 miles off the Venezuela coast and was originally part of the South American mainland. Its flora and fauna include many South American species not seen elsewhere in the Caribbean. It also has such strange natural features as mud volcanoes and an asphalt lake.

But of all its natural wonders, the most spectacular is the bird life. More than 425 species from North and South America and the Caribbean meet here in the forested mountains and mangroves. Of special note is the nightly sunset arrival of hundreds of scarlet ibises, the national bird, to roost in a sanctuary of the Caroni Swamp only 7 miles south of the capital. Guided boat trips through the swamp end where the birds return daily.

Information

Trinidad and Tobago Tourism Development Company;
P.O. Box 222, Level 1, Maritime Centre, 29 Tenth Avenue, Trinidad, W.I.;
(868) 675-7034, (800) 816-7541; Fax: (868) 675–7432;
e-mail: info@tdc.co.tt; www.goTrinidadandTobago.com

ASA WRIGHT NATURE CENTRE

Port-of-Spain, Trinidad, W.I.

Deep in a rain forest on the slopes of the Northern Range at 1,200 feet overlooking the Arima Valley is the Asa Wright Nature Centre, a bird sanctuary and wildlife reserve with an inn. Built about 1906, the inn is in the Victorian estate house of the former coffee, citrus, and cocoa plantation, now mostly returned to the wild. It is surrounded by dense tropical vegetation; sitting on its veranda is like being in an aviary, except that the birds come and go freely from the surrounding rain forest.

The centre, a private institution unique in the Caribbean, was established in 1967 on the Spring Hill Estate by its owner, Asa Wright, an Icelandic-born Englishwoman whose rugged manner may have helped give rise to many tall tales about her. She acquired the 197-acre property upon the death of her husband and was persuaded by naturalist friends to create a nonprofit trust to preserve the area and make it a study and recreation center.

The inn is rustic but comfortable; services are minimal. Most of the rooms are in bungalows, furnished with a bureau, desk, chair, and reading lamp and have attractive bedcovers and curtains; all have private bath and international phone service. The rooms also have screened porches or outside areas where you can enjoy the birds and the great outdoors in privacy. Wi-Fi service is available for a fee in several of the rooms as well as throughout the manor house and veranda.

At the entrance to the manor house, beyond the office where useful nature books can be purchased, are the main house's two bedrooms. Directly on, a hallway leads into the parlor and, to one side, the dining room. Both rooms are comfortably furnished in a traditional, homey manner as they might have been in their plantation days. On the veranda outside the parlor, guests gather for afternoon tea and at other times to watch birds, as well as nightly before dinner for the inn's complimentary rum punch. Full bar service is available throughout the day and at meals, including a selection of fine wines.

All meals, fresh and hearty, are served in the dining room buffet style. The kitchen will prepare picnic baskets if you want to spend the day hiking and birding or drive to the beach on Trinidad's Caribbean northern coast.

Natural history programs with slides, lectures, and videos are usually scheduled in the evening. But by evening, after an active and exhilarating day with nature, you will probably be happy to go quietly off to bed.

The centre has its own guides and five hiking trails, which day visitors may also use for a small fee. (E-mail dayvisit@ asawright.org for information; reservations for lunch are required.) The trails, ranging from half-hour strolls to difficult three-hour hikes, are designed to maximize viewing of particular species. Maps are available for self-guided forays into the rain forest.

With ease you will see tanagers, thrushes, trogons, blue-crowned motmots, many species of hummingbirds, the beautiful crested oropendola, and dozens of other bird species. The trails pass through magnificent rain forest; the upper-story canopy is often more than 100 feet above you. North of the centre are other trails at 1,800 feet, where you can spot species that prefer high elevations. Generally the best weather, and thus most favorable time, to see the greatest variety of birds is from December to March, although an interesting variety of tropical birds can be seen year-round.

The most celebrated species at Asa Wright is a nesting colony of oilbirds, which make their home in a cave located on the property. This rare bird is found only in Trinidad and in northern South America. The site can be visited only with a guide. A guided tour of the centre grounds and visit to the oilbird cave is included only on stays of three or more nights due to capacity limits the centre uses to control visitation to the oilbird colony. While the inn takes guests on an individual basis, most people staying here are likely to be part of a natural history or birding group from the United States, Canada, or Britain. The Asa Wright Nature Centre is unique, though obviously not for everyone. For bird-watchers, naturalists, and hikers, it's nirvana. And I believe this quiet, friendly inn should also appeal to anyone—age eight to ninety-eight—who is a true nature lover.

Asa Wright Nature Centre (S) 🖌
7¾ miles, Blanchissuese Road, Arima, Trinidad & Tobago, W.I.
Phone: (868) 667-4655 (for voice messages only); Fax: (868) 667-0540; e-mail: asawright@caligo.com; www.asawright.org

Owner: Asa Wright Nature Centre, a nonprofit trust

General Manager: Ann Sealey

Open: Year-round

Credit Cards: MasterCard and Visa for incidentals

U.S. Reservations: Caligo Ventures, 426 Petronia Street, P.O. Box 6356, Key West, FL 33041-6356; (800) 426-7781; US/ Canada; (305) 292-0708; Fax: (305) 292-0706; www.caligo.com/trinidad/index.html

Deposit: $100 per person

Minimum Stay: None

Arrival/Departure: Transfer service arranged for fee

Distance from Airport: One-and-a-half-hour drive; taxi one-way, $30

Distance from Port-of-Spain: Two-hour drive. From Arima: 7¾ miles (thirty minutes); taxi one-way, approximately $20

Accommodations: 25 rooms, most with terraces (two in main building, 21 in bungalows; 19 with twins, two with kings, three singles with air-conditioning)

Amenities: Ceiling fans; bath with shower only; phones in rooms; no television, radios, air-conditioning (except in singles), or room service

Electricity: 110 volts

Sports: No facilities; natural pool for wading; Caribbean coastal beaches less than an hour's drive

Dress Code: Very casual

Children: Over eight years of age

Meetings: Up to fifty people

Day Visitors: Yes

Handicapped Facilities: Very limited

Packages: Natural history and birding tours

Rates: Per person, daily, AP. *High Season* (mid-December–March 31): $200 (double), $275 (single). *Shoulder Season* (April 1–30 and November 1–December 15): $155 (double), $210 (single). *Low Season:* $125 and $155, respectively

Service Charge: Included

Government Tax: Included

TURKS AND CAICOS ISLANDS

A diver's paradise lying at the end of the Bahamas chain, the Turks and Caicos (pronounced KAY-kos) have been dubbed the Caribbean's Last Frontier. A British Crown Colony made up of eight islands and several dozen cays, the islands stretch across 90 miles in two groups separated by the Turks Island Passage, a deep-water channel of 22 miles.

To the east is the Turks group, which has Grand Turk, the capital with about half of the colony's population of 20,000; and neighboring Salt Cay, an old settlement with windmills and salt ponds, declared a Heritage Site under UNESCO's World Heritage program.

To the west are the Caicos Islands—South, Middle, North—which form an arch on the northern side of Caicos Bank. The small archipelago is surrounded by virgin reefs, most uncharted. Provo, as Providenciales is known, is the commercial center and the site of most of the resort and commercial development. North of Provo is Pine Cay, home of the Meridian Club and Parrot Cay.

The islands are not richly blessed with tropical vegetation, but they do have a surprising variety of flora. Coconut palms, casuarinas, sea grapes, and palmettos give them a rugged, windswept beauty. Middle Caicos and North Caicos have fertile soil with lush patches of citrus and fruit trees.

The islands have some exceptional natural attractions: almost 200 miles of untouched beaches, acres of tropical wilderness and wetlands, and magnificent seas with some of the most spectacular marine life in the world. Several locations are national parks and bird sanctuaries (two islets in the Turks and eight locations in the Caicos), and a nature lover's paradise.

Grand Turk is a long, skinny island of 9 square miles along the Turks Island Passage. This and Salt Cay are great places for whale-watching in spring and autumn, when the passage becomes a thoroughfare for migratory humpback whales and giant manta rays.

Information
Turks and Caicos Islands Tourist Board, Lincoln Building, Suite 2817, 60 East 42nd Street, New York, NY 10165; (800) 241-0824, (646) 375-8830; e-mail: tci.tourism@caribsurf.com; www.turksandcaicostourism.com
(Also see Nikki Beach Resort on p. 310 and Seven Stars Resort on p. 311 in On the Horizon.)

AMANYARA

Northwest Point, Providenciales, Turks and Caicos Islands, B.W.I.

Opened in March 2006, the first member of the aesthetically sensitive Amanresorts group to be built in the Caribbean, Amanyara is set in an isolated coastal area on the northwest end of Providenciales (better known as Provo), far removed from major development on the eastern part of the island. The resort is reached by an unpaved road through a remote area covered with native bush and stunted trees. Its pavilions and private villas can barely be seen in the woods surrounding them. Its small, secluded beaches hidden in rocky ironshore coves overlook the 4,168-acre Northwest Point Marine National Park with some of the world's best wall and reef diving. But there is nothing about this Amanresort that would have you thinking "dive resort."

Amanyara is exquisitely beautiful. Its name, meaning "peaceful place," derives from *aman,* the Sanskrit word for peace, and *yara,* the word for place in the Arawak language. It is well named, but perhaps, too peaceful for most people.

Upon arrival, you enter the resort through a large, very high ceiling reception pavilion that opens onto a formal reflecting pool landscaped with trees. The setting is so serene, so perfectly symmetrical and harmonious, it's like walking through the gates of a Shinto shrine.

The reflecting pool is framed on one side by the library and a boutique, and on the other, by the restaurant and bar. As your eyes lead you through these rooms, you are awestruck by the rich, intricately laid wood that dominates the space and is the singular important element in the simple but elegant decor. Everywhere, Amanyara is open to the elements—the sun, reflections from the pond, the breeze, and the sounds and sights of the ocean.

All the lines are straight until you reach the Bar—what drama! The circular room sits under a soaring roof that is a magnificent work of art for its intricately assembled slates of beautiful wood. Surrounding the bar at the center are oversize lounging day beds.

The restaurant provides a choice of dining settings: The first part is open to the breezes; the second, air-conditioned. The open setting leads down onto a terrace with outdoor seating beneath two large trees. Both areas have views to the ocean. The air-conditioned section also opens to an outdoor balcony that enjoys views across the reflecting pool. The menu offers a selection of Asian and Mediterranean fare with an emphasis on local seafood, served in portions almost as sparse as the decor. The staff, you will notice, is mostly Asian.

Beyond the restaurant and bar is another drama. A long, narrow black stone swimming pool (164 feet by 26 feet) with a terrace alongside a long sundeck looks out over the sea. On either end of the pool are two lounge pavilions from which shallow entries to the pool also provide for water lounging. There's a third lounge pavilion closer to the ocean and an outdoor shower.

On a dune above the white-sand beach is the Beach Club, an informal lunch dining venue open throughout the day for grills, sandwiches, salads, and occasional informal beach barbecues in the evenings. The interior is terraced with a bar in front, or lower terrace that leads to a large wooden deck. At the beach, equipment for snorkeling, sailing, kayaking, and other sports is available.

Beyond is a grassed courtyard and Amanyara's Dive Centre, operated by Ocean Vibes, whose instructors offer scuba diving for beginners to advanced and specialty courses. A 5-mile-long fringing reef parallels the coastline. Ray, dolphins, and hammerhead, reef and lemon shark have been sighted; humpback whales pass through during their winter migrations.

The Library, with its reading terrace overlooking the reflecting pool, has books on the Turks and Caicos, along with novels, magazines, newspapers, CDs, DVDs, and board games. Next door is the Boutique, with a small selection of resort wear, jewelry, gifts, and sundries. There is also a thirty-seat screening room where movies are shown regularly.

Amanyara's accommodations are found in forty wood-shingled pavilions, each measuring 1,250 square feet and identical in layout and design. They best capture the Aman aesthetic with a simple palette of colors and materials, the finely finished wood of the furniture, and floors of polished sand-colored terrazzo with teak inlays.

The pavilion sits on a platform either at the edge of a tranquil pond with a wooden sundeck extending over the water, or atop the ironshore in dry-wood vegetation with the ocean peeking through, here and there. Three sides of the pavilion are mostly glass, bringing the outdoors inside, and an overhanging roofline shades its three outdoor terraces. Glass doors slide open to catch the sea breezes, when that's preferred to the air-conditioning. Rocky paths lead to an occasional sandy cove hidden in the ironshore by the sea.

The room interior (about half of the pavilion overall) has a king-size bed at the center; behind it sits a writing desk and chair. To one side is a cabinet with a minibar. One corner of the room has a reading chair with a footstool and an entertainment console housing a flat-screen television with a Bose DVD/CD player and sound system. The bathroom, separated from the bedroom by a decorative wooden screen, has a free-standing bathtub. Twin vanities, hair dryer, umbrella, makeup mirror, shower, and separate toilet are found on either side of the bathroom, as is a dressing area and closet with a safe, bathrobes, slippers, and beach bag. The bedroom/living room opens onto the three outdoor wooden decks: One has twin banquettes for lounging or dining; another, two day beds; and the third has a sunken table with cushions (sunken so as not to obstruct the view from the bed).

On the south side of the property, Amanyara has three-, four-, and five-bedroom villas, each sitting on about an acre and a half of land in dry tropical vegetation, either along the oceanfront or by a pond; some have internal reflecting ponds. The villas are centered around a rectangular or square infinity-edged swimming pool in black volcanic rock surrounded by hardwood decking. The free-standing bedroom pavilions are similar to those of the resort with some having an outdoor bathtub and shower. All villas have a large living and dining pavilion, outdoor dining area, fully-equipped kitchen, cook, and housekeeper. Each villa also comes with two, four-seat golf cars, and guests have access to the resort's facilities and services. Some villas have an additional bedroom suitable for up to four children and a nanny. The Fitness Centre has exercise equipment—treadmills, bikes, elliptical trainers, rowing machines, a range of resistance training machines, dumbbell set, incline bench, body bars, and mats, and offers aerobic workouts. A personal trainer is available upon request. Racquets and balls are available for use on the two flood-lit, Har-Tru clay tennis courts. Spa treatments and services by Amanyara's team of therapists are available in guest pavilions and the resort's temporary spa villa, until a permanent facility is built. There is no hair salon.

Snorkeling from the beach at Amanyara is super. The sandy bottom declines gradually until the reef wall falls away dramatically into a sheer vertical drop. Additionally, the rock formations surrounding the resort are home to many small fish; excellent snorkeling is found in there. The Turks and Caicos Islands have some of the finest deep-sea fishing grounds in the world. Both light tackle and game fishing charters can be arranged.

Amanyara is so beautiful aesthetically, don't pass up an opportunity to see it. But this resort is clearly not for everyone. Aman-resort habituées (who like to call themselves Aman-junkies) relish it. But such serenity can be intimidating and barely talking above a whisper tiring. You may want peace and quiet, but 24/7 for a week or two? Think about it.

Amanyara
Northwest Point, Providenciales, Turks and Caicos Islands, B.W.I.
Phone: (649) 941-8133; Fax: (649) 941-8132; e-mail: amanyara@amanresorts.com; www.amanresorts.com

Owner: Caicos Resorts Ltd.

Management: Amanresorts

General Managers: John Vasatka and Tania Rydon

Open: Year-round

Credit Cards: Most major

U.S. Reservations: (866) 941-8133

Deposit: Three nights (two nights May 1–October 31)

Minimum Stay: Eight nights over Christmas/New Year's; five nights over President's Weekend and Easter. Minimum stays also apply in the villas.

Arrival/Departure: Private transfer included in rate

Distance from Airport: Twenty-minute drive

Distance from business center: Thirty-minute drive

Accommodations: 40 pavilions; 15 three-, four-, and five bedroom villas (to be increased to 33 villas)

Amenities: See text

Electricity: 110 volts/60 cycles

Fitness Facilities/Spa Services: Gym, tennis; spa villa and in-room treatments

Sports: See text

Dress Code: None

Children: All ages but some pavilions not suitable for toddlers

Meetings: Theater style for thirty

Day Visitors: Lunch and dinner reservations, subject to space

Handicapped Facilities: No handicap-modified rooms; one bathroom in public area

Packages: Five-night Wellness; seven-night Romance

Rates: Per pavilion daily: Christmas/New Year (December 18–January 2) $1,980–$2,550. *High Season* (January 3–May 31): $1,550–$2,150. Villas, $7,000–$15,250 and $5,600–$13,950. *Low Season 2009,* inquire. Rates include airport transfers, minibar, nonalcoholic drinks, local and long-distance phone calls, wireless in-room Internet access, yoga classes, nonmotorized water sports, tennis courts/equipment/hitting partners.

Service Charge: 10 percent

Government Tax: 10 percent

GRACE BAY CLUB
Providenciales, Turks and Caicos Islands, B.W.I.

Situated on one of the most beautiful beaches in the world—powdery porcelain sands that run for 12 uninterrupted miles washed by gorgeous, reef-filled turquoise waters, with slightly more than six acres fronting 1,100 feet of the pristine shore— the 11-acre Grace Bay Club is a hideaway that is elegant yet casual, sumptuous yet understated and refined.

The Grace Bay Club is designed for affluent, sophisticated international travelers who appreciate quality along with tranquillity. It was the first luxury resort to open on Provo (Providenciales on the map), and although many others have popped up on this newly discovered island, there's little likelihood that any of them will surpass this impeccably designed and superbly maintained beauty by the bay.

Set in gardens on the beach, the Grace Bay Club suggests a gracious Spanish village in stucco the color of the late-afternoon sun. Red tile roofs at staggered levels, terracotta or marble floors, stone balustrades, wrought-iron balconies, and shaded terraces are interlaced with lush courtyards, splashing fountains, and arched pathways framed in bright bougainvillea. The graceful setting is enhanced by elaborate landscaping and hidden corners.

With its recent expansion, Grace Bay offers accommodations in three different sections. Grace Bay Club Hotel (the original buildings where major renovations have recently been completed) is the adults-only section. Here, no two suites are alike, and range from 700-square-foot studios to 1,700-square-foot two-bedroom penthouses. Ground-floor units boast patios with private solariums and paths leading to the beach, all hidden from view in tropical landscaping.

The major change in these units was the bathrooms which were made much larger and now have dual vanities, marbled tub, and separate shower and toilet. The suites are self-contained retreats with oceanfront terrace or patio, kitchenette refrigerator, microwave. The larger units have dishwasher, and washer and dryer.

Another section called The Villas at Grace Bay Club, is the family area with four four-story buildings, each with nine large, luxurious condominiums that are either junior, one-, two-, or three-bedroom suites and the penthouse, a four-bedroom suite covering the entire floor. All accommodations have air-conditioning and a ceiling fan, a direct-dial phone, flat-screen television, DVD, and CD player.

The third section is the new The Estate at Grace Bay, four six-story buildings with twenty-two ultra-elegant condominium suites that were priced from $3.5 to $8 million. They range from oceanfront junior suites (800 square feet) with bed/living room, terrace, minibar, bathroom, and outdoor rain shower encased in glass and stone to a 7,000-square-foot penthouse with four oceanfront bedrooms with terraces, living room, dining room, media room (or optional bedroom) and private study with terraces; Jacuzzi tub, grill, and rain shower on terrace, and private elevator access.

Most suites measure about 3,700 to 4,700 square feet with three or four bedrooms; some are anchored by an infinity-edge plunge pool. They have a Bose speaker system, wireless Internet, and kitchen fitted with Wolf & Sub Zero appliances, custom Italian cabinetry, wine chiller, elegant minibar, and Grohe faucets, among other fine features. After their sale, the Estate suites are put into Grace Bay's inventory for rent. A limited number of private beach cabanas, spacious enough for spa treatments and dining are available to Estate guests. The cost is $200 day use, which can be credited against food, bar, or spa services.

When you enter the air-conditioned reception, furnished like the living room of a home, you will be greeted by the concierge or an attendant with a refreshing cool drink and a cold hand cloth while you check in. You will be assigned a "personal concierge" who is a combination butler and concierge, able to take care of your needs from unpacking to arranging a party or sightseeing, who will accompany you to your suite. He will give you a cell phone and number to call anytime you need his services.

A design masterpiece, the Anacaona Restaurant, named for the Lucayan Indian goddess (her name means "flower of gold"), consists of palapas strung along the beach. In the evening tiki torches cast a romantic glow, enhanced by flickering candlelight from each table. The main palapa's thatched roof (built by Seminole Indians from Florida) and recently redesigned with new lighting and blue and gold decor, is supported by a ring of classic white columns, and arranged on four levels, so that diners on each have front-row views of the tranquil turquoise-turned-lavender-turned-silver waters of Grace Bay, framed by floodlit palm trees and smoke from the flaming torches. To complement its redesign, the restaurant has a new menu created in collaboration with celebrated chefs from around the world. It also offers "Private Island" dining—a service, available only for one group or couple each evening, that comes with a private butler, chef, and customized menu. Beachfront tables are decorated in fine-dining style and adorned with tiki torches.

A recent addition is a black marble bar that stretches 90 feet across the beach from the restaurant to the water's edge. It's probably the longest bar in the Caribbean. Designed by Keith Hobbs of United Designers, noted for his work with Nobu and the London W Hotels, the black marble creates the illusion of water with the structure floating above the beach into the ocean. During the day, the bar is shaded by canopies, but in the evening, it is open to the sky and offers full restaurant service and a special cocktail menu.

The Lounge is a contemporary beach oasis at the water's edge with lounge chairs, sailcloth canopies, and evening sunsets to watch by flickering torches and glowing fire pits. The open-air space has a martini menu and serves tapas, accompanied with live music from local musicians during the week.

The Grace Bay Club layout stretching along its long beachfront made it easy to provide all the villa accommodations with ocean views, and the addition of an on-the-beach family swimming pool and the outdoor, casual-dining waterfront grill cleverly helped separate the two areas: the villas, the new section, is active with children and their families, while the hotel, the original section and its freshwater swimming pool, form an adult area for those who prefer tranquillity.

The resort's Kid's Town offers a variety of outdoor activities for kids and teen guests, such as hikes, snorkeling, semi-submarine treks, kayaking, horseback riding, and sailboat and other excursions. Prices range from $39–$135. Family adventures can also be arranged with a local ecotour company. The Kid's Town "V.I.K." Club (Very Important Kids Club) for children ages two to twelve costs $180 per child and includes a personal greeting by a Kids Coordinator, a stuffed animal, and fruit punch upon arrival, a Kids Town bathrobe, VIK card for one daily slushie at the pool bar, nightly turn-down service, unlimited use of the Kid's Town playroom, and gifts such as hats, T-shirts, and maps of the Turks and Caicos islands.

Grace Bay's other amenities include a Jacuzzi overlooking the beach and two lighted tennis courts. There is a small video and book library as well as backgammon, chess, and other games. The former reception, an attractive open-sided area, is now used for groups. It houses a small business center with two computers with free Internet access for guests. The resort's boutique is there, too.

The Anani Spa offers a wide variety of services, including aromatherapy, massage, reflexology, facials, wraps, pregnancy massage, waxing manicures and pedicures, as well as special treatments for men. The spa uses Elemis products. The fitness center has a full daily schedule of classes from yoga and Pilates to children's ballet and karate.

Complimentary windsurfing, Sunfish sailing, and snorkeling gear, along with a full range of water sports and bone-, bottom-, and deep-sea fishing are available. Day sails and small-boat excursions to nearby uninhabited islands are popular. Scuba—some of the best in the Tropics—and golf just across the road can be arranged.

Grace Bay Club ****
P.O. Box 128, Providenciales, Turks and Caicos Islands, B.W.I.
Phone: (649) 946-5757; Fax: (649) 946-5758; e-mail: info@gracebayclub.com; www.gracebayclub.com

Owners: Mark Durliat and Partners

Managing Director: Nikheel Advani

General Manager: Anderson Howard

Open: Year-round

Credit Cards: MasterCard, Visa, American Express; personal checks by prior arrangement only

U.S. Reservations: (800) 946-5757

Deposit: Three nights; for December 16–January 1, cancellation must be received before November 1

Minimum Stay: Ten nights during Christmas/New Year's; five nights, winter

Distance from Airport: 10 miles; airport transfer included

Distance from Business Center: 3 miles

Accommodations: 59 oceanfront suites (junior and one–four bedrooms), all with one or more private terraces or balconies; all with king-size beds (convertible to twins) and some with queen-size pullout sofa beds. 22 Estate suites (junior to four bedrooms, combinable to five and six bedroom suites)

Amenities: Air-conditioning, ceiling fans; direct-dial telephone, flat-screen cable television including DVD/CD players, complimentary high-speed wireless Internet access; iPod docking stations; safe; refrigerator (some with ice maker); bath with tub and shower, bathrobes and slippers, hair dryers, Elemis bath amenities; room service 7 a.m.–10 p.m.; daily maid service, nightly turndown service; daily *New York Times*

Electricity: 110 volts

Fitness Facilities/Spa Services: Full-service spa and fitness center

Sports: Two swimming pools and Jacuzzi; two soft-surface, lighted tennis courts; complimentary water sports including windsurfers, Hobie cats, kayaks, bicycles, snorkeling; scuba diving, and sailing arranged for additional charge; free shuttle to Provo Golf Club, where guests receive reduced green fees and priority tee times

Dress Code: Casual sportswear by day; elegantly casual in restaurant for dinner; long pants, collared shirts

Children: All ages; Kid's Club, see text

Meetings: Boardroom for up to twenty persons

Day Visitors: Welcome

Handicapped Facilities: No

Packages: Honeymoon, wedding, golf, spa

Rates: Per room, double, daily, CP. *High Season* (mid-December–mid-April): $864–$1,579. *Shoulder Season* (April 1–May 31; November 1–December 19): $666–$1,183. *Low Season:* $501–$952. Airport transfer included. MAP available. Rates for two–four bedrooms Villas and Estate suites, inquire.

Service Charge: 10 percent

Government Tax: 10 percent

THE MERIDIAN CLUB ON PINE CAY

Pine Cay, Turks and Caicos Islands, B.W.I.

Since the only way to reach Pine Cay is by boat or private plane, you could say the Meridian Club is remote and exclusive. But what really sets the resort apart and makes it one of the truly great hideaways is its refreshing simplicity and its wild natural setting along one of the world's most gorgeous beaches.

The small, unpretentious resort belongs to the homeowners of an exclusive residential development on Pine Cay, a privately owned 800-acre island—about the size of New York's Central Park—floating on spectacularly beautiful aquamarine water between Provo and North Caicos.

Set on two uninterrupted miles of pristine white sand washed by clear, languid water, the club is comprised of a clubhouse and clusters of cottages less than a stone's throw from the beach. Some of the private homes also are available for rent. No cars are allowed on the island; you get around on leg power by walking or biking or, when available, by golf cart.

The clubhouse is the reception and social center, with an indoor-outdoor dining room on the first floor and an attractive upstairs lounge with a bar, corner library, and veranda. Guests and homeowners—a well-traveled, well-heeled, and somewhat intellectual group—mingle here nightly for cocktails hosted by the manager and for after-dinner socializing.

The clubhouse opens onto the pool, which has a wide terrace used for breakfast, lunch, and tea, and for barbecues on Wednesday and Saturday night. Dinner is an informal affair in the dining room. The food is good, not gourmet. The resort has a visiting chef program during the season.

The beachfront cottages are connected by a walkway lined with local flora. Most guest rooms are large junior suites, tastefully furnished. They have a king-size or twin beds, a separate sitting area, a large bathroom with shower, and screened porches facing the beach. There is also an outside shower with hot and cold water and each suite has its own thatched beach hut with lounge chairs for two.

At the end, a bit separate from the group, is Sand Dollar, a hexagonal cottage that honeymooners like for its privacy. The rustic cottage has stone floors and a tiled bath with an enclosed outdoor shower. It has its own thatched beach hut just large enough to shade two.

Recently, the resort was given a complete renovation and upgrade that included freshening the twelve guest rooms, Sand Dollar Cottage, and common areas with new decor inside and out; the reconstruction of the lobby and the gift shop; new furnishings of the bar and outdoor lounge and dining areas; and the installation of a new pool filtration system.

The resort has added four new boats for guest transport, snorkeling, and other activities. Use of water-sports equipment and daily excursions to nearby cays for snorkeling are included in the room rate. The snorkeling, with the reefs rich in marine life, is some of the best you will ever find. Bonefishing, which is said to be outstanding in May, is also available, as is deep-sea fishing. The resort also arranges for golfers to play at the Royal Turk Golf Club on Provo.

But of all the changes, perhaps the most important has been moving reservations to ring directly at the Club, enabling the resort to provide more personalized service and a quick response to inquiries with greater knowledge regarding the resort and the island.

Several features set the Meridian Club apart from other retreats. The untamed appearance of Pine Cay is the most apparent and the one the homeowners are determined to maintain. Strong-willed environmentalists, they have resisted the temptation to expand and, instead, have converted about two-thirds of the island into a national park. They are equally vigilant about the coral reefs protecting the island.

Covered mostly with dry scrub, Pine Cay has freshwater lakes and gets its name from a type of tree that covers vast areas of the Caicos. It has a nature trail, and any dirt road can be used by birders to spot some of the 120 bird species found here.

The camaraderie between owners and guests is unusual, too. (In most resort developments the residents and resort guests seldom see one another.) The congeniality and high number of repeat visitors are also reflected in the warm relationships between guests and staff members, who, if not polished to Savoy shine, are attentive and caring.

Although the Meridian Club is barefoot living most of the time, it maintains a certain gracious style and civility. Its small size makes it easy for guests to feel at home quickly. In addition to homeowners and their affluent friends, your companions are likely to be professionals, business executives, eastern establishment types, and a titled European or two. Times may be changing, but not on Pine Cay; there are still no cars, no television, and cellular phone use is discouraged. If you find it necessary to use your cell phone, you will be asked to make your phone calls by the tennis court—away from everyone—and not in your room or on the beach as a courtesy to other guests.

The Meridian Club on Pine Cay ** 🖉
Pine Cay, Turks and Caicos Islands, B.W.I.
Phone: (866) PINE CAY, (746-3229); (781) 828-0492; e-mail: reservations@ meridianclub.org; www.meridianclub.com

Owner: The Meridian Club

General Managers: Beverly and Walter Plachta

Open: November 1–July 31

Credit Cards: Visa, Master Card, American Express; personal checks accepted

U.S. Reservations: (866) PINE CAY (746-3229), (649) 946-7758; or reservations@ meridianclub.com

Deposit: Three nights; forty-five days cancellation, subject to a 4 percent service fee. Policy may vary during holiday periods.

Minimum Stay: Seven nights during Christmas

Arrival/Departure: For stays of seven nights or more, the club provides either boat- or air-taxi transfer at its discretion between Provo and Pine Cay. Inquire from reservations.

Distance from Airport: (Provo Airport) 10 miles; taxi to boat dock one-way, $35; resort has 2,500-foot airstrip used by private planes, small charters, and interisland carriers

Distance from Provo Town Center: 15 miles

Accommodations: 12 suites in beachfront bungalows, all with terrace or patio; twin beds or king. Private home rentals available.

Amenities: Ceiling fans; bath with shower, refrigerator, standing fan, hair dryer, bath robes, in-room safe, toiletries; ice service, nightly turndown service, room service for breakfast; afternoon tea; no air-conditioning, telephone, television, VCR, radio, clock

Electricity: 110 volts/60 cycles

Sports: Freshwater pool; tennis and equipment, bikes, boating, snorkeling and equipment, sailboats included; wilderness trails and birding; deep-sea fishing, bonefishing, tarpon fishing, reef fishing, scuba, and golf on Provo arranged

Dress Code: Always casual, but no tank tops. In the evening, chic casual for women, slacks and collared shirts for men

Children: No children under twelve years of age except during Christmas/New Year's Week and Family Months of June and July when children six years old and up are permitted. Those under eighteen not allowed in bar after 6:00 p.m. unless accompanied by an adult family member

Meetings: Up to twenty-six people

Day Visitors: Day Pass available with prior arrangements. $85 per person including lunch, plus tax and service. Transfers not included.

Handicapped Facilities: No

Packages: Hideaway, Shell Seeker

Rates: Two people, daily, AP, for week's stay (one to three, or four to six nights are slightly higher). *High Season* (mid-December–March 31): $1,055–$1,205. *Shoulder Season* (November 1–December 22): $765–$915. *Low Season* (April–July 31): $775–$925. Rates include transfers from Provo airport to Pine Cay via taxi and boat. For information on cottages and rates and hotel packages, see Web site.

Service Charge: 10 percent

Government Tax: 10 percent

PARROT CAY
Providenciales, Turks and Caicos Islands, B.W.I.

This secluded, exclusive, private-island hideaway zoomed to the top of the charts as the place to see and be seen almost from its first day, thanks to its well-known, well-heeled owners, who have a loyal, and often royal, following, and prices likely to make everyone take notice.

Parrot Cay actually began in the late 1980s, when a wealthy Kuwaiti constructed the resort on the uninhabited islet. By

1991, the resort was completed and scheduled to open, but before the first guests were to arrive, the Gulf War erupted.

Parrot Cay remained shuttered and desolate for the next seven years, when it was purchased by an unlikely twosome, Singaporian Christina Ong—owner of London's Metropolitan and Halkin, as well as prestigious hotels in Asia—and British entrepreneur and founder of the Hard Rock Cafe and Planet Hollywood restaurant, Robert Earl, who no longer is an owner but maintains a home at Parrot Cay.

They realized the potential and lure of this abandoned getaway rapidly approaching a state of decay, with a 3.2-mile-long ribbon of powdery white-sand beach, bordered by crystalline azure waters. The infrastructure was already there; all that was needed was some imagination and an infusion of millions.

And did they ever. When the word got out, the beautiful people and celebrities came running. On a single day in its first spring, Bruce Willis, the Saatchi family of advertising fame, and noted fashion designer Jean Galliano were all in residence in their respective beach suites.

Located on an almost inaccessible 1,000-acre island in the Turks and Caicos, Parrot Cay is elegant in its simplicity. It is designed for those who demand anonymity, yet want to be in the company of trendsetters who must be the first to discover the newest playground.

Aside from the privacy, the lure—especially when you're luxuriating in a beach suite or being indulged by the largely Indonesian staff—is the aura of casual elegance achieved by British interior designer Keith Hobbs of London's United Designers.

Hobbs took the elements of traditional colonial decor and artfully blended them with Asian simplicity—four-poster beds and a lavish use of white fabrics, especially gossamer-thin netting around the beds and as curtains. The effect is romantic and soothing, not to mention sensuous. Teak furniture with woven reed seats and backs in the simplest of Asian lines is everywhere.

The main building, where designer Roth Rothermel was in charge, is an updated version of Caribbean colonial architecture, set high on a hill overlooking the Atlantic on one side and the inlet that separates the cay from the larger island of North Caicos on the other. Rothermel gave the original dark-wood building a lighter look by painting the railings of its multilevel terraces white, set off by the blues and aquas of the water.

From the main building, sited at the top of a 50-foot rise (the highest point of the island), the rooms and suites in two-story, red-tile-roof buildings cascade down the hill toward the sea. Along the beach are the newer cottages, all with one- and two-bedroom suites and by far the most desirable—and expensive—of Parrot Cay's sixty accommodations.

The original swimming pool was covered over and serves as a gigantic flowerpot with five palm trees shading the zero-entry pool. Alongside is Lotus, the poolside restaurant and bar—only steps from the water's edge. A few steps away near the beachside suites is the fitness center, with a full complement of weights and exercise equipment.

Beyond lie the one- and two-bedroom beach suites, each with direct access to the beach. The two-bedroom units have private pools. The most private are the three-bedroom villas, which have their own pools.

In 2008, The Sanctuary, a new eight-bedroom rental property with two infinity pools and Jacuzzi, opened. It is actually two, four-bedroom villas with one common area called the pavilion, but the two houses must be rented together. Situated on the most private part of island, farthest from the hotel, The Sanctuary has an eclectic decor with elements from Bali to Africa in East meets West harmony.

And now, you can buy your own perch in paradise—beachfront villas are being offered for sale are situated a short buggy ride from the main hotel. For a cool, $9 million for three bedrooms or $11 million for four bedrooms, the price, includes the land, the home, furniture, fixtures, and butler's quarters.

If you must stay in touch with the outside world, multiple international direct-dial phones with dataports are strategically placed in each room and suite, while the daily *New York Times* fax is presented at breakfast. Televisions and DVDs are in all rooms.

Wending your way to Parrot Cay, has become easier in recent years as scheduled, direct air service is available from Miami, New York, and other major gateways to Providenciales, or Provo, as it's known by aficionados. After being met by the resort's greeter and assisted into a waiting van, you'll have a fifteen-minute cab ride to the Parrot Cay's private dock, where one of the resort's cruisers will whisk you over smooth, translucent, inside-the-reef waters to Parrot Cay in about thirty-five minutes.

At the dock you're greeted by the staff and driven in Parrot Cay's version of a stretch limo—an elongated golf cart (there are no cars on the island)—to the main building, where a chilled face towel and cold drink await you. You'll immediately sense that you've chosen well. From here it's on to your suite or room, where your luggage is already in place.

Life on Parrot Cay is as you please. There are two lighted tennis courts, an armada of small watercraft, a well-stocked library and lounge, and a large, circular bar to enjoy before and after dinner—which, by the way, is served in the dining room one floor below.

Parrot Cay's Asian-style spa, the COMO Shambala Retreat, will pamper you with body treatments of imported herbs, spices, and flowers and massage techniques and other spa rituals to induce deep relaxation and promote revitalization. Along with these are such Eastern-inspired therapies as Thai and Shiatsu massage, body realignment, and yoga—and all this less than two hours from Miami.

Parrot Cay ****
P.O. Box 164, Providenciales, Turks and Caicos Islands, B.W.I.
Phone: (649) 946-7788, (877) 754-0726; Fax: (649) 946-7789; e-mail: res@parrot cay.como.bz; www.parrotcay.como.bz

Owner: COMO Hotels and Resorts

General Manager: Crawford Sherman

Open: Year-round

Credit Cards: All major

U.S. Reservations: Direct to hotels, (649) 946-7788; toll free: (877) 754 0726; Fax: (649) 946-7789; or e-mail: res@parrotcay .como.bz. Or online through Leading Hotels of the World, http://www.lhw.com

Deposit: Three nights; thirty days cancellation

Minimum Stay: Ten nights during Christmas/New Year holidays; five nights during certain holiday; three at other times

Arrival/Departure: Transfer from Providenciales Airport included (see text)

Distance from Airport: (Providenciales Airport) 15 miles

Accommodations: 58 units (25 garden-view rooms, 17 deluxe ocean-facing rooms, 4 one-bedroom suites, 9 one-bedroom beach houses/villas with plunge pools, 2 two-bedroom beach villas with private pools, 1 three-bedroom villa with pool). Separate from main resort: Parrot Cay Estate, 3 privately owned, three-bedroom villas in resort's rental pool; The Residence, a complex of five-bedroom house along side 2 three-bedoom villas can be taken individually or as a complex; and The Sanctuary, 2 four-bedroom villas with one common pavilion, must be rented together.

Amenities: Hotel rooms: air-conditioning, ceiling fan; direct-dial telephone with dataport; safe; bath with tub and shower, hair dryer; tea and coffeemaker; room service; television, radio, CD player, DVD; library

Electricity: 110 volts

Fitness Facilities/Spa Services: See text

Sports: Hobie Cats; lighted tennis courts; air-conditioned gym; nature trail; snorkel-

ing, windsurfing, waterskiing, diving; golf in Provo at additional cost

Dress Code: Smartly casual

Children: All ages; babysitting

Meetings: No

Day Visitors: No

Handicapped Facilities: No

Packages: Romantic getaways and others (see Web site)

Rates: Per room, per night, FAB. *High Season* (early January–mid April): $775–$3,500. *Shoulder Season* (April 19–May 31 and November–December 20): $650–$3,000. *Low Season* (June 1–October 31): $575–$2,600. Two-to eight-bedroom villas; inquire.

Service Charge: 10 percent

Government Tax: 10 percent

THE REGENT PALMS
Providenciales, Turks and Caicos Islands, B.W.I.

The multimillion-dollar luxury resort, which opened in early 2005 on Grace Bay Beach, became a member of Regent Hotels in 2007. The Regent Palms combines classical design incorporating elements from the islands' colonial British connection in the architecture, building materials, and interiors, and modern amenities with a fine attention to detail.

You enter The Regent Palms through a coral stone gateway, leading down a tree-shaded drive to the reception, a formal Palladian edifice styled after a plantation manor house. The reception opens onto the prettiest setting of the resort—an interior courtyard and formal sunken garden with a fountain in the middle. In perfect symmetry

along the sides of the garden are tree-shaded, colonnaded walkways under lattice trellises covered in vivid bougainvillea and fronting small stone cottages housing upscale boutiques.

At the far end of the garden is the graceful two-story Mansion, classic in symmetry and detail. Open-air and terraced on the first floor, the coral stone building houses the main restaurant, Parallel23, and bar on the ground floor and a 2,000-square-foot ballroom with balconies on the second floor. On the back side of the building are the business center and an Internet room with computers and printer for guests' use. High-speed Internet access is also available in the suites and there is wireless Internet access poolside and at the beach.

The twelve-acre site, which was little more than sand when building began, is now graced with hundreds of palm trees and gardens of flowering shrubs, orange trees, and perennial flowers.

From the Mansion, foliage-lined walkways lead to the large, irregularly shaped infinity pool with big round, cushioned pods for sunning at the center and wooden decks for people-watching at the front. A large Jacuzzi sits in the middle of the pool and is reached by a bridge; to one side is a swim-up bar, four concrete banquettes and tables in the water for lunching without leaving the pool.

Next to the pool, the sunken terrace of Plunge restaurant provides for barefoot snacking on Caribbean-flavored dishes, salads, and pizzas. In the afternoon pool attendants circulate with fresh fruit kebabs, aromatherapy spritzing, cold water, and chilled towels. The pool is crowded when the resort is full, especially with families and kids.

Five large, coral stone five-story buildings with one-, two-, and three-bedrooms and penthouse suites form a tight U around the pool. The suites, some more than 1,500 square feet, have truly elegant appointments and sumptuous baths. Carved four-poster beds with hand-tufted mattresses and custom-made linens of 488-thread-count Egyptian cotton are the sort of details that signal the luxurious nature of these suites.

Throughout, the architecture reflects the classical elegance of British colonial buildings of the Caribbean. Creamy, textured coral stone quarried on Barbados is the dominant building material. White stepped Bermuda roofs top the residence structures; other buildings have native cedar shingle roofs, open verandas, and wraparound porches—characteristics of Great House designs. Unseen is an underground network of tunnels for services and personnel.

Interior design and furnishings, art and accessories, such as traveling chests, campaign chairs, and blue Chinese vases, reflect the eclectic mix found in colonial estates across the British Empire, including the Caribbean. White and neutral colors, including the crown moldings, walls, curtains, and vaulted ceilings, lend a refined touch. Floors are a mix of pale limestone and travertine marble. In contrast, bed frames and other custom-made furniture are dark mahogany, intricately carved and inlaid with exotic veneers.

Rooms have private balconies with outdoor seating and are furnished with flat-panel LCD television, DVD/CD player, a microwave, refrigerator, and coffee machine. Some have full kitchens, others kitchenettes, and all are equipped with Viking appliances.

The eight penthouse suites with great views of the sea and offshore islands come with vaulted ceilings, keyed elevator access, a study (or extra bedroom) with high-speed Internet access, large travertine terraces with a pergola, an interior "water room" with waterfall shower, and an adjacent SunSuite with an outdoor shower, garden, and Jacuzzi. Butler service is available for an extra charge. Large suites and penthouses have full-size chef's kitchens so guests can retain a personal chef for meals and entertaining.

The Mansion, the centerpiece and social hub of the resort, houses the resort's (very expensive) restaurant, Parallel23, open for breakfast and dinner year-round. Its continental buffet breakfast is included in the room rate. The restaurant offers tropical fusion cuisine and an extensive wine list in a casually elegant setting, indoor and alfresco on the terrace overlooking the gardens. It also has a display kitchen with a wood-burning oven. The Green Flamingo bar next to Parallel23 has indoor/outdoor seating and is a popular pre-dinner or late-evening meeting venue.

The scent of burning incense mixed with the fragrance of flowers and the soothing sound of fountains and waterfalls greet you when you enter the Regent Spa. Housed in a separate building covering an acre near the resort's entrance, the spa is an oasis of serene gardens, reflecting pools, and unusual treatment rooms in coral stone structures surrounded by water.

The reception area, fitness center, yoga pavilion, beauty salon, and spa boutique face a quiet courtyard and a formal Japanese garden beside a large reflecting pool. The men's and women's changing rooms flanking either side of the yoga pavilion have secluded sunning terraces. On the other side of the changing rooms is the inner sanctum of the spa. A lovely central palm-lined promenade with three treatment cottages on each side are reflected in the dark pool waters with such perfect symmetry it seems to be a mirage.

The cottages are architectural gems: The back wall of each treatment room slides open revealing a reflecting pool that is surrounded by a privacy wall and fountain. After sunset, lit oil lamps in the fountain add another exotic element. At the end of the promenade are two larger private spa suites where couples can be pampered for a half or full day. The suites have a shower, treatment area, and private garden terrace for sunning or dining under the stars. Sliding window walls open onto the reflecting pool on one side and the garden on the other. The spa has four new Zareeba cabanas providing the most exotic treatments of all. Forming the backdrop of the spa is an 8-foot-tall/80-foot-long wall with cascading water.

The spa menu offers Sonya Dakar products and treatments, such as Mother of Pearl Body Exfoliation, the signature treatment. It incorporates native elements such as hand-crushed local queen conch shells mixed with an aromatherapy oil to polish and soften. There's a new men's treatment room and a menu of treatments, including a classic razor shave and a new line of men's care by Art of Shaving.

The yoga, Pilates, and meditation pavilion offers daily classes. Other facilities include a beauty salon and a fitness center with state-of-the-art equipment and daily classes. Private classes and personal trainers are available.

While you are being pampered in the spa, your kids can have a great time in the Conch Kritters Club, with a kids' playroom and scheduled activities for ages four to twelve years. The playroom has board games, computer and video games, and toys. The trained staff also offers yoga and Pilates for club members. The club is open in season from 9:00 a.m. to 4:00 p.m. and 6:00 to 10:00 p.m. Full-day sessions cost $90 per child; half day, 9:00 a.m. to noon, $45; and evenings, which include kids-only dinner and a movie, $70 per child. Babysitting services are also available.

The resort has a tennis court for day or night play and Hobie Cats, snorkel gear, kayaks, windsurfs, floats, and children's toys available for use. Golf at nearby Provo Golf & Country Club course is only a few minutes away and diving can be arranged.

Upon arrival you'll find chocolate chip cookies and two bottles of water in your suite. Upon departure, your farewell bag will have bottled water and a granola bar for the trip home.

The Regent Palms ****
Providenciales, Turks and Caicos Islands, B.W.I.
Phone: (649) 946-8666; Fax: (649) 946-5188; e-mail: info@thepalmstc.com; www .theregentturksandcaicos.com

Owner: Stan Hartling.

General Manager: Diderik Van Regemorter

Open: Year-round

Credit Cards: Most major

U.S. Reservations: (866) 877-7256; Canada: (800) 567-5327

Deposit: Three days; twenty-one days cancellation. Christmas/New Year's reservations require 50 percent credit card deposit at booking and full payment by November 1. Cancellations after October 1 and no-shows will not be refunded.

Minimum Stay: Three days at Thanksgiving; seven days at Christmas/New Year's

Arrival/Departure: Meet/assist service and transfers included in rate

Distance from Airport: 8 miles

Distance from business center: 4 miles

Accommodations: 72 one-, two-, three-bedroom, and 8 penthouse suites

Amenities: Hand-tufted king bedding; fine linens, bath sheets; minibar, flat-panel television; safe; high-speed Internet; complimentary water, nightly turndown. Master bath: hydro-massage bathtub, separate marble shower. Penthouse: full kitchen with Viking appliances

Electricity: 110 volts

Fitness Facilities/Spa Services: See text

Sports: Swimming pool, tennis court lit for night play, croquet lawn. Nonmotorized water sports: Hobie Cats, snorkel equipment, kayaks, clear canoes, windsurfers, floats; children's beach toys; diving, sailing, golf arranged

Dress Code: Smart casual

Children: All ages. Conch Kritters Club playroom and supervised program for ages four to twelve

Meetings: Up to 160 people

Day Visitors: Spa and dinner with reservations

Handicapped Facilities: No

Packages: Spa, honeymoon, wedding

Rates: Per room, per night, double. *High Season* (January 3–April 14): $640–$990; suites $1,180–$4,880. *Shoulder Season* (April 15–May 27; October 29–December 19): $450–$690; suites $830–$3,600. *Low Season* (May 28–October 28): $380–$570; suites $1,170–$2,930. Rates include continental buffet breakfast in restaurant and nonmotorized water sports. For Christmas season rates, inquire.

Service Charge: 10 percent

Government Tax: 10 percent

U.S. VIRGIN ISLANDS

Topside or below, few places under the American flag are more beautiful than our corner of the Caribbean. Volcanic in origin, the Virgin Islands are made up of fifty green gems floating in a sapphire sea; only three are developed. They are only a short distance apart, yet no islands in the Caribbean are more different from one another.

St. Croix, the easternmost point of the United States, is the largest. A low-lying island of rolling hills, it was once an important sugar-producing center. Many plantation homes and sugar mills have been restored as hotels, restaurants, and museums; Christiansted and Frederiksted, the main towns, are on the National Register of Historic Places.

St. Croix offers an impressive variety of activities, from hiking in a rain forest to turtle-watching, but its most popular sports are snorkeling and scuba diving. The island is surrounded by coral reefs; off the northeastern coast is Buck Island Reef National Monument, the only underwater park in our national park system.

St. John, the smallest of the trio, is truly America the Beautiful. Almost three-quarters of the mountainous island is covered by the Virgin Islands National Park. Around its edges lovely little coves hide some of the most alluring porcelain-white beaches and aquamarine waters in the Caribbean.

The National Park Service Visitor Center in Cruz Bay schedules ranger-led tours, hikes, and wildlife lectures and publishes a brochure outlining twenty-one trails. Cruz Bay, the island's main town, is booming from new popularity and rapidly losing its tiny-village charm to traffic. The ferry from St. Thomas takes twenty minutes.

St. Thomas floats on a deep turquoise sea with green mountains and an irregular coastline of fingers and coves sheltering idyllic bays and pretty white-sand beaches. Only 13 miles long, it seems larger because of its dense population and development. Its capital, Charlotte Amalie, is the busiest cruise port in the Caribbean.

St. Thomas offers good facilities for water sports and for tennis and golf, but it is best known for its smart boutiques with clothing, accessories, perfumes, and jewelry from world-famous designers.

The Virgin Islands, as U.S. territories, have a special tax status that gives returning U.S. residents a $1,200 exemption from customs duty rather than the $600 applied to visitors from other places.

Information

U.S. Virgin Islands Division of Tourism, One Penn Plaza, New York, NY 10119-0002; (800) 372-8784, (212) 502-5300; Fax: (212) 332-2223; www.usvitourism.vi, www.stjohnusvi.com.
Offices also in Atlanta, Chicago, Los Angeles, Miami, Washington, D.C., and San Juan, Puerto Rico.

THE BUCCANEER
Christiansted, St. Croix, U.S.V.I.

At The Buccaneer you could roll out of bed to play golf or take a swim at one of the two pools before breakfast, explore some of the Caribbean's best reefs fronting three white-sand beaches before lunch, and then enjoy a game of tennis before dinner—all within eyeshot of the pink palazzo whose history stretches back 340 years.

Spread over 340 tropical acres near Gallows Bay on St. Croix's northern coast, The Buccaneer was opened in 1948 as an eleven-room inn in a seventeenth-century estate house by a family whose origins on the island date from the same period. The building's thick walls and graceful bonnet arches are still visible in the French Wing; the Cotton House serves as administration space; and the eighteenth-century sugar mill is the venue for the manager's weekly cocktail party and weddings.

Now greatly enlarged and developed into a complete resort, the main building sits on a rise with commanding views. The roadside entrance passes along a drive lined with royal palms and well-kept gardens bright with bougainvillea and a great variety of tropical trees.

Some of the accommodations are in the main building, while others are housed in a variety of cottages and bungalows near the fairways and tennis courts and in terraced gardens cascading from the main building to the sea. All have terraces. If you are a beach body, you may prefer the rooms that snake along the seashore. They have high, cedar-beamed ceilings and stone terraces overlooking the sea and pretty sunsets. Oceanfront rooms have marble floors and bathrooms. Three deluxe one-bedroom suites, Ficus (two bedrooms) and Frigate (one bedroom), are furnished with four-poster beds, two baths, and a living room.

The most luxurious accommodations are twelve beachside units, called Doubloons, in keeping with the resort's tradition of naming rooms for gold coins rumored to have been buried by the buccaneers who sailed these islands. The large rooms are housed in a marble-terraced villa that echoes the island's Danish colonial architecture. Each has king-size four-poster beds or two queen-size beds, wide terraces or balconies with beach and sea views, picture windows with window seats, walk-in closets, and spacious bathrooms with whirlpool tubs and double showers.

Thirty-two rooms on the second floor of the main building have marble floors, carved four-poster beds, and doors made of solid mahogany. Originally known as the Hamilton Wing—for Alexander Hamilton, who spent his childhood here when the property was called Estate Shoys—the second story follows the contour of the original seventeenth-century foundation, which results in a group of rooms that each have a different shape and size; all have great views.

Another historic group, the four Widow's Mite rooms—originally built in the 1700s and so named because their expansive sea views recall rooms used by a ship captain's wife awaiting her husband's return from a long voyage—now have marble floors, newly outfitted bathrooms, all-new furniture, and a window seat tucked into the panoramic bay window.

The Buccaneer's tennis complex is the largest on the island. The eighteen-hole golf course (5,810 yards, par 70) dips and dives from hilltops to the water's edge. For fitness folks a 2-mile, eighteen-station par course jogging and exercise path winds through the hilly terrain. Those with something less strenuous in mind can join the weekly art class or check their e-mail on a computer provided for guests.

At the improved Hideaway Spa you can iron out the kinks and enjoy a massage, sauna, seaweed wrap, or other pampering while your kids participate in a free program that includes crafts, supervised snorkeling, sing-alongs, parties, and their own daily newsletter.

One of The Buccaneer's two pools is by the main building, set into seventeenth-century foundations. The second is a free-form pool on quiet Beauguard Beach next to the Grotto, where burgers and snacks are available.

The Beach Shack, the water-sports center, offers staff-led snorkel and kayak tours. Lunch is served daily at the Mermaid, a breezy beachside restaurant, which is also the setting for some evening meals, especially enjoyed by families and guests preferring a light meal.

At breakfast in the open-air Terrace in the main building, you'll enjoy views of the fairways and the sea; in the evening the lights of Christiansted twinkle in the distance. Dinner offers a continental menu with West Indian flair. The Brass Parrot is a separate air-conditioned restaurant adjacent to the Terrace, serving as the resort's banquet and meeting room. Both restaurants were redesigned to provide more seating to take advantage of their commanding views. Nightly the Terrace bar hosts live musical entertainment by different combos.

The Armstrong family, now the third generation to operate the hotel, is a family of naturalists. General manager Elizabeth Armstrong leads free weekly nature walks. The golf course is a popular birding spot.

The Buccaneer is a member of the Historic Hotels of America, so named by the National Trust for Historic Preservation.

A quiet, self-contained, family-owned and -operated resort with a casual and friendly ambience, The Buccaneer is suitable for all ages and all situations, from singles to families. It appeals most to travelers who want an active vacation with a wide range of sports. Many guests are repeaters; some are from families that, like the owners, are into the third generation.

The Buccaneer ****

Box 25200, Gallows Bay, St. Croix, U.S.V.I. 00824-5200

Phone: (340) 712-2100, (800) 255-3881; Fax: (340) 712-2105; e-mail: mango@the buccaneer.com; www.thebuccaneer.com

Owners: The Armstrong family

General Manager: Elizabeth Armstrong

Open: Year-round

Credit Cards: All major

U.S. Reservations: Direct to hotel, (800) 255-3881

Deposit: Three nights winter; one night summer; five nights Christmas/New Year's

Minimum Stay: One night

Arrival/Departure: Transfer service included in honeymoon packages

Distance from Airport: 10 miles (thirty minutes); taxi one-way, $20 for two, $10 each additional passenger; private car, $42 for up to four people

Distance from Christiansted: 2 miles; taxi one-way, $7; hourly hotel shuttle to town, $3 per person, one-way, $5 round-trip

Accommodations: 138 rooms and suites, all with terraces (50 oceanfront, 34 Great

House, 12 Doubloons, 12 ridge rooms, 12 tennis units, eight family cottages, five suites, and five units in various locations); 54 with kings, 84 with two queens

Amenities: Air-conditioning, ceiling fan; safe; telephone, satellite television; refrigerator; dressing area; bath with tub and shower, basket of toiletries, hair dryer; ice service, nightly turndown service, room service at specific hours; boutiques

Electricity: 110 volts

Fitness Facilities/Spa Services: Health club; spa treatments (see text)

Sports: Two freshwater pools; parcourse exercise path. Tennis: Eight Laykold tennis courts (two lighted), pro shop, fee for courts, lessons, equipment. Golf: Green fees, charge for equipment, caddies, carts, lessons. Snorkeling, kayaking: Free lessons

and equipment. Day and evening cruises, fishing, horseback riding arranged.

Children: All ages; activities program; cribs; babysitters; during summer children eighteen and under stay free in room with parents

Meetings: Up to ninety people

Day Visitors: Yes

Handicapped Facilities: Limited

Packages: Golf, tennis, honeymoon, wedding, family

Rates: Per person, double, daily, FAB. *High Season* (mid-December–March): $340–$1,045. *Low Season* (mid-April–mid-December): $295–$730. Weekly rates available in summer; inquire.

Energy Surcharge: 6 percent

Government Tax: 8 percent

CANEEL BAY, A ROSEWOOD RESORT
St. John, U.S.V.I.

Consider these numbers: 166 rooms on 170 acres and a staff of 400, and seven beaches. Not bad odds, you could say. But these are only some of the elements that have made Caneel a legend.

Opened in 1955 as the late Laurance Rockefeller's first Caribbean venture, Caneel was the first of the ecologically built hideaways of the RockResort style. Caneel is built into the ruins of an old sugar plantation within the Virgin Islands National Park. It's sprawled on a peninsula scalloped with seven flawless beaches protected by coral reefs that are also part of the national park. Indeed, the fact that Caneel is framed on all sides by the

national park forever ensures its pristine quality.

The Caneel appeal is immediately apparent, with acres of carpetlike meadows, artfully arranged shrubbery, and gardens of tropical flowers. Guest rooms are clustered in cottages of natural rock and weathered wood. They're all but hidden in the vegetation and are widely scattered. Some rooms are in the hillside tennis gardens, but most are set directly on the beaches.

The Cottage Point area on a bluff facing the water is the most requested honeymoon spot for its seclusion. Paradise Beach is next to the famous Cottage 7, formerly the Rockefeller home and now luxury digs for visiting bigwigs. Scott Beach, where units are in single-story buildings, is popular for its afternoon sun and lengthy beach. And cozy Turtle Bay Beach boasts the best snorkeling.

Regardless of locale, Caneel's rooms are airy and spacious and remain no-nonsense affairs with walls of louvered and screened windows for cross ventilation, and private patios. Recently, all the accommodations were refurbished with a new retro "beach house" design featuring handcrafted furniture and fabrics inspired by the Caribbean palette in refreshing sea-foam greens and blues. Thirty additional rooms were made connecting.

Although there still are no telephones or television in the guest rooms, Caneel has made several nods to the twenty-first century. Air-conditioning has been added to all units, and bathrooms have been renovated and upgraded. There are outdoor phones with AT&T direct at each of the clusters of buildings, and you can now get a complimentary cellular phone from the front desk if you really must stay connected to the outside world. And now, Wi-Fi is available throughout the resort and is offered on a complimentary basis. A business center in a private room by the front lobby has a computer, printer, Internet access, and telephone.

Breakfast and lunch buffets indulge guests with many choices. If you prefer a light lunch, the open-to-the-breezes bar by the central building is a delightful setting in the shade by day and popular for drinks in the evening. If you prefer quieter, air-conditioned comfort, Turtle Bay Estate House serves breakfast and a midday meal during the winter season. You can also return there for afternoon tea or for the weekly wine tasting in the Wine Room, where 2,000 bottles of wine are displayed.

Caneel is at its most magical at night, when the grounds are aglow with low "mushroom" lamps, and Polynesian-style torches hidden in the thick foliage light the paths near the activities building. A laid-back combo completes the mood with light dance music.

Dinner is served in three locations, all with a view of the twinkling lights of St. Thomas in the distance. The casual Beach Terrace on Caneel Bay Beach has an open kitchen with a wood-burning stove and rotisserie. It serves a buffet breakfast and lunch and the Monday night grand buffet. Equator, in the flower-festooned ruins of an eighteenth-century sugar mill, offers a cornucopia of Caribbean and other specialties and a fun Caribbean carnival decor in which to enjoy it—but all, naturally, in the low-key style that is Caneel's trademark. The third venue is the enormous eighteenth-century manor house, site of the more formal, romantic Turtle Bay Estate House, where it's time to dress up and sit down to a five-course meal.

Caneel offers a host of water sports and a variety of sail excursions and charter cruises. Beach Hut staff members are trained to give lessons in the use of snorkeling equipment and in windsurfing, Sunfish sailing, kayaking, and aquafins. The resort has eleven tennis courts and tennis pros who arrange round-robins, hold clinics, and are available for lessons. You'll find jogging paths (and hiking trails in the national park) and an air-conditioned fitness center with cardiovascular training equipment. Aerobics classes are one of a changing selection of daily activities. You'll also find the Self Centre, where yoga, meditation, and relaxation techniques are offered from $35 per session. In 2008, the centre introduced new wellness programs including qi gong (pronounced *chi-kung*), a holistic practice; yin yoga, designed to release tension in the joints; and astrology consultation, among others.

Caneel is trying to handle a growing demand from guests who want to bring their children, and at the same time accommodate those who come to Caneel to get away from children—theirs and anyone else's. The program selects beaches appropriate for families and those seeking tranquillity. There are also two beaches for those over twelve years of age. Also, the resort has created the Teen Center, which is equipped with Ping-Pong, a pool table, computer with Internet access, and a jukebox.

Finally, Turtle Town, a children's center at one end of the property, has a full-time director and a staff of one counselor to every five children. Each day's program has a theme with special stress put on environmental appreciation of the resort and of St. John.

Whether you fall into the with-kids or no-kids group, contact the manager in advance and be specific about your needs. Fortunately, Caneel is large enough and so spread out that it can accommodate guests of all ages without anyone trampling on others, provided the resort is informed of guests' needs in advance.

Caneel Bay, A Rosewood Resort ★★★★
P.O. Box 720, St. John, U.S.V.I. 00831-0720
Phone: (340) 776-6111; Fax: (340) 693-8280; e-mail: caneel@rosewood-hotels.com or www.caneelbay.com

Owner: CBI Acquisitions

General Manager: Nikolay Hotze

Open: Year-round

Credit Cards: All major

U.S. Reservations: Rosewood Hotels and Resorts, (888) ROSEWOOD, (888) 767-3966; Fax: (340) 776-6111

Deposit: Three nights; twenty-eight days cancellation for December 19–April 15, fourteen days for balance of year

Minimum Stay: Ten nights during Christmas

Arrival/Departure: Transfer on Caneel Bay's cruiser from St. Thomas five times daily and Little Dix in Virgin Gorda twice weekly

Distance from Airport: (St. Thomas Airport) 12 nautical miles (see Arrival/Departure, above)

Distance from Cruz Bay: 3 miles; taxi one-way, $5 per person

Accommodations: 166 rooms in one- and two-story cottages with terrace (33 ocean view, 55 beachfront, 37 premium, 5 in Cottage 7, 10 courtside, 26 tennis/garden)

Amenities: Air-conditioning, ceiling fans; bath with shower (few with tub), hair dryer, toiletries, iron and ironing board; safe; coffeemaker, minibar, sodas and ice service; nightly turndown, room service with charge for breakfast; no telephone; television in Estate House Lounge and Beach Bar; nightly movies; business center, Internet

Electricity: 110 volts

Fitness Facilities/Spa Services: Fitness center (see text); massage on request

Sports: Freshwater swimming pool; eleven tennis courts; tennis and nonconcession water sports included in rate; deep-sea fishing, boating, golf in St. Thomas arranged; dive shop offers resort course, certification; clinic; jogging path, hiking trails

Dress Code: Casual by day; in evening men required to wear collared shirts and trousers

Children: Year-round (see text)

Meetings: Up to 100 people

Day Visitors: Welcome in certain areas only

Handicapped Facilities: Limited

Packages: Dive, tennis, sailing, honeymoon, wedding; Simply Caneel (with Little Dix)

Rates: Per room, daily, CP. *High Season* (December 19–March 31): $500–$1,400. *Shoulder Season* (April 1–April 30 and mid-November–mid-December): $395–$1,050. *Low Season:* $350–$875

Service Charge: 10 percent

Government Tax: 8 percent on room only

MAHO BAY CAMPS HARMONY, AND ESTATE CONCORDIA PRESERVE
St. John, U.S.V.I.

Folks, we're talking camp here. Camp as in *camping*—no private baths, no hot water, not even running water, except in the communal bathhouses.

This escape to paradise means tented cabins, which you'll probably share with friendly little lizards, mosquitoes, and other bugs. Getting to this heavenly rest takes seven hours or more via plane, taxi, ferry, and another taxi. On the last stretch—a bone-cracking ride on the wooden seats of a converted flatbed truck—self-doubt may set in. At Maho's reception area you'll be checked in by a friendly attendant, who'll give you the dos and don'ts about Maho and about protecting paradise. Then you'll lug your luggage up (or down) the hill to your abode.

It's obvious that Maho Bay Camp is not for everyone. What may be less obvious is why I have included Maho in this book in the first place. But, you see, many people think Maho offers the greatest vacation in the Caribbean. They come from all over the United States and all walks of life. Maho has one of the highest winter repeat rates—80 percent—in the Caribbean. The staff is made up mostly of folks who came as guests and decided to stay.

Maho Bay, a private campground in the Virgin Islands National Park, is unique in the Caribbean. It was created in 1976 by engineer-ecologist Stanley Selengut, who is now teaching the world that being an environmentalist can be good business. The camp enjoys a gorgeous setting on a wooded hillside that falls to a small beach and overlooks an exquisite bay of reef-protected turquoise waters and expansive scenery of mountainous green neighboring islands. Maho Bay has none of the amenities of a typical tropical retreat. On the other hand, true campers call it luxurious.

Accommodations are in tented cabins, all but hidden in the thick foliage that climbs the hillsides, and are connected by a network of boardwalks and wooden steps. The dense woods help ensure privacy but sometimes obscure the view. Each cabin, made out of a translucent water-repellent fabric, is built on a 16-by-16-foot wooden platform suspended above the ground on wooden pilings, like a tree house. It is surprisingly roomy and quite comfortable.

The tent has a sleeping area with twin beds; a sitting area just large enough for a trundle couch that sleeps two; a small kitchen unit with a two-burner propane stove, electrical outlets, cooler, dishes, and utensils; and an outside deck, which makes a great perch for watching the sunset or counting the stars.

There are five bathhouses with sinks, toilets, and showers at various locations around the property; a grocery store, which is neither nonprofit nor cheap; a multipurpose outdoor community center for meetings, seminars, and weddings; barbecue areas; and a cafeteria-style restaurant and bar in an outdoor pavilion with spectacular vistas where breakfast and dinner are available.

If you are more a beach person, you might prefer the camp's lower reaches, but if you don't mind the hike to heaven, the tents higher up are the most desirable, both for their wonderful views and because they have high ceilings with ceiling fans, which stir the air and help keep away mosquitoes.

Maho's greatest innovations are at Harmony—perfect for people who love the idea of camping but can't hack the inconvenience. Selengut, in conjunction with the U.S. National Park Service, built six units, each with two large guest rooms, following the *Guiding Principles of Sustainable Design*. The units are built totally from recycled materials, partly to prove that it can be done and partly to test products in the school of hard knocks of the Caribbean.

If no one had told you, you probably would not realize that these units were anything other than attractively furnished hotel rooms with a kitchen and dining area, a bath, and a large terrace. The hot water in each unit is powered by sun; some of the original solar use has given way to standard electricity to provide consistency in guest comfort. If you go with the spirit of adventure and curiosity and if you truly care about the environment, you will enjoy your stay.

Maho has a craft center, focused principally on glassmaking as part of its Trash to Treasures recycling program, with demonstrations daily by artists-in-residence. Craft classes in pottery, glassblowing, painting, and fabric printmaking are offered each week. A list of classes/times being offered for the year is available from the Web site. Some works of art can be purchased at Maho and online.

Maho also has a program for children six years and older, offering classes in pottery, paper making, papier mâché art, and more, to teach children the potential for recycling in a fun and creative way. Nothing goes to waste at Maho, if it can be recycled. Nothing.

As St. John beaches go, Maho's isn't much, but there are two longer white-sand stretches a short walk or swim away. All three beaches are great for snorkeling. The resort offers scuba, sailing, windsurfing, and kayaking at an additional charge. But the highlight is hiking on any of the national park's twenty-one trails.

Maho protects the environment with missionary zeal—and with the national park's rules. Evening programs are usually eco-oriented and may feature presentations by staff from the national park service or a visiting expert. Maho also hosts conferences on ecology.

Maho's taxi service makes trips every two hours into Cruz Bay during the day, but if you want to take in the town's nightlife, transportation in the evening can be a problem unless you rent a vehicle. Jeeps are recommended.

Always the innovator, Selengut has developed another tented resort, Estate Concordia Preserve, located on a hillside on the less traveled southeast corner of St. John near Coral Bay and abutting the Virgin Islands National Park's Salt Pond and Ram Head areas. It's something of a combination of the first two—not as basic as Maho and not as deluxe as Harmony.

In 2005, Estate Concordia added seven innovative eco-tents (now with a total of twenty-five) with comforts that go beyond ordinary camping such as fully equipped kitchens, solar-powered refrigerators, solar-heated showers, and private composting toilets. Each unit is designed to accommodate a family of up to six. In addition to the eco-tents, there are nine Concordia studios that range from a single room to a two-floor duplex with kitchen, bathroom, and private deck.

In 2007, Concordia added Café Concordia & Meeting Pavilion, a remarkably innovative, new multiuse green building that has a well-stocked grocery store, café offering alfresco dining, events pavilion, and large open space with extensive panoramic views. The wheelchair-accessible structure is topped with a 1,500-square-foot greenhouse roof-covered deck. The pavilion and open spaces provide a stunning setting for functions from yoga classes to island weddings and can accommodate fifty for meetings and workshops.

St. John architect Glenn Speer used green building techniques throughout. To reuse existing materials, the pavilion deck was built entirely of rock filled gabion (large cage) baskets excavated from the site. Baskets are planted with native vines and hanging plants to blend into the natural landscape. Water is collected from the roof and processed to potable standards on site. Glass blocks admit natural light and lighting fixtures and decorative touches were made at Maho Bay Camps recycled arts center.

Estate Concordia was instrumental, with the help of volunteers with mobility disabilities, including wheelchair-users, in testing some newly designed accommodations that have walkways for convenient access and living quarters with wide doorways, large bathrooms with spacious shower stalls, and utilities within easy reach. Some volunteers using assistive/adaptive recreational equipment also had the chance to swim, snorkel, kayak, sail, and even scuba dive, fulfilling lifelong dreams. Details on facilities and prices are available from Maho Bay Camps.

If you understand that Maho is a campground, and that's the type of vacation you want, you will not find better facilities in a more beautiful setting in the Caribbean. Unfortunately, many people not suited for Maho—perhaps having a romanticized notion of what it is—go there anyway, attracted by the low price and the illusion that they can hack it.

Maho Bay Camps, Harmony, and Estate Concordia Preserve (S) 🖋
Cruz Bay, St. John, U.S.V.I. 00830
Phone: (340) 776-6240; Fax: (340) 776-6504; e-mail: mahobay@maho.org; www.maho.org

Owner: Stanley Selengut

General Manager: Adrian Davis

Open: Year-round

Credit Cards: Most major

U.S. Reservations: Maho Bay Camps, Inc., (800) 392-9004, (340) 776-6240; Fax: (340) 715–2020

Deposit: Half of reserved stay; fourteen days cancellation less 50 percent of room cost

Minimum Stay: Seven nights holiday weeks

Arrival/Departure: No transfer service; twenty-minute ferry ride from Red Hook dock on St. Thomas to Cruz Bay, $5; forty-five-minute ferry from Charlotte Amalie to Cruz Bay, $10

Distance from Cruz Bay: Maho, 8 miles; taxi one-way, $14 for one, $10 shared; Maho's service, $8. Concordia, 12 miles. Car rental advised; arriving guests are given detailed driving instructions.

Accommodations: Maho-114 tent cabins, all with twin beds and trundle couch for two; 12 guest rooms in 6 Harmony units. Estates Concordia: 25 eco-tents; 9 studios.

Amenities: Maho Fans (seven with ceiling fans); showers in communal bathhouses. For Harmony and Concordia, see text.

Electricity: 110 volts

Sports: Hiking in national park; boating, snorkeling, diving, windsurfing, kayaking, deep-sea fishing available

Dress Code: Informal

Children: All ages welcome

Meetings: Up to 125 people

Day Visitors: Welcome

Handicapped Facilities: No facilities at Maho; one unit at Harmony. Facilities at Concordia, inquire

Packages: No

Rates: Two people, daily, EP. Maho, **High Season** (mid-December–April 30): $135–$145; $15 each additional person; **Low Season** (May 1–mid-December): $80. Harmony, **High Season** (mid-December–April 30): $220–$250; **Low Season** (May 1–mid-December): $130–$155. Concordia, **High Season,** eco-tents $155–$185, $15 extra person; **Low Season,** $105, $15 extra person. Studios, $150–$250, $25; $105–$160, $15, respectively

Service Charge: None

Government Tax: 8 percent

FRENCHMAN'S REEF AND MORNING STAR MARRIOTT
St. Thomas, U.S.V.I.

A multi-million dollar renovation in 1998 transformed this old white fortresslike structure into a pretty pink edifice with white trim and natural stone accents set in landscaped, flowering gardens. And the transformation was in much more than the facade.

Frenchman's Reef and Morning Star, its adjacent sister resort on the beach—both Marriott franchises since 1992—were badly damaged by Hurricane Marilyn in 1995, but remained open throughout the crisis to house rescue workers and hotel staff who had lost their homes. Finally, after St. Thomas had fully recovered, the hotel closed for eight months to make the transformation. Now, the resort has undergone a two-year, top to bottom $25 million

renovation that was completed in summer of 2007.

A palm-lined driveway leads to the entrance where you step into a beautiful lobby, open and airy with views that extend all the way out to the sea. In the latest refurbishing, the lobby has been enhanced with new brightly colored, contemporary Caribbean furniture in pod-style seating arrangement, meant to encourage guests to take advantage of the lobby as a public space for socializing or conducting business.

A double stairway leads down to bars and restaurants on the first level, which overlooks a pool area that wraps all around the building's sea side. On the lower level are two adjacent swimming pools with a waterfall at one end, a fountain at the other, a swim-up bar at the center, and views to infinity at every turn.

At the far side of one pool, another set of steps leads down to a third level with another waterfall and an extension of land along the rocky coast at the edge of the cliff, where there are two Jacuzzis. To one side of the pool complex is a fitness center with steam rooms, spa treatment rooms, and a sauna; and on the other side you'll find Sunset Terrace and the new Sunset Bar and Grill. It's amusing to be here in the late afternoon, watching the cruise ships sail out of the harbor at sunset: The passengers on the ships are taking as many pictures of the resort as the hotel guests are of the ships.

A pretty gazebo on the southern side of the pools is used for weddings (the hotel does such a huge wedding business that it has a special department, Weddings in Paradise, to handle them). Here, too, steps lead down to Morning Star Beach; another swimming pool; two lighted Omni-turf tennis courts; the two- and three-story Morning Star Villas; a beachfront snack bar, Coco Joe's; and Star Market, a small convenience store.

Windows on the Harbor, the main dining room, with a popular Friday-night seafood buffet and Sunday brunch got a major face-lift complete with a new menu, which includes a "Fit for You" section featuring low cholesterol, carb-conscious, and low-fat options. Other Frenchman's Reef eateries are the Captain's Cafe, serving light fare; and the Presto Marketplace, a snack bar and convenience shop by the lobby. The Pirates Den is a nightclub with live entertainment and a sports bar. Another wing of the restaurant level houses a ballroom and meeting rooms, a separate area for group check-in, and a business center.

In the earlier redesign of the resort, twenty-two rooms of the old hotel were eliminated to make way for eighty-eight luxury suites and a new floor was added on the top of the hotel to create a group of bi-level suites with living rooms and loft bedrooms, and seventeen royal suites with cathedral ceilings, Jacuzzis, and a spiral staircase that winds up to the bedroom. In the latest renovation, all guest rooms in Frenchman's Reef as well as in Morning Star Beach Resort, got new "Revive" bedding, mahogany furniture, and new window treatments, along with new bathroom amenities. Each guest room has a minifridge, separate icemaker (the only one I've seen in a Caribbean hotel), hair dryer, coffeemaker, iron and ironing board, telephone with voice mail and data lines, safe, television, chaise longue, desk, balcony, and twenty-four-hour room service. Frenchman's Reef's clifftop location affords most rooms spectacular views.

The water-sports center offers snorkeling, diving, kayaking, windsurfing, parasailing, sport fishing, and sailing excursions. Free clinics for tennis, snorkeling, and diving are offered, as are aerobics and jazzercise. A ferry shuttle departs from a special dock several times a day for Charlotte Amalie, eight minutes away by boat.

From the front desk to the restaurants to housekeeping, all personnel have participated in special training programs that have raised the hotel's service to a level that has been significant in creating the new Frenchman's Reef.

Frenchman's Reef and Morning Star Marriott Beach Resort ***

Marriott Beach Resorts, P.O. Box 7100, St. Thomas, U.S.V.I. 00801
Phone: (340) 776-8500; Fax: (340) 715-6191; e-mail: resorts@marriott.vi; www .frenchmansreefmarriott.com

Owner: Marriott International

General Manager: Jose Gonzalez

Open: Year-round

Credit Cards: Most major

U.S. Reservations: (800) 223-6388

Deposit: Two nights; seven to fifteen days cancellation, depending on season

Minimum Stay: None

Arrival/Departure: Transfer arranged upon request

Distance from Airport: (Cyril E. King Airport) 6 miles; taxi one-way, $10 for one person, $8 each for more than one. There is also a fee for baggage (large bags are $4 each and small bags are $2 each).

Distance from Charlotte Amalie: 3 miles; taxi one-way, $8 for one person, $6 each for more than one

Accommodations: 356 rooms and suites at Frenchman's Reef; 96 villa units at Morning Star

Amenities: Air-conditioning; direct-dial telephone; safes; cable television, movies; icemaker; refrigerator; twenty-four-hour room service; bath with tub and shower, hair dryers, toiletries; iron and ironing board; shops; beauty salon; full-service business center; wedding service

Electricity: 110 volts

Fitness Facilities/Spa Services: See text

Sports: Two freshwater swimming pools; two tennis courts; free clinics; water sports

Dress Code: Casual

Children: All ages; under eighteen years old stay free in room with parents

Meetings: Up to 1,000 people; audiovisual facilities

Day Visitors: Yes, with reservations

Handicapped Facilities: Yes

Packages: Golf, family, honeymoon, wedding, dive

Rates: Per room, single or double, EP. **High Season** (late December–mid-April): From $595–$639. **Shoulder Season** (mid-April–June 1): From $529. **Low Season:** From $463

Government Tax: 8 percent on room

THE RITZ-CARLTON, ST. THOMAS
St. Thomas, U.S.V.I.

Commanding a magnificent setting at the eastern end of St. Thomas with expansive views of the U.S. and British Virgin Islands, the Ritz-Carlton with its Italian Renaissance style and hilltop location could easily have you imagining that you are somewhere on the Italian Riviera.

Terraced in thirty acres of lavish gardens, the elegant resort was designed by Barbadian architect Ian Morrison, whose signature is the adaptation of various Mediterranean architectural elements to Caribbean settings. The main building and centerpiece of the resort suggests a Venetian Renaissance palace outfitted with a prince's ransom of Italian marble. Its red tile roof and ochre stucco facade are reminders of the Mediterranean style.

From the hotel's impressive entrance reached by a long, flower-lined driveway, you arrive at an imposing valet-attended porte cochere and step into the palazzo and onto beautiful Portuguese marble mosaic floors. These lead you through graceful arched and columned hallways to the reception desk.

This, it turns out, is the upper level of the palazzo, with high-arched Palladian windows that open onto spectacular views of the resort and the islands dotting the turquoise Caribbean waters below. At the center of the building is a small inner courtyard; one of its walls has several lion-head fountains with water cascading gently from one to another.

This imposing structure holds the administrative offices, several fashionable boutiques, a concierge desk on the top level, and the Ritz-Kids room on the lower. The rest of the resort spans the hillside in both directions and falls to the beach via a flower-festooned stone stairway and a magnificent pool.

Over the last several years, the hotel has had a $40 million renovation during which a Club Lounge and new Club Level accommodations and were added and others enhanced, the restaurants were redesigned; and the first Prada Spa in the Caribbean was introduced.

Rimming the southern side are multilevel beige stucco buildings with flower-filled terraces, resembling large villas on the Italian Riviera; each is named for a tropical flower. They house the large guest rooms with fresh new decor. All have large balconies with fabulous views, air-conditioning, ceiling fans, coffeemakers, hair dryers, and enlarging mirrors.

Each room has marble floors and is furnished with a flat-screen television, high-speed Internet, stocked minibar, a desk and chair (some have one or two love seats with a coffee table), a Sealy Posturepedic® Plush bed designed for The Ritz-Carlton, with 400 thread-count linens and down feather pillows. There are three telephones—by the bed, on the desk, and in the bathroom. In the closet you will find an umbrella along with a digital safe. The marbled bathroom has a long, narrow shelf over two separate sinks along with toiletries, a pair of monogrammed seersucker bathrobes, and iron and ironing board.

To the last two of these villas, two floors were added and a new five-story villa was built between the two villas, connecting the three buildings. The new villa houses four Presidential Suites and the large private key-activated Club Lounge. Together the three buildings now house fifty-five Club Level rooms, fifteen executive one-bedroom suites and four, 3,000-square-foot presidential suites. The latter have two-bedrooms, a dining and living area, fitness room with treadmill, and bath with rain showers and soaking tubs. The Club Lounge has a dedicated concierge and offers five food presentations daily.

On the northern side of the palazzo, the former small spa was converted into a much larger spa with fourteen treatment rooms and a large lounge. The spa offers aromatherapy and other spa treatments, as well as those available through a partnership with Prada Beauty, a leader in scientifically advanced skin care.

The fitness center has exercise and weight-training equipment and a personal trainer on request. The Motion Studio, a new facility located near the fitness center, is used for aerobics, yoga, Pilates, and other classes such as African drumming.

The resort's new restaurants include Sail's, the oceanfront restaurant that was enlarged with an extended roof cover and offers open-air dining during the day. The expanded area also houses a new indoor air-conditioned steak and grill restaurant. In-room dining is available around the clock. Bleuwater, enhanced by floor-to-ceiling French doors that open onto a view of the bay, is the resort's sophisticated, signature restaurant, specializing in fresh local seafood choices created by Executive Chef Jasper Schneider. The vegetables it serves are delivered weekly from The Chef's Garden in Huron, Ohio, which practices sustainable agriculture, ensuring maximum flavor and nutrients. The restaurant is open daily for breakfast and dinner; reservations are required. The Great Bay Lounge, which has an outdoor deck for dining, serves sushi and an eclectic menu of small plates and cocktails. It has a billiards table and board games and features nightly live entertainment.

The hills rimming the Ritz-Carlton form something of an amphitheater cupping the beach. To the south is a mangrove pond with ducks and other birds and at the center is a gorgeous 125-foot-long free-form swimming pool with a vanishing edge on the side toward the sea, allowing the water to spill over like a waterfall—when you look across the pool, the water seems to disappear into the sea.

Snorkeling, windsurfing, Sunfish and Hobie Cat sailing, as well as dive instruction, certification, and excursions are all available for an additional charge. The hotel's 53-foot catamaran, *Lady Lynsey,* offers day sails and cocktail cruises. Nine moorings are available for guests who want to arrive by boat. The tennis complex has lighted Astroturf courts. A horticulturist leads walking tours. For more sedate activity, a resident artist offers watercolor classes upon request, for $65 per person.

The Ritz-Kids Club, a children's program for ages five to twelve, is available daily, Monday to Friday, 10:00 a.m. to 4:00 p.m. On Tuesday it is also available 6:30 to 9:30 p.m., and on Thursday during the evening

hours only. The program is supervised by trained counselors and offers a wide range of fun and educational activities. The cost is $75 for a full day including lunch. Babysitting services are also available.

The Ritz-Carlton should appeal to just about anyone who likes a stylish atmosphere and can afford the tab. Bear in mind that you will need to do quite a lot of walking. There are golf carts to fetch you from your room to the palazzo, but they tend to function on island time—which is to say, slow.

The Ritz-Carlton, St. Thomas ★★★★
6900 Great Bay, St. Thomas, U.S.V.I. 00802
Phone: (340) 775-3333; Fax: (340) 775-4444; www.ritzcarlton.com/resorts/st_thomas

Owner/Management: THC St. Thomas Corporation

General Manager: Marc Langevin

Open: Year-round

Credit Cards: All major

U.S. Reservations: (800) 241-3333

Deposit: Three nights; thirty days cancellation

Minimum Stay: None, except during Christmas; inquire

Arrival/Departure: Transfers available

Distance from Airport: (Cyril E. King International Airport) 13 miles (thirty minutes); taxi one-way, $15 per person, plus charge for luggage

Distance from Charlotte Amalie: 6 miles (twenty minutes); taxi one-way, $14

Accommodations: 180 rooms and suites (including 55 new club rooms, 15 new executive suites and 4 new presidential suites)

Amenities: Air-conditioning, ceiling fans; three international direct-dial telephones; marble bath with tub and shower, two sinks, separate toilet, hair dryer, toiletries, bathrobes; twice-daily maid service with nightly turndown service; stocked minibar; coffeemaker; iron and ironing board; clock, CD player, radio/cable television; safe; beauty salon; laundry and valet service; twenty-four-hour room service

Electricity: 110 volts

Fitness Facilities/Spa Services: See text

Sports: Freshwater swimming pool; snorkeling, windsurfing, Sunfish sailboats, Hobie Cats; scuba instruction, full certification, dive available for additional charge; lighted Astroturf tennis courts, equipment, lessons; golf at Mahogany Run and deep-sea fishing arranged

Dress Code: Casual by day; casually elegant in evening

Children: All ages; Ritz-Kids Club, age five to twelve; babysitters

Meetings: Up to 200 people

Day Visitors: No day passes

Handicapped Facilities: Entire property is wheelchair accessible. Rooms available for physically challenged. However, be aware that property is on hillside and very spread out.

Packages: Honeymoon, wedding, dive, others

Rates: Per room, daily, EP. *High Season* (mid-December–April 30): $545–$2,000. *Shoulder Season* (May–early July and October–mid-December): $350–$1,200. *Low Season:* $250–$750

Service Charge: $55 per person, per day resort fee

Government Tax: 8 percent

ON THE HORIZON

This section features resorts that hold the promise of being among the best.

Antigua
HERMITAGE BAY
St. John's, Antigua, W.I.

Hidden in a secluded cove on Antigua's west coast, Hermitage Bay is set between tropical clad hills and a beautiful beach. The property is the essence of understated luxury. Comprised of twenty-five individual cottages built in dark tropical hardwoods that blend into the natural landscape, the cottage suites combine a contemporary minimalist style in decor with echoes of Antigua's colonial past—and all with panoramic views of the Caribbean Sea and neighboring islands in the distance.

The luxury begins at check-in when you are greeted by a Room Ambassador who checks you into your Cottage suite, while you enjoy a cool drink. If you wish, she will unpack for you.

This all-suite, all-inclusive boutique resort offers five Beachfront Cottage Suites (900 square feet); three more located directly behind them near the main infinity-edge, freshwater swimming pool; and seventeen Hillside Cottage Suites (1,000

square feet) set against hillside in terraced gardens, each with panoramic views of the Caribbean Sea and private infinity-edge plunge pools.

The restaurant and bar overlooking the beach serves international cuisine with a Caribbean flair. Dining is a la carte and includes breakfast, lunch, afternoon tea, and dinner, as well as a selection of house wines and most beverages. Meals and beverages can be served in suites for an additional charge.

Nonmotorized water-sports equipment is available on the beach—along with staff for instruction—and is included in the all-inclusive price. The resort has a full-service spa and a boutique.

Care was made to preserve the natural setting and to keep in harmony with it. The resort has a gray-water system to conserve water, and has taken steps to protect the mangroves and wildlife. To contribute to the local economy, the resort obtains the herbs, jams, and fresh provisions from local farmers.

Hermitage Bay
P. O. Box 60, St. John's, Antigua, West Indies
Phone: (268) 562-5500; Fax:(268) 562-5505; info@hermitagebay.com; www .hermitagebay.com

Reservations: Direct to hotel

Owners: Andrew and Alex Michelin

General Manager: Keith A. Martel

Rates: Per suite, double occupancy, all-inclusive: *High Season,* $800–$1,600; *Low Season,* $700–$1,000. Service charge 10 percent; government tax, 10.5 percent. Tipping is not encouraged.

HODGES BAY CLUB
St. John's, Antigua, W.I.

On the northern shores of Antigua, a ten-minute drive from the airport, are the white-washed villas of Hodges Bay Club, a multimillion-dollar luxury, beachfront development scheduled to open in fall 2008.

The resort is eco-conscious, using state-of-the-art products and materials in its design and its facilities. The resort aims eventually to grow most of its own produce.

The Club's contemporary, sophisticated style blends stone and hardwoods with stainless steel and glass. Surrounded by tropical gardens, the resort has ninety luxuriously furnished hotel suites and twenty-four ocean-front apartments and houses, a beachfront infinity pool (one of three swimming pools), a spa and fitness center, two tennis courts, and four dining options ranging from casual to fine dining.

The four accommodation types—all with terraces—include hotel suites with a contemporary bathroom with a Jacuzzi bath or spa pool; ocean suites; apartments with a fully equipped kitchen and bathroom; and ocean-front houses and penthouses with an open-plan living/dining area, fully equipped kitchen, bathroom, and private spa pool. All houses and penthouses have a maid and private parking. A personal chef can be requested.

Fathoms, a three-floor house available from December through April, sleeps up to eight adults in four bedrooms, each with bathroom, *al fresco* shower, an infinity spa pool, and expansive terraces with ocean views.

The resort offers a choice of three restaurants, an extension spa, and a kids club—Pelicanos—for children ages two to eleven.

Hodges Bay Club
P.O. Box W 1273, St. John's, Antigua, W.I.
Phone: (268) 462-2300; Fax: (268) 462-1333; www.hodgesbayclub.com

Reservations: Direct (268) 462-2300 or reservations@hodgesbayclub.com

Owners: EMC Group

Managing Director: Ross Justice

Rates: To be announced

Barbados
ALMOND CASUARINA BEACH RESORT
St. Lawrence Gap, Christ Church, Barbados, W.I.

Those who knew the old Casuarina Beach, one of Barbados' most popular small hotels, will be anxious to see its multimillion-dollar reincarnation as the all-inclusive Almond Casuarina Beach, the fifth member of the Almond group and the third in Barbados.

Ideally located on the south coast in the St. Lawrence Gap—Barbados' action central—and fronting a stretch of the beautiful Dover Beach, the new Almond Casuarina Beach is equidistance from Bridgetown and Grantley Adams International Airport, about a fifteen-minutes drive.

Set on eighteen acres of tropical gardens and committed to continuing the environmental mission for which the old hotel was famous, the new Almond Casuarina has extensive facilities for couples, families (there is a Kids Club and a Teen Center), and even singles—an unusual offering for an all-inclusive resort. Its 289 air-conditioned rooms come in five categories from standard rooms amidst the tropical gardens to deluxe ones overlooking the pools, superior deluxe with larger bedroom, superior deluxe in the newly constructed beachfront block, and one-bedroom pool/garden suites with spacious bedroom and living area. All rooms have balcony or terrace.

In addition to three freshwater swimming pools, there's a children's wading pool with a waterfall and an array of land and water sports. The Spa offers a full range of beauty treatments and spa services, which can be prebooked.

The resort offers four restaurants and a British-style high tea is served in the afternoon. For an alternative lunch and anytime snacks, there's the Beach Grill and a Kids Club buffet. Room service is available only for lunch and dinner. Guests also have access to the three restaurants at Almond Beach Club and six at Almond Beach Village. Nightly live entertainment includes a live band, floor shows, and a late-night piano bar.

The "For You. About You" concept (Almond's answer to a concierge) is a support team to assist guests in planning their vacation even before they leave home and to handle special requests like reservations for spa treatments, dinner, sightseeing, limousine airport transfers, birthday celebrations, and more.

Almond Casuarina Resort
St. Lawrence Gap, Christ Church, Barbados, W.I.
Phone: (246) 428-3600; Fax: (246) 428-1970; www.almondresorts.com/Resorts/AlmondCasuarina; email: info@almond resorts.com or ACBForYouAboutYou@ almondresorts.com

Reservations: 1-800-4ALMOND or www .almondresorts.com.

Owner: Ralph Taylor

General Manager: Frank King

Rates: Per room/suite, per night, standard double occupancy, all-inclusive: *High Season,* $900/$1100. *Low Season,* $700/$1,000. Service charge included; government tax: included. No tipping allowed.

Curaçao
RENAISSANCE CURAÇAO RESORT & CASINO

Willemstad, Curaçao, Netherlands Antilles

Scheduled to open in historic Willemstad in late 2008, the Renaissance Curaçao Resort & Casino is as colorful as Curaçao's famous waterfront and its architectural design takes its cue from the historic setting, blending it with contemporary features. But what makes this resort truly unusual is a different piece of history—it's built into the Rif Fort, a nineteenth-century landmark designated as a UNESCO World Heritage site.

The Renaissance Curaçao is part of a retail and entertainment complex adjacent to the cruise port. It has a manmade beach, a waterfront promenade, and The Renaissance Mall with fifteen restaurants, lounges and bars, shops, a casino, and six movie theaters with a full-service restaurant and bar and which intend to show the latest releases.

The hotel has 237 rooms and suites, a spa and fitness center, and is set to offer a cool nightlife. The accommodations come in three categories of guest rooms and four types of suites. The guest rooms either overlook the atrium or have balconies with island or ocean views.

The Renaissance Curaçao's freshwater infinity pool overlooks man-made Eternity Beach with its waterfalls and endless view of the Caribbean Sea. The resort's spa will offer a wide range of treatments, while the fitness room is fitted with treadmills, step machines, workout stations, exercise cycles, and weights.

The resort's conference and banquet facilities include a 3,600-square-foot atrium, a 2,700-square-foot ballroom, two boardrooms, coffee lounge, business center, and indoor and outdoor function space. The pool and private beach area provide additional space for outdoor events. The 15,000-square-foot Carnaval Casino with its Carnaval decor and ambience will have a variety of machines and table games.

Renaissance Curaçao Resort & Casino
The Rif Fort, Otrobanda
Curaçao, Netherlands Antilles
Phone: (599-9) 435-5000; Fax: (599-9) 435-5025; www.renaissancecuracao.com; email: info@curacaorenaissance.com

Reservations: (599-9) 435-5000

General Manager: Maylin Trenidad

Rates: Per room, double occupancy: *High Season* (January–April 30): $364. *Low Season* (May 1–December 21): $267, plus tax and service 23.05%.

Dominican Republic
THE WESTIN ROCO KI BEACH AND GOLF RESORT

Punta Cana, Dominican Republic

Situated on 2,700 acres of tropical vegetation and fronting a 4-mile beach, the Westin Roco Ki Beach and Golf Resort is the first hotel opening in Roco Ki, a major new resort development on the Dominican Republic's popular east coast and the Westin chain's first resort in this country. When it opens in summer 2009, the hotel will come with a magnificent Nick Faldo–designed championship golf course, a full-service spa, seven restaurants, four bars, four swimming pools, and a commitment to environmental preservation. Over the next decade Roco Ki will see the addition of a world-class marina, hotels, up to three more championship golf courses, retail shops, condos, villas, and beachfront homes.

Located on Macao Beach, 20 miles north from the Punta Cana International Airport, Roco Ki, a Starwood resort, is set in the natural vegetation of protected mangroves, long stretches of white-sand beach, and dramatic cliffs overhanging the ocean. For more than 2,000 years, the site was the heart of the Taino Indian culture. Pre-Columbian artifacts discovered here and the area's natural beauty and diversity were incorporated into the resort's character and ambiance. There is even a Taino Interpretive Center and Museum on the property.

The resort's accommodations include 157 hotel rooms and suites; 32 Jungle Luxe® bungalows with sea and gardens views; 20 cliffside, 3,400-square-foot, villas overlooking the ocean; and two- and three-bedroom resort condominiums. Guests will have a choice of seven restaurants and bars.

In addition to the 11,500-square-foot Heavenly Spa™ (Westin's first in the Caribbean), there are tennis courts, a watersports complex, a wildlife sanctuary, and a Westin Kids Club® and Activity Center.

The state-of-the-art conference center, accommodating up to 700 guests, has fourteen rooms equipped with wireless Internet, and outdoor venues for theme parties and special events.

The Westin Roco Ki Beach and Golf Resort
Macao Beach, Dominican Republic
Florida Office: 2901 SW 149th Avenue, Suite 320, Miramar, Florida 33180
Phone: (954) 624-1771; Fax: (509) 278-5589; www.westin.com/rocoki

General Manager: Randy Ha

Rates: Per room, double occupancy: **High Season** (late December 2009–April 2010): $569–$759. **Low Season** summer 2009 from $389 and autumn $339.

Grenada
MOUNT CINNAMON
Grand Anse, Grenada, W.I.

The retro-looking fridge in the kitchen is tangerine orange or electric blue; French doors open onto a large patio with arches framing wide-angle views of the sea and Grand Anse Beach just a five-minute walk away. At Mount Cinnamon, twenty-one one-, two-, or three-bedroom suites in white villas with red tiled roofs and arched balconies are terraced down a hillside overlooking the sea as bougainvillea, hibiscus, and other tropical flowers spill over walls.

Everything about the rebirth of this twenty-year-old villa property, a ten-minute drive from the airport and from St. George's, conspires to amuse with happy hues of lemon, fuchsia, lime, and whimsical touches that make you smile, like gaily-painted tin fish wall hooks holding wicker beach bags and wood oars standing in tall wicker baskets.

A canvas of white walls, crisp white linens, and red tile floors show off joyful colors that cover the beds, furniture, puffy pillows, carpets, and locally produced art work; adobe walk-in showers are hand-rubbed with fuchsia or gold or blue; and Roman-striped pillows sit on bright blue cushions.

The pool, off the open-air lounge area of the main building and reception, offers a quiet respite steps from the villas. White canvas umbrellas and orange, turquoise, and green wicker-style lounge chairs add splashes of color to the patio. The Beach Club, a short walk from the villas, is set up with a covered patio, tables, lounges, and a dining area where you can order lunch and drinks.

Moi Spa at Mount Cinnamon is small, but like everything else here, designed to evoke the senses with lots of candles, abstract art work, and subdued lighting. Savvy, Mount Cinnamon's restaurant, has received rave reviews since it opened.

Future plans, to be completed in the next two years, include a beachside luxury hotel catering to families. Water will meander all the way to the sand with a series of pools and waterfalls surrounded by flowers and tropical plants—all natural.

Peter de Savary's $555 million Port Louis Grenada—an investment twice the annual budget of Grenada—is a mixed-use seaside development, now under construction. It will have a 300-slip marina for mega-yachts; individual homes and villas; and several hotels including a 180 room/suite Nikki Beach, which recently formed a partnership with the De Savary Group. (www.portlouisgrenada.com)

Mount Cinnamon
P.O. Box 3858, St. George's, Grenada, W.I. Phone: (473) 439-9900; Fax: (473) 439-7000; www.mountcinnamongrenada.com

Reservations: (473) 439-9900 or e-mail: reservations@mountcinnamongrenada.com

Founder/Chairman: Peter De Savary

Operations Manager: Chris Ghita

Rates: Range from $400–$600 per suite to $500–$950 per villa, plus 10 percent service charge and 8 percent government tax. Rates include breakfast; MAP rates available. Children up to age twelve are free.

Puerto Rico
THE CERVANTES
Old San Juan, PR

Situated only a few blocks from the cruise piers and at the heart of San Juan's best restaurants and nightlife, the small hotel is ideal for those who want to spend a few days in Old San Juan before or after a cruise.

Set in a former bank building dating from the late 1800s, the twelve-room/suite hotel is the handiwork of Nono Maldonado, Puerto Rico's best-known fashion designer. From the classic, colonial exterior with arched windows and wrought-iron balconies, you step into interiors that combine a modern classic ambience with cutting-edge cool. High quality furnishings throughout reflect Maldonado's refined, elegant couturier designs. Silk, taffeta, suede, and other rich fabrics in topaz, copper, bronze, and gold are used on clean-lined couches and chairs, with splashes of color in original art on the walls and pillows and throws on the beds. The reception and bar's counter tops are onyx; some restaurant table tops are pure silver.

The hotel's entrance opens onto the small area with the reception desk and elevator to one side and a small lounge and bar on the other. Behind is Panza, the hotel's award-winning restaurant, popular with local patrons for sophisticated Caribbean/Asian fusion cuisine. It opens to the public for lunch and dinner; breakfast, included in the rate, is for hotel guests only.

The hotel's accommodations are situated on the top four of the six-floor building, starting with the large, bi-level Penthouse suite which covers the entire sixth floor. It has a large living room, guest bath, roof-top terrace, bar, and dining table seating ten on the first level. The bedroom and bathroom are three steps up on the second level. The marbled bathroom is a triumph with a Jacuzzi tub and a separate sauna shower with massaging jets and rain-shower head. The suite, popular with honeymooners and celebrities, can be reserved for small parties and dinners. Other floors house three types of accommodations: Master or junior suites and superior or standard rooms.

The Cervantes was named by its owner, Puerto Rican–born and New York–bred James Sanchez, general manager and president of C Group Hotels, who was inspired by Cervantes' *Don Quixote de la Mancha,* to follow his dream in creating the hotel. Sanchez has two other hotels in the making near The Cervantes and by 2010, plans to have fifty rooms/suites in his boutique collection. He also owns three Las Casitas villas at El Conquistador (see page 190) on the east coast, enabling the hotel to offer "town & country" packages combined with the Golden Door Spa there. The Cervantes is designed for adults; it welcomes children, preferably three years and older, but has no facilities for them.

The Cervantes does not have a concierge, rather, the front desk personnel are jacks of all trades and cheerfully handle normal daily requests, arrange transportation, sightseeing, golf, and appointments at the Secrets of Eden spa, a full-service spa next door. Although the accommodations are deluxe, The Cervantes' informal structure resembles a European pension or small country inn rather than a fancy hotel.

The Cervantes
329 Calle Recinto Sur, Old San Juan
Phone: (787) 724-7722; Fax: (787) 289-8900; e-mail: reservations@cervantespr.com; www.cervantespr.com

Reservations: Direct to hotel reservations@cervantespr.com; or (787) 724-7722

Owner: C Group Hotels

General Manager: James Sanchez

Rates: Per room, single/double, CP. *High Season* (December 24–May 30): $225–$425; Penthouse suite $975. *Low Season* (June 1–September 30): $195–$400 and $900, respectively, plus 9 percent government tax and $2 per person per night city tax. A 9 percent service charge included in rate.

LA CONCHA, A RENAISSANCE RESORT
San Juan, PR

Condado, San Juan's prime resort area which, after almost a decade of decline, has made a comeback thanks to major hotel renovations, the addition of high-end boutiques—Ferragamo, Chanel, Gucci, among others—and most important, the rebirth of La Concha after being an empty eyesore for ten years.

The hotel's opening in December 2007 marked, almost to the day, forty-nine years when the original hotel opened and was hailed as the masterpiece of the "Tropical Modernism" architectural movement in the Caribbean. Today's La Concha, set on six tropical oceanfront acres, has maintained many of the original design elements, while redefining them for the twenty-first-century traveler. Marketed under Marriott's Renaissance brand—the first in Puerto Rico, the hotel is only Phase One of a huge project that will see the addition of a condo-hotel tower on La Concha's east flank and to the west, the restoration of the Vanderbilt mansion as the centerpiece of another hotel and condo-hotel complex, opening in 2009.

Already a mecca of urban seaside chic for hotel guests, visitors, and Condado residents is La Concha's five restaurants, elegant open-air plaza with cascading waters, fountains, and pools on one side of the expansive, open lobby. There are 248 spacious, contemporary guest rooms, including sixteen suites.

In addition to a multilevel infinity swimming pool and Jacuzzi, La Concha's gym enables guests to work out while enjoying expansive views of the sea. A full-service spa is scheduled to open in 2009.

La Concha's meetings and banquet facilities also provide panoramic ocean views, as well as qualified staff for planning and support for weddings, high-tech conferences, and events.

La Concha, a Renaissance Resort
1077 Ashford Avenue, San Juan, PR 00907
Phone: (787) 721–7500, toll-free: (877) 524-7778; Fax: (787) 724-1949; e-mail: info@laconcharesort.com; www.laconcharesort.com

U.S. Reservations: (877) 524-7778

Managing Company: International Hospitality Enterprises

General Manager: Eddie Sipple

Rates: Per room, single/double, EP, from $249 to $599 year-round, plus: 11 percent service charge and 12 percent government tax.

St. Barts
LE SERENO
Grand Cul de Sac, St.-Barthelémy, F.W.I.

Shortly after it opened, Le Sereno quickly appeared on top-ten lists, the A-lists, the "hot" lists of fashion and travel magazines, newspapers, and the Internet. Divinely simple and simply divine sums up typical descriptions. What brought all this attention was the resort's designer—the ultra-cool French interior designer Christian Liaigre, who has been called the hautest of haute designers.

Actually, Le Sereno is a reincarnation of Hotel Le Sereno, a St. Barts stalwart for more than three decades, but the similarity is in the name only. The new resort has thirty-seven new, spacious beachfront suites and villas of very clean modern design inside and out. They overlook the sheltered, 600-foot palm-shaded, reef-protected beach of Grand Cul de Sac on the east end of St. Barts and as its name implies, is a haven of serenity. The beachfront gem has been well described as being like St. Barts itself—a contradiction of luxury and simplicity.

All the stylish suites and villas have ocean views, private terraces, and landscape gardens by Venezuelan landscape architect Fernando Tabora, known in the Caribbean for his beautiful gardens of several Barbados hotels. Liaigre's minimalist, custom furnishings conform to his signature white against dark wood furniture and trim, with taupe and cream accents. They are complemented by signature robes and linens made for Le Sereno by D. Porthault. All units are air-conditioned and provide complimentary wireless high-speed Internet access, cordless phones, flat-screen satellite television, personal iPods/docking stations, safe, hair dryer, deluxe toiletries, and twice-daily housekeeping service.

Le Sereno's Beach Club has a beachfront, freshwater infinity swimming pool and equipment for snorkeling, kayaking, and others water sports. The Fitness Center offers equipment and can supply fitness trainers. In-room spa treatments are provided by Ligne St. Barth, the long-established local company that makes skin-care products from natural ingredients.

Le Restaurant des Pêcheurs with an eclectic mix of Liaigre-designed furniture, captures an outdoors feeling in a stylish yet relaxed setting for breakfast, lunch, and dinner. As the name implies, its specialty is fish supplied daily by local fishermen. The resort also offers a "Beach and Pool" menu of light fare, available from noon until sundown. The Lounge, next to the restaurant, and Martini Bar are opened throughout the day and evening.

In addition to its much praised accommodations, Le Sereno receives good marks for its high quality service by a well-trained, around-the-clock staff.

Le Sereno
BP 19, Grand-Cul-de-Sac, 97133 St.-Barthélemy, F.W.I.
Phone: (590) 590-298-300; Fax : (590) 590-277-547; e-mail: info@lesereno.com; www.lesereno.com

Reservations: reservations@lesereno.com

Owners: Ignacio Contreras and Ricardo Dunin

General Manager: Jacques Roy

Rates: Per room, per night, including continental breakfast, tax and service charges, round-trip airport transfers, **High Season** from €680 suite to €2,180 villa; **Low Season** €480 to €1,780. Holidays have special rates and required five night minimum stay; inquire.

St. Lucia
THE LANDINGS ST. LUCIA, A ROCKRESORT
Rodney Bay, St. Lucia, W.I.

After an absence of thirteen years, Rock-Resorts returned to the Caribbean with the opening of The Landings St. Lucia in December 2007. Located on nineteen acres fronting 800 feet of beachfront on Rodney Bay in the island's northwest corner, The Landings, a condo-hotel, opened with 62 suites of the 231 one-, two-, and three-bedroom suites to be completed in three stages by 2010. Phase Two added 65 suites in September 2008.

Built around a marina and lagoon, the resort has an airy, five-story welcoming pavilion. The resort's facilities include the Yacht Haven restaurant, a spa and fitness center, a marina with sixty private yacht moorings, swimming pools, tennis courts, water sports, and beach services.

All suites have oversized terraces or landscaped patios and some have plunge pools. All one-bedroom suites are ground floor with harbor views and furnished with king bed. Two- and three-bedroom suites are found on all floors and face either the harbor or beach.

Yacht Haven offers casual dining for breakfast, lunch, and dinner daily. The Viscount Lounge in the main lobby is the venue for afternoon tea along with views of yacht basin; it features entertainment in the evening. The Compass Terrace, tucked behind the Welcoming Pavilion and facing west, is a large outdoor space with a fountain and ideal for receptions, weddings, or watching the sunset. To take advantage of your gourmet kitchen, the resort will stock it with your selections prior to your arrival. The resort is not an all-inclusive, although meal plans are available.

RockResorts Spa® boasts eight treatment rooms, including one for couples, a full-service salon, and state-of-the-art fitness center. There are lounge chairs and umbrellas at the beach and the beach concession offers a variety of water sports. You can swim at the beach or at one of several pools. There is a kids' program geared to educational and environmental programs.

There is no golf course, however, the resort provides transportation to the nearby eighteen-hole, championship golf course of the St. Lucia Golf Club.

The Landings has an environmental agenda. Among its green initiatives are solar energy to help power the resort and partnerships with local farmers to purchase their produce.

The Landings St. Lucia
Rodney Bay
Castries, St. Lucia, West Indies

Phone: (877) 657-ROCK; (758) 458-7300; www.thelandingsstlucia.com; http://landings.rockresorts.com

Reservations: (877) 657-ROCK, (758) 458-7300

Developers: The Landing Ltd, a St. Lucian registered company

Management: RockResorts International

Managing Director: Gary Thulander

Rates: Per room, per night, double occupancy, one bedroom: *High Season* (January 5–March 31; May 2–11): $350. *Low Season* (April 1–May 1; May 12–November 26): $225. Taxes and gratuities are additional. For two and three bedroom, inquire.

Turks and Caicos Islands
NIKKI BEACH RESORT TURKS & CAICOS
Leeward, Providenciales, Turks and Caicos Islands, B.W.I.

In April 2008, Nikki Beach Resorts, best known for its Nikki Beach Clubs in Miami's South Beach and a dozen countries around the world as a trend-setting lifestyle and entertainment brand, launched its entry into the resort business with the opening of its first hotel in the Turks & Caicos. It is the first phase of a major 423-acre resort and residential development in the Leeward area on the northeast tip of Providenciales (better known as Provo) and the first luxury resort to open in this area. Phase Two, to open in 2010, will add a 110-room hotel, casino, and spa.

Aimed squarely at young, urban sophisticates in their twenties and thirties, the $100 million dollar Nikki Beach Resort Turks & Caicos is the first of twenty new resorts which the Nikki Beach group is developing worldwide. Some of the glamour, for which the Nikki Beach Clubs are known, starts for guests upon arrival at Providenciales International Airport, where they are met and assisted by a hotel representative and led to a chauffeured stretch limousine for the transfer to the resort. On the twenty-minute drive, guests can sip champagne and select their music preference for listening, and watch a video of party life at various Nikki Beach Clubs while completing their check-in. Upon arrival at the hotel, a personal assistant, who is a combination concierge and butler, is available for each guest 24/7.

Set on a man-made beach facing an inlet that opens to the ocean, the resort has a colorful façade painted in coral, mustard, and tan and trimmed with white balustrades and railings of the terraces; red-tile roofs add a Mediterranean touch. There are forty-eight deluxe studios and one-, two-, and three-bedroom suites—all with ocean or water views; all suites have terraces or French balconies.

The resort's facilities include an infinity-edge swimming pool with a swim-up bar along side the beach. One side of the bar is surrounded by a flagstone terrace with double-bed lounges. On the other side and beyond the pool, a terrace extends to three open-air cabanas furnished with sofas and lounges—and yours for $1,000 to $5,000 a day, depending on the time of the year.

Café Nikki, an open-air restaurant with a large circular bar serves three meals daily; a second venue by the water is added during the winter season for breakfast and lunch. Menus offer an interesting selection of contemporary cuisine, including sushi. Nightly entertainment and special events are staged throughout the year and the signature Nikki Beach Club and VIP Ultra Lounge host late night and Sunday beach parties in Nikki Beach style.

With Island Global Yachting, a premier mega-yacht marina operation, Nikki Beach is developing the Turks & Caicos Yacht Club, a 110-slip mega-yacht marina accommodating vessels up to 200 feet, adjacent to the hotel. Said to be the world's first eco-marina designed and built.

Nikki Beach Resort Turks & Caicos
Leeward, Providenciales, Turks and Caicos Islands, B.W.I.
Phone: (649) 941-3747, (866) 720-2613; e-mail: info@nikkibeachhotels.com; www .nikkibeachhotels.com

Reservations: (649) 941-3747 or e-mail: info@nikkibeachhotels.com

Owner: Nikki Beach Hotels & Resorts

General Manager: Gregoire Poirier

Rates: Per suite, double occupancy, all-inclusive: *High Season,* from $1,000; *Low Season,* from $700, plus service charge and government tax

SEVEN STARS RESORT
Grace Bay, Providenciales, Turks and Caicos Islands, B.W.I.

Opened in July 2008, the new Seven Stars Resort is located on Grace Bay, part of the Princess Alexandra Park, a protected marine reserve on the northern coast of Providenciales. The hotel sits on twenty-two acres fronting one of the longest beachfronts of Grace Bay Beach's famed 12 miles of powdery white sand.

Named for the seven stars in the Pleiades constellation, the resort is comprised of three buildings enhanced by courtyards, fountains, and tropical gardens with 115 residential units. The units break out to 165 spacious oceanfront/ocean-view studios measuring 620 square feet and one- to four-bedroom suites and penthouses, ranging from 700 to 6,000 square feet. Most have uninterrupted sea views; some have garden or island views; and all have wraparound terraces or balconies.

Seven Stars has two restaurants: the open-air Sand Dollar, a pool terrace restaurant where light lunch of salads, sandwiches, and a daily hot special are offered; and La Pergola and bar, the fine-dining venue open nightly for dinner and serving contemporary Mediterranean cuisine and Caribbean influenced selection.

The hotel's large heated saltwater pool and cabanas are surrounded by tropical landscaping under the shade of palm trees. Dune pavilions with an Indonesian hardwood frame and tiki roof over a double mattress are strategically placed in the dunes to enjoy the transquillity of the expansive beach and sea views. The pool bar is open from 10:00 a.m. to sundown, and a flag placed in the sand alerts beach attendants who also dispense refreshing sprays.

The hotel's Tour Desk can arrange water sports, especially fishing and scuba diving, for which the Turks & Caicos are famous. Other options include day sails, cruises to other cays and islands, and car rentals. The resort has two floodlit hard-surface tennis courts and golf is available at the nearby Provo Country Club on the Karl Litton–designed eighteen-hole championship course; golf clubs can be rented.

The Seven Star's Spa has four treatment rooms, each with its own bath and outside terrace. Using Paris-based Yon-ka products, it offers a menu of treatments done by trained therapists in one of the spa rooms or in the guest's room or terrace. The Fitness Center is furnished with a full range of Cybex equipment. The resort has a children's play area with several Jungle Jims, a boutique, and can handle small meetings and weddings.

Seven Stars Resort
P.O. Box 432, Grace Bay Road
Providenciales, Turks and Caicos Islands, B.W.I.
Phone: (649) 941-7777; Fax: (649) 941-8601; email: sevenstars@sevenstarsresort.com; www.sevenstarsresort.com

Reservations: (866) 570-7777 or (649) 941-7777

Owner/ Developer: Sodalco Development Company Ltd.

Managing Director: Duncan MacArthur

Rates: Per studio/suite, per night, **High Season** (January 3–April 4): $610–$940/$825–$1,110; **Shoulder Season** (April 20–May 31; November 1–December 18): $485–$750/$660–$975; **Summer** (June–October): $365–$560/$495–625. For larger suites, please inquire.

INDEX

THE BEST OF THE BEST

This chart is not intended to be a complete inventory of each resort's facilities. Instead, it indicates the especially strong features of each establishment. For example, most beachside resorts in this book offer scuba diving or can arrange it; however, the chart notes only those resorts focused primarily on diving or that have a particularly outstanding dive facility.

	Beachside	Hillside	All-inclusive	Budget	Value	Honeymoon	Romantic	Wedding	Children's Program	Families	Singles	Sports/Active	Dive	Golf	Tennis	Marina	Spa/Fitness Center	Nature Lovers	Hiking	Birding	History	Cuisine	Entertainment	Casino
Almond Morgan Bay (St. Lucia)	•		•		•				•	•	•	•												
Altamer (Anguilla)	•		•				•																•	
Amanyara (Turks & Caicos Islands)	•						•										•	•						
Anse Chastanet (St. Lucia)	•	•				•	•	•					•		•			•	•					
Asa Wright (Trinidad)		•		•	•					•								•	•	•				
Biras Creek (British VI)	•		•			•	•	•			•					•		•	•					
Bitter End (British VI)	•	•				•	•		•	•	•	•	•			•								
The Body Holiday (St. Lucia)	•		•		•	•	•				•	•	•		•		•							
British Colonial Hilton (Bahamas)	•			•	•																•			
Buccaneer (USVI)	•					•	•	•		•		•		•	•		•				•			
Calabash (Grenada)	•					•	•			•					•			•						
Caneel Bay (USVI)	•					•	•			•		•			•		•	•			•			
Cap Juluca (Anguilla)	•					•	•	•							•							•		
Capt. Don's Habitat (Bonaire)	•				•								•											
Carlisle Bay (Antigua)	•		•			•	•			•							•							
Casa de Campo (Dominican Republic)	•			•	•		•		•	•		•		•	•	•	•						•	•
Casa Colonial (Dominican Republic)	•					•	•										•					•		
Cobblers Cove (Barbados)	•					•	•			•					•							•		
Coco Palm (St. Lucia)			•	•	•		•	•																
Coral Reef Club (Barbados)	•				•				•	•	•	•		•	•		•					•	•	•
Cotton House (The Grenadines)	•	•				•	•	•				•			•	•		•						
Couples San Souci (Jamaica)	•	•	•			•	•						•				•							

The Best of the Best — Caribbean Resorts comparison chart

	Beachside	Hillside	All-inclusive	Budget	Value	Honeymoon	Romantic	Wedding	Children's Program	Families	Singles	Sports/Active	Dive	Golf	Tennis	Marina	Spa/Fitness Center	Nature Lovers	Hiking	Birding	History	Cuisine	Entertainment	Casino
Couples Swept Away (Jamaica)	●		●			●	●					●	●		●		●						●	
CuisinArt (Anguilla)	●					●	●					●			●		●					●		
Curtain Bluff (Antigua)	●	●	●			●	●					●			●		●					●		
Dunmore Beach (Bahamas)	●								●													●		
Eden Rock (St. Barts)	●	●				●	●					●										●		
El Conquistador (Puerto Rico)	●	●				●		●	●	●		●	●	●	●	●	●						●	●
El Convento (Puerto Rico)				●	●							●									●	●		
El San Juan (Puerto Rico)	●					●						●					●						●	●
Fairmount Royal Pavilion (Barbados)	●					●	●	●				●										●		
Four Seasons Exuma (Bahamas)	●					●	●	●	●	●		●		●	●		●							
Four Seasons Nevis (Nevis)	●					●	●	●	●	●		●		●	●		●							
Frangipani (The Grenadines)	●			●						●														
Gallery San Juan (Puerto Rico)				●								●									●			
Galley Bay (Antigua)	●	●				●	●					●			●		●							
Golden Lemon (St. Kitts)	●					●	●															●		
Golden Rock (Nevis)		●		●		●	●			●	●								●	●		●		
Grace Bay Club (Turks & Caicos Islands)	●					●	●					●	●		●		●						●	
Graycliff (Bahamas)		●								●											●	●	●	
Green Turtle (Bahamas)	●				●		●			●		●				●								
Guana Island (British VI)	●	●	●				●					●						●	●	●				
Half Moon (Jamaica)	●					●	●	●	●	●		●	●	●	●		●						●	
Hermitage (Nevis)		●		●														●	●	●		●		
Hôtel Guanahani (St. Barts)	●	●				●	●					●			●		●							
Hyatt Regency Aruba (Aruba)	●					●			●	●		●	●	●	●		●						●	●
Isle de France (St. Barts)	●	●				●	●					●			●		●					●		
Jamaica Inn (Jamaica)	●	●				●	●	●							●									
Jumby Bay (Antigua)	●					●	●	●	●	●		●	●		●		●	●	●	●				
Kura Hulanda (Curaçao)				●		●	●										●				●			
Ladera (St. Lucia)		●				●	●										●	●	●	●		●		
La Samanna (St. Martin)	●	●				●	●					●			●							●		
La Source (Grenada)	●		●			●	●					●					●							
Le Cap Est (Martinique)	●																●							
Le Toiny (St. Barts)		●				●	●														●	●		
Maho Bay (USVI)	●	●		●						●	●							●	●					
Malliouhana (Anguilla)	●	●				●	●		●	●		●			●		●					●		
Marriott Curacao Beach (Curaçao)	●					●			●	●	●		●				●							●
Marriott Frenchman's Reef (USVI)	●	●				●	●		●	●		●	●		●		●							●
Meridian Club (Turks & Caicos Islands)	●	●					●											●	●	●				
Montpelier Plantation (Nevis)		●				●	●					●			●			●	●	●	●	●		
Necker Island (British VI)		●	●			●	●			●		●			●							●		
Nisbet Plantation (Nevis)	●					●	●	●				●												

316   THE BEST OF THE BEST

	Beachside	Hillside	All-inclusive	Budget	Value	Honeymoon	Romantic	Wedding	Children's Program	Families	Singles	Sports/Active	Dive	Golf	Tennis	Marina	Spa/Fitness Center	Nature Lovers	Hiking	Birding	History	Cuisine	Entertainment	Casino
One&Only Ocean Club (Bahamas)	•					•	•	•							•	•						•		
Ottley's Plantation (St. Kitts)		•				•	•	•		•			•				•	•	•			•		
Palm Island (The Grenadines)	•		•			•						•	•				•	•			•			
Parrot Cay (Turks & Caicos)	•					•	•										•	•						
Pasanggrahan (St. Maarten)	•			•						•														
Peter Island (British VI)	•	•				•	•						•		•	•	•	•	•					
Petit St. Vincent (The Grenadines)	•	•				•												•						
Pirates Point (Cayman Islands)	•				•								•					•				•		
Raffles Beach (The Grenadines)	•	•					•														•		•
The Regent Palms (Turks & Caicos Islands)	•						•	•	•	•					•									
Renaissance Jaragua (Dominican Republic)			•	•			•			•				•			•					•	•	•
Ritz-Carlton Grand Cayman (Cayman Islands)	•							•	•	•			•	•			•					•		
Ritz-Carlton Rose Hall (Jamaica)	•					•	•	•	•	•		•	•		•		•							
Ritz-Carlton San Juan (Puerto Rico)	•	•					•	•	•	•					•		•					•	•	•
Ritz-Carlton St. Thomas (USVI)	•	•				•		•	•				•	•			•							
Rockhouse (Jamaica)		•		•	•	•				•														
Rosewood Little Dix (British VI)	•					•	•		•				•		•	•	•	•						
Round Hill (Jamaica)	•	•				•	•		•						•		•							
Royal Plantation (Jamaica)	•		•		•	•									•		•							
Royal Plantation Island (Bahamas)	•					•			•			•			•		•		•	•				
Sandals Dunn's River (Jamaica)	•		•		•	•							•										•	
Sandcastle (British VI)	•	•				•				•														
Sirena (Anguilla)	•				•				•	•	•													
Sivory Punta Cana (Dominican Republic)	•					•							•			•		•				•		
Small Hope Bay (Bahamas)	•		•	•		•			•	•			•											
Sofitel Bakoua (Martinique)	•					•									•		•							
Spice Island (Grenada)	•			•		•	•										•							
Strawberry Hill (Jamaica)	•	•															•							
Sugar Mill (British VI)	•	•																						
SuperClubs Breezes Runaway Bay (Jamaica)	•		•	•	•					•		•		•	•		•						•	
SuperClubs Grand Lido (Negril)	•		•		•	•		•			•	•	•		•								•	
Tensing Pen (Jamaica)				•	•	•	•		•			•												
Tortuga Bay (Dominican Republic)	•						•				•			•			•							
Tryall Club (Jamaica)	•	•				•	•		•	•		•		•	•		•				•	•		
Twelve Degrees North (Grenada)	•	•		•						•							•							
Village St. Jean (St. Barts)		•			•	•				•														
Young Island (St. Vincent)	•	•				•	•			•							•	•	•					

ABOUT THE AUTHOR

Kay Showker is a veteran writer, photographer and lecturer on travel. Her assignments have taken her to more than one hundred countries in the Caribbean and around the world. She has appeared as a travel expert on CNN, ABC, CBS, and NBC, and radio stations across the country, as well as guest host on America Online and the Travel Channel.

She has authored fourteen travel guides, including *Caribbean Ports of Call: Western Region; Caribbean Ports of Call: Eastern and Southern Regions* (winner of the Best Guidebook Award by the Caribbean Tourism Organization); and the *Unofficial Guide to Cruises* (named "The Best Guidebook of the Year" by the Lowell Thomas Travel Awards when it was first published in 1996). She served as a senior editor at *Travel Weekly* and has written for such leading travel publications as *National Geographic Traveler, Travel and Leisure,* and *Caribbean Travel and Life* among others. She was a member of America Online's creative team for "Cruise Critic," for which she wrote the "Ports of Call" segment.

A native of Kingsport, Tennessee, Ms. Showker received a master's degree in international affairs from the School of Advanced International Studies of Johns Hopkins University in Washington, D.C., and a B.A. from Mary Washington University; she also studied at the American University at Cairo, Cairo University and Georgetown University. She is the recipient of numerous awards for her travel writing and was the first travel writer to receive the *Sucrier d'Or*—a professional achievement award given by the government of Martinique. She is a member of the Society of American Travel Writers, the American Society of Journalists and Authors, and the New York Travel Writers Association. She has served as a consultant to government and private organizations on travel and tourism.

Ms. Showker lives in New York City and St. Petersburg, Florida.